D1086715

Dear God,
I'm only a boy.

G Schmidt
Henderson, Neb 68371

MENNO DUERKSEN

CASTLE ♛ BOOKS

ABOUT THE AUTHOR

In an age when there was no television to lure him away he devoured books and magazines by the hundreds. He resolved to become a newspaper man.

It was a career that would span 39 years, including seven years as a correspondent for United Press in Europe and the Middle East. He became involved in the drama of history being made, the chaos in Germany at the end of World War II, the Nurnberg war crimes trials, the birth of the State of Israel. At times, the drama lapped so closely upon Menno's heels he could smell the breath of death. Some of that drama is reflected in the later stories in this book.

Since retiring from active newspaper work Menno has been doing magazine writing, mostly in the field of motor car history. He has twice won the prestigious Karl Benz Award, offered each year by the Society of Automotive Historians for what is judged to be the best magazine series of the year in the field of automotive history. The last award, in 1984, was for a four part history of General Motors.

But for years, memories of the drama of his life, from the Oklahoma childhood to the battlefields of Palestine, whirled through the author's mind and he decided to write it down. Perhaps others may wish to learn a few of the lessons he has learned, sometimes so painfully. For example - One should never pick up a skunk by its tail.

H L Schmidt

by Menno Duerksen

Copyright©1986 by Menno Duerksen

ALL RIGHT RESERVED

This book may not be reproduced in whole or part without the express permission of the publisher.

Cover picture by Paul Penczner

CASTLE 🏰 BOOKS
233 Crestmere Place
Memphis, Tenn.
38112

Printed in the U. S. A.   ISBN 0-916693-07-4

Dedication

This book is dedicated to my wife, Thea, who believes in miracles and who loved me enough to encourage me to write it, even when there were parts of which she did not approve.

THE SETTING

God was in his heaven and sometimes rode about, thunderously, in his big Newton farm wagon. On stormy days it could be heard and seen below, the clatter of the steel shod wheels, striking giant sparks which danced on the rocky "gyp" hills.

Down below, on the Oklahoma prairie, every man was a Job, fated to endure his share of the drouths, hail storms, dust storms, pestilence and blizzards. Even the lightning which sometimes struck dead the peaceful cows, grazing along the fence rows. It was all the hand of God.

Across those prairies strode the tight lipped Mennonite father images, armed with pliant but tough mulberry switches, under command by God to apply those switches vigorously against the back sides of their erring children.

Into this world, in 1916, the author of this book was born.

A child is always compliant, in the beginning at least, to the shaping forces of his environment. If, in time, there comes rebellion, is it not, perhaps, because the bursting force of a growing child mind is too explosive to be confined in a pre-formed pattern so small?

In time, Menno Duerksen did rebel. But he knew, too, the joys and love of his noble dog, Pedro, who almost died on a cow barn gallows. He fought with the "devil horse Reuben." He gloried in the two frolicking colts, Pat and Sam - before they plunged into quicksand. He knew the dubious "joy"of trapping skunks to obtain a bit of spending money. He learned the tender joys of love from "the greatest mother who ever lived."

Chapter One - Reuben

Reuben was the wildest sex fiend I ever met.

In fact he tried to kill me one day when I interfered with one of his sex adventures.

And yet, somehow, there was something so utterly fascinating about him. You could hate him, so passionately, and then be forced to stand there and glow at his fire and spirit.

I was only eight when I first saw Reuben.

It all came about because of another of those "itchy foot" pilgrimages my Dad made. My father, the man of the eternally restless soul. Ever the anxious pilgrim, making his family the victim of those cross country treks as he searched for the holy grail, spiritual and material, which he hoped would somehow bring peace to his unresting soul.

But Reuben.

Dad had just brought his family, and that included me, his eldest son, back to Oklahoma after that last effort at finding greener pastures in Oregon. We landed at Grandpa Friesen's, as usual. There really wasn't any other place to go. I knew there had been an exchange of letters in an effort to make peace with Grandpa.

Grandpa and Grandma had opposed that marriage from the beginning, my Dad and my Mom, their daughter. And then, afterwards, all those fruitless pilgrimages simply alienated Dad from Grandpa even further, reinforcing the belief of Grandpa and Grandma that they shouldn't have allowed that young Duerksen guy to marry their Mary. When Dad had set off to the promised lands of

California or Oregon, he returned each time poorer than before. We, the family, suffered.

I believe that to obtain even a half way reconciliation with Grandpa, Dad had been forced to swear, most solemnly by mail, that he would settle down and stop all that pilgrimage stuff.

Since Dad was more or less broke when he landed back on Grandpa's doorstep, it meant Grandpa would have to help out in getting him back on his feet. Dirt farming. It was about the only occupation the Mennonites considered honorable.

Grandpa probably never would have admitted it, even to himself, but I have always believed that Reuben was a punishment he inflicted upon Dad. If Dad were to get back into the farming of that stubborn Oklahoma soil he would have to have at least one team of horses. And they would have to come from Grandpa.

For the record, Grandpa pleaded that he was a bit short of horses at the moment but he could let Dad have Reuben and Mike. This story really wouldn't quite float because Grandpa always had plenty of horses. He had a huge black stallion painted on the side of his barn, proclaiming to all folks passing by that here lived Jacob Martin Friesen, prideful of his horse flesh, breeder of fine horses. Work horses, that it. There wasn't much riding in those purposeful days. Horses were for plowing. And harvesting. Perhaps, marginally, to pull a buggy.

Dad had enough experience with horses to know that Reuben was a monster of a black stallion. Folks didn't normally hitch stallions to plows but that is exactly what Grandpa was proposing that Dad try. Take it or leave it. Dad didn't have much choice.

Mike, now, was something else. Very nearly as big as Reuben but properly gelded so the fiery juices didn't make him a devil monster like Reuben. Grandpa insisted that Reuben was broken to work. This, we learned, was true to a point. But God, what a beast.

The second part of the suggestion was that Mike had been "worked in" as the other half of the team and that Mike would have a steadying effect on the black monster. Which was also true, to a point. But oh, beyond that point.

All of which led us to about three or four years of some of the most hectic farming ever inflicted upon a man. Or boy. For I, as the eldest son, would be involved, too.

At the beginning I didn't even know what made Reuben such a wild, unbroken and nearly unmanageable giant. A boy

8

growing up in a proper Mennonite home wasn't told what made the
difference between a horse that had its balls and one that didn't.

Even when one of the neighbors brought a mare over to be
"served" by Reuben, on those occasions when he was called on for
that "other kind of duty," it meant that we kids got herded into the
house and Mom was alerted to keep her eyes out so we wouldn't
peek out the windows.

We could hear Reuben screaming that wild, primeval sex
challenge as he was led up to the waiting mare and once or twice I
managed a bit of a peek but it still remained something mostly on the
mysterious side.

I even asked Dad about it but that didn't produce much of
anything by way of enlightenment. I guess it started the day I first
rode to town with Dad on the wagon behind Reuben and Mike.

I believe Dad would have preferred to leave Reuben home
but since he had only one wagon, and that was a two horser, he
didn't have much choice in that, either.

It was a cool spring morning. As we swung out of the
driveway onto the road, Reuben was prancing like crazy, almost
leaping out of his harness. His tail was switching wildly and his
rear haunches were leaping up and down in short, nervous hops.
He was screaming his wild, whinnying challenge to the winds. He
was trying to run and Dad was pulling on the reins furiously,
fighting to overcome the plunges of that wild, snorting animal. I,
too, had grown up around horses but here was something, a horse,
unlike anything I had ever seen before.

And then there was Mike, patiently and quietly trotting along
beside Reuben as any well behaved horse really should. The
contrast was a bit much for the curious brain of a kid of eight.
Finally I said it.

"What's the matter with Reuben, Dad? Why is he so wild?"

"Oh, he's been penned up in the barn all night and he just
wants to run. He'll settle down after a while," said Dad. But Mike
had been penned up in the barn, too. I wasn't quite satisfied with
this answer. But Dad wasn't telling me any more. Not then.

But if Reuben was going to calm down I thought he was
taking a long time about it. The distance to town was five miles and
I know we had gone more than half that distance before he even
acted half way like a normal horse. Until me met another farmer
coming to meet us in a wagon drawn by two mares.

As the mares came within seeing, and smelling, distance,
Reuben began his crazy act all over again. Bucking, plunging and

9

screaming that wild, frenzied whinny that simply left so many questions unanswered. Mike was having none of it. But Dad, his feet braced against the foot board was sawing on the reins and trying to keep that wild devil horse under control.

Looking back on it now, I'm certain that neither of those mares was even in heat but they were female and that was enough for Reuben. It seemed he was on the verge of leaping right out of his harness. I would suggest it is no easy task for a horse to rear up on his hind legs while strapped into a heavy harness and hitched to a wagon with another horse with that heavy tongue pole between them. But Reuben managed it. By this time, that kid sitting on the wagon seat next to Dad was scared all the way into the middle of his gut and was hanging on almost as if he were astride that mad monster.

Thank God, Dad was an experienced horseman and none of the reins or harness straps broke. Else Reuben might have simply taken off, like Pegasus, rocketing over the wagon tongue.

Later, as we neared town and encountered other wagons and teams, Reuben simply kept his wild act going. Even if the other horses were males and geldings, Reuben somehow felt the need to hurl his screeching challenge to anything on four feet that looked like a horse. To the mares he was doubly wild.

All of this was a bit much for my puzzled brain. I guess, at that time I barely knew the difference between a mare and a "horse." Farm folks seldom ever used the word "gelding." Not to speak of stallions, or mares in heat. I just knew we had a crazy horse on our hands. Wild crazy. A horse that seemed to go berserk every time a strange horse came near. Mare, gelding, whatever. And when a mare in heat came close - well, I was about to begin my education on that.

They still had the old fashioned hitching rails on Main Street and Dad made the mistake of assuming he could safely hitch Reuben and Mike to it.

Oh, he tied them on well enough. Especially Reuben. And then he handed the reins to me. "You stay with the wagon and watch the horses," he said. He had a bit of grocery shopping to do and then we would drive down to the feed store and load some hay on the wagon, our real purpose for taking the wagon to town.

"Gee, Dad," I had protested. I had hoped I could at least go look in the store windows, at all the goodies we couldn't buy. Maybe I even hoped for a nickle and the big, fat candy bar I could buy with it. Now I was stuck with the reins. And the horses.

10

"If they try to get away, just pull down hard on the reins," said Dad, ignoring my plea. He had no surplus nickles in his pockets those days anyway.

At first, Reuben satisfied himself with twisting his neck around and screaming every time a team went by. I did a bit of jerking on the reins. Things remained under control. For a while.

I didn't know it then but, looking back on it now, I am certain some farmer came to town with a mare in heat hitched to his wagon. Usually it would be safe enough. Hardly anybody ever drove a wagon to town with a stallion hitched to it. Maybe, like Dad, the guy didn't have but two horses and little choice. All I knew then was that another team came by and Reuben exploded into action.

He began leaping and surging against the railing. All this accompanied by that unholy shrieking and screaming whinny. If you could call that wild mating cry a whinny. I tried to do my duty by jerking on the reins and hollering but I doubt if Reuben was even aware of my efforts.

Poor Mike. He was almost as helpless as I. He had probably been suffering those outrages from Reuben for years and had perhaps tried, in his tame horse manner, to act as a steadying influence on his crazy team mate. But what could he do now? Reuben weighed nearly 1,800 pounds and was exploding with frenzied energy.

When the two of them, Reuben with malice aforethought and Mike passively, dragged along unwillingly, surged against that hitching rail the posts snapped and the rail splintered. The town folks who had built that railing had probably never visualized an emergency like this.

The sidewalk beyond that railing was perhaps six to eight feet wide. Beyond that, the big plate glass windows of the C. R. Anthony Dry Goods Store. I remember the huge shards of razor sharp glass flying through the air as the steel shod end of the wagon tongue rammed against the glass. I, some seven to eight feet behind the end of that tongue pole, escaped the flying glass.

Somewhere in the midst of all this exploding action I heard Dad yelling. Apparently he had not been far away and when he heard Reuben's scream, and the crash, he knew he'd better go to the rescue. That Dad of mine never had the most commanding voice in the world but he was shouting in desperation now, at the horses, perhaps the closest I ever heard him come to a curse. He leaped right into the middle of it all, somehow got his hands on Reuben's reins and dragged the bleeding horses backwards out of the wreckage.

In a moment it was all over. The townspeople had gathered in a circle around us to stare at this outrage to their peaceful day. Someone brought a cloth to wrap around the worst of the cuts on Mike's neck. Poor Mike, the innocent sufferer, had once more received the worst wounds. Reuben, the devil horse who had caused it all, had escaped with minor cuts.

Perhaps the most outraged man of all was the manager of the Anthony store. "My window. My window," he shouted. "That will cost you." It did.

Poor Dad, what could he do? Only the best he could.

I'm not sure I remember all the details now but it went something like this: "I'll have to come back to talk to you later. Right now I must get this crazy horse out of town." And we made our escape.

As we drove down the street I could almost literally feel the hostile glances of all those townspeople, aimed at our helpless backs.

It was the look of defeat on Dad's face which told me the most. He had not only been humiliated, he had been struck another terrible financial blow at a time when he had virtually nothing. If I had been able to read his mind, I am certain I would have found a desire to kill Reuben. God's wrath, I am sure, he must have implored that day to be showered upon the head of that wild animal.

The drops of blood dripping from the monster's neck could never be sufficient unto the sin. On the other hand, he couldn't kill Reuben if he wanted to. He hadn't paid for the horses yet. Reuben still belonged to Grandpa.

Somewhere in the middle of it all, on the way home, Dad turned to me and shouted, "Why didn't you hold them?" "I told you to hold them if they tried to get away."

So now I was being blamed, too, for the sins of that mighty devil horse. Heck, I probably weighed all of 70 or 80 pounds. A boy against nearly two tons of wild, plunging horse flesh.

I know Dad went back to town the next day, in the Model T Ford that had brought us from Oregon, not the wagon, to make his peace with the townsfolk. I found out later that he had been forced to sign a note at the bank to pay for the smashed window. And the hitching rail. Plate glass windows didn't come cheap even in the 1920's. And here Dad was, trying to make a new start at dirt farming to feed that big family of ours, 10 of us then, counting

Mom and Dad. I also heard that Dad had to go back to Grandpa for more help, too, before we harvested our first crop.

God save us if any more help from Grandpa came in the form of more Reubens. If Grandpa Friesen had indeed, subconsciously or otherwide, intended Reuben as some sort of punishment to Dad, that punishment had begun in good measure. And there was more to come.

I know it was weeks before Dad ever dared go back to town again with the horses. But there were times when the wagon, to carry the larger loads, was simply a must. But in the meantime, when he had gone by Model T, he apparently had scouted the alleys of Weatherford for a safer place to tether his horses. I know the next time we drove to town Dad headed straight for an alley more than a block from Main Street and headed up to a huge power pole. There he tied the horses to that stout pole. He had even brought a heavy rope halter for Reuben to add to the bridle reins to make sure the black devil would never break away again.

But Dad had also purchased something else to control that wild animal, a thing called a "bicycle chain bridle bit."

Bridle bits for horses came in various styles. For the tamest of horses there were the straight bar bits. For horses just a bit more difficult to manage there were the hinged bits, jointed in the middle so that when you pulled on the reins it pinched a horse's mouth. A bit of pain, and control. Then there were the yoked bits, with a yoke, or prong, in the middle. That yoke would, when you pulled on the reins, poke at the roof of a horse's mouth. Oh, it was rounded and smooth but could inflict pain. And then there was the bicycle chain bit. It was the most cruel of all. Whoever had invented that thing must have known another Reuben.

The bit was indeed patterned after a bicycle chain, with the links running through the mouth of the horse. It had two modes of use. One side of the links were smooth but the other side had teeth, like the teeth of a saw. Oh, no, not so sharp as on a saw, only dulled vee edged teeth. But cruel enough. With the teeth turned to the rear, you could darned near saw the lower jaw off a horse.

These bicycle chain bits have probably long ago been outlawed by the humane societies, concerned about the welfare of horse flesh. But then I doubt that the good men and women of such societies ever had to fight a battle with a horse named Reuben. And I'll have to say, in defense of Dad, that he was not without mercy. He used that bit judiciously and never "sawed" any more than he had to in order to control that devil. On the other hand, when

Reuben really went wild it was only a bicycle chain bit that could force him under control.

Mike, meanwhile, was privileged to wear between his teeth the tamest of all bits, the smooth bar. He never burdened the trust. In fact, we never used those bicycle chain bits on any other horse until years later, after Reuben's two mighty sons were born and grew into fiery replicas of their father, despite their gelded status. But that is another story.

Somehow, in the days to come, Dad managed to fit Reuben into the picture of tilling the soil on the old Kroeker farm we had rented.

But even when he labored, Reuben managed to do it in a manner so different from that of other horses. So utterly different, so challenging, so completely beyond the scope of normal horse behavior.

The first half hour of plowing on a chill morning would be a series of explosive events. Lumped together, an exhausting chain of frustration.

Events they were.

It was a trial of its own, among the trials of Job, just to get that horse hitched and straightened out in front of a plow. And when the huge animal did begin pulling he lunged forward in a frenzy of energy which seemed to say, "Well, if I, the noble stallion must needs be humbled at the front of a plow, I shall demonstrate that I am no ordinary horse. If I must plow, I will plow it all at once. Now. Fast. Let fly the black earth. Plunge, plunge."

And for the man behind the plow - later it would be a boy - one could only live in the hope that after a time, perhaps in an hour or so, that bedeviled mountain of horse flesh would somehow begin to calm down and work as a normal horse.

At last, he would slow. For one thing, Dad, in an effort to control the nearly uncontrollable, had engineered a bit of revenge of his own. Extra holes drilled into the hickory double-tree from which the two horses pulled the plow. Off center, those extra holes. The first one by perhaps three inches, the second at six. And Reuben would always get the short end of the double-tree.

An engineer with a slide rule could, perhaps, calculate the amount of extra load Reuben had to pull by getting the shorter end. At three inches, bearable. At six, a cruel punishment. It was at six inches that Reuben had to start on those chill mornings. Later, after perhaps an hour of heaving and the devil sap beginning to wane, Dad would bring it back to three. It was seldom indeed that

14

Reuben, the mighty king of horse muscle, ever got to do his labors at even-steven, the bolt in center position as it was for normal horses.

In those early days of our sojourn on the Kroeker farm, the days when we had only Reuben and Mike for traction power, Dad never entrusted me with the reins or the plow. I was too small. The horses too big. And Reuben too evil.

It was not until I had grown a bit and the picture had also changed a bit that I was finally trained to operate a plow - and trusted with the reins of the devil horse.

Perhaps the biggest dimension that changed in the picture was the acquisition of two more horses. They were sorely needed for there were so many jobs on a farm that called for a four horse hitch. A gang plow, for example, a two bottom tiller of earth. A single shared plow, with two horses, was simply not adequate if a respectable farmer intended to make a living.

But from the stand point of putting up with Reuben, the biggest change in the equation, one which threatened to throw everything out of control again, was the fact that the two new horses were mares. Lady horses, to put it simply. Big, broad, sturdy of muscle and nearly as big as Reuben and Mike. Destined, in the future, to become the mothers of Reuben's mightiest and most spirited sons.

Meanwhile, with a desperate courage born of necessity, Dad determined to employ those two mares, Daisy and May, on the same hitch with Reuben and Mike. Possible, perhaps, by a man with such horse experience as Dad had acquired in his years. Possible, perhaps, with a sufficient use of that cruel, bicycle chain bit. By use of the off-center double-trees. By judiciously posting the long suffering Mike between Reuben and the mares.

At first, Reuben seemed to blame Mike for standing between him and the mares. He would bite, snap and snarl at his patient companion. Dad solved that part by making a sturdy stick with a harness snap on each end, to fasten betwen Reuben's and Mike's bridles. It was punishing to poor Mike but at least Reuben couldn't bite him any more.

It all worked, after a fashion, and Dad was able to unite the savage and wild energy of Reuben with the willing efforts of Mike and the two good mares.

Oh, Dad would never have gotten away with such a hitch if the mares had been in heat. In their "safe" periods, Reuben wouldn't have done much if he had been able to get to them. Except snort, scream, prance and make a general display of his sexual potential. Perhaps nip the mares a bit with those huge teeth of his. He was good at that.

If the mares did come in heat during the work season it simply meant all four-horse-hitch work had to come to a halt. One of the changes Dad had been forced to make when he acquired Reuben was a remodeling of the horse barn. He had knocked the partitions out between two horse stalls, making a double stall. Then the walls of that big stall were reinforced with sturdy two-by-eight planks. An extra wall was added to make it a complete enclosure, with a heavy plank reinforced door.

During the "in heat" periods for the mares, Reuben was locked into that big stall and the mares kept at a distance from the barn. Not that it calmed Reuben a damned bit. He could smell a mare in heat for at least a half a mile and on more than one occasion, when he picked up that scent he splintered those big planks on the walls of his "cell" in his furied efforts to break out.

The coming of the mares to the farm had also forced Dad to make other changes. It was simply out of the question to turn Reuben out into the pasture with the other horses. In fact, he sometimes made display of his devil spirit by chasing the cows, trying to attack them even if they couldn't become objects of his sexual assaults.

So Dad had been forced to build a special fence around a six acre pasture plot separate from the regular pasture. Instead of a normal three wire fence and post every 20 feet, for the Reuben pasture we had to use five strands of barbed wire and a post about every eight or 10 feet. More of that penalty Grandpa had inflicted on poor Dad. He paid and paid for the privilege of owning that crazy devil.

And even.this wasn't always enough. There were occasions when Reuben caught wind of a mare in heat, somewhere in the neighborhood if not at home, and simply slammed his way through that high, reinforced fence to escape.

Dad was almost as stubborn and refused to admit defeat. His next step was to hobble the monster while "en pasture." He buckled a leather strap between Reuben's front ankles with a length of steel chain linking the straps, just long enough to allow him short steps for grazing. No normal walking or running. Just short, hobbling limps. Dad thought that made it impossible for Reuben to break out of his special paddock.

Even that didn't work. There would come that inevitable day when a neighbor would call to tell us that our sex fiend was at their house, or barn, fighting to break in and get at one of the mares, which happened to be in a sexually receptive mode.

When Dad went to get Reuben he found the hobbles broken, dangling from one foot. And the only consolation one could derive from this was that when Reuben tried to walk or run, with that chain dangling from one foot, it would whip and bring pain to his other front leg.

Then there was the time when one of Reuben's breakouts and sexual assaults was aimed at one of our own mares. It nearly killed her.

This was Dolly, a smaller black mare Dad had acquired recently. Inevitably she, too, would come in heat. I guess it was the snorting, challenging whinnies of our big devil monster that alerted Dad and he went running to the "rescue." And this time, a rescue operation was truly a necessity.

Reuben had broken out of his paddock and had made his way across some 600 yards of wheat field to reach the fence of the regular pasture where Dolly had been locked up. Dolly had met Reuben at the fence and the crazy monster had somehow managed to mount her across the fence. But in the process, Dolly had become tangled into the strands of the barbed wire fence and her hind legs were cruelly slashed. I was sure that if Dad had not arrived when he did she would have bled to death.

She almost died anyway when her wounds became infected in the fly infested summer. Dad, and Uncle Jake Schlichting, who doubled as a farmer and a sort of self trained rural vet, nursed her patiently for weeks and she finally recovered. But, after the gaping wounds healed, it left Dolly with one stiff leg, unbending at the joint. Another penalty inflicted by our terrible Reuben. Dolly eventually had to be destroyed. Oh, Lord, how long wilt thou torment us?

I supposed, through all these experiences, I was slowly learning that Reuben not only wasn't a normal horse, he wasn't even a normal stallion. I have been around other stallions and none was quite as wild, quite as crazy, quite such an eternal devil as our Reuben.

I know that any horse with his balls can become wild, often unmanageable or even dangerous when in the presence of a mare in heat. But I have seen stallions so tame people trusted their children around them, to play with them or ride them as pets.

But somewhere in Reuben's heritage a set of wild, crazy genes must have combined in his blood to make him more a devil than a horse. A fierce, unmanageable monster. A cruel plague of an albatross forever hanging around the neck of the man who owned him. Somehow, as I said, I was never able to eliminate from my mind the suspicion that Grandpa had known it all the time and had inflicted Reuben upon Dad intentionally.

And then there would finally come that day when Reuben would try to kill me. And may have come closer than I was willing to admit at the time.

It happened on a day when Dad wasn't home. And Uncle Dave Bushman, on the farm across the road, wasn't home either. Nor his son, Ike, who was older than I and might have been of some help.

In any case, the old country wall phone impatiently signalled our ring that day and Mom answered. It was Aunt Bushman on the phone.

"Your Reuben is over here tearing our barn down. Send someone to get him quick," she pleaded.

That was when Mom called me. Me, just a kid, maybe nine or 10, weighing perhaps 80 or 90 pounds.

"You'll have to go get Reuben," said Mother. I tried to argue but there wasn't much use. Knowing Mom, who was pretty self-reliant herself, I believe she would have gone with me if she had known what was going to happen. Both Mom and Dad expected quite a lot from their eldest son, even before he had a chance to grow up, so Mom must have believed that I could handle it.

She said hurry but I knew that for me to go over there and tell Reuben to go home would be like telling a tornado to go away. I'd have to go well armed. So while Reuben continued slamming against Uncle Bushman's barn, I delayed long enough to find a good, stout stick. It would have to be long enough to keep Reuben's flying hooves out of range. And strong enough to prevent its breakage when I tried to use it. I had to be given credit for not going unprepared.

Sure enough, by the time I got there the barn boards were splintering under Reuben's attack. Uncle Bushman had a mare in heat. He didn't want her bred. He had penned her in the barn so she would be "safe." From the what I could see as I came on the scene, she wasn't going to be safe very long.

18

For once, Dad's hobbles had held. Reuben's front legs were still shackled. That much was in my favor. But despite those hobbles, when I came up to Reuben, waving my stick, he charged me. Up on his hind legs and those huge front feet high in the air, menacingly. He was walking, almost running, on those hind legs. With those threatening front feet came that ungodly scream from his powerful lungs.

My heart was pounding and I was scared. Plenty scared. But I knew there was no retreat. Mom and Dad simply expected me to do what they told me to do. I spread my stubby legs, braced myself and when Reuben came within range I whacked him across his neck and chest as hard as I could. The blow landed with a good, whacking thump and I knew I had hurt him. I had to. Anything less was a waste of time. And dangerous.

I worked my way between the barn and the raging monster. Then I began whacking him with the stick as fast and as hard as I could. Whack, whack, whack. Luckily, most of my blows were striking home.

After a whole series of these blows Reuben finally began backing away. He would bear the marks for weeks. I got him turned around and headed for home. He had gone perhaps 50 yards when he suddenly cut loose with one shrieking, challenging whinny once more. He turned and charged me again, up on his hind legs and with those manacled hooves swinging.

But again I was ready, my stick slashing across his neck and chest. And again the cruel blows overcame that primeval sex power in his blood and sent him hobbling home again.

At least three or four more times he tried it. I, my heart pounding with fear, but also with anger now, was ready each time. Whack, whack. I was thankful that my stick did not break. It was green, pliant and sturdy.

We were almost home when that final moment of truth came. I guess I had decided he had given up and may have relaxed my vigil, just a bit. I knew I had been hurting him with the stick. He had gone several hundred yards without making another attack. And since we were so close to home I had assumed I had that battle won.

Then it came. That last and final attack from Reuben. Accompanied once more by that wild, shrieking whinny from an 1,800 pound sex maddened beast.

Up he went, on those powerful hind legs of his, his head now towering some 10 feet high in the air. He lunged towards me, those two giant front hooves swinging like maces above my head.

This time, Reuben almost got me. I was forced to back up as I tried to get my stick into play and I stumbled. There I lay on my back, staring up at those great hooves coming down at me.

To this day I don't know how I escaped. I just know that a kid of nine or 10, especially a scared kid, is pretty good at scrambling, even when down on the ground. I simply rolled out from under those crashing hooves as they hit the ground where I had been lying. If those hooves missed me only by inches, it was enough.

And somehow as I scrambled I managed to keep my grip on my only weapon, that stick. It had been a wisdom born of cold necessity. By the time Reuben made his next lunge I was ready. My feet braced and my stick whistling through the air.

I suppose I never hit an animal harder in my life. I didn't give a damn if I killed him, although that probably wasn't possible. Now it was anger, more than fear, which drove me furiously to the attack. I wounded that big animal cruelly. Blows to his head, his ribs, his neck. Any place I could land a blow. I was raising welts that would astonish even Dad.

Why had I beaten Reuben so hard? Dad would ask. When I explained Reuben had tried to kill me he didn't press the matter. After all, Dad had suffered his defeats at the hands of Reuben and bore him little love or compassion.

But the blessed truth on that day was that after that last attack Reuben did give up and go home. I managed to get him into the barn and locked up in his plank cell.

As I stood there, panting and trembling, I was so wrung out I could barely savor my narrow margin of victory. It was when I saw him starting to lick at his wounds that a torrent of profane anger whirled through my mind. "I don't care if you die, you sonofabitch." I didn't.

Suddenly, in that aftermath, I became aware of the stick I still clutched tightly in my hands. In that long journey home I had not dared drop it for even a second. Now, suddenly, I hated the stick, too, and I flung it on the ground. I stumbled toward the house to tell Mother that I had carried out her orders and had brought Reuben home.

Once more, Dad had to pay, for the splintered walls of Uncle Dave's barn. It was not much afterward, I came home from school one day and found Reuben gone. I asked Dad about it and he hesitated. He didn't like to talk about things like that.

"I sold him," he mumbled and left it at that. It was only later that I learned, from one of my uncles, that Reuben had indeed been sold, to a rendering plant. Dad had simply faced the inevitable and Reuben was now gone forever.

Perhaps one reason Dad felt free to make that decision was because Reuben had, in the meantime, sired two magnificent colts by those two broad hipped mares. They were in the barn now, growing up and giving so much promise, if that were possible, of being even bigger and stronger than their mad sire.

But Dad had learned his lesson and those sons of Reuben would be properly gelded in their time. He didn't want to take a chance on any more devil horses around the place.

As for me, at the news of what had happened to Reuben, I should have been glad that the crazy beast who had tried to kill me was gone. But suddenly my emotions were mixed. I, the red blooded kid, growing up with a hero worship for the bold, the tough and the magnificent, wasn't really sure I was glad.

Crazy, wild and mean, that he had been. But also so big, so strong, so magnificent, so wildly untamable. In a sense, at least, something to bring a lump to the throat.

Why did he have to be so different? Chained eternally to his burden of an unbroken will. A fate which would lead, inevitably to his destruction.

For a time, that five wire paddock and the planked stall remained to remind us of the big devil horse that had been such a huge part of our lives for years.

Eventually, Dad converted that big stall back into double stalls, for Reuben's great sons. Posts and wire from the paddock were scavenged for making repairs on other fences.

As for me, I needed no paddock and no stalls to keep alive forever the memory of the great black stallion who had tried to kill me.

Reuben the terrible.

Chapter Two - Hell

Hell was 30 feet deep. Right behind the cow barn.

Those slippery poles, right on the brink, were all you had to cling to when you were dangling over the edge. Devil things were pulling on your legs, trying to pull you down.

Those cow barn poles supporting the roof, worn smooth by the endless rubbing of the cows, were so slippery you could feel your fingers slipping, slipping, as you fought and struggled to keep from going down. The smelly old cow barn would have been a blessed sanctuary at that moment, if only you had been able to drag yourself into its covering protection.

Thirty feet deep and perhaps 60 yards wide. Maybe 100 yards long. Roughly the size of a football field. Only nobody was playing football down there in that profane pit.

Everything that was going on down there was programmed at the unholy level of exquisite suffering, before death. The heat. The pain. The red glow of perpetual fires. Death held constantly just beyond the edge of fulfillment of prayers coming endlessly from the lips of the writhing, tortured victims. No, they must not die. Death would bring a blessed end of pain - that would violate the entire concept of the plan. It would no longer be hell.

If you could have somehow hovered in the sky, say, at the altitude of about a mile, you could have looked down to behold the fiery shimmer of that strangely glowing pit. From that distance it might have appeared something like the red eye of a rectangular and inverted subterranean Mars. Perhaps even embodying a certain mysterious beauty.

But if you then dropped down to, say, 100 feet you would then have known the evil contents of that pit. The unending glow of that red fire, fed by some kind of mysterious, inexhaustible fuel that covered the entire floor of the pit.

The great shock would come from seeing the figures of human bodies, somehow made nude and sexless, lying in the glowing coals of that huge bed of fire. Hundreds of them. Perhaps thousands. The number somehow infinite, as if to symbolize all the condemned sinners of the world.

They writhed endlessly, these inhabitants of hell, in an effort to relieve the pain. And yet they did not run or try to flee, or climb those 30-foot walls. They lay in the blistering coals, immobilized - in the grip of some immutable law that kept them from moving beyond the prescribed motions for suffering. The movements of their bodies were like the eternal movement of the waves of a sea.

All so evenly programmed. For them to have dashed madly about, scrambling at the walls, or to try to attack the devil creatures hovering over them with glowing tridents, even to have screamed in terror, would have somehow violated the concept of eternal suffering. They were allowed only to moan, at a carefully modulated level of sound. But it was enough to tell me, clinging so desperately to the slippery pole, that the pain was real. And to warn me that I must not allow the devil creatures to drag me down.

Perhaps I was only eight, not more than nine, when I began fighting that battle of the slippery poles in my dreams. My tender, fearing soul did not have to be told what that evil thing down there was. I knew. I knew so well. From the very beginning, from the first tentative awakening of my child mind, I knew that hell was down there. Perhaps not in such clearly defined shape and size, or quite so hot, but there.

Dad had made certain of that. And to some degree even my gentle, loving mother. And the people of the churches to which I was carried, beginning at infancy. It had begun to be part of my consciousness, perhaps when I was only four, or five, or six, at those roaring prayer sessions of the Apostolic Faith Mission in Oregon. Those hundreds of voices sounding together, an undulating cacophony of sound but each individual voice praying his own personal prayer. The passionate messengers of God were making certain, so utterly certain, that hell would remain vivid and alive in my childish consciousness.

There was something so confusing about it all, too, to the awakening child mind. The ultimate symbols, one was told, were love, mercy and goodness in a triumph of sinlessness over sin. Trumphant over the devil. Over hell.

Jehova's image which began to emerge in my new awareness, from the endless Bible tales my mother told me at night at my bedside, was somehow at odds with love, mercy, charity and compassion. He was a Jehova of wrath, anger and punishment in a flaming hell.

The courageous Samson who loved and served God but who must at last die because he had disobeyed God. The long suffering Job, cast forever into a morass of suffering. Adam and Eve, driven from the beautiful garden. King Saul, dying upon the point of his own sword. Even the noble Moses, condemned to die after only a glimpse of the promised land. Abraham, commanded to slay his own son. And when the plunging knife was stayed, at the last moment, a gentle and innocent lamb must die instead. Still, the frightening image of a father, with a knife poised over the breast of his little son. John the Baptist, gentle prophet who baptized Christ but fated to die, his head served up on a platter. And even Jesus, the ultimate symbol of love and forgiveness, condemned to die, impaled upon a rending cross.

Was it somehow because love was not sufficient unto the needs of a boy's birthing soul? Must all these contradictions of evil, and suffering, the wrath of Jehova, the scourging of whips upon Christ's body, the thorns upon his head, must all these things be part and parcel of the image of love, of gentleness, of charity of the spirit?

From the preachers, the evangelists, the eternal message of hell. The ominous pacing, the shouting, the vividly painted charts showing devils with horns, the thunderous stomping of feet on the plank platforms in their revival meeting tents. All this had pressed itself upon my child mind so much. More deeply than the message of love.

God is love. God is gentle. God is merciful. God is forgiving. Yes, I could hear it all. But the part that was shaking me the most, the part which pierced so deeply into my boy soul, was the sound of thunder and lightning, the stomping of feet. The sweat glistening on the brows of the gesticulating preachers, these messengers of God, as they hurled their threats of wrath. Of hell. Eternally hell. The hell of the never dying fire, the hell of eternal damnation and suffering.

"You will pray. You will plead. You will entreat for one drop of water to cool your burning tongue. But you will not get that drop of water."

24

And if all the shouting was not enough, those preachers had their vividly painted canvasses, with lurid details. The hells. The fires. The devils. Nobody need tell a kid any more about the face of hell.

"Surely goodness and mercy shall follow thee all the days of thy life." Just as surely - evil and anger, and wrath, and hell shall follow thee. Close behind.

There were times when it could have been fun. Was fun, in a way. The way all those things had their beginnings. Like the morning when Dad told me he was going to town with the hay wagon, because of its extra wide bed, to help haul some of the trappings of a coming revival meeting up there on the hillside by the church.

The huge canvass tent, the loads and loads of benches, the big wide planks for the preaching platform. Dad, and all the other leading members of the little white Mennonite church on the corner of Kroeker farm, were drafted into service to prepare for the big event. Especially Dad, because he was not only a son-in-law of J. M. Friesen, pastor of the church, but also earmarked as the understudy, to take over when the patriarch would no longer be able to do his duties. But preachers were not paid in the Mennonite church. They had to farm like everybody else and somehow find time to preach as well.

Dad's mission of the moment was to go to the lumber yard to pick up the lumber and planking. The church people really weren't buying the lumber. They borrowed it. That, too, was one of those little rituals of rural farm community. Knowing that all these Mennonite farmers were customers, when they needed lumber, the lumber people would lend them the planking for revivals.

"Just don't drive any nails in it," they would admonish. "If you put nail holes in it we can't take it back."

I didn't quite comprehend how you could use lumber without driving nails in it but these Mennonite carpenter-farmers knew that trick, too. They would purchase a small portion of the lumber for the framing. The framing was fashioned to hold unnailed planks captive but virgin of nail holes.

It was this loose planking which always added a bit of drama to the sermons. For when a real fiery preacher had worked himself up into a proper frenzy in the selling the messages of the Lord, started shouting, waving his arms and stomping back and forth, the loose planks would rumble an accompaniment. The thunder and lightning.

The huge tent, ah, what an adventure for a kid to see that thing coming to life. Big enough to cover a quarter of the church yard. Watching the men working under the direction of the evangelist's front men, lace the sections of the huge tent together. It was the biggest tent I had ever seen, a three poler. Big as a circus tent but I had never been allowed to go near a circus. They were sinful, our solemn fathers assured us.

But this was almost as good as a circus. Twenty or 30 men pulling on the ropes, lifting, hoisting the huge billowing sections aloft. A monster that almost came alive as the Oklahoma winds tugged and waved the seeming acres of canvas. And even when finally in place, firmly anchored by the big steel shafts driven into the sod, it would continue the undulating movement. A thing alive. Something to bring alive the fires of Jehova. That hell.

After the huge canvas was safely in place, then the job of lugging all those benches. Watching the men fashioning that plank platform with its railings. Lugging the pedal organ from the church over to the tent. The shiny, varnished pulpit, so out of place in that rustic tent setting.

All this in anticipation of the arrival of the star of the show, Evangelist Schultz. He was a great one, the men would say, as they worked. He could make your hair stand on end. He would make the sinners shake in their boots. So spoke our neighbors as they tugged on the ropes, pounded the stakes and "created" the stage for the big show.

I was becoming anxious to see this "great preacher." And when he finally did arrive, after all the stage setting was done, I was a big disappointed. I had thought he must be at least taller than my handsome, white bearded grandfather who was well over six feet tall.

Barrel chested, short, stumpy, with short cropped gray hair, this Preacher Schultz. But he would live up to his billing, we would soon discover. He would make the fires come alive.

It was a custom that each family in the church must issue a dinner invitation for the great visiting evangelist during the course of the two weeks "crusade." Revival meetings, folks called them in those days. To revive the spirit of the church folks, to round up the straying sinners and get them back into the fold.

Actually, there were too many families and the great preacher had to reject a lot of the invitations. But we were among the lucky ones because of Dad, I suppose. No. 2 man in the church. The "rejectees" grumbled a bit, perhaps. Having him in your home might leave a bit of the holy spirt that had rubbed off. Or was it only the pecking order syndrome?

Anyway, it was a big occasion and fun when Preacher Schultz showed up at our house for dinner. Mom had killed all of three fat chickens for the occasion. The platter heaped high with the golden offering. Corn. Potatoes. Gravy. Pie. Oh, wow, was it good to have a bigtime preacher to dinner.

When it came time for the blessing, Dad asked Preacher Schultz to do the honors. I don't remember what he prayed about but I do remember it was a lot different than when Dad did it. Sounded like real glory stuff. After all, wasn't he a pro?

And then the big show. The revival.

One might have expected that we small fry would receive strict orders from Mom and Pop to sit up front. But in our world of Mennonite culture things didn't quite work out that way. It was, in a way, a hierarchy thing. It was the elders who sat up front and the closer you sat, the rule seemed to be, the more secure your position in the rank of the God things. As if, somehow, the blessings would be dispensed in order of nearness to the "throne." Even this kind of throne.

Some of the real important elders almost staked out "dibs" on their front row seats and a guy could catch a bit of hell fire right there if he happened to snitch somebody's staked out seat. In any case, it was on occasion when the moms and the dads were content to allow the kids to sit in the back, under the fringes of the big top.

That way it gave us a chance to do a bit of our kid talk stuff, if we didn't make it too loud. Especially before the "show" got under way. Or during the singing, which always preceded the preaching. It would drown out our yak.

Some of the older boys were openly testing their courage. "Old Preacher Schultz ain't going to get me up there," they would be boasting.

"Up there" was mourner's bench territory. The long bench set up right in front of the platform, with a goodly layer of sawdust sprinkled on the ground to protect the knees of the penitent sinners. The "sawdust trail."

The bench was really the focal point, the entire purpose of the whole show. In fact, a preacher's worth, his entire reputation, might rest on the "score" of the sinners he could lure up to "get saved." Born again.

"I hear he got 57 saved up at his last meeting," one of the church elders could be heard to say. "Reckon we'll get that many?" "Naw, I doubt it. We'll be lucky if we get 25 or 30." "Some always backslide, anyway."

That backslide thing. Such an ominous and secret evil attached to it. Seems like the church folks didn't really like to discuss it much. At the beginning I didn't even quite understand. But I learned. The backsliders were the ones who hit the sawdust trail, got hooked onto the Glory Road but who didn't have the guts to stick it out. Succumbed to a bit of sinning. A "save" which had failed to take.

I always figured the braggers among those older guys were the ones who had never "hit the trail." But when that brag talk warmed up I would always see a few more hanging around who wouldn't say much. When the sin braggers got loud they would sort of slink away. I always figured that these "slinkers" were the backsliders. Their conscience was giving them pain.

Or maybe they were indeed among the souls counted as "saved," but who simply lacked the courage to stand up to the boasters of sin.

As for me and my compatriots of the younger set, say, age eight to 12, we were not really considered serious candidates for the sawdust trail. It was almost as if the older folks thought we hadn't developed a soul yet. Before "the age of accountability," that was the formal term those grownups used. Before a guy had a conscience. Before he could feel the twitches of pain in the soul when he violated one of the rules on the sin list. .

When I heard the older boys boasting that they would never tread that sinner's trail to salvation I sort of kept my mouth shut. My buddies, Albert, Paul, Harvey, Raymond, cousins, buddies, didn't have much to say, either. It was still a bit over our heads. We talked of other things. And listened.

Someone might suggest that as flighty brained kids, on the fringes of the big show, we might not even be drawn into the spirit of the thing. That we might not even listen to Preacher Schultz. But somehow we did. There was the curiosity of the drama being played out there, front stage. The lure of something new, unknown.

And then, since Preacher Schultz was indeed a master of his craft, we were inevitably drawn into it all. If nothing else, those vivid pictures they had hanging up there. Jesus, hanging on the cross. The devil. The angels of heaven. The evil spirits of hell.

The heavenly angels were white and the hellish angels were black. The brimstone. The smoke. All a surrealistic hodge-podge. But luring. A panorama of fascination for a kid brain, trying to comprehend.

The first week was only a warm up. No calls to the mourner's bench. But in the second week things began in earnest. At the end of each sermon designed and calculated to poke red hot needles into the souls of sinners, those calls began. Mournful, haunting but also luring.

At the end of his sermon, after he had thundered his last warning, stomped his last crash on the rattling planks, Preacher Schultz would call for one of those famed "sinners call" songs by the choir, and the organ.

"Softly and tenderly, Jesus is calling. Calling, dear sinner, come home. Come home. Come home."

Or, "Why not tonight?" Or, "Almost persuaded." "Why do you wait, dear brother?"

Right in the middle of one of those haunting songs, Preacher Schultz would raise his hand. The melody would stop. He would do a recap on his final plea.

"I want to tell all of you young people out there who haven't given your hearts to God, there is never a chance like now. If you wait, if you postpone it, it might be too late. Nobody can know whether you will be here tomorrow. God's judgement might come tonight. You might not see tomorrow's rising sun. I know the devil is tugging at your heart, telling you not to do it. Telling you that you still have time for "fun." But believe me, folks, I know. I have seen young people die suddenly, in a single night. Something can strike you down and you would be damned to eternal hell. To burn forever. No one can save you then. It will be too late."

Even I, a child not yet credited with the age of accountability, was frightened by such threats. The "Softly and tenderly" part sounded good. But the hell fires were something else.

"Saved." Such a tremendous weight of fatefulness tied up in that word. Folks of a later age would talk about being "born again." And it was true, our preachers used that term at times. Wasn't it, after all, in the Bible? They would read the Holy Scripture and there would be Jesus, talking about it, "Ye must be born again." But in that Mennonite-Christian-Protestant culture of our day, the key word was always, "Saved." The big word. "Are you saved, brother?

29

Are you saved, sister?" Saved. Saved. Saved. I must have heard that word a million times.

Even for me, hanging around those fringes of the big show, listening to the powerful cries of the full voiced Preacher Schultz, the threats of hell and damnation, a new factor was entering my soul. I was becoming aware of sin. If I had not, indeed, reached my age of accountability, it was coming. Fast.

No, I did not hit the sawdust trail and kneel at the mourner's bench. But, before that big show ended I was thinking about it. I felt a strange tugging at my soul. A new fear I had never known before.

The strange lure and beauty of the other end of the question was attracting me, too. I wanted to be saved - and experience that wonderful glow of love, beauty, tenderness, the forgiveness they were promising me. That moment of glowing light that would enter my soul like a mantle of peace at the moment of salvation.

Perhaps it was my childish shyness that held me back. Perhaps even the fear of the taunting from the "big boys." Once or twice when the pleadings of Preacher Schultz, and the haunting melodies of the choir, almost became irresistable one of my buddies would tug at my sleeve and ask if I wanted to go. The implied promise, that they wanted to go, too. We would go together. But even this was not enough. I found myself pulling free. Giving a shrug. Fearful. Embarrassed. Ashamed to expose my soul before the eyes of all these folks.

And then it was over. Preacher Schultz packed up and left town. The big tent came down. It wasn't quite as glamorous any more. The mystery, the anticipation, were gone. And in their place a gnawing, troubling worry. A fear. A fear of hell.

Oh, it had been there before, at least in a sense. Mom and Dad had been taking me to church ever since I was born. A babe, in mother's arms. I had been hearing all those words from the beginning of any awareness at all in my mind.

And even beyond that, the religion thing occupied such an enormous place in Dad's life. He held two Bible reading and prayer sessions for the family every day. But every day. Not to speak of his prayers at mealtimes. Church every Sunday, rain, shine or ill. Plus prayer meetings every Wednesday.

But it had never really had a living presence in my soul, especially the hell and fear part, until after the Preacher Schultz revival. Now it had become a gnawing, fearful thing.

Perhaps it was inevitable that the night would come when I went to hell. So real you could smell the burning flesh. Hear the wails of the souls in eternal torment. And now hell suddenly had new dimensions. Thirty feet deep. That 60 yards in width and 100 yards in length. I was gripping that slippery pole, my legs dangling over the brink. An evil black thing was clutching at my legs, pulling me down, down.

I woke up screaming. Cold sweat was pouring down my face. My screams awakened my brother, Ernie, lying beside me. It awoke Mother and Dad asleep in their own bedroom. Mother came running.

"What's the matter son? Are you sick?" she demanded anxiously.

It was Dad, sleepy eyed, who suggested, "Maybe it was a bad dream." It was indeed.

Somehow I never had the courage to tell them the truth. That I had been in hell. Or at least dangled over the brink of it. Felt the heat and heard the moaning of the burning souls below.

But to my child being, my newly awakened soul, it was more than a dream. For even the next day in the daylight of a new day, the reality, the fear, remained alive. It remained with me for days.

Until it happened again. It may have been less than two weeks after that first visit to hell that I made the journey once more. In the night. The awakening screams. The sweat. The terror which I could not reveal to my parents.

And now my hell retained its living presence by day. Something indelibly etched upon my consciousness and becoming more real each day. The terror renewed by each visitation to my hell.

And I continued to go. The identical vision each time. Thirty feet deep. Sixty yards wide. A hundred yards long. The glowing fire. The writhing souls. The endless moans. The slippery poles of the cow ban. The devil creature pulling at my legs. I began to fear, each night as I went to bed, that I would see and feel my hell once more. And I did, at least once every two or three weeks.

But now, driven by the terror, I also began to remember the other side of the picture. That peace and heavenly light Preacher Schultz had promised, which my Dad and his Bible eternally promised, if I would ask God to forgive me. To save me. To place

31

me in that promised state of "being saved." I desperately wanted something to save me from those incredibly fearsome visits to hell.

I thought about it for days. For weeks. Perhaps months. Trying to summon the courage to take action. And finally, one night I did that, too.

Dad and I had been out doing some late chores. It was dark. Dad was carrying the kerosene lantern for light. And something demanded our presence in that smelly old cow barn. The barn of the slippery poles. So close to my hell.

Perhaps it was the very fact that we were physically present in that old barn, that symbol of my visitation to hell, that forced the decision. And the action. With a courage born of desperation, I said it to Dad.

"Dad," I said, a new trembling in my voice. "I want to be saved."

Dad stopped suddenly. We had been about to head for the house. He looked at me searchingly, questioningly. Could it be true that his oldest son, barely nine, was asking to enter the kingdom of the Lord? It would become, if not then, one of the most urgent longings of his life.

"Are you sure?" he asked. "Do you know what you are asking?"

I nodded. I could not even look at his face, the face of my own father, in that trembling moment. But I had to escape those visits to hell. To escape the fear that was becoming a part of my waking hours.

There had had always been some sort of a gap between my father and myself. I had never felt close and tender towards him as I did to Mother. Mom was different. I really loved her and when she took me in her strong arms to hug me, it was a glowing feeling of peace. Of being loved. Of being protected. Perhaps I should have talked to Mom about getting saved. But somehow the rules of the game dictated that it be done through father. He was the God image in the family.

Perhaps my feeling of distance, of repulsion, towards my father may have come from the fact that he was the one who punished me. Whipped me when, in his judgement, I had done wrong. The ritual, the religious connection, he made of those whippings, carrying out the will of God, had made my father a source of terror, too.

But now I had committed myself into the quest for salvation through my father.

"Let us pray," he said, setting the lantern down. We were near the edge of the cow barn, where the manure was not so heavy. Where it was more dry. And clean.

By the flickering light of that lantern we knelt and prayed.

"Our Heavenly Father, look down upon us with mercy tonight. I come with my young son who asks to give his soul to your service. Have mercy upon him. Forgive his sins. Allow him to be saved."

Forgive me my sins? What sins?

Perhaps this was the key to the whole thing. I must confess my sins. But what were they? True, I realized that I sometimes made Dad angry. I had been whipped, along with my brother and one of my sisters, for using Dad's new straw stack for a coaster slide. It had been a lot of fun but it had also wrecked all that careful stacking work Dad had done. I had been whipped when Dad had found one of the nail tipped arrows from my home made bow and arrow set, sticking in the side of one of the horses. It hadn't penetrated deep and hardly hurt the horse but maybe that had indeed been a sin. I had snitched several handsful of cherries from Uncle Dave Bushman's orchard, which I had gobbled up as fast as I picked them. Now that might have been a real sin for it had been stealing.

Maybe I had lied to Dad a few times when he asked me if I had completed some ordered chore, and I hadn't. But real sins, the kind that would earn God the right to hurl me into that fiery pit, I could not bring to my mind at that moment.

Dad prayed that I should be saved. That curiously magic word, the seeming key to the whole God business. And I asked it, too, although I may not have given it proper articulation. Maye I didn't even understand it completely. All I knew was that I wanted to be saved from those visits at night to that glowing hell. One day that black devil creature might indeed succeed in pulling me down.

Hesitantly, fearful of allowing the words to pass over my lips in audible fashion, I did try to confess some of my sins that night. The ones I could remember. I did earnestly pray to God, "Please, save me."

But it was taking so long, the praying. The beseeching. I had thought it would all be over in a few minutes. I am sure Dad had believed the same thing. It wasn't.

For I had been promised something which did not come to me now. The picture the Bible people, Preacher Schultz and my Dad, had prepared for my expectations was that in a certain moment, when God accepted my application, that he would reach down with some sort of magic, nay spiritual, wand and touch my body and soul, and I would suddenly be transported into the state of being saved. That moment, I had been promised, would bring a glow of light, peace and salvation.

I was now waiting, and praying, with tears in my eyes, for this visitation of the spirit of God into my yearning soul. And it was this that did not come to me that night.

In fact, the whole process was taking so long I heard Mom calling from the kitchen door, asking anxiously why we didn't come in. Dad rose for a moment from his prayer rite, went to the edge of the cow barn and shouted, "We'll be there in a minute."

We weren't. And now I was becoming nervous. Hurry and come, I was saying in my heart to that holy package of peace and light that was supposed to descend upon me and fill my soul. I truly waited. And it didn't come.

After more long moments a thought began to creep into my mind. We couldn't stay out here in the cow barn all night. In a few minutes Mom would probably come to see what was going on. It was time for the evening bed time worship in the house and my siblings were probably waiting, too, anxious to get to bed. They dare not without that prayer session. I, too, was longing for bed and sleep.

Maybe, that thought was telling me, I would simply have to tell Dad that I had received God's gift, that I was saved, so we could stop all this painful bargaining with a God who, for reasons of his own, was not answering our prayers. Certainly not mine.

Sure, it would be "faking it," but what else was I to do? I could promise myself that I could try again later, on my own. But then, a more frightening thought. If I made such a false confession of being "saved" could not that, too, be a terrible sin? Something that God would mark up in big letters on my sin scoreboard up there in the sky? Maybe holding it against me in any future "save" session.

I couldn't know. I just knew I couldn't kneel there on that dirty cow barn floor forever. I couldn't keep Dad there all night. I couldn't face an anxious Mom, coming out to see what was wrong. I had tried. I had done my part. I was becoming desperate and I had to do something.

In the end, I weakened and blurted out those fateful words, "I'm saved, Dad. I feel good now."

34

Dad's face burst into a smile of triumph. His prayers had been answered. His eldest son, the center of his universe - other than God, of course - had entered the Holy Kingdom. Lord be praised. He praised.

When we got to the house Dad announced the joyful event to Mom, to the whole family. This was the part that embarrassed me the most. I couldn't feel that triumphant joy that Dad and Mom were expressing. Mom hugged me and kissed me. And I could only feel ashamed, mostly because of that lie.

Then, at the final bedtime prayer session, Dad went through it all again. Thanking God for the new blessed event in the Duerksen family. The crossing over by his eldest son, from sin to salvation.

At least I didn't go to hell that night. I was too exhausted. But the next morning, when I awoke, it was with the sudden realization that now I was truly on the spot. Both Mom and Dad and the other kids, knew all about it. It would be announced in church. But most significant of all, so far as I was concerned, was the fact that I would now be expected to live a sinless life. I must be a "perfect" boy. No longer would I be allowed the luxury of even a grumble when Dad assigned an unpleasant task.

No longer could I dawdle when I was supposed to be working. I would have to watch my language when playing with my buddies in school. I'd have to trot home after school every day and do all the work that Dad had laid out.

In short, I'd just about have to stop being a boy. A child. If I was saved I would have to act like it. All the way. It might not have been so bad if I had truly received into my soul that big ball of peace and light, the joy floating around in my innards. It might have given me the strength to live up to the image. But now the terrible burden in my soul was the knowledge that I really didn't have it. It was all a lie. How long can a boy live with such a lie?

I had even heard somewhere the mention of the "unpardonable sin." Had I, perhaps, committed it? Was lying to Dad, in God's presence, that unpardonable sin? I began to feel that sin thing itching at me again. The fear I had felt and which had driven me towards that session with Dad in the cow barn. Now the whole thing was becoming more of a burden than a blessing. What had I done to deserve this?

As weeks went by, I found it was impossible to live that image of perfection. I tried, but it didn't work. It would have meant killing all the boy, the child, in me. Nature simply would not permit it.

The problem was that Dad saw what was happening, too. I was not the little holy angel flitting about, never grumbling, doing his and God's will, 24 hours a day.

One day Dad caught me in some innocent little prank and he then raised the question.

"You haven't forgotten that you were saved, have you?" he asked, tentatively.

And then, those horrible words, "You aren't backsliding, are you?"

Now I had it. That terrible word, "backsliding." In church they had always spoken about it as if it were worse than a sin. The ultimate, the terrible, the hell condemning sin. And now Dad was asking, suggesting that I might be guilty.

"No, Dad, I'll try to be good," I said. I was trapped. What else could I say?

I did try again. And perhaps for a few more weeks I was able to embody that image of perfection which would keep Dad from making that horrible suggestion again. I even kept my promise, the one I had made that night in the cow barn, to pray to God on my own about it. Giving God another chance. Not once, but a number of times I held my own private prayer sessions with God.

I believed. I wanted to believe. I wanted that package of salvation. I begged and pleaded for it. I shed my own private tears. But someone up there refused to mail that package.

And then it happened. Something I had hoped would never happen again. The whole reason why I had gone through all that soul baring ceremony and ritual out in the cow barn had been the hope that it would banish that ultimate horror from my soul.

It was once more in the middle of the night. Once more I awoke with a terrible scream. Once more I awoke my brother, Ernie. And Mom and Dad who came running. My sisters sleeping upstairs had, hopefully, not heard it.

But now it was I, the cold sweat once more upon my brow, who must allay everyone's fears. I could not tell the truth. It would have revealed too much.

"I guess it was something I ate for supper. I just had a bad dream" I said. One more lie.

So everybody went back to bed and to sleep. Except me.

It seemed as if I lay there awake for hours, sleepless. In a cold sweat of fear. It was almost as if the door of the sleep chamber had been slammed shut and locked forever. In fact, I'm not sure whether I ever fell asleep that night.

For that terrible thing had happened to me once more. I had gone back once more to the slippery pole, the grabbing hands of the devil creature, the yawning pit of fire waiting below for me.

I had gone once more to hell.

Thirty feet deep, behind the cow barn.

Chapter Three - Whip

I just stood there, looking at Uncle Dave Bushman's belly, trying to make my mouth work. It wouldn't.

All I could do was blubber. I was scared stiff.

And all I could see was a cross.

It seemed that he had ripped the front on that faded old pair of bib overalls he was wearing and Aunt Bushman apparently had put on a patch of new denim, in the shape of a cross. That patch was right at eye level for me and filled my field of vision. The dark blue of the new cross over the faded old bib.

To look at his face I would have had to look up and I couldn't do it. I was upposed to apologize for stealing cherries out of his orchard, even if I did gobble them up at the scene of the crime. There were witnesses. Two of his little nieces, visiting, had peeked through the hedge and saw us. They blabbed.

I already had one licking for stealing the cherries. Now, if I failed to apologize, I'd get another. Dad had made that clear when I tried to beg my way out of it.

That first licking had been a blister banger, because stealing was way up near the top of the whipping grade sins. My butt was still burning and I didn't want another licking but now I couldn't make my mouth work.

I stood there a long time, looking at his rotund belly and the cross. In a sense it was almost as if I were hung up on that cross. It took so long that Uncle Dave finally decided he'd better break the impasse.

"Well, son, what can I do for you?" he asked. He knew darned well what it was all about. Dad, who had done the butt

38

blistering, had already talked to Uncle Dave about it. But now he had this second stage of ritual to go through.

"I'm sorry I stole the cherries," I finally blurted out. His words had given me courage.

"We've got plenty of cherries. You could have some if you asked. But stealing, it is not good," he said.

I barely heard those last words. I was already gone. Freed from my terrible burden, I was streaking for home like a scared rabbit. My sin paid for. Twice.

First, that godawful whopping. And now, being "hung up" on that cross. Seemed like it, anyway.

Those whippings. My fanny still twitches, just remembering.

My Dad had a thing about whipping his kids, all eight of us. God told him to do it so he did. He had that God command thing well documented.

But he was the only man I knew who made such a holy ceremony out of it. So deliberate and formal, like the Supreme Court handing down a judgement.

Most dads I ever heard about who whipped their kids, did it as a part of anger. Temper. Reprisal. When they caught Johnny in the act. I know about that because I checked it out with some of my buddies. I believe it must be easier for a a dad, doing it that way. That slow, deliberate ritual method Dad used must have been tough on him, too.

Oh, Dad go mad sometimes. You could see it. The anger lines coming in at the edge of his mouth. The trembling lips. But he always managed to jerk up on his own reins and get himself under control. He had to. Because that was in God's command book, too. The Bible.

During all the years I was on Dad's whipping list I can remember only one occasion when he whipped while he was angry. That one was more of a beating than a whipping. But then, when it was all over - I could hardly believe it - he suddenly realized what he had done and apologized. To me, just a kid. Oh, not for the whipping. I probably would have gotten that anyway. But because he had done it in anger, before his "wrath" had a chance to cool off. So you could see he was as tough on himself as he was on us, the kids.

But that cool, deliberate method of Dad's was tough on a kid's psychological stability. When he caught you in the act of one of those whipping grade sins, or found out about it later, he just told you, almost formally, that you had earned a licking and were going to get it.

"Well, son, it looks like I'll have to whip you again." But not right then. In fact, he almost never did it when he passed judgement. There had to be that "cooling off" period first. Usually he did in the evening, just before bed time. That meant if your "sin," and the judgement, came in the morning you had to live with that horrible "thing" hanging over your head all day long. No fun that day. Talk about the "Sword of Damocles."

Sometimes it was Mom who caught you, and passed judgement. But she almost always left the actual whopping to Dad. "I'm going to tell Dad about this when he gets home and he'll have to whip you."

Oh, no. It almost made me wish, sometimes, that Dad wouldn't come home at all.

"Why can't you do it, Mom?" I would plead.

No mystery about this. I had learned, long ago, that Mom didn't whip as hard as Dad did. If it was just a little "sin" she might agree but if she figured I need a good whopping I'd just have to wait for Dad. More Damocles.

But Dad wasn't so dumb either. He was well aware of the fact that Mom never laid her hands on like he did. I can remember more than one occasion when Mom gave me a licking and then, when Dad got home, he gave me another on. Just to make sure I got the message.

By doing it at bed time it gave Dad the opportunity to go through the whole ritual. That was real important to him.

Dad and Mom, all of us, had to go through the "family worship" thing at bed time, every night. But every night. Dad never skipped. If things got a bit hectic and it was late, he might cut it short but then he'd make up for it next time. Skip it? Forget about that.

First Dad would read a chapter from the Bible. Then, "Let's pray." It meant all of us had to get down on our knees by our chairs and listen while Dad, sometimes Mom, went through their prayers. It wasn't any of this "God bless our food, Amen." Dad prayed about everything.

If the weather was dry, he prayed for rain. If it rained too much, he prayed for God to let up. If anybody he knew was sick, he prayed for them. If somebody in the neighborhood died, he prayed for their soul. If a bank note was due and he didn't have the money, he asked God to help out on that, too. He prayed for the heathen. He prayed for the sinners.

If something bad happened, like the time the lightning struck a fence out in the pasture and killed three of our best cows, Dad would also remind God about that. Humble like. But insistant, too.

"Oh, Lord, in thy wisdom thou hast allowed this painful thing to happen to us. If it was because we have sinned, Lord, forgive us and show us thy will. Thou knowest, Lord, that we are poor. We pray that thou willst protect us from harm and evil."

And then he always prayed about us, the kids. Mostly for God to look after us, to keep us "free from evil" - whatever that was - and for God to talk to us and make us give our souls to Him.

On whipping nights there was always a special ritual. The stuff he would read from the Bible would always be especially selected to deal with the whipping matter. He wanted to make sure, quite sure, that we understood. It was not Dad's will that we were getting it, but because God had commanded it. For our own good. He had it all down pat, those Bible verses, and they clanged home like the clanging of a hangman's bell.

"He that spareth the rod hateth his son; but he who loves his son chastises him."

I never could understand why a man had to hate his son if he didn't whip him.

"Chasten thy son while there is hope, and let not thy soul spare for his crying."

Oh, wow. That explained why crying never helped. God told him not to listen if we yelled.

One of the real toughies went like this, "Withhold not correction from the child; for if thou beatest him with the rod he shall not die. Thou shalt beat him with the rod, and shalt deliver his soul from hell."

No way you could argue with that one. One thing for certain, Dad was going to keep us out of hell, if whipping would do it. But I never could figure out the part about how whipping a kid would keep him from dying.

"The rod and reproof giveth wisdom; but a child left to himself bringeth his mother to shame."

So - these lickings were supoosed to make me a wise guy. As for Mom, I certainly didn't want her in a state of shame but why did a kid have to be whopped all the time to keep her out of the shame business?

41

After he had read off a string of those Bible whipping quotes, Dad would start the prayer end of the ritual. Here it came all over again. "Lord, we love our children but we know we must carry out thy command to punish them. Lord grant us wisdom to do what is right in thy sight."

First he made darned sure we understood that it was God who was making him do it and then he asked for wisdom to decide. Who was doing the deciding?

Mostly, at that point, as I knelt at my chair and trembled in anticipation, I just wanted to get it over with and it was almost a relief when, after the prayer, Dad would light the old kerosene lantern and we'd head for the barn.

Then came the problem of the weapon. That was tough, too, especially the way he handled it. He would hand me his pocket knife and tell me to go cut a switch from the big mulberry tree beside the barn. Man, my Dad sure knew how to lay on the agony. And stretch it out. Like making a condemned man furnish his own rope to be hanged with. And maybe even make him tie the knot.

Cutting that switch posed a dilemna, too. Self-preservation would suggest that you cut a small one. But if it was too small Dad wouldn't accept it. We had been through that before. On the other hand, a thin one, even if it was barely big enough to pass Dad's inspection, would bring regrets because it would cut. And hurt. Wow, those welts. But if you cut one too heavy, too thick, that would hurt just as bad, from the whomp.

Sometimes Dad used a leather strap from the horse harness. He usually doubled it and it was bearable until it struck with the edges, instead of flat. Ouch.

Dad had his favorite "whipping corner" of the barn. It was where you had to bend over the feed box. "Bend over the box," he would command.

I'd make my last desperate plea. "Please, Dad, I'm sorry. I won't do it any more." I'd start blubbering. But it was a waste of time and emotion. Dad had his orders to "spare not for his crying." I bent. He whopped.

The size of the whipping depended a lot on Dad's cool judgement. If, in his opinion, your sin was a good sized one, you got a good whacking. If it was a sort of border line transgression, you might get off with a few licks.

For example, snitching something - stealing - was up near the top of the list and you could count on some blisters on your butt.

I only got caught stealing that one time, those cherries from Uncle Dave Bushman's orchrd. And got the blisters.

The biggest thing I resented about the deal, aside from that painful apology episode, was the fact that it had been my cousin, Frank Friesen, who had talked me into it. He didn't get a whipping, or have to go apologize. Cousin Frank got by with all sorts of things. He even bragged about the watermelons he stole in the summer time. And then there was the time he took a guy's love letter out of our neighbor's mail box, tore it open, read it and then burned it. The neighbor's son had a big love affair going and was getting letters from his sweetie.

I heard you could go to jail for stealing mail. I waited to see if he'd go to jail but he never did. Frank was pretty big and he even bragged that when his dad tried to whip him he grabbed the broomstick his dad wanted to use, jerked it out of his dad's hands and chased his dad out of the house with it. Frank was a bully who made it rough on the smaller kids in school. And here I was, the one who kept getting the licks.

Using profanity was way up at the top of the list, too. I found out about that when my Cousin Irvin tried to run over me with his horse and I called him a, "Goddamned son of a bitch."

Some of my sisters heard it and told Dad. Man, that one really brought on a big ceremony.

That one happened while we were on our way home from school, on one of the days when Cousin Irvin rode a horse. It was another one of those crazy ideas a young character gets when the hormones start popping. Irvin was older than I but he wasn't even mad at me. He probably simply wanted to show off, to impress the girls. Told me he was going to run over me on his horse.

He'd charge at me with the horse but he really should have known better. Most horses don't like running over people and the horse wouldn't stomp me. Besides, I grew up on a farm and had been around horses all my life. I wasn't afraid of a horse. If I had done battle with Reuben, the big devil horse, I could handle Irvin's horse. When he got too close I simply grabbed the bridle rein of the horse and gave it a couple of yanks. It made the horse rear and almost threw Irvin off. That was when he really got mad and tried for keeps to make his horse run over me. And that was when I called him a sonofabitch. And then I got out of his reach by scrambling under a fence. The horse wouldn't jump the fence.

But I could even feel it, in my mouth and in my heart, when I shouted those "profane" words at him, that I was committing a sin.

43

I wasn't used to using such words. They left a strange, bitter taste in my mouth.

I tried to tell Dad about what Cousin Irvin had done and felt I at least had mitigating circumstances. It didn't matter, I had taken God's name in vain and would get my whopping.

"Do you know what a bitch is?" Dad asked solemnly, there in the barn, just before the licks started. I didn't and that was when he explained that a bitch was a female dog and calling Irvin a sonofabitch was calling his mother a female dog. Well, I was sorry about that because Aunt Friesen was a pretty decent woman and had even given us cookies sometimes. I wasn't mad at her. I was mad at Irvin but I doubt if he even got a licking for his horse play.

That licking, the one I got, was one of the hot ones. I had welts on my butt for days.

As time went by I figured I didn't deserve at least some of the lickings I got. I even figured maybe Dad was taking that God command stuff a bit too seriously. At other times? Well, maybe so.

Like that time, on Halloween, when a gang of us went over to the Barkman farm and threw a lot of his corn out of the crib, into the mud. I figured, even while we were doing it, I would get popped if Dad found out. He did. And I got my licks.

Usually, when several of us were involved in the same "misdemeanor," Dad took us to our licking ceremony separately. You see, Dad learned some things along the way, too. If he herded us together we'd watch to see who got whopped the hardest and then complain, "You didn't whip her (maybe one of my sisters) as hard as you whipped me."

Heck, sometimes we even counted the licks to see if he was being fair. I remember one time when I and my brother and two of my sisters were all involved in the same "sin." That was one time he took us all down into the cellar together.

The biggest thing I noticed that time was that the girls didn't get licked nearly as hard as we, the boys, did. I really didn't mind that part so much. Somehow, it seemed, the girls shouldn't be whipped as hard as boys. Funny how I was willing to concede that, even at the tender age of eight or nine.

Unless I happened to be mad at one of my sisters and hoped Dad would really pour it on. Maybe after we had been fighting.

One thing Dad wouldn't allow when he whipped us, was resistance. Fighting or squirming to get out from under. Dad even said it, "If you fight you'll just get it harder." He meant it. But

God, just laying there and taking it. It violated all the laws of nature.

There was one strange aspect to those whipping episodes with Dad, the physical contact thing. For example, in the days when I was just a little squirt, before the feed box period, when Dad would bend me over his knee to do the spanking. I found myself physically repulsed by that contact with his knees, his arm around me to hold me.

Even later, during the feed box period, when the licking was over Dad always wanted to put his arms around me, hug me and kiss me to prove he still loved me, despite the licking. And he kept reminding me that he was only doing it to keep me out of hell. Because God had made it so clear that was the way to do it. But I couldn't stomach that body to body contact with Dad. Never could.

Now, with Mom, that was different. In the first place, she never whipped as hard as Dad did. In the second place, somehow, it felt good to feel Mom's arms around me. I could feel the love coming through. When Mom put her arms around me and kissed me I felt warm and loved and protected.

On a few occasions Mom even interceded with Dad, to talk him out of a licking for me. And a few times Dad even let me get by with a warning when she did. Oh, how I loved Mom then.

I must have been all of 11 or 12 when that "anger" incident took place. I was considered big enough by now to work in the fields, like a man. Even with a four horse span on the gang plow. But it got, as the old cliche goes, "hot as hell" out there under the Oklahoma sun in July and August. Sometimes that thermometer would squirt up over the 100 mark for days on end.

And, since Dad always farmed with horses - he hated mules - it meant we had to stop after every two or three rounds and let the horses blow. Sometimes Dad would even come out to the field carrying a couple of big buckets of water to give the big animals an "in between" sip of water. The sweat would be dripping off those beasts.

But Dad always wanted to keep his eye on things so he always told me to do the "blow" thing on the home end of the field. That way, if he was doing some chores in the yard, he could keep and eye on me. But the thing I didn't like about it was that the home end was right out under that blazing sun. I was a real red head, with sensitive skin, and all I had for protection was a big straw hat and that thin muslin shirt.

That was when I noticed that by mid-afternoon those big tall cottonwood trees edging the south end of the field, would cast their shadows out over the plow area. Why not do my horse resting act down south, in the shade? I know I should have said something to Dad about it. But I didn't.

Oh, how good that shade felt. As I sat there a few minutes I guess I even dozed a bit. Those farm work days were so terribly long for a kid. But Dad was watching a lot closer than I thought. And here I was in this shaded spot that wasn't even in sight from the house.

I didn't hear Dad coming. I didn't even hear the shouting he swore he did. It had been all that shouting, with no response, that got his steam up. He was wondering why it was taking so long to make my round of the field.

The first thing I knew, I had been jerked off that plow seat, hurled down on the ground and Dad was standing over me with a stick, a big stout one, and was whaling the tar out of me.

I could see he was angry this time. But for real. He was gasping for breath and screaming, "Why didn't you answer me? Why didn't you answer me?" He didn't even give me a chance to answer, to say anything. Just whopped and screamed.

And then, so suddenly, as quickly as it began it was all over. He stopped. Almost as if some mysterious force had grabbed him and locked his hand. He was still breathing hard but now I could see something changing in his face. As if, so suddenly, the realization had come to his soul that now he had sinned. The voice of his God, "Lift not thine hand in anger."

Very quietly, but earnestly, he said it, "I'm sorry I whipped you while I was angry."

That was the only time in his life that Dad had touched me in a fit of anger.

As for me, just a kid and hurting from the heated blows he had rained upon my body, I couldn't explain what was going on inside my own soul. All I knew was that suddenly I wasn't so angry with Dad after all. Hurt. Offended. True. But, after all, that was what he was apologizing about.

I suppose that in any father-son whipping situation there has to come a time for the last whipping. I've sometimes wondered which it is that makes the decision. Somehow, I suspect, in most cases it is the son. I know it was in my case.

Father never was a big man. Probably in those days he never weighed more than 140 pounds. But as I grew, it became apparent that nature intended me to be bigger than my Dad. By the time I was 15 I was as big as he, and very strong.

It was not a simple decision on my part. Nor one I made in a moment. I thought about it a long time. One of the things that brought the decision was the feeling, on my part, that Dad had sometimes whipped me when I really didn't deserve it.

In other cases? Well, I knew I had violated his rules, his code of conduct, but I decided I had just reached an age when I didn't want to be whipped any longer. Part of it may even have been pride, the fact that I felt I was getting too old, too big, to be whipped like a kid. In any case, I had simply decided that there would be no more whippings.

After I made that decision, I knew it was only a matter of time until the big confrontation would come. I wondered how Dad would take it. Would he fight? Would he physically try to reassert his authority? If so, would I fight back? Strike my father?

My decision, if it came to that, was that I would not hit my father. I would simply grab his stick, hold it and hold him off me.

The strange thing about it all is that I cannot even remember what my "sin" was that did bring that final confrontation. But I remember the confrontation, almost as clearly as if it had happened yesterday. As usual, Dad had informed me that I had done something wrong and that I would be whipped. He ordered me to come to the barn with him.

I went. I didn't want to create a scene that any of the family, especially Mom, might have to witness. I certainly did not want to humiliate Dad in front of her. So we went to the barn. Dad had his stick and ordered me to do the bending, over the rim of the horse stall. And that was my moment of truth. It took all the courage I had but I said it.

"Dad, you're not going to whip me."

Now it was almost as if I were the aggressor, and that I had struck him across the face with his own stick. That hurt look in his eyes. But after a moment it was almost as if he, too, had been thinking about it, had been anticipating this confrontation.

But he wasn't ready to surrender so easily.

"What do you mean, I'm not going to whip you? I'm your father and you've got to obey me. You're not a man yet," he replied stubbornly.

"You're not going to whip me," I repeated. I guess I was trembling, too, but I was also determined.

This was open rebellion against a parental authority that had been enforced, by the whip, for so many years. Perhaps ever since I was one or two years old. I didn't even remember the beginning. I would remember the end and it had now ended.

Dad did try a bit further but I could see the stubborn resolve was slowly melting. It was no longer strong enough to break my will. He ordered me once more to bend over the crib. I stared into his eyes and said it once more, "You're not going to whip me."

That was when our eyes locked contact for several minutes. Long minutes. At one point he even made a move toward me, with the stick. But then, perhaps, he knew he had lost.

Dad was tough, for a small man. And he had courage. I would even learn more about that later. But at that moment he suddenly found he did not have the courage to physically do battle with his oldest son.

Looking back on it even today, from a perspective of so many years, or even as of the moment itself, I believe I was suffering, too. It is not easy for a boy to humiliate his father in this fashion. I've even heard men boast that if one of their teen aged sons ever tried a trick like that on them they would wait until that son was asleep in bed, get a baseball bat and, "Beat hell out of him."

I doubt if very many fathers ever carried out a threat of that kind. I know my father would never have done it. That whipping thing had been a part of his life, a part of his religion, almost a religious rite. In challenging him in this manner I had challenged one of the most basic principles of his life. And he wasn't prepared to cope with it.

I had won. But it was not a proud victory. In fact, for a moment, it was almost as if I was back there in Uncle Bushman's back yard again. Hung up on that cross.

Chapter Four - The Skunk Tail Bit

It was my Uncle Dave Friesen who first told me about that skunk tail bit.

Uncle Dave had squinty eyes that made him look as if he were smiling all the time. Even when he wasn't. Most of the time he was. But it was tough on a kid, looking at those squinty eyes and trying to decide whether to take him seriously or not. A kid had to be careful about things like that.

Uncle Dave's farm wagon came rattling down the road that morning, behind that unmatched team of his, a roan and a bay. Uncle Dave was clucking the horses along in a shuffling half trot. And trotting along behind, in the cloud of dust following the wagon, came his two big hounds. Those hounds went just about every place Uncle Dave went.

He had his carpenter tools in the wagon, and some lumber. He was coming to our house because our old wheat granary, sitting there on the side of the gyp hill with its faded coat of red barn paint and patched cedar shingle roof, needed some patching. Just old age. Uncle Dave was "Carpenter Uncle" in the family clan and was going to help Dad patch the granary.

Out in the fields the winter wheat was greening for spring. In a few weeks it would be harvest time and no time for granary patching. It was in the early spring when folks, especially uncles, helped each other with chores like that. Nobody got paid. If Uncle Dave's granary needed patching, Dad would help him. Just a part of the old barn raising tradition of the prairie frontier.

But the big thing that happened that day was something those two hounds of Uncle Dave's got themselves involved in out there in the fruit orchard. Something a hound, or any dog for that matter, just wasn't supposed to become involved in. Absolutely and positively, not.

No sooner had Uncle Dave stopped and tied his horses than those hounds started prowling the new territory. Somewhere out there in the orchard they jumped a big fat skunk and chased him into his den. They were now furiously digging, trying to get their teeth into his smelly hide.

All this action had turned it into a skunky sort of day. The moist spring air out in the orchard, in fact our whole front yard, was hanging heavy with that choky, pukey smell of skunk. All because those crazy hounds were out there violating all the laws of normal dog behavior.

Taylor's Trapping Guide and all the other animal books were very clear on that. A skunk was a very stupid animal, the Guide said, because he could afford to be. Equipped with that horrible super stink weapon he didn't have to be smart. No man, beast or any would-be skunk eater could stand up to the yellow, pukey stuff a skunk could squirt with such deadly accuracy, up to 15 or 20 feet.

As Taylor's Guide put it, "Once he has faced that terrible weapon, any sensible dog will make a wide circle around a skunk." Just proved Uncle Dave's dogs didn't have any sense.

And the stuff was terrible, all right. That much I knew.

Maybe I was only about 10 or 11 years old but I had already served my time in the "skonk works." It was the lure of money that got a poor country kid into a mess like that. Taylor's, or even the local hide dealer, would pay several bucks per hide for a good skunk fur. Man, those were the days when a kid was lucky if Dad gave him a nickle on Saturday to buy a candy bar. Two whole bucks for one fur? Maybe even more if he was a big one and didn't have too much white striping on him. And if you didn't cut any holes in his hide when you skinned him.

Was it any wonder that a youngster could lose his sanity and go skunk trapping?

Oh, but the irony of it all. For it was true about how stupid a skunk was. You didn't have to be a smart trapper and learn a lot of tricks like you did when you were trying to trap a coon or a coyote. The coyotes were the smartest of all, almost impossible to catch. But a skunk, you just set one of your Oneidas in the mouth of a fresh skunk den and the stupid skunk would walk right into it.

That was the easy part that helped lure you into it. But oh, God, what happened after that.

DEAR GOD, I'M ONLY A BOY

Most kids, my age or bigger, who fell for the lure of those big bucks dangling out there in front of their eyes and tried skunk trapping usually gave up after one or two of those repulsive experiences. My brother, Ernie, for example. He didn't have the stomach for it. But everybody said I had some sort of stubborn streak in me. Even my sisters agreed to that. If I made up my mind to do something I usually did it. Or got bloodied in the try. Or "stunked." It was that stubborn streak that was going to get me into a lot of "stunkem" trouble.

I remember how crazy I was when it all started. Actually felt, for a few minutes, at least, that I was lucky when I caught one of the stinky beasts. Usually, you could tell by your nose, long before you got to the scene. After that was when the fun began.

So, you've got Old Mister Skunk caught, with one of his legs firmly gripped by the jaws of your Oneida, but how do you kill him and skin him without getting skunked? But good.

It's incredible how many rounds of "skunkem" a skunk can fire without running out of ammunition. For one of the early bright ideas I came up with, in dealing with a trapped skunk, was to stand upwind and out of range, then chunk rocks or hunks of wood at him. Knowing that he would cut loose with a barrage every time a rock landed near him. Or on him.

After about 20 or 30 chunks, you would notice that the squirts were becoming weaker and weaker. For it was after I was certain he had fired his last drop from his skunk cannon that I would move in, cautiously, to finish him off with a club.

But, no, no, no. Every time, but every time, that beast would somehow manage to come up with one more squirt as soon as I got into range.

And then it became some sort of an insane, furious and stubborn anger that would take over, forcing me to throw all caution to the wind, wade into the face of his horrible weapon and take it while I whacked him to death.

And thus turned myself into a pariah. For, no matter how cold it was Mom would simply, but firmly, bar the house door. It meant taking a tooth chattering bath with lye soap out in the tool shed.

Then, after putting on clean clothes you'd have to soak your contaminated overalls, shirt and every stitch you had on, down to your underwear, in kerosene for several days before Mom would dare try to wash them.

51

But now there were those crazy hounds of Uncle Dave's, out there doing battle with a well armed skunk. And stubbornly defying all the laws of normal dog behavior. They were staying with him despite their reception of several well aimed blasts of skunk ammo. Smack in the face. The eyes. The nose. The mouth.

In the end, the dogs smelled worse than the skunk.

There wasn't enough room in the entrance to that den for both dogs at once so they took their stubborn turns at the punishment. One dog would dig furiously for a few seconds and then, after receiving several blasts of the skunk skokem right in the face, he would back out, clawing his paws at his burning eyes. Cough, sneezing, choking, wheezing, slobbering.

Then hound Number Two would dive in and give it a try until he, too, had received his quota of torture. One-two, one-two.

Everybody - Uncle Dave, Dad, Mom, the whole family and I - knew what was going on. Lord, how could you help knowing. Downwind, you could smell that stuff for half a mile.

Several times while the battle was going on I sneaked up as close as I dared, to try to get a look. Not too close. I didn't want to get banned to Siberia out of skunk trapping season. No money in that.

From the depth to which the hounds had progressed into the tunnel it was clear that Mister Skunk and acquired, under the press of this emergency, a bit more than his normal quota of intelligence and, while not abandoning all hope in his ultimate weapon, he must have begun doing a bit of digging of his own. Deeper and deeper into the mother earth.

My reaction to all this, based on my past skunk experience, was one of pure admiration for the gutsy behavior of Uncle Dave's hounds. How could they keep diving in for more when they were almost literally being suffocated by that evil liquid? My dog, Pedro, was a gutsy dog, too, but he had enough sense not to tackle a skunk.

I'm not sure exactly how long that crazy, insane battle lasted. It may have been an hour. Two hours. Maybe even more.

But I do know the hounds finally won it when one of them managed to get his teeth into the smelly hide of that black beast and came out of the hole dragging that clawing, spitting, fighting and squirting skunk. I guess even a skunk would fight when he had to.

But, once clear of the tunnel, the skunk was no match for two angry hounds. Faced with the bared fangs of those dogs, the skunk was quickly slain and the dogs then dragged the smelly body up into the front yard.

In the manner of victorious dogs in the presence of their master, that final gesture of dog triumph, the hounds dragged their odorous prey up to Uncle Dave and attempted to lay their booty at his feet. It was one time when Uncle Dave, normally quite proud of his two brave hunting dogs, didn't want a damned thing to do with them, no matter how glorious their victory.

And, considering the caliber of the awful cannon, it really hadn't been such a one sided battle.

After a rejection from their master, the hounds were willing to lay the "offering" at Dad's feet. When he chased them away, they came to me but I was equally rejective, no matter how much I admired their guts.

The dogs finally dragged the smelly body out to the middle of the yard and left it lying there while they went slinking off to nurse their burning eyes and sorely offended nostrils. They certainly made no attempt to eat their fallen enemy.

It was Dad who finally had to dig a hole, then get a long handled pitch fork, careful lift the stinking body and deposit it in the hole. A goodly portion of earth was then shoveled over.

It might be the produce of an over stimulated imagination if I suggest that, for weeks after that, every time I went near that skunk grave I could smell the odor of skunk seeping up through the earth.

As for the fruit orchard and the area of that battle scarred den, it required no imagination to perceive that this field of battle smelled mightily and malodorously for weeks.

But then there had been that other little fateful item which had surfaced on that day while the hound-skunk battle had been going on. Somewhere along the way, as the battle progressed, Uncle Dave had made a somewhat off-hand remark which was going to stick in my mind for a long time. It would lead me to a certain fateful day. "You know," he said, casually, "folks say that if you grab a skunk by his tail and jerk him off the ground before he can pee on you, it will paralyze his squirt machinery. The skunk can't pee on you unless his feet are planted solid on the ground."

I pondered that remark, as best a kid could ponder. I looked at Uncle Dave's squinty eyes. I tried to decide whether he was kidding me or not. I couldn't tell.

I didn't want to argue with Uncle Dave but even I, a snotty kid, knew that when a skunk fired that smelly stuff at you it wasn't pee. All skunks, male and female, had regular pee machinery just like other animals. The skunkem stuff came from special glands and was squirted through a special squirt hole located just below his tail. On a papa skunk, for example, the pee machinery wouldn't even be aimed in the right direction.

Then you had to consider the source, too. Uncle Dave was just a bit of a maverick in our tightly knit Mennonite clan. He didn't come to church every Sunday like he was supposed to. Not even if his dad, my grandpa, was the preacher. Folks said Uncle Dave was known to swig a bit of home brew - the only kind you could get in those days when all beer or liquor was illegal. And sinful, too, if you asked Dad or Grandpa. There were even rumors that Uncle Dave made a bit of of the stuff.

Beyond all that, to all of us young squirts, nephews and such, there was an aura of glamour hanging around Uncle Dave's head. Much of it based on the notoriety he earned one day when he became involved in a fight in our town in which the weapons were carpenter hammers. A pair of smoking six-guns would have made it a bit more exciting but even a hammer can acquire a certain measure of glamour under proper circumstances.

Uncle Dave showed up wearing a bandage on his head. We didn't mind that when we also got word that his opponent had to be carted off to the hospital with an even bigger bandage. The grownups never did tell us kids all the details. It seems there was a big dust-up with the law over that one. Mennonites were't supposed to get into trouble with the law. The clan was proud of the boast that no Mennonite had ever seen the inside of the Custer County jail.

Word got out that the whole deal was settled on some sort of a "self-defense" plea, but none of that distracted from Uncle Dave's stature in the eyes of his youthful beholders.

Later, if the subject of that fight ever came up, Uncle Dave never said much. He just looked at you with that squinty face of his and you could never be sure whether he was smiling or not. I rather suspect he was.

But all this was part of the reason why a kid had to be careful in considering any remark Uncle Dave made about skunk tails.

Not that the idea didn't have its allure. Especially to a kid who also happened to be a skunk trapper. It was more or less moot at the moment. Because the skunk trapping season, the cold weather when the furs were prime, was still months away. But I wanted to believe it and somehow the idea just wouldn't go away. It just got stuck there in my mind.

Gosh, if it were true it might solve my problems about getting stunk up during the trapping season. Somehow, maybe. But the big problem still remained as to how one would manage to get close enough to a skunk to grab his tail without getting skunked. That would take a bit of doing.

One thought that came to mind was to enlist the help of my brother, Ernie, to distract the skunk while I sneaked up to him. But Ernie wasn't the daring kind. I then considered inventing some sort of long pole with a tail grabber on the end of it. But before I got involved in anything like that I wanted to have more evidence that it would work.

I asked several grownups about it, starting with Dad. He was a farmer and while he had never trapped skunks I figured that anybody who grew up out there on that Oklahoma prairie must have had his encounters with skunks.

Dad was noncommital. "I don't know. I never heard of it," he said. And then he added, "I never tried it." He paused a moment and then he added, for emphasis, "I know I never will, either."

End of skunk tail interview with Dad. He had stopped just short of flatly forbidding me to try it. Perhaps he thought his eldest son had enough sense not to.

I asked several other grownups about it. Most of them, like Dad, were sort of in the middle.

One thing for doggone sure, nobody seemed eager to try it. About the most encouraging answer I could get went something like this - "Well, I never heard of that one but you know, come to think about it, it might be true." All of which only made me more curious than ever.

Oh, God, if only that skunk hadn't been out in the cow pasture that day. If everything hadn't been such a perfect set-up. Sometimes, when I think back about it now, it almost seems as if fate had been planning that one for a long, long time.

It was a Sunday afternoon and such a beautiful day. One of those early summer days when the weather was not too hot and the whispy white clouds were playing tag with the sun. And for some now forgotten boy reason I was out in the pasture without being under any orders from Dad. Just on my own.

My dog, Pedro, was out there with me but he was off sniffing for rabbits somewhere. Even if he had been at my side he wouldn't have been of much help because, when it came to skunks, he wasn't on the gutsy side. For all practical purposes I was alone out there on that pasture hilltop. A hilltop dented with a few of those little gyp stone caves, or dens.

Alone, except for the skunk

When I first spotted him he was just standing there in the entrance to his rocky den. It was nature's architectural design of the scene which made everything so perfect.

Just a small cave, with an entrance about six or seven inches high and perhaps a foot wide. Flatter than tall. The roof of the entrance was the top of the hill, then that sharp little vertical drop for about a foot, with that entrance cut by nature into the side of that tiny cliff.

The skunk heard me coming and reacted as any normal skunk will do upon the approach of any possible danger. He raised that plumy tail of his. Straight up. I was quite familiar with that sign. It meant he was ready, his firing piece cocked and waiting. He hadn't fired a barrage, yet. He would wait until I was well within range. Oh, I knew all about skunks. Well, almost all. I did know he could fire in a split second.

But when he cocked that weapon, by raising his tail, it meant that the tip of that tail was protruding over the edge of that little ledge above his den door. My heart suddenly was pounding with the exciting prospect of what was about to happen. I had come to my moment of truth. I would have to make a decision, very quickly. And the opportunity was so perfect. So damnably perfect.

All I had to do was sneak around to the rear of the den and come back towards him from the rear, with that little overhang giving me perfect protection from being struck by his stink barrage. I could simply reach down and grab the end of that raised tail without being in the line of fire.

He would have to come out of his den entrance to be able to aim his artillery fire at me on top of his den. I would have the protection of that overhang to duck for cover if I saw him coming out.

No, I cannot explain it. I couldn't then and cannot now, more than 50 years later. On that day it simply seemed as if I were being driven by some mystic hydraulics of compulsion. I couldn't stop myself. I just had to do it.

The skunk cooperated perfectly. Perhaps that age old assumption of immunity and impudence, the inbuilt skunk knowledge that he was safe so long as he had that terrible weapon cocked and ready, was making him so brave.

56

As I carefully approached I could see that skunk tail protruding over the lip of the rock roof. The air was so clear and I was so close I could almost count the hairs on the plumy tail, waving gently in the breeze.

And then I did it, just reached down and grabbed his tail and jerked. That skunk was off the ground!

Oh, Mama, please, why did it have to be so terrible? So awful? So pukey?

Not once, but twice. Three times. Or more. I couldn't be sure.

I do know it was more than once for my stubborn brain was still working while it was going on. The first fleeting thought was that perhaps he had managed to fire his first blast before his feet left the ground and that after that first blast the punishment would stop.

After all, my mind was telling me, in a logic so perverse it nearly became the ultimate self punishment, I had already suffered that first blast. A second could hardly be worse. And if I wanted to prove, once and for all time, whether Uncle Dave had been wrong, I must suffer the ultimate. I would have to hang on.

What lunacy can possess the mind of a stubborn child?

Yes, I had been sorely punished by skunks before. But on those previous occasions the "direct hits" had been mostly in the form of a few drops on my trouser legs. Or on the sleeve. This time I was getting it straight in the face.

How can one truly describe it to people who have never had this ultimate experience?

Doctors sometimes talk about a thing called "exquisite pain," an area of pain so intense that the human brain becomes a quivering mass in which all other thought processes stop. Out on that Oklahoma hill top that day, I was suffering the exquisite revulsion - if not pain. My eyes aflame. My nose rebelling beyond rebellion. Lungs heaving. Choking. Convulsed

Oh, God! Mama! Uncle Dave! Why did you have to tell me?

Chapter Five - Horse Biscuits

The devout Mennonite fathers who founded Friesen School, District 12, could only have gagged righteously in their beards at the suggestion that one day there would be included in the learning process of the school a lesson in the art of eating horse biscuits. Or horse balls. Oh, well, horse turds if you insist.

And yet, school was where I was forced to learn it.

Oh, the teacher never had a hand in it. In fact she never knew. She was probably busy inside, grading papers, the day it happened. It was too revolting for me to tell her and it would have required using that word a kid didn't use in front of a proper lady of our day.

Besides, even if I had had the nerve to tell her it would have gotten my Cousin Frank Friesen into trouble. And then I would have been in worse trouble. For Cousin Frank would have probably beaten me until I wasn't able to crawl. He was the one who stuffed those horrible "biscuits" in my mouth.

Forcibly, of course, and with the help of his kid brother, Paul. Frank never would have been able to do it by himself, even if he was bigger than I and was always knocking the smaller kids around. The school bully, Frank.

Most kids, after they are no longer kids, usually have a few fond remembrances of the old one room country school - ours had two rooms - where they acquired their rote in "reading, 'riting and 'rithmatic." Other than the the horse biscuits, and a few more unpleasant things, I suppose I have my share of happy memories about that school.

For one thing it was my Grandpa Friesen who donated the land upon which that school stood, a little corner out of the 160 acres of prime farm land he had homesteaded just before the turn of the century.

Folks said that little corner of land was the highest hill in the county and if you stood on that school yard on a clear day you could see darned near all of Custer County. If you climbed into the bell tower you could see even further than that. So flat was Western Oklahoma.

That big bell in the tower would have to be part of the picture for it was one of the rigidly enforced rules that the teacher had to ring that bell at 7:30 every morning, half an hour before school time, to remind all the kids in the neighborhood that if they were not hoofing it on the way to school, they'd better get hiking. While teacher stoked up a fire in the big pot bellied stove.

If that Oklahoma wind wasn't howling in the wrong direction you could hear that bell all the way to the Kroeker farm, where we lived, nearly two miles away. On the down wind side, you could hear it farther than that.

The memories aren't quite so fond when you start remembering how cruelly cold that wind could be on a January morning. How hard it blew. So hard it almost felt like something solid and you almost had to cut your way through it. You'd arrive at the schoolhouse door barely able to move. The skin on your cheeks more burned than frozen. Your breath coming in gasps which left the sensation of icy knives carving at your lungs.

But then there was spirng and fall, too, when the weather would be balmy enough to play baseball, or even a tamed down version of football, out on the playgrounds. Or, turd ball. Agghh!

But fall, winter or spring, it seemed that we were always walking, walking, eternally walking to or from school. It is true that on a few occasions, if it were pouring down rain and the roads were a sea of mud, Dad might hitch up the horses and take us to school in the wagon. We'd huddle under a sheet of canvas in the grain box, shivering with cold and wet.

On still other rare occasions, if some sort of an emergency made us late, Dad might even crank up the Model T Ford and take us. It might be one of those bitterest of cold days when the very forces of nature would decree that doing the morning chores took a bit longer. Chopping the ice in the watering tank so the cows and horses could drink. Thawing things out in the kitchen so Mom could cook breakfast.

59

On the coldest of such days the old Model T wouldn't want to go. Then Mom would have to heat up several gallons of hot water to pour into the radiator and warm up the engine block.

Dad would crank and crank until a lung gasket would almost blow. We'd be standing there, all bundled up, knowing that every minute of cranking was making us that much later to school.

And then there were occasions when, despite the hot water and the back wrenching turns on the crank, the old car simply refused to go. Which meant no reprieve from school, merely that now we had to walk after all. In the bitterest cold and with the certainty now that there would be a tardy mark on the report card.

Some of the memories might have been a bit more fond if, in the better weather times, we had been allowed to dawdle a bit on the way home, with all our friends. But Dad's orders were carved in stone, one had to hike his butt home from school, but pronto. Work to be done.

"You can plow until dark," he would say. Or pick cotton. Or mend a fence. But fun after school? We never had enough time for that.

Study time was after supper. If we complained that we could not see to read or write, Dad would patiently go through his lamp cleaning routine, trimming the wick of the kerosene burner and polishing the glass chimney with with a wadded up hunk of newspaper. All this careful ministration might allow an extra candlepower or two to escape from the flame. Back to the books.

Oh, but it really wasn't all bad. Not even Dad could take our 20 minute recesses away from us, morning and afternoon. Or that hour for lunch. If you bolted your lunch from the lunch pail in 10 minutes it left us 50 minutes for a hurry up game of "corners," our country brand of baseball. Or a stretch of "choose-up football." Even if the football was nothing but a home made bag of denim, stuffed with straw. It might make the punts a bit wobbly and short but still fun.

Corners. Football. Chase the kitty. And - turd ball.

No mystery as to why we had a lot of horse turds at school. Horses went to school, too.

Oh, not to learn. The nags were transportation for the kids who lived a bit further, maybe three or four miles from Friesen School.

Some of them rode two, or even three, on a horse. Others rode to school in buggies.

What it all meant was that when those founding fathers built that school they also had to erect a horse barn on the corner of the school yard, to house the horses while the kids hit the books.

Not a real cozy barn. Tin roof and thin board walls on three sides, including a wall facing north, fountain of those evil winds. An open side facing south. The kids who came, via horse, had to bring their own hay for the animal to munch on as he served his waiting period.

It was another rigid rule at Friesen that nobody was allowed to play with the horses, ride them or take them out of the "barn" during school hours or recess. But they forgot to make a rule about playing with those turds scattered so plentifully around the barn.

Fresh ones, stale ones. The fresh ones were the smelly ones. At least the horses were kind enough, by nature, to form their excreta into hard little egg shaped balls. Not as messy as the cow stuff. Messy enough.

My memory is not completely clear as how the horse turd thing got started. Most of it simply stemmed from the fact that Cousin Frank was a stinker, a bully. He didn't have to have a reason.

Some days he wasn't as bad as he was on others. On his good days he might even be friendly enough to join in our corners game like a normal guy. Or football. Except that he was big and he could always insist on playing fullback so he could run over all the smaller squirts. And he did. Also big enough to enforce his interpretation of the rules, if he got caught cheating.

On his worst days he simply made life miserable for the smaller kids. Which was most of us for he was about the biggest hunk of boy in school. He enjoyed his role. "I can lick any kid in school," was his perennial boast. He just about could.

Some days he'd simply choose to knock some small kid down, just for the hell of it and then dare anybody to do anything about it.

Oh, he was careful enough to do it when "teach" wasn't looking. And if the kid went squealing to teacher it merely meant double trouble because Frank would waylay the victim again, off the school grounds, and give him a double dose of knockdown. So the kids didn't snitch much. A reign of terror and Frank enjoyed it.

There came those days when some of us smaller characters would get our heads together and try to figure out how to get revenge on Frank. We never could quite come up with the right solution.

61

True, several of us could have ganged up on him and probably licked him but then always that fear of his special revenge. Waiting his opportunity to catch us alone, one by one, whammo.

I believe some of us even seriously entertained the thought of killing him. That would have ended the tyranny forever. But we didn't say much about it, out loud. There was too much of the Mennonite puritanism burning in our souls. And the fear of God. You'd not only go to jail, you'd go to hell. It was probably even a sin to think about it.

If somebody did blurt out the thought, "I'd like to kill him," everybody understood it was not in earnest. Except, perhaps, to fulfill the psychological need of the moment. Not with blood and all that.

Some of us, and that even included me, even tried the opposite tack. Trying to toady up to him. Be his friend. Run his errands. Give him his little coterie of "servants."

Looking back on it now, it is disgusting to contemplate the cowardice of such an approach. But what could a kid do with a stinker of a bully like Frank around. You had to save your hide somehow. But even the toadying didn't help much. He never let up for long. The ego part of him needing feeding with a constant diet of domination over his weaker peers. At times it bordered on the sadistic. Like that horse turd thing.

As I said, Frank was a head taller than I and outweighed me by at least 20 pounds. His brother, Paul, was my age but also a bit taller and a bit heavier. But I could lick Paul. At least most of the time.

We were pretty evenly matched. Sometimes he would lick me and sometimes I would lick him. But I was slowly learning how to take care of him.

The crazy part of it all was that I didn't even want to fight Paul. And Paul didn't really want to fight me. He wasn't the bully type like his brother. When Frank wasn't around we got along fine. But somehow, it seemed, in order to keep his ego nourished, Frank felt it necessary to see me and Paul fight. He was always knocking our heads together.

He might tell me, for example, that Paul had said something nasty about me. That I was a coward, maybe. Or, mostly vice versa. It was easier to tell Paul that I was the one who had been spouting off. And then Frank would come dragging brother Paul, point to me and say something like this, "He said you were a yellow belly and he was going to lick you. Go get him."

Then he'd almost literally bang our heads together. If we didn't start punching eagerly enough, Frank could always slip in a few punches of his own to get the dander up and the fight started. Sometimes the hurt would bring anger and then we, normally friends, would really start slamming away at each other in earnest. A bloody nose. A black eye. A few good bruises. Frank just never got enough. It seemed to satisfy his sadistic soul just watching the two of us whaling each other.

I even tried the tactic of allowing Paul an easy victory so the two of them would leave me alone. But then you had to swallow all that crowing Frank would do for his brother in front of the other kids.

"Paul licked him. Paul licked him," he'd crow.

Oh, how tortured the soul of youth. Why did God, or some kind of fate, allow such misery for a kid who didn't even hate anybody? Unless it was a bully named Frank.

And then that final act of sadism - the horse turds.

Perhaps it was inevitable, with so many of those horse biscuits lying around, and given Frank's inventive disposition for evil.

In any case, it was during a recess one day. A bunch of us were playing near the horse barn. Frank got into one of his moods when he wanted to see violence between Paul and me.

Suddenly, just like that, he turned to Paul and said, "Stuff a horse turd in his mouth." God knows where the idea came from but once Frank said something like that, his ego demanded the performance of the thought. Once more the "provocation ritual," rubbing our noses and slamming us together.

This time, with the thought of that horse turd in my mind, I fought for real. I had had enough experience with Frank to know it was no idle threat. I also knew that Frank was not above helping his brother, if necessary. But for that moment I was busy trying to lick Paul. And I did. I managed to knock him down and was astride him, pinning his flailing arms when sudden I felt those other arms pulling at me.

I didn't have to be told what they were. Frank was simply up to his old tricks. If Paul couldn't take care of me alone, Frank would make sure his orders were carried out. I was fighting with the wild fury of a cornered rat now but it was impossible to win against the two of them. Frank managed to pull me off his brother and turn things around so I was on the bottom and Paul on top.

Then Frank grabbed a fresh, smelly horse biscuit, handed it to Paul and said, "Stuff it in his mouth."

We had an audience. Nearly every student in the school was standing in a ring around the scene of battle, watching as if bewitched, somehow fascinated, entranced, by the ultimate vulgarity, the gagging repulsiveness of the thing. I suppose it is safe to say that none of them had ever seen a horse turd stuffed into anybody's mouth and maybe such a notable event would indeed take place that day.

With that horrid thing being smeared in my face I was able to fight with the strength of at least a small Samson. Fired with that burst of adrenalin induced by fear, I could easily have thrown Paul off me and escaped. I almost believe I could have even licked Frank that day, alone. But against the two of them - it was simply too much. Even Paul was now, somehow, committed to the act. Perhaps for him, too, the entrancing fascination of this ultimate sadism was dragging him along.

Helpless at the overpowering strength of the two of them, I nevertheless continued to fight with desperation. I must, I must get free. Somehow, to avoid this awful fate. My thoughts may not have been specific during those moments of battle but in looking back on it now, I was, in a sense, being raped.

I know, the soul of a sensitive woman might rebel at the suggestion that what I was suffering that day could be compared to rape But it was. Robbed, if not of my pure virtue, of my budding manhood. Could anything be more degrading? More bitter? Especially with all my school comrades, including the girls, standing there with their mouths agape. If I were forced to eat that horse shit, could I ever be clean again? Acceptable as a friend or playmate?

To their eteranl credit it must be said that a few of my friends were protesting, begging Frank to give up this degrading act. Especially the girls. I also seem to remember one of my best friends, one of the boys, protesting, too. But none of them were willing to challenge Frank. Physicially. His reputation, his strength, his evil kingship, were simply too well entrenched. A deterring thought to them, perhaps, that even if they ganged up on him and forced him to stop, in the end he might force them to eat a . horse turd, too. In any case, nobody stopped Frank and Paul. My teeth were tightly clamped with the strength of a bulldog. I was determined that even if they smeared the crap on my face my lips I would never allow it to go past my teeth. Into my throat. But, faced with my tightly clenched teeth which I did not loosen, Frank's evil mind came up with even more cruelty. He began slugging me unmercifully.

"Open your mouth, you bastard," he gritted at me. "If you don't open your mouth I'll kill you."

Oh, he probably didn't really mean that. Even Frank the bully was not willing to commit murder. Inside, he probably didn't even want to. He merely wanted to add more verbal drama to the "rape."

Perhaps I might even have succeeded in keeping that terrible filth from passing beyond my teeth but Frank had one more moment of inspiration. A new weapon.

He grabbed a sharp stick lying nearby, forced the sharp end between my teeth and pried them apart.

And then, into my mouth, over my tongue, came that gagging filth. The rape had been fulfilled.

I prefer to believe that I never really "ate" any of it. That I somehow managed to keep it out of my throat and to keep from swallowing any of it. Under the circumstances it was impossible to be sure.

And, in a sense at least, the worst was still to come. For now, the sadistic act completed, Frank and Paul set me free. I was standing there, spitting, gagging, coughing, trying to clear my mouth and throat of this unspeakable filth. And then I was forced to listen as Frank did his crowing in front of his kingdom.

"See, we did it. We made him eat horse shit."

In that moment, I felt that I would bear the mark of that indignity forever. I would be the "marked man," or boy. The only boy in school, perhaps anywhere, who had been forced to eat shit. Could anybody live with that?

Perhaps it would be sweet to say that somehow, eventually, I managed to get my revenge on Frank. But, in a physical sense at least, it was not to be.

For a time I even thought about killing Frank. Somehow. The vision which entered my mind most often was that of splitting his head with an axe. Such was the rage which this ultimate indignity had forced upon my soul.

But in the end, that would not come to pass either. My Mennonite upbringing was still too strong. One could never commit this extreme act of revenge. I would be damned forever to a burning and living hell. But from my wounded soul I could not banish the wish, the will, to do it.

In a sense, however, Frank was punished for his act. Perhaps it was poetic justice. It was my friends, or more, almost the entire student body of the school that brought it about.

For somehow, in bringing that disgraceful act to its ultimate climax, Frank had descended to a depth which now marked him as the guilty one. Of having committed some kind of an unpardonable sin. To these kids at least.

I doubt if they planned it. And the weapon they used was only a psychological one. It was silent. But it was complete. A revolt of the spirit from these kids.

They never tried to beat up on him. They never snitched on him. They simply ceased to serve as knights of his perverse kingdom. In a figurative, even physical, sense they turned their collective backs on him.

After that, when Frank approached a group of these youngsters they would simply and silently slip away. If they were forced to play in games in which he took part, they did it in a manner which indicated they did not see him. The invisible man. The pariah. All unspoken. But so utterly effective.

The thing he had done had been just a bit beyond the acceptable. Too obscene. Too much the ultimate act of filth. He must now serve his times as a pariah.

I am sure that Frank was doing his suffering, too. If he was capable of that. There were times when the snubbing act from the kids was so complete you could see the puzzling hurt on his face. Did he ever regret having done what he did? I could never be sure but I believe he did.

There came a few occasions when he tried to fight back.

"What's the matter with all of you?" he would shout angrily. Did he have to ask? He knew.

There were a few occasions when he even resorted to threats, an effort to regain his bullying stance. "I'll lick every one of you ," he shouted. But the imperious weight of the threat was, somehow, no longer valid. He never tried it.

And somehow Frank was never again able to establish his bullying reign of terror. Not completely, at least. Faced with that unified wall of silent rebellion, he now seemed baffled. Wounded. The bully king whose crown had toppled.

As for my friends, my pals, they remained my friends and my pals. I was never made to feel the disgrace of what had happened. Perhaps, the friendship was even a bit warmer now. And the horse turd incident was never mentioned.

And then, since Frank was in the older group, two grades ahead of me, there would come the time when he would graduate and be gone from the school. And since I still had two more years to go, it was a two year reprieve from the bully's oppression. I was among friends and school was a lot more fun now.

In the end it was a parting of the ways. I went on to attend high school in Weatherford. As I recall, Frank didn't even go to high school. I did encounter a few more bullies along the way. But none who even contemplated, or threatened such an ultimate evil as I had been forced to accept from him.

Frank moved away, too. I heard later that he had gone to California and was a bus driver. Somewhere, some time, I believe I was even told that he had changed. That he was a pretty decent sort of a guy after he had grown up. I didn't really care. I seldom inquired about him. And it was inevitable that each time I heard his name, a gaggy, choking thought would come into the mind. The horse turds.

There would even come a time, many years later, when I would receive the news that he had died. Of cancer.

The news did not make me happy. My soul, or perhaps my psyche, had long ago passed beyond the need for revenge. Even such revenge one might accept by knowing that a man, once a boy, who had committed the ultimate act of disgrace, was dead. And I, somehow, had survived him.

But neither did I weep. Nor feel the urge to. How could one weep for a person who had once stuffed a horse turd in one's mouth?

It would be many years later - I had gone so far and to so many places - before I would find myself back in Oklahoma once more, for a family reunion. And I found myself steering the car back to that gentle hill. The old Friesen School hill.

The building had been torn down and those few acres of school yard had been merged into the wheat field which surrounded it. Not even a fence, or a post, to mark the spot.

It was fall. The earth had been plowed, awaiting the seeding for a new crop of winter wheat.

I climbed over the fence which now bordered the field and walked out onto that fertile Oklahoma soil which had produced such bountiful harvests of grain.

In my memory the chimes of that vanished bell. Of those bitter winds of January. A more pleasant memory of the time when I won a prize for being the best speller in the third grade. Another prize I had won at Christmas for reciting a short poem about "Little Bill," a boy who became so good just before Christmas that his dog thought he was ill.

From the hilltop I could see, less than half a mile away, the farm house and the barn my grandfather had built. Where he had lived and where he had died. Still further, to the south, the white house, the Kroeker place, from which I had trudged to school. The sturdy house was being used for a granary now.

As I wandered, a bit aimlessly, my toe stubbed against something hard, something solid on the ground. I picked it up and saw that it was a fragment of the cast iron scroll work from the legs of an old school desk. Could it have been my desk?

Or?   The impulsive thought - perhaps the desk of Frank Friesen?

It was inevitable. Into my mind crept the picture, the memory, of the round, brownish green horse biscuit. I didn't even like to call it turd any more.

If I kicked around a bit more, would the toe of my shoe uncover, perhaps, the remains of some of those detestable objects? I knew, of course, almost before the question formed that this could never be. A horse turd is, after all, bio-degradable.

Gone forever when exposed for a few months to the winds, the rains, the plow and mother earth.

Only the memories are forever.

Chapter Six – Gun

My father strode towards me with a gun in his hands.

I could feel a new beating of the heart. Fear? Of my father? I had to know that he wouldn't shoot me, his eldest son, no matter how bitter our relationship had become, at times.

What was happening? Was not pacifism a major part of his soul?

The drama of that day was provided mostly by the fact that, to my knowledge, my father had never touched a firearm.

You had to know Dad, and the Mennonite story, to even begin to understand why these questions suddenly became so turbulent in my mind at that moment.

I suppose the place to start would be to say, simply, that Dad had been reared as a Mennonite. The movement gave him the name for me, his eldest son. That should say it all, except that it doesn't.

Somewhere in the misty past of the 16th Century, the 17th Century and the 18th Century and even the 19th Century, in places like Friesenland of Northern Europe, in Switzerland, East Prussia and even Czarist Russia, the stage had been set for one of those strange historical - or was it religious? - dramas that would cost so much in the stuff of human souls. And blood. A good deal of it. Another revolt against the autocratic powers of the Catholic Church which almost parallels, in intensity if not in size, Martin Luther's rebellion.

The issue at first was the act of Baptism. Later, another issue, the refusal to bear arms, would be added. In the cost, an endless migration of people seeking freedom and the blood of those caught in the revenging net of the Catholics, the arms rejection issue may have overshadowed the Baptism matter.

69

But in the beginning it was a man named Menno Simon and other men of "the church" who concluded from a study of the Bible that the baptism of infants was not the will of God.

In fact, for a time, after the revolt started, the revolutionists - if such a term could be applied to men of peace - were known as the Anabaptists. The double, or repeater baptizers. The quoters of John the Baptist, who baptized only adults and then only upon confession of an allegiance to God and their repentance for their sins. The quoters of Christ, who subscribed to the practices of John the Baptist.

Using the Scriptures, these men had a good case.

In time, Menno Simon would bequeath his name to the new movement which would go down in history as the Mennonites.

It was a revolt which would cost many an Anabaptist his head by the dreaded sword, and would place a price on the head of Menno Simon himself, who was forced to flee. He was sentenced to death in absentia.

This pacifism argument. Again, citing the Holy Scriptures, the words of the Great Prince of Peace, the call to turn the other cheek, to "love thine enemy," to forgive "unto 70 times seven," these Anabaptists, these Mennonites, again had a good case.

Any man who should take sword - or gun - in hand, must die by the sword.

It was a time and a place in history when the conscription of men to bear arms was simply a premier institution in the laws of the lands of Europe. And now these Mennonites were revolting against even that. In essence, they affirmed, "Never shall any son of the Mennonites take a sword or a gun into his hands. To deal death to any man made in the image of God."

For the principles of baptism by choice and the refusal to bear arms, these stout hearted Mennonites were willing, if necessary, to die. And die they did, by the hundreds and thousands. The authorities of Catholic Church dominated governments hounded them and put them to death.

After that it became a search and a pilgrimage for these men and women of peace. Constantly they searched for a country, a land, where they would be allowed to worship in peace. No sword in their hands.

For a time, the kings of East Prussia gave these pilgrims this freedom. In return for which the Mennonites, mostly agrarians, made the land fruitful with their labors.

When the Prussians, in time, withdrew the bounty of peace, the Mennonites sent a delegation to Russia to plead with Catherine the Great and they "found favor in her eyes." In return for their promise to make the somewhat barren wastes of the Ukraine bloom and bear harvests, she would grant them immunity from the hated conscription.

But a time would come when even that promise would be revoked and then, late in the 19th Century, it became America, that shining land of freedom, which lured these constantly trekking Mennonites. Kansas, California, Oklahoma, Pennsylvania and other states would soon have their "colonies" of Mennonites. These tightly knit communities of people with a faith in the God of peace. A people who were granted, by the Constitution of the United States, the freedom to practice their religion, responsible only to God in matters of the soul.

Dad's father, his grandfather and even long before that, had all been Mennonites. On Mom's side the same. Members of one of those tight little communities. First in Kansas and then, when the Federal Government opened the prairies of Oklahoma to non-Indian settlement, in Oklahoma. Custer and Washita Counties.

So it was no wonder that Dad exploded with righteous wrath when his eldest son of 14 acquired a shotgun. He found it hidden in the barn. He sternly ordered me to get rid of it. Quickly. "Now."

Otherwise, I would get another of his effective lickings. He'd lay on the rod until I obeyed.

In fact, I almost got into double trouble over the shotgun. Dad couldn't believe that I had acquired the gun honestly. Which would have meant I was a thief. That would have been even worse than being a gun owner. So I had to tell him about old Mr. Jantzen, our neighbor, who wasn't a Mennonite.

In a way, it was Dad's fault that I had started dreaming about owning a gun. He and his Mennonites should have set up separate schools for us Mennonite kids and kept all that romantic frontier history stuff away from us. In fact, they did that in other parts of the country but, in Oklahoma, when the state government set up school districts and decreed that all kids had to go to school, the Mennonites decided it would be cheaper to let the State educate us. They probably didn't suspect that a country district school could be so "subversive."

But there I was in Friesen School, District 12, with access to a library full of books about Teddy Roosevelt hunting bears and buffalo out west. There were stories about the "Thundering Herd."

71

Books about the furies of battle in the Indian wars. "At War With Pontiac" was a book that set my heart to pounding. I know that by the time I was 11, I had read every book in that small library.

I really wasn't mad at the Indians and didn't really want to shoot any of them. Living in Oklahoma we had Indians all around us. For the most part, they seemed a peaceful lot. Except on Saturday nights, maybe, when a few of the "bucks" would get a belly full of "Fire Water" and try to tear the town up.

In fact, some of the white folks - not the Mennonites, though - even married Indians. One of my buddies in school bragged that he was one-eighth Indian. You could see it, too. He had dark skin, hair and eyes. We kept waiting for him to act like an Indian but he never did.

When I ran out of reading material in school, there was my cousin, Ike Bushman, who lived right across the road. He was older than I, had a private room and had it stacked full of wild West magazines. When I begged, he let me borrow some of them.

Wow, all that six gun justice stuff.

To keep Mom and Dad from finding out what I was reading, I put Literary Digest covers on them. But I got caught a few times, anyway, and it ended in a fine dust-up. My fanny got whopped and then I was in trouble with Ike Bushman because word of it got back to his Dad, too. And Uncle Bushman was a devout Mennonite, just like Dad. Ike wouldn't let me have any more of his magazines. Maybe he didn't have them anymore.

In any case, under the circumstances, it was inevitable that I end up dreaming about owning a gun. If for no other reason than the fact that we had all those jack rabbits loping around the pastures and wheat fields. I saw other guys hunting them. Why couldn't I?

Maybe it wouldn't have all turned out the way it did if it hadn't been for that "golden opportunity" which suddenly slammed me right in the face. When I was 14.

There was Old Man Jantzen. He was our next door neighbor after we moved into town. His wife had died and all his children were grown up, living somewhere else. But he was a friendly old character. He had a lot of fascinating junk around his place - like that old .12 gauge Winchester Model 97 hanging on the wall of his attic.

My brother, Ernie and I often went over to visit Old Man Jantzen and one day he took us up into his attic. I don't remember why. But I wasn't in that attic more than a minute before I spotted that big gun hanging there. It was sort of dirty and rusty, as if it had

72

been hanging there for a long time. But it was for real - a man sized gun.

"Whose gun is that?" I asked.

"Mine," he said.

"How come you got it hanging up there? How come you don't use it?"

"It's broke. It won't shoot."

"Mind if I look at it?" I bravely asked.

The old man hesitated a moment. Then he reached up, took it down and handed it to me.

Wow, this was something. A really, for sure, man sized gun in my hands. Just about the first one I had ever held. Oh, maybe I had handled a little .22, once or twice, when we visited kids whose parents weren't quite so Mennonitish.

But this old 97 was a big shooter. Man, would I like to own it. My brain was working like crazy.

Some folks said I was a natural born mechanic. When I was five or six years old, I had already made some of my own toys. Dad never had much money to buy any. By the time I was eight, I had made a pretty good replica of a tractor, that big Oil Pull Rumley that Grandad used on the threshing rig at harvest time. The drive wheels were some old Model T Ford timing gears I scrounged from somewhere.

I guess I was about nine or 10 when Jake Kroeker came out to overhaul the engine on a Fordson tractor and I spent a couple of days lying on my back under the tractor with him. I must have asked him a million questions and by the time he was through, I knew all about gears, pistons, connecting rods and all that.

By the time I was 14, I could take a tractor carburetor apart and clean it. I could lace and true bicycle wheels. I was even working part time as an apprentice in Charlie Kendall's motor machine shop. So I had acquired pretty good credentials, even as a kid, for looking at a broken shotgun.

I eyeballed the thing hard, trying to figure out what was wrong with it and after a few minutes I had it figured. A hunk of steel was broken out of the slide action. A pretty important piece.

But my boldness stuck out a mile. "I can fix it," I said.

"I don't think so," said Mrs. Jantzen. "I already took it to a shop, years ago, and they said it couldn't be fixed without some new parts. They cost too much. The gun's not worth it."

Wow. Old Man Jantzen was taking my bait.

"Mind if I try?" I asked.

"It's no use. You can't fix it," he insisted. "It's no good."

I waded right in. "If I can fix it can I have it?"

Jantzen hesitated. This was something he had not anticipated and he didn't want to answer the question. But I kept boring in. Finally he said it.

"Okay, take it and try but I know it won't work," he said. I guess he figured it a safe bet that no kid my age could fix that gun.

But I certainly wasn't going to give him a chance to reconsider. I grabbed the gun and took off like a streak, through the orchard. Then, when I was about half way home, I slowed down. I remembered Dad. And his thing about guns. So I sneaked around carefully, behind the barn, made sure Dad wasn't around and I found a hiding place. Behind some boards covering a wall.

Then, later, when I got a chance, I sneaked out, wrapped it up in some paper and took it down to Charlie Kendall's shop. Charlie was the one who had taught me how to lace and true bicycle wheels. After that, I did all his bicycle work. Charlie knew just about everything there was to know about mechanical things. He even had patents on some auto motor gadgets. He even knew about guns.

When I showed him the old 97 he didn't say much. "Humph. Broke pretty bad."

I didn't ask him to fix it. I was going to do that myself. And I did. I cut and filed away on a hunk of steel for hours until it was the exact replica of the piece that was broken. Charlie did give me a bit of advice a few times. But I did it. Then, when I put the whole thing back together and tried the slide action, I let out a whoop of joy. It worked like a new one. I had me a gun.

Well, I almost did. I was honest enough to take it back and show it to Mrs. Jantzen. He tried to back out of our agreement.

"I've got it fixed," I said when I showed it to him. He took it in his hands and worked the action. When he saw how smooth it worked, he wrinkled his nose a bit.

"You did that?" he said, unbelieving.

To which I proudly asserted, "I sure did."

Then, "You want to try it?" I asked him. I had bought a half dozen shells.

"Naw, I'm not sure I trust it," he said. "You shoot it."

The truth was, I had hoped he would try it first. Mean of me, I guess, if it would blow up. But I wasn't about to let anybody put me in the "fraidy cat" barrel.

I set an empty tin can up on top of a fence post, about 25 feet away, loaded and started to take aim.

"Better be careful. That damn thing might blow your head off," he said. That didn't help my pounding heart a bit. Especially when he stepped back a few steps.

I swallowed hard and took aim. My courage was bolstered by the fact that, in working on the gun, I had assured myself that the piece I had made was not really an essential part of safety. Only the action of closing and locking the breech lock. I was certain it was safe. But still the heart pounded wildly. I had never fired a shotgun in my life. And this was a big .12 gauge. Not a kid sized .410.

But I had gone too far to chicken out. I took aim and pulled the trigger. "Bloom!"

For a few seconds, I almost believed the damned thing had blown up. I wasn't very big and that old fire piece kicked like a mule. The fact that I hadn't been able to clean all the rust out of the barrel didn't help, either. That blast knocked me about three steps backward. My shoulder was hurting. But I wasn't wounded. My head was still in place. Above all, the tin can was blasted to shreds.

Now came the argument about who owned the gun.

"You said if I could fix it I could have it," I reminded him.

"Naw, I never said that," he insisted.

"Yes, you did." Luckily, my brother, Ernie, had tagged along, equally fascinated by the gun and he stood by my side, agreeing that this indeed had been the bargain. It helped.

But Old Man Jantzen was stubborn, too. He started towards me and reached for Old Model 97. That was when I had to make a decision, but fast. I did. Just took off running through the orchard with the gun.

The old man started after me a few steps. Then he stopped. What could he do? I guess he just had to figure he had lost a bet.

Oh, he could have gone to Dad and claimed the gun. And Dad certainly would have made me give it back.

In any case, that was when I hid the gun in the barn and that was where, a few days later, Dad found it.

So this was all the story I had to tell Dad now. Well, maybe I did leave out the part about the argument over ownership. At least it got me off the hook so far as being a thief was concerned. But Dad was still adamant about not allowing a gun on the place.

I had to get rid of it - or, else.

I finally slunk off with the gun, headed towards Mr. Jantzen's place. I suppose I was just about the unhappiest kid in

Custer County at that moment. I really didn't know how to handle this one. But the closer I got to Mr. Jantzen's house the more I was trying to figure out how to get around Dad. I was, somehow, going to keep that gun.

I knew Mr. Jantzen was a bit hard of hearing. It gave me an opening. A slim one but maybe it would work.

I figured if I just tapped lightly on the door he might not hear me. Especially if I tapped on the front door. He almost never stayed in the front part of the house. We had long ago learned to knock on the back door. And loudly.

The strategy worked. I tapped, not too hard, on the front door. No answer. I tapped again, gently. I had fulfilled the requirement of my conscience. I could tell Dad, if he caught me with the gun again, that I had tried to take it back. Sure, I could have left it on Mr. Jantzen's back porch. But then somebody might come along and steal it. Not that we had many thieves in town. Or the edge of town.

The next part of my strategy, to keep from lying to Dad, was to get a piece of canvass, wrap the gun up to keep water off, in case it rained, and then hide it in the weeds just inside Mr. Jantzen's yard fence. In a spot where I was certain he would not find it.

Now I could truthfully tell Dad I had taken it back to Mr. Jantzen's place.

Meanwhile, I could sneak over once in a while to make sure it was still there. And on occasion, when Mom and Dad were not home, I'd even sneak it out and go rabbit hunting. The big problem being that even when I shot one I couldn't bring it home.

Other than sneaking over to my hiding spot, just inside his property, I avoided Mr. Jantzen after that. I didn't want to wake up any sleeping dogs.

It was one of my sisters who snitched on me and got me in trouble with Dad again. She had seen me with the gun and everybody in the family knew about the argument and the dictum.

Dad was pretty angry. And stubborn.

"But Dad, I did take it back. I knocked on the door, twice. He didn't answer. So I just kept it awhile."

That didn't help much. Dad wasn't budging. Period. Period. Period.

But my mind was clicking again and I tried one more tack. I knew how well Dad knew about the value of the dollar in those hard times. And how poor we were.

"But Dad, that thing is worth money. And it's mine. Mr. Jantzen said I could have it if I fixed it. If I sold it I could get money for it."

Wow. It worked.

"Well, all right," Dad said. "But sell it quick."

I had a reprieve. A "legal" one.

Later, when Dad would bring it up again I would always have some sort of a lame excuse. I hadn't been able to find a buyer, yet, I would say.

Meantime, I decided the best strategy was to keep the thing out of sight. If Dad didn't see the thing he might forget about it.

And that was the way it worked. Time more or less settled that argument. I was growing older, nearly as big as Dad, and it wasn't easy for him to whop me any more. Besides, I was a good worker and kept things going around the place. Fixed the car and other things. I know it was tough on Dad but eventually the whole thing sort of settled into a standoff.

I didn't flaunt the gun around Dad and he didn't push the matter. Eventually, it was simply an unspoken understanding that I owned a shotgun and Dad still hated guns. Nobody was going to get shot over the issue.

I learned a lot about guns from Old Model 97. I suppose one of the best lessons came the very first time I tried shooting a rabbit with it. I had spotted the rabbit in his hiding place in some brush behind the barn, sneaked the gun out, loaded it, took aim and fired. God, what a mess.

Talk about pulling a rabbit out of a hat. I had just done the opposite. I made a rabbit disappear.

When I walked over to pick him up I saw a big blasted place in the ground, some remnants   of ears and feet. That was about all. I had simply pulverized that rabbit. Mark up lesson Number One about shotguns. Never shoot a rabbit from a distance of 10 feet.

So deadly and devastating is a shotgun, especially a big .12 bore at close range, it is almost unbelievable. At 25 or 30 feet, you might have a bit of rabbit meat left. But better make it 25 or 30 yards.

At first, because of the explosive issues surrounding that gun, when I did kill game I never brought it home. At least not at the beginning. But this was at the bottom of the Great Depression. There were days when there was nothing to eat on the table. Or almost nothing. Maybe some bread pudding and milk.

So, one day I happened to spot a small flight of ducks circling to land on the pasture pond. I ran for my shotgun and sneaked up to the dam, carefully crawled up and peeked over. There were four ducks, two of them close together. I aimed at the two and blam! I had two ducks.

In times like ours it would have been a sin to throw them away so I took them home and offered them to Mom. She hesitated a moment. I didn't push. I knew what must be going on in her mind. But then she took them, cleaned them and when she called us for supper that night there was that platter of roast duck on the table.

Now it was Dad's turn to make up his mind. I was watching him carefully.

First, he said his grace, thanking God for our food. He always did that. But, since he didn't exclude the ducks, it seemed he had thanked God for the harvest of my Old Model 97.

The step was taken. The exclusion could still come if Dad refused to eat the duck. He hesitated. I could see him looking at me out of the corner of his eye. But then he reached out, took a hunk of duck and started eating it. We had reached a plateau in our gun battle.

But there was still that final little drama to come. The day when he would carry that gun in his own hands.

The Great Depression was getting worse, instead of better. We were back on a scraggly farm near Clinton, trying to scratch out an existance - you couldn't call it a "living." Wheat was selling for only 25 cents a bushel, barely enough to pay for the tractor fuel to harvest it. Not to speak of planting more.

Saturdays came when Dad would haul the weekly offering of butter fat to town and get, perhaps, $1.25 with which to buy groceries. Such were the times when Dad and Mom could no longer afford the luxury of a protest if I brought home a rabbit from the fields. Or a quail. Or a duck.

Except that, even at 75 cents for a box, I could seldom afford shells for the gun. On that particular day I was down to my last shell.

I was out in the field plowing corn with Pat and Sam, the horses. Dad had been busy with other work around the barn. A spring day, still filled with the chill of the sweeping winds across the Oklahoma plains. I had my heaviest coat on as I plowed.

And then, as I turned the corner of the field, I saw Dad trudging toward me. He was carrying something. At that distance I couldn't make out what it was. Something long and dark.

It was only as he came closer that I saw it was my shotgun.

A strange confrontation. I wasn't frightened. I knew Dad had no malicious intent. And yet, there had to be a bit of drama in the thing, too. What was he doing with my gun? Certainly he wasn't going hunting. I doubt if he ever fired a gun. In fact, I'm certain. He didn't even know how. But here he was, the man who had never touched a gun, hated all that guns stood for, bearing all the faith of his soul to a principle which forbade the bearing of arms - and now a gun in his hands.

Maybe, somehow, that gun had ceased at that moment to be a weapon.

I stopped the horses and waited. Silently he came towards me. He must have realized that I, too, was puzzled. Surprised. His last steps became a bit hesitant. But he had passed his milestone in taking that gun in his hands. He would be as resolute now, in carrying out his purpose.

He handed me the gun. He fished from his pocket that last cartridge that I still owned. His speech was simple but eloquent unto the moment.

"Mother says she doesn't have anything to cook for dinner today. She thought maybe you could find a rabbit. I'll take over the plowing while you go."

I guess our eyes did finally meet for a moment. I knew what it had cost him to come trudging across that field carrying the gun. I didn't intend to make it any more difficult for him.

So I silently handed him the reins, took the gun and headed for the pasture. The slopes of the pasture gullies would be the most likely place to find a rabbit. There weren't so many around any more. Almost as if they, too, were somehow starving in the Great Depression. Or more hungry people were now hunting them.

Suddenly , the challenge had been handed to me. Dad had walked his mile. Now I must walk mine.

I had a single shell left. One shot. No more. What if I didn't jump a rabbit? What if I jumped one and missed him?

I really wasn't that good a shot at a moving target. That much I had already learned. A bounding, leaping, zig-zagging cotton tail was not the easiest target in the tall grass.

But my little moment of reality had to come that day. As I skirted a ravine, a cottontail did leap and began his zig-zagging through the grass. I had only a second of opportunity. I aimed and fired.

79

He flipped and lay still. We would have food on the table that day.

That should be the end of this story - but I still had something to discover that day.

Many people, not wise in the ways of guns, including my mother, do not know that while a rifle fires a single bullet, a shotgun shoots a whole handfull of tiny pellets. Depending on the shot number you ask for when you buy your shells, even as many as several hundred. The whole concept being that by sending out a spray of shot that covered, say, roughly a circle of 30 inches at 40 yards, a shooter had a better chance of hitting a moving target. The hope, that at least half a dozen of those little pellets, maybe even a dozen or more, will strike the target.

But as I skinned and cleaned that rabbit that day I couldn't find a single pellet wound on his body. Nowhere. And yet there had to be. He had been so frisky - but when I fired he tumbled so quickly.

It was only when I made a final examination that I found a single pellet had penetrated one of his eyes, killing him instantly. Not another mark or wound on him.   I had, for all practical purposes, missed that rabbit. Only a single stray pellet out of the shot pattern had found its mark. So narrow had been my margin of success.

Mother was standing and watching, waiting as I cleaned the little animal. She saw the lone pellet wound, too. Then, in the nature of mothers who are not supposed to know about such things, she said, "My, that was a good shot. How did you do it?"

I decided it was one question best left unanswered.

It would have to be sufficient unto the day that my father had made a difficult decision. And that there would be food on our table for dinner.

Chapter Seven – Pedro

Pedro, the lovable imp, whose mother died of a hanging. By the neck, with a rope, until dead.

A shattering, shocking sight to a boy of 10 who stood watching. Unbelieving. Eyes popped open. Frozen into immobility. But somehow entranced by the horror of it, impelled to watch. Even impatient for the final death. Why doesn't she die? Please.

Pedro was scheduled to die on that same gallows his mother died on - a roof pole in a cow barn - but he got a last moment reprieve when I pleaded for his life.

It was a probationary reprieve, depending on his recovery from that evil scourage, the mange.

If I reveal that it was my Dad who was the hangman, perhaps a reluctant and revolted hangman, but the executioner nonetheless, then I suddenly find I must make an apology for him.

I believe the whole thing pained Dad more than his pride would allow him to admit. Especially when it took so long for the bitch to die. It appears that a dog's neck does not break easily and Dad was forced to make some rather gruesome assists. I believe he was even relieved of the immediate pressure to do a repeat job when I pleaded with him for little Pedro's life.

It wasn't really necessary to forgive Dad for what he did. He only did what, in his mind, was necessary. A frontier farmer on the western prairie with a soul that could be passionate but tough. His will steeled to the occasional necessities of things less than pleasant.

I was assisted in my own personal forgiveness by the fact that Pedro did, eventually, recover from the mange. His reprieve stretched into nearly 20 years. Thus Pedro gave me the companionship, nay the friendship, of the most lovable, the most willing and the most intelligent dog that ever lived.

If such a broad statement precludes all other dogs in this world, then so be it.

I believe it is the prerogative of every dog owner to exclude all other dogs - and all other dog owners - in such a declaration of faith, fidelity and love towards his own, his very own dog. Furthermore, I feel the facts will bear me out in this case.

I have owned and lived with many dogs in my lifetime But there was only one Pedro. Could there ever be another such as he?

Pedro really was supposed to belong to my youngest sister, Lillian. They were born almost exactly at the same time. There was the suggestion that they could grow up together, the two of them. He, the round bellied, furry, self-propelled bundle of energy. A living toy.

But somehow girls don't seem to need dogs as much as boys do. The relationship between puppy and baby Lillian never really flourished the way it had been hoped. However, Pedro and I sort of gravitated towards one another in a relationship which would inevitably make him my dog. At least 80 per cent of him. The other 20 he gave, quite willingly, to the rest of the family. All nine of them.

It was Sam Randle, the feed store man, who had given puppy Pedro and Happy, his mother, to Dad one day. The reasons why Mr. Randle wanted to dispose of the mother dog have become somewhat obscured through the long passage of time. But she came with what, for a small town dog, was quite a distinguished reputation. She caught and held a burglar who had broken into the feed store one night.

It would have seemed that Mr. Randle would have wished to retain the services of such a noble dog. But he offered puppy and mother to Dad and he came home with them. I don't even know if Pedro had any brothers or sisters.

The tragic part was that, soon after they arrived on the farm, both mother and puppy began showing signs of mange. Their hair began to fall out. We would never know whether they had picked it up in the feed store or acquired it on the farm. We never had any other mange on the farm.

Mr. Randle, when informed of the malady, promptly gave Dad some smelly sulphur base ointment with which Dad tried valiantly to cure the dogs.

It didn't work very well. The mange got worse. In time, both Pedro and his mother were completely naked. Their skin scabby and scaly. An ugly case. The mother even worse than Pedro.

That was when Dad decided that the two of them would have to be disposed of. The question then became one of how to do it. Dad's Mennonite religion precluded the ownership of a gun. A knife or an axe were a bit too bloody for Dad.

He could have gone down the road to Uncle Jake and asked his help. Uncle Jake, despite the fact that he was also of Mennonite heritage, had somehow come to terms with his conscience and the Mennonite anti-gun thing, to the extent that he kept a pistol hidden in his house. He brought it out at hog killing time. I heard him boast that he would use it on a chicken thief if he ever caught one in his hen house.

If it had been a horse or a cow which had been crippled or ill, and needed disposing of, Dad would have gone to Uncle Jake. I know he did it once when one of our mares became hopelessly crippled. But for a dog? Somehow Dad had decided he shouldn't bother Uncle Jake about a dog and he decided to do it himself, with a noose. Looking back on it now, I am certain that if he had known how rough it was going to be, on himself as well as the dog, he would have gone to Uncle Jake.

But then if he had done that, Uncle Jake would have simply fired two shots and there would have been no Happy - and no Pedro.

An ironic blessing that would give me my beloved dog. It was inevitable that I forgive Dad.

Actually, when the pup arrived on the farm he had no name. It was my oldest sister, Martha, I believe, who came up with that name, Pedro.

From where came the name? We had no Spanish or Mexican connections in our family. But there it was, a name for a dog - and it stuck. No matter to me, it would always be associated with the most lovable dog of all.

At first it was mostly play. The fun part. If one could somehow summon the services of a time machine, taking you back half a century to that Oklahoma hillside, you would focus in on the bright green grass of a morning in spring, the blue sky whisped with the fragments of snow white clouds. In the center of the picture sits a boy and his dog.

I would sit cuddling the pup in my arms, scratching behind his ears - he always loved that. I would stroke his fur and whisper little crazy thing into his dog ears. After a minute or two, his dog soul filled to the exploding point with joy, he would leap out of my arms and begin running in frantic circles around me. Then, after four or five circles, he would come charging straight at me, leap into my arms, his tongue lapping at my face and making those little yip-yip sounds that only a happy dog can make. The ultimate communion of a boy soul and a dog soul, in moments which would be captured, in memory at least, forever.

It is when I reveal the ancestry of my dog Pedro that it is certain I will bring pain to the hearts of fine dog breeders. The mother, a tawny bulldog type. A bit longer, of body and leg, than an English bulldog. In shape more like a boxer but with a stubby, bulldog type mouth and nose.

The father, Mr. Randle had said, was a collie. A geneticist's nightmare. But all of these strains showed in Pedro the pup. The short legs and the stubby nose of the bulldog. The hair of the collie, long and silky. And those legs, they really weren't quite as short and stubby as the bulldog's. Just a bit of the collie, perhaps.

It was Pedro's color which provided one of those mysteries of dogdom nobody can ever explain. As a puppy, before he lost his hair to the mange, he had been on the tawny side, a bit lighter than his mother. The color of a Jersey cow. One color, all over.

But after Pedro began to recover from the mange, which had completely denuded him, he was transformed. Now he was much darker, almost black on most of his body with lighter hair touches more tawny tan than black. There were even a few white spots, including a white throat. How strange are the mysteries of nature.

The lack of patrician breeding never bothered me. If nobility rests on character - on wisdom, performance, loyalty and lovability - then Pedro was the most patrician of dogs.

In fact, I have long harbored a belief to which even some dog breeders agree, that a mixed breed dog - a mongrel - is often tougher in physique, more resistant to disease and more intelligent that a dog of pure breed.

In health, for example, Pedro was, after he recovered from the mange, just about the healthiest dog that ever lived. I don't recall that he ever became ill. He never saw a vet in his life. He never saw a single can of dog food. He never had an inoculation of any sort. And he lived to be nearly 20 years old.

So far as his diet was concerned, it would give indigestion to the dog purist. Only table scraps and bones. Millions of chicken bones. I know, folks say you should never feed chicken bones to a dog. Get stuck in their throats and kill them, they say. Somebody forgot to tell Pedro about that. He learned to chew and eat those chicken bones when he was a puppy - with no problem. No problem at all.

Oh, Pedro got hurt once. Pretty badly. He was still quite young. It came after we had moved to town. My brother, Ernie, and I were prowling the country far to the east and crossed that famed traffic artery, U. S. Highway 66. We were returning home when it happened.

Apparently, Pedro wasn't used to the higher speeds of cars on this route and he miscalculated as he attempted to dash across. A screech of brakes. A cloud of dust. A thud and young Pedro went sailing into a ditch, yelping with pain. The driver speeded up and was gone.

I dashed to the yelping dog and felt him for broken bones. Several ribs were broken. You could feel the sharp edges sticking up through the skin. There was blood on his mouth. One of his hind legs also seemed broken. It was crooked.

I wasn't ready to write him off, however. I cradled him in my arms and carried him all that mile or more back home. A little yelp of pain every time I shifted his body in my arms.

Back home, I laid him gently in the hay in the barn and we nursed him as best we could. A vet was out of the question. First, we didn't know of a vet and, if we had, there was no money for one. It was up to Pedro to pull through.

On the ribs there wasn't much one could do. They just healed and later your could feel the knots on his chest where the breaks had been.

As for the leg, I had watched Grandpa Schlichting put splints on brother Ernie's arm that time when he fell out of the apricot tree and broke his arm. So, feeling with my fingers as best I could, I straightened Pedro's leg out and clamped splints on it.

The fact that Pedro recovered his health, completely and without the services of a vet, may be some sort of a minor miracle. Or perhaps he wasn't hurt as badly as I had thought at first. Just those knots on his ribs and that right rear leg just a bit off center.

But none of that stopped Pedro from becoming just about the runningest dog in the state of Oklahoma. No, not the fastest. But the runningest.

I knew when I started all this I was compromising any credibility I had, simply by calling Pedro the greatest dog that ever lived. I compromise it further by now insisisting that Pedro could catch a jack rabbit.

Please, I never said he could outrun one. I merely said he could catch one. A matter of endurance. For Pedro could run farther, without stopping, than any dog I ever knew.

All of which calls for a bit of explanation. Most westerners, who know the habits of jack rabbits, will know whereof I speak. When a jack rabbit is confronted with danger he simply makes use of the most potent weapon he has, speed, to get away from danger. But once having outrun his pursuer, if any, Mr. Jack Rabbit makes his fatal error. He stops, hunches up on his hind legs, cocks those long, mule-like ears, looks and listens to see what happened to whatever "thing" it was that spooked him.

If that "thing," which might be Pedro, or a coyote, is still coming, Mr. Jack Rabbit just takes off again, kiting at jack rabbit speed for two or three hundred yards and then repeats that stop-look-and-listen routine.Then again. Most country dogs, after two or three rounds of that stop-and-go routine, will give up. They'll decide it's no use trying to catch any animals that can travel so fast.

Apparently, that confused set of genes that combined to create a dog like Pedro had forgotten to install the idea that he should give up after two or three goes at the rabbit. Maybe it was the bulldog in him that kept him going. All I know is that Pedro never stopped running, even if the jack rabbit was out of sight. He always knew that over the next hill he would see it again.

Pedro's speed may be estimated, if one is generous, at half the speed of a jack rabbit. But during those seconds when Mr. Rabbit was in the look-and-listen mode, Pedro was still moving. Making up for lost time.

There would simply come a time when, after perhaps a dozen or so of those sprints, even a tough old jack rabbit would begin to wonder just what kind of a crazy dog it was that didn't obey the rules. And just never stopped coming.

Perhaps by this time Mr. Rabbit was also becoming aware of the fact that his bursts of speed were not quite so lightening fast. That his lungs were beginning to gasp for air. With that short legged bulldog type still coming.

I know it happened because it was a scenario I personally witnessed so many time. Pedro would jump a jack rabbit and the two of them would disappear over one of those gyp hills a half a mile away. Then I would hear, in the distance, only that little yip-yip sound Pedro gave when on the chase. In time that, too, would fade away.

So far they would run. A mile. Two miles. Three. Whatever it took. Those plains rabbits didn't hunt for cover as rabbits do in most parts of the country. The plains jacks just ran, depending on that speed to save them. Unless they ran up against something like Pedro.

Pedro might be gone a half hour. An hour. Or even more. But you could almost bet on it that when he did come back in sight again, topping a hill, he would be dragging his prey. It was a pretty tough haul for some of those rabbits were very nearly as big as Pedro. Ask any Texan how big they grow their jack rabbits. The Oklahoma jacks are just as big.

And it wasn't all an exercise in futility, either. For Pedro those rabbits were food. Not that we were starving him. He got his scraps, and those perennial chicken bones. He had simply developed a taste for rabbit.

Especially well cooked, dog style. Which meant digging a hole and burying the rabbit. Then allowing several days for "cooking." So amusing to watch Pedro during his cooking process. After a rabbit had been in his hole a day or two Pedro would wander, sort of casually, over to the site of his cache, sniff a bit and then walk away. Later, next day perhaps, when his educated nose told him the rabbit was just at the right stage for eating, he would dig it up, eat a portion and then rebury the remainder. For another meal next day, coming back each time he was hungry. Then, with the rabbit consumed, he would start his hunt for a fresh one.

But I suppose the one thing I remember most fondly about Pedro was his fabulous ability to handle cows.

Ah yes, it is the oft told tale. The unbelievable wizardry of the collie types in handling cattle and sheep. If I must insist upon a retelling of the tale, a la Pedro, it is simply because, despite his dubious ancestry, Pedro turned in a performance which left no room for challenge. Perhaps, only perhaps, I might concede that other dogs may have matched him. I shall reserve my rights to doubt.

You see, Pedro did not have to be taught to manage cattle. He taught us. I would suggest he was almost born with his Ph.D. in the art. In fact, at the beginning, it never even occurred to us to attempt to train Pedro to help with the cattle. We only had a small milking herd. They were kept, for the most part, in the fenced pasture and we were accustomed to the idea of doing all the handling ourselves. Even when Pedro trotted along with us, as we went to bring the cows home for milking, we somehow overlooked any potential abilities in this area. Perhaps it was his stubby nose, and the somewhat bulldog form of his body which had led us to believe he hadn't been born to be a cow dog. Until he decided it was time to teach those dumb humans that is was a dog's perogative to do the cow work. A subtle lesson in dog wisdom.

For example, that business of bringing the cows in from the pasture at milking time. Dad had always relied on Ernie and me to do this job. And when young Pedro romped along it was because he was our playmate, our pal.

But almost without our realizing it, Pedro just started taking over the job. There were times, for example, when the eating was lush and the cows didn't want to come home. They might skulk off into the brush. Then, armed with long sticks - to scare them mostly - we'd beat the bushes and run our legs off trying to get the beasts rounded up and headed for home. Pedro found this great fun. We might be puffing and panting, trying to head off a stubborn cow when suddenly we would find Pedro far ahead of us, easily outrunning the cow and heading her off. Yipping with joy at this game we played with cows.

It was only a matter of weeks before we, Ernie and I, mostly went along for appearance sake, to give Dad the idea we were obeying his orders to bring the cows home.

Pedro did all our work and with the greatest of joy. He came to know each of our cows by sight recognition and knew when one was missing. He would then dive into the bushes and come out with the errant cow. Then, after forming them all in a tight little herd he would head them for home. And if Pedro found it great fun, as his happy yipping suggested, we were even happier, for he had taken over one of our drudging chores.

But even more unforgettable was Pedro's exclusive methods of dealing with an unruly cow which did not wish to cooperate. It was inevitable that some of the cows would come to resent that yapping little busybody, nipping at their heels, and try to make a fight out of it. They might charge him, try to kick him, or if they had horns, try to horn him. It didn't work and Pedro quickly invented a trick to deal with it.

That cow herding part undoubtedly was a part of his collie heritage. That "reprisal" trick must have been something the bulldog part of his nature came up with. Pedro would simply make a flying leap and a quick grab, with his teeth, at the cow's tail. No, not the lower bushy part where there was no pain. He went for the upper tail portion, the bone and muscle part.

Then he'd clamp down with that famed bulldog tooth grip and hang on, riding along on the upper portion of their rear legs, out of reach of their kicks. A cow on the receiving end of this trick simply went wild. With pain, fear and frustration at that little devil imp clinging to her rear.

The cow would buck, leap whirl and run in an effort to shake him off. It never worked. Pedro always hung on until he was certain old madame cow was ready to obey his marching orders and then he turned loose. Just dropped off, landing on his feet and heading the cow back into the herd.

One lesson per cow was usually enough. Even the meanest of the dog haters learned after two or three lessons. And while it seemed Pedro was enjoying it all, I must insist that he never pulled that trick on any cow that behaved. Only the unruly ones that tried to make a fight out of this herding process. Oh, they learned to respect that little dog, those cows did.

I'll never forget how amazed Dad was when he first saw Pedro's tail trick. He could hardly believe it and at first he tried to get Pedro to stop it. He'd hurt the cows. But that was one time when I intervened on behalf of Pedro, explaining that he only did it to the cows that tried to make a fight out of it.

One of the amazing aspects of this tail trick was how quick and accurate Pedro was, despite his somewhat stubby legs. He could move like lightning when a cow tried to kick him, or horn him. I can remember no more than two or three times when a kick landed in his ribs and when it did Pedro quickly got his revenge - a la tail.

And the same on his aim when he made that flying leap. I can remember only two or three occasions when he missed. And when he did it was only a matter of seconds until he had made his second try. And whammo.

That tail trick almost became a legend in our neighborhood. Other cow owners, with a few unruly cows of their own, could only shake their head in disbelief and wish mightily that they had a dog like Pedro.

It was, perhaps, inevitable after watching Pedro show us how good he was with cows that a couple of lazy farm kids like Ernie and me should stumble onto the idea that maybe, just maybe, Pedro could do that roundup job without us tagging along. All that walking for nothing. It was worth a try.

I remember we'd start down that fenced lane, leading to the pasture and after getting out of sight of the house I would simply speak to Pedro. "Go get the cows, Pedro. Go get the cows."

He'd start off down the lane, alone, but then, after going perhaps a hundred yards or so he'd stop, turn and look to see if we were coming. Gosh, how could those stupid humans want to miss all the fun? After all, he liked our company too. But no, we had other things on our minds and I would repeat the order, "Go get the cows, Pedro."

And he did. Just like that. And so, with Pedro taking over our chore, it gave Ernie and me a bit of extra time to goof off. Until Dad caught on about what was going on. He was happy enough to learn that Pedro could go bring the cows home, but now came the sad part when Dad gave us something else to do - while Pedro rounded up the cows.

So far as Pedro was concerned, he was in dog heaven. It seemed it was only a matter of days until he would become nervous about cow fetching time and would come bounding up with that look of anticipation on his face. "Isn't it time to go get the cows, yet?" he seemed to be saying.

And when the order finally came, "Go get the cows, Pedro," he would go bounding down the lane, yippity yip. Telling us so eloquently how much this happy dog loved it all.

Oh he wanted his pay. When he got back and the cows were safely penned in the barn for milking, he'd come charging towards me with such eagerness it almost seemed as if he wanted to knock me down. It was the signal for me to brace myself for his charge which would carry him all the way up my legs to my face where he would try to lap my face with his happy tongue.

Now he was saying, "See what a good job I did. I'm the greatest, no?" He was. And I told him so.

I'd give him a generous dose of scratching behind the ear, stroke his head and tell him, "Good dog, Pedro. Good dog." These were the moments of happy communion between dog and boy. Joyful the merged spirits. Happy the dog because he had been granted the privilege of serving his masters.

Perhaps it is even a sacrilege to suggest that I, or we, were his masters. I never really felt that way. True, I told him to do things and he almost invariably did them.

But if he did so it was only because he wanted to. My wishes were his wishes. At times, if this were not also a sacrilege, I was tempted to think of him more as a brother than as a dog. I'm sure Pedro felt that way about me. So how could a boy fail to honor the unspoken wish of such a dog as Pedro?

But, back to Pedro's education, or ours. The next step in his cow herding came again almost as a natural for Pedro, the super dog.

Fences were expensive and scarce in those hard time. Many times, even if you could afford them, there were situations when a fence was needed only temporarily and wasn't worth the effort to build them.

This came when Dad might plant two crops adjacent to each other, one of which would be the type on which cows were granted temporary grazing rights. The othere, a no-no crop for cows. Which, automatically, would bring up the toughest kind of cow herding. For a boy, at least. Standing guard on the unfenced border and keeping the cows on the right side of that boundry. Your marching orders, "Keep the cows out of the corn."

It could be exasperating. The cows were not so stupid either and they would try to outflank you. Maybe two or three cows would go slowly grazing off to your right and another small group go sneaking left, closer and closer to that forbidden fruit. Then they'd finally make the dash across the line. You'd jump up, run like mad to head them off and then you would realize that the other little group had outflanked you and were now busy chomping the corn. Oh, how Dad hated that. And we hated the guard job passionately.

In any case, it shouldn't be hard to guess who took over that nasty chore. It might have taken Pedro all of 20 to 30 minutes to learn about that boundry line and on which side of it the cows were supposed to graze. After that, nobody even had to give orders. He would just sit there, on the boundry, watching like a hawk . The moment any cow made the slightest move to cross that boundry he was off in a flash. His warning bark was usually enough for those cows had long ago learned to respect that canine sentry. And if they didn't move fast enough there was always his hole card weapon, those teeth on the tender parts of their tails.

After that, the boundry herding job became a pushover. One kid, with that dog, was enough. After all, Pedro did all the work.

But there is one more cow herding story about Pedro which tops even all of these - the broken fence story.

We had plenty of broken fences in those depression days when there wasn't a nickle for new posts or barbed wire. You simply had to make do with the old ones. Which meant an unending round of patch, patch, patch with rusty wire. At times, it seemed that the cows knew how weak the fences were.

There would come those times when the grass in the pastures, perhaps in the long, dry summers, simply couldn't fill the bellies of the cows. They would begin to eye the green corn or cotton growing on the other side of the fence. Oh, yes, cows love those tender young cotton plants, too. The cows would simply push a bit on the rotten fences and something would snap. Out into the corn, or cotton.

It meant we had to keep a close eye on the fences and the cows. Then, when they made one of those break-throughs, it meant rounding them up, herding them back through the broken fence gap and another round of fence patching.

Oh, sure, we were well aware of Pedro's cow herding ability by this time and it simply became routine, on one of those days, to call Pedro to help round up the poaching cows and get them headed back through the break in the fence. And Pedro did it with his usual finesse. Good dog, Pedro.

But I doubt if anyone was prepared for what happened one Sunday when the whole family went to church and the cows chose that holy day to make one of their fence breaks.

When we came home from church, Pedro wasn't there to make his usual "yippity yip" welcome at the gate. But then, after we got out of the car we could hear him, far out in the corn field, yipping to let us know where he was. But he didn't come.

When Dad and I went out there, the signs were there to tell us what had happened. The cows had broken out and Pedro, somehow sensing it, had gone out there all alone, with no one to give him orders, to take care of the situation.

He had rounded up the sinful cows, sent them packing back through the fence break and then simply mounted guard on the gap while he waited for us to come home from church to patch the fence once more.

God, what more was this fabulous dog going to do for us?

I believe that was the day when even Dad had to pay his respects.

"You know," he said, "having that dog around is like having an extra hired man on the place. Only you don't have to pay him."

Oh, yes, he did get paid. All the pay he wanted. It was love he wanted. Those little ear scratch sessions, those assurances from us that he was a good dog and we knew it. Perhaps the knowledge on his part that he was a well loved dog. I'm sure Pedro felt he was the best paid farm hand in the world.

It is, perhaps, at this point where someone will have decided that I have been building up on the message that Pedro was all gold and guts. But he did have his black marks, his impish or devilish side. For one thing, he hated and killed cats.

So, now I have probably tarnished the lovable Pedro image forever.

I haven't the slightest idea where Pedro's deathly hatred of cats originated except that it seems to be the nature of dogs, most dogs at least, to hate cats. And to chase them. Most dogs are satisfied with a short, furious chase and when faced with an angry cat in a corner will often as not abandon the chase.

Not all dogs. Not Pedro. When it came to people, Pedro had nothing but love in his dog heart. But with cats it was murder in that heart of his. He followed through on that hate as persistantly as he did when he started chasing a rabbit. His crusade against the feline race got us into trouble on more than one occasion when he killed the wrong cat.

I saw one of Pedro's cat slaying episodes one day, the whole drama, after he had chased and cornered a huge tomcat, almost as big as he was. It was such a mean looking beast I even had a few fears of my own that Pedro might have tackled more than he could handle. But almost as if hypnotized, like the day I watched the execution of Pedro's mother, I stood and watched.

By this time, I was a teenager and perhaps had accumulated a bit of macho mischief in my soul, too. I wanted to see how this battle was going to end. If Pedro got himself into more trouble than he could handle, I might even be able to rescue him. That part was never necessary.

Pedro had his technique down pat. He apparently had been through this many times before, even if his foes had not always been so big and so vicious. In any case, for what seemed like minutes and minutes there was no real action. The cat was virtually motionless, except for its yellow eyes which never left the dog. And an occasional hissing snarl as it bared its huge fangs. Pedro, meanwhile, was doing something that reminded me of a pantomime. He was pacing, oh, so slowly and carefully back and forth in a right angle arc in front of the cat, perhaps four or five feet away.

It almost seemed as if it went on for hours, although I am certain it was not more than 10 or 15 minutes. It was clear the cat was not going to charge unless attacked. And Pedro? It seemed as if he would never make his move. I became impatient for action. It was the look in the dog's eyes that became so fascinating. He seemed to be watching for some kind of a signal from the cat. The tiniest flicker in its eyes. The faintest trace of motion.

I never saw the signal but apparently Pedro did. The action, when it came, was so sudden it was like a bomb exploding. Pedro simply made his charge like a striking rattler, so fast that he became a blur. In a fraction of a second he had his jaws clamped on the backbone of the huge cat and I could hear the crunch of breaking bones.

Pedro then gave two or three mighty twisting jerks with his jaw and tossed the cat aside. That body flew through the air for about six feet and landed with a thud. It hardly twitched. The big tom had been dead almost at the instant when Pedro's jaws struck. Its backbone was not broken, it was crushed.

I had known for a long time that Pedro was a true cat killer but I had never seen the entire drama as I did that day. So sudden, so final. The cat, big and strong as it appeared to be, never had a chance and Pedro never even received a scratch. He was the master of his game, savage and tragic. It was one side of Pedro's character I never really admired, except in a grudging respect for the finesse with which he carried it all out.

But Pedro's crusade against cats brought a minor crisis to our house, one day. It was during a period when we lived in one those shotgun shanty type farm houses near Clinton - it was all Dad could manage for. We discovered the shanty was infested with mice. Mom wanted a cat to control them. But we all knew about Pedro's passion for cat slaying. Bring a mouse killer cat home? How?

We could, of course, always keep the cat inside. Pedro was never allowed inside the house, anyway. That was part of Dad's dictum. Dogs were never allowed inside the house no matter how much you loved them. Pedro was well aware of this and never even made the attempt to cross the threshold.

I can remember only one occasion when Pedro invaded the house - but that is another story. As for a cat, it had somehow been accepted that cats could remain indoors. But we also knew it would be inevitable that Pedro would, one day, find a way to get the cat. You couldn't keep a cat forever locked up.

Mom decided to talk to me about it. She was well aware of the fact that, by osmosis or otherwise, Pedro was my dog. If he would obey anyone he would obey me.

"If I bring a cat home, do you think you could persuade Pedro not to kill it?" she asked.

That was strange way to put it. And yet, the idea intrigued me.

I knew you could almost talk to Pedro as if he were human. He clearly was the most intelligent dog that ever lived. It was always a challenge to see just how far you could go with that dog.

In any case, I told Mom to get her cat and I'd take care of Pedro.

It was really a kitten, not a cat, that Mom showed up with. A lovable little beast, about half grown and from a family of good "mousers." A solid, dark gray, almost blue. Gentle and playful. A guy could become attached to such an animal. But if Pedro ever got his jaws on such a gentle little beast it would be worse than murder.

First, I began playing with the cat indoors, to gain its confidence. Oh, that was easy. Then I took it carefully in my arms and walked outside. Pedro was waiting. He was always waiting for me. At the sight of the cat he bristled. I could hear a slight muttering in his throat. The hair on the back of his neck rose ominously.

I'm sure that most of it was simply his inbuilt hatred for cats. But then, perhaps, he also sensed that the cat was about to usurp some of my affection for him.

I held him off with a sharp command. "No, Pedro. No." It was a tone of voice I had seldom used on him and now it was his turn to be puzzled. But, at least, he obeyed and did not try to get at the cat.

Then I gestured with the cat, making sure Pedro knew what I was talking about.

"Pedro," I said, sharply, "Don't kill this cat. No, no, no."

My sharp and commanding tone was enough to convince Pedro that he was dealing with something special here. I believe, he understood. But to make sure, I repeated it several times, then took the cat back in the house. I was taking no chance. I repeated this little act for several days.

Finally, I took the step that could have been fateful. I took the kitten outside and placed it on the ground, repeating my orders to Pedro once more. That little episode could have indeed been dangerous. For the playful kitten apparently had little fear of the dog and started playfully towards him. I was ready to grab the cat but Pedro had understood me.

Oh, no, he didn't accept the cat's playful little advance. His acceptance hadn't gone that far. But instead of attacking, he simply backed away.

Somehow, looking back on it even today, I find it almost unbelievable the way that worked. Later, when the cat might be outside, sleeping on the porch for example, if Pedro's travels took him that way he simply made a circle around the cat

Ah, so you cured Pedro of killing cats, you suggest ? Oh, no.

Perhaps we did hope so for a little while, at least. But it was only a matter of weeks before we learned that he was on his cat killer campaign, as always. He hadn't changed a bit. He had simply obeyed orders not to kill one little bluish gray cat.

Such was the loyalty and obediance, the understanding this dog was capable of. And the incident never spoiled my relationship with Pedro one bit. We were still friends. Pals. One cat off limits to his jaws.

And then there was Pedro's big dog fight. But here we discovered a real mystery about Pedro's character.

By this time we've undoubtedly left the impression that good old Pedro was really macho. All guts. Warrior without peer. Not afraid of the biggest and toughest cats. Not afraid of the meanest cow. But it was when Pedro had to face challenges from another dog that his tough character underwent such a change. Humiliating to me and my own teenage ego.

For when Pedro faced a challenge from another dog he simply turned tail and ran.

It was inevitable that times would come when Pedro would encounter those other male dogs of the macho type. And times when they would come charging, head on. And there would be my Pedro, of whom I was otherwise so proud, his tail tucked between his hind legs and running for cover. The very best I could do was cringe.

But then, one day, something happened to change the picture.

It was that big brindle bulldog hound type that belonged to Mr. Pearson, who lived a mile and a half down the road. A true macho dog. When Pearson would come rattling down the road, on the way to town with that team of his pulling his beat up old wagon, the big brindle was always with him, trotting along under the wagon for shade on those hot summer days. And every time they went by, if Pedro was in sight, here came the big brindle in a challenging charge. Pedro always ran for cover. Brindle usually gave up after a good charge or two, his ego satisfied that he had sent his adversary running for cover.

And when that happened, there would be Mr. Pearson, sitting on his wagon, grinning with his own little share of macho pride. He probably got his kicks from watching his brindle chase other dogs and, on occasion, chew them up.

Several times he even had to rub it in, if I were within earshot.

"Hey, son, it looks like your dog hasn't got much guts." I had to swallow that bitter hunk of crow too. What could I say?

But then that day. A day on which Mr. Pearson's destination was our farm. He had arranged with Dad to borrow the wheat seeder. He and Dad were busy hooking the seeder onto the back of his wagon, for the trip home, when the big brindle spotted Pedro and made his usual charge. But being deep in his own yard changed the scenario. When Pedro ducked into the tool shed to get away and backed into a corner, the brindle made the mistake of going in after him.

The first thing I knew about it was when we heard a commotion in the tool shed. Mr. Pearson ran to look and began screaming.

"Your dog, he's killing my dog. Come get him off," he shouted. Now that was a switch for you. The guy had always smirked so broadly at his dog chasing mine. Now he was screaming for help to save his dog from Pedro.

By the time I got there, Pedro had the brindle by the throat in that classic bulldog "death grip." Well, after all Pedro was half bulldog, no? He was now in the process of killing himself a dog.

I really didn't give a damn if he did. In fact, I probably hoped he would. But with Mr. Pearson raising such a ruckus, and Dad joining in, I decided I had to do something.

First, I simply tried to pry Pedro's jaws open. No chance. Next I grabbed Pedro by his hind legs and dragged him out of the tool shed. That meant dragging the big brindle along, too, for Pedro never loosened his grip by an ounce.

Out in the open we tried to pry them apart. I finally told Mr. Pearson to grab his dog by the hind legs and pull. I grabbed Pedro by his and we tried to jerk them apart. Still no go. Impossible. And in the meantime the brindle was passing out.

His tongue was hanging out and it was apparent that in a moment he would be dead. Pedro showed no signs of turning loose.

It was then, in a panic because of the way Dad and Mr. Pearson were carrying on, that I did something I would be ashamed of the rest of my life. I grabbed the only weapon handy, a hunk of two-by-four, and began beating Pedro on his neck, shoulders and head. I probably didn't even realize it then, how cruelly I was hurting him. I know now and it hurts just to think about it.

In any case I must have knocked Pedro nearly unconscious for he did eventually turn loose of the brindle. The brindle was unconscious. Not dead but very near it. Mr. Pearson lifted his dog into the wagon and drove off.

Poor Pedro, bleeding from the cruel wounds on his head and shoulders, simply went slinking away. Unable to understand the crazy ways of humans, especially the ones who told him they loved him.

Eventually he forgave me. What else could a lovable dog do? I took him in my arms, nursed his hurts, and showered him with apologies.

As for the brindle, he eventurally recovered and continued to trot along with his bosses' wagon. But how his behavior changed. Every time their wagon came near our yard old brindle was skulking, not under the wagon but on the far side of it. Never venturing a glance in the direction of our yard. It was almost the same for Mr. Pearson. Never again would I have to cringe at his taunting words, "Your dog ain't got much guts, has he?"

As for me, it could only be a pyrrhic sort of victory. I had to savor it as long as I could. I had hoped that now my Pedro might stop running from other dogs but he didn't. I had to be content with the memory of that day, knowing that Pedro would fight if he had to. And could lick a dog nearly twice his size.

There was one other aspect of Pedro's life of which I could never quite be sure whether I was proud or slightly embarrassed. His love life. Ah, what a Casanova. He always seemed such a shy and retiring type around the girl dogs.

City folks, with their antiseptic handling of dog sex, or lack of it, might have a bit of trouble understanding all this. But anyone growing up out in the country would know.

At any time when a bitch in the neighborhood might come in heat, ready for the big love go, every male dog in the area would catch wind of it and start hanging around. Amusing to watch. But it could go on for hours, even days, before any action came.

Just a single girl dog, heated up by the functions of her nature, sort of lolling around with anywhere from five to10, or even more, male dogs in a congregation around her. She would wander about, a bit aimlessly, sheepishly, with all those machos trotting along behind. Perhaps the bitch even enjoyed all the attention, the seemingly endless foreplay.

And with all those machos it seemed the same. Instead of going about the love business aggressively, as one might expect, they all acted somewhat indifferent about it all. They might sniff a bit. Rub up against her a bit. But occasionally, when one of the machos might get a bit too close, the others would snarl and charge at him, not her. Sort of challenging the aggressive one.

And while all this was going on, there would be my Pedro, as part of the macho gang, too. Or, more accurately, on the fringes of it. If the other dogs lacked aggressiveness, Pedro seemed downright shy. I sometimes wondered why he even joined the ritual, unless there was something in his glands which simply decreed that he must.

If you really wanted to catch the dogs in the final, climactic love act, you had to wait a long, long time. Anybody waiting to see it would have long ago become bored by the slowness of the process and forgotten about it. But eventually it would happen, the final coupling. I suppose I even witnessed that a few times in my life. But never with Pedro. It always seemed he was being shoved aside by the more macho types. But the amazing part of it was the results.

As anybody knows, after a bitch has been "served" and a period of nine weeks has passed, a litter of pups will be the result. And, lo, almost invariably when it happened in our neighborhood, the puppies turned out to look like Pedro. The sly lover boy.

I would, in fact, harbor the guess that out in Custer County, Oklahoma, today there are hundreds of dogs which can trace their ancestry to Pedro.

And what of the "vigil" story, Pedro style? Yes, books are full of dog vigil stories. Stories about faithful dogs who fasted themselves to death atop the graves of their dead masters. I cannot tell such a tale about Pedro simply because I didn't die. And Pedro eventually did. But, yes, there is a Pedro vigil story.

I believe it all started when we moved to Gyp Corners, about three miles from Weatherford. I got a job in town. I was driving back and forth every day and the only thing I knew about it, so far as Pedro is concerned, is that he was waiting at the gate for me every evening when I came home. Yippity, yip.

It was Mom who first told me about the other aspect of it.

"Did you know," she said, one day, "every afternoon about 4 o'clock, Pedro goes out and sits on the cellar roof, looking down the road, waiting for you?"

No, I didn't know but after that, every evening when I topped that gyp hill about a half mile away, I would strain my eyes towards the cellar roof. Sure enough, there was the tiny form of Pedro, shrunk in the distance, sitting and waiting.

But always, by the time I was at the gate he was there, too. Yipping his love. Something to warm the ego part of a guy's heart. But there was more to come.

That summer, at the time in a young man's life when certain stirrings of his genes sent him venturing out into the world, I trekked off to work in a riding stable in Akron, Ohio. Again, it was Mom who told me about it, by letter.

Every afternoon, Pedro would mount his vigil post, she wrote, looking down the road, waiting for his absent master. Far into the night he would sit, she said. Wondering, in his dog soul, why it was the humans were so unfaithful.

It was late that fall before I finally made it home. It was long after dark when my car turned into the driveway. And sure enough, there was my Pedro running to meet me.

But his yapping voice was making the sounds he reserved for strangers, warning the folks inside that someone was coming.

Perhaps I was a bit disappointed but I stopped, rolled down the window, and said one word, "Pedro." Now my heart was warm again for he exploded into a frenzy of joy. When I jumped out of the car he almost smothered me with his happiness. Jump, jump, jump. Trying to jump all the way into my face to kiss me with happiness.

Hell, how could a guy ignore something like that? I simply kneeled down on the ground, put my arms around him and hugged him tight. Yes, Pedro, I loved you, too.

But then it was time to go into the house and tell Mom I was home. To take her in my arms, too, to tell her hello and that her oldest son, for whom she had wept a few tears of her own at the departure, was back. But it was in the midst of all this, while hugging Mom in the kitchen, that I suddenly became aware of a commotion around my feet.

It was Pedro, still trying to cling to me.

It wasn't such a big deal until I remembered that Pedro had never before been allowed inside the house. That dictum from Dad had always been rigidly enforced. And Pedro had honored it with impeccable fidelity. Until that single night, the night I came home from Ohio. Pedro had simply barged through the door and clung to me, for the single time in his life that he forgot.

My lovable, lovable imp.

Chapter Eight - Jinks

After my brother-in-law, Jinks Harris, came zooming down from the skies and landed his airplane in the cow pasture behind Grandpa's barn, I asked him if he would give me a plane ride. I had never been up in a plane.

"I'll have to ask God about it," he said.

Oh, heavens, he has to ask God about giving me a plane ride.

It was obvious he didn't want to say yes. He had hesitated when I asked the favor. One moment. Two moments. Then he answered. He scrambled for an "out." But I hadn't expected him to reach that high.

Considering the circumstances and knowing Jinks as I did, I should have expected that kind of an answer. I didn't like Jinks and I guess he knew it.

Some guys my age, in their teens, might have considered it a bit on the glamor side to have a former bank robber and ex-con from San Quentin, a former Hollywood movie actor, for a brother-in-law. I didn't. I was strictly a white hat guy.

My heroes all came from Zane Grey and the Old West pulps where the good guys were always straight. Real straight. They didn't shoot anybody except the stinkers. I liked them that way.

True, I had to consider the fact that Jinks had "fessed up" on his sins while he was locked up in San Quentin. He got himself a parole and was now billing himself as the ex-con who got right with God. A flying evangelist on top of that. Using all his sin and glamor background to lure in the crowds.

But I considered Jinks to be a bit of a phony and I wasn't convinced that he really had a direct line to God. Especially not a two-way line.

I'm sure Jinks didn't like me much either. He probably had me labeled as a snotty teenager. A smart ass.

Oh, he wouldn't have admitted it. If you worked the God circuit you had to go along with all that "God is love" business. Which included loving sinners and teenage brother-in-laws.

But that didn't stop him from using God as an "out" to keep from giving me a plane ride.

I later found out that Jinks wasn't really quite as much of a phony with his faith as I thought he was. He proved that before he died. But I'm still convinced - that airplane ride stuff happened long ago - that Jinks was a bit on the arrogant side when he promoted himself so high in the ratings with God. He assumed a heckuva lot in his relationship with the Man up there.

In fact, I got the impression that when God didn't quite fall in with what Jinks thought his line had to be, Jinks wasn't above making decisions of his own and crediting them to God. It didn't always work but that didn't keep Jinks from working at it.

I suppose the reason I didn't like Jinks was because I had never forgiven him for what he did to my sister, Martha. She had always been a pretty good guy in my book and he had dragged her through some of the nastiest corners of hell.

If that wasn't enough, he turned out to be one of of those guys who thought he was too good to get his pinky clean hands involved in anything that smelled of work.

This part I learned about several years after that "kidnapping," when he had bamboozled Martha into marrying him. Things had cooled off a bit but while Mom and Dad were still pretty hot about it, Jinks was using our place as a free motel stopover when he happened to be in that area. He didn't mind shoving his feet under our table, stowing away the grub and sleeping in one of our good beds.

But then one day I was out at the barn, unloading some hay, and Jinks was sort of hanging around, as if he enjoyed watching somebody else do the sweating. I asked him if he would lend me a hand. That was when he snooted off and made it clear that a man who was as close to God as he was, one of God's consecrated preachers, didn't touch anything that smelled of manual labor.

That did it. He had committed the cardinal sin of the western plains country.

Grandpa was a preacher but he scooped wheat at harvest time. Dad was a preacher, too, but he slaved like two dogs. It was an old Mennonite tradition that preachers worked and were not paid for preaching.

You just didn't eat a man's chow, sleep in his bed and then snot off when it came to helping out with the chores. I was so mad I was about ready to ram my pitchfork up his butt.

I never did like Jinks Harris. Never did.

It had all started back in 1930 when Jinks first came to town and the newspapers started writing about this former outlaw who had joined the God team and was now out rounding up sinners in his evangelistic meetings. It was pretty clear that Jinks didn't mind cashing in on his old time sin image of a former bank robber turned "flying evangelist." It attracted crowds - and offerings.

A part of his crowd, so far as our town was concerned, included a good portion of the Duerksen family. My sister, Martha. Dad, who was doing a bit of preaching himself and was one of the eternal seekers of the great truth, fell for it.

It was even Dad who persuaded Martha to get up there on the platform with Jinks, to play the piano and sing to put a bit more of the pizzazz into the proceedings. Martha was pretty good at both.

Martha, who was 24, had never shown much interest in boyfriends up to that point. But she admitted later that she had been strangely attracted to this tall, gangling, reformed outlaw with his polished cowboy boots and the big white Stetson hat. He, at least, took his hat off while he was preaching.

She had been an honor student in high school and was a bit shocked at first at the somewhat crude grammar he used from the pulpit but, then, grammar wasn't everything.

As for Jinks, he was wowed over her from the start. I have always suspected that a big portion of that "big love" was due to the fact that he sorely needed somebody like her, who could make with the proper sounds on the piano and warble those old time religious songs the way my sister Martha could.

He started wooing her - whoosh,. All out and no holds barred. At the time, I was under the impression it all happened in about four hectic days. Actually, it took a bit longer than that.

When Jinks decided he was hooked on this girl, he managed to book more of his preaching campaigns in nearby towns, starting with Clinton, Weatherford, then Cordell and Bessie, so he could hang around the area and work on Martha.

The whole woo campaign almost got shorted out when Martha discovered that Jinks was divorced. Not once, but twice. Marrying a divorced man was way high on the taboo list in our God system in those days. Especially in the old stiff backed Mennonite world Martha had been born into.

Martha did, in fact, tell the guy to get lost. That should have settled it, except that when Jinks once had his claws out he didn't pull them in. Even if his grammar wouldn't gram, he could still make with the logic. Even if he had to invent it. If four plus four didn't equal eight, you could always make it 16.

Jinks finagled until he managed to get Martha alone in a borrowed car. Then he demanded that she marry him. Then, when Martha, in great defense of her righteousness, reminded him of his two divorces and Jehovan laws which forbade what he demanded, Jinks came up with that logic he had invented.

Maybe Martha was asking for it. If so, she got it.

Jinks informed her that his first wife had divorced him, not he her. Then, when the gal remarried, that made her the adulterer, not Jinks. He had not sinned. He had been sinned against. He was pure as a lily. Jinks, the innocent party in the eyes of the Lord.

As for his second wife, she had stuck with him until he got religion in San Quentin. It was his "born again" happening which imposed upon him the duty of confessing his sins, not only to God but to the "sinned against," his wife. When he began reciting his "sleeping around" sins while while married to her, she also up and divorced him. Then remarried. Again making her, not him, the adultery commiter and leaving him home, scot free. No sin spots on his ledger.

"I wanted to believe this theory but it was not easy," Martha wrote, years later. She should have had a bit more stiff in her backbone.

"You'll get to travel throughout the United States, to sing and play in some of the biggest auditoriums all over the country," the great persuader told her. This veteran slicker from Hollywood and the wooing wars, was a smoothie.

At first, sister Martha had the courage to shrug off the bait, told the guy to bug off. He didn't.

"Little country girls don't always know what they want," he declared as he bounced off the ropes for more.

Martha did have spunk enough to postpone the thing, make her own sojourn to the wilderness, pick out her own rock of Abraham for an altar and pray about it.

"Dear God, before you allow me to make the wrong choice, strike me dead."

No strikes. No deads. So she married the guy. Especially after he showed up with a marriage license, already made out, hustled her into a car and took off so fast she didn't have time to ponder his logic any further.

"The Lord told me to do it," he declared, for a clincher. And since obeying the Lord included her in, she would have to agree. The Lord's will, Amen.

It was when Mom and Dad learned about what had happened that they "blew." The furies of God's wrath they would bring down upon the head of this "kidnapper."

In any case, the fact that Martha was 24 and legally entitled to make her own mistakes, didn't slow Mom and Dad down a bit.

Mom, who was a pretty good sized lady, expressed some of her wrath by use of a broom, which she grabbed out of Jinks' hands. She and Dad tracked him down in a meeting hall in Cordell, where he was preparing for more preaching services. Mom chased the bridegroom into a closet with the broom. He skulked there, waiting for her to cool off.

Maybe Martha should have seen some handwriting on the wall. Jinks left her out there alone to face her irate Mom and Dad while he, the new husband, hid out in the closet. His "hero" role wasn't too bright at that moment.

The upshot of that confrontation was that Martha went home with Mom and Dad that night. The next day they visited a lawyer in Clinton, asking to see if they could get Martha's marriage annulled.

The whole matter would have been quite simple if they had known then what they learned later. But the information came too late. Jinks hadn't served his time when he was released from prison. The terms of his parole specifically denied him the right to marry until his parole expired.

Jinks, who understood very clearly where he stood on the parole rules, retreated for a few days, hitchhiking to Tulsa, where his parents lived. But after a few more days, he sneaked back into our home town, managed a few tricks to get back in touch with his bride, and by the time the smoke cleared away, Martha had changed her mind once more. She would cleave to her new husband and find out if he could fulfill those promises of a glamorous future. For better or worse.

Mostly worse, dear Martha would so bitterly learn over the next 15 years. Much worse.

For the moment, since the terms of his parole also decreed that he could not leave the State of Oklahoma, his home state, until his parole expired, the first stop was the poor scrub oak country in the desolate hills near Tulsa. Scrub oak country in a time when the worst economic depression of all history was beginning to slam home with all its fury.

You could live on gravy and biscuits if you had to, not necessarily enjoy it. A hunk of jackrabbit meat might sweeten the pot occasionally, if somebody was lucky. Water, you hauled by the bucket from a well outside. Winter and summer.

Go someplace? By hitchhike only. No car. No gas if you had one. The rude awakening. Where was all the glory, the huge auditoriums, the crowds, the money, the airplane that Jinks had promised Martha?

In the beginning, Jinks could blame it all on the parole board, the mandate that he stay inside the state. When he did try a bit of campaigning on the God circuit in scrub oak and jackrabbit country, the pickings were no more than nickles.

If the poor folks had a dime they would spend it on a bit of flour for their gravy, not give it to a preacher with fancy dreams who didn't even have a car, much less an airplane now. Jinks could only dream about California and live for that date on the calendar when his parole would expire. That had been his stomping grounds in his glory days. Out there he would make it big once more. He somehow failed to comprehend that the depression had hit California, too.

For sister Martha, the waiting was only a new nadir, a new bottom, somewhere out on the Texas plains near Shamrock. On a night when the icy winds and rains of December would sweep down upon the figures of a tall man in a cowboy hat and boots and the slender girl-woman beside him. The kind of cold and wet that would first chill the body and then the soul, creating rebellion against a dream that had so quickly turned sour.

For Jinks' big day had come. His parole had expired and he was heading back towards his "promised land." California, here we come. They had gotten as far as Shamrock by hitchhiking.

Oh, it had started a bit more auspiciously. Jinks had even been able to save a few bucks. To celebrate his new freedom he had hired the services of a pilot named Muzzy who happened to own an old Swallow airplane powerd by an ancient OX-5 engine from World War I. A plane which had a reputation mostly for forced landings in weed patches and cow pastures. The plane was supposed to take them to California but it only survived as far as Stillwater, Oklahoma, where it reverted to its old habits of conking out.

After that, a spell of hitchhiking dumped Jinks and Martha onto the cold, wind and rain swept shoulders of Route 66, somewhere near Shamrock. The storm had dwindled traffic nearly to a halt. When no cars would stop to offer them a lift, the merciless pelting of the cold rain and the wind began to alter the direction of this man's will, even Jinks Harris, guided by God. He suddenly turned and ordered Martha to follow him. He strode off in the direction of the Shamrock railroad yards.

It was here that reality suddenly descended on Martha. She realized that she, a tenderly reared young lady, was going to be asked to "ride the rails." She managed to summon enough courage for one of her first major rebellions against this domineering man of God. She demanded to be allowed to go home.

Came a new, revealing facet of her husband's soul. He brusquely ordered her to repent. That was God's language. She must repent of her "grumblings" and her rebellion.

"You're going with me," he declared and she did. Riding an empty box car on which one door refused to close.

"We had to run back and forth (inside the box car) almost all night to keep from freezing," she would remember, years later. As they rolled across the icy Texas plains, the beginnings of the long, bitter harvest of regrets.

California, land of the glorious promises. California, writhing now under the burden of crushing economic disaster. Writhing even further under a new burden of the dispossessed of the Dust Bowl. The hungry and the expectant who had come to trample out their expected share of the flowing milk and honey. But trampled instead by the wrath of the curdled milk and the souring grapes.

Jinks Harris would rely on his street wits and his newfound faith in God to trample out his own brand of redemption for body and soul, in a poverty stricken California which he remembered as the stage of his earlier triumphs.

He trampled mightily and his faith endured - of this, even I had to agree - but the fruits of that faith largely eluded both of them. For by the time they reached California, Martha, too, was committed. She had passed her point of no return.

But not before her bitterness had reached such depths, in 1933, that she actually contemplated suicide. And rationalized to her own soul that God would forgive her when He contemplated the terrible circumstances which had driven her to this desperate measure. She contemplated but the flesh would not slay her.

If she attempted to fight back against Jinks, she was met by a torrent of Holy Scripture, unanswerable, which could be distilled into a single essence, "Wives, be subject to your husbands."

The Holy Scripture had been wrought in the image of male chauvinism.

A time would even come when Jinks would blame the failure of his own evangelism on the failure of my sister, Martha, to obtain the baptism of the Holy Ghost.

Oh, God, how does one explain that one?

Only the people of the Pentecostal Holiness Church and a few other "far in" fundamentalist faiths could explain that. The Father, the Son and the Holy Ghost? Too simple.

Well, the world mostly knows about the "born again" thing. After Jimmy Carter, they should know. The act of becoming "saved," of passing from the state of sin to salvation. Of passing from unbelief to belief. From doubt to faith. From bad to good. From untruth to truth.

And then the baptism. No mystery here. Even the Catholics believe in baptism, a form of it, anyway. The water on the head. Or the dunking. A ritual of consecration of the soul to God.

But then that Holy Ghost thing. To the Pentecostal people, a third step into the realm of God, a step even more profound, more demanding, more trying to the soul. An utter surrender and the ultimate coming of the spirit. Something far beyond the "born again" status. You could go to heaven on the born again ticket but to become the ultimate being of God, well, you had to take that third step.

I had seen some of the Holy Ghost experiences as a kid, watching the Pentecostal Holiness people, the "Holy Rollers," babble in tongues, jump over benches and roll on the floor, or in the dirt, under the influence of the Holy Ghost. At least they said it was the Holy Ghost.

In any case, no matter what the real definition is, Jinks suddenly decided that Martha had not achieved it and that God was therefore withholding the supreme success of Jinks' evangelism work because his wife, his "helpmeet," had not achieved her final status as a God creature.

It was while on a "crusade" in Phoenix, where, perhaps, things were not going quite as he had expected, that Jinks issued his ultimatum, his edict, to Martha.

She must return to California and do whatever was necessary to obtain that final visitation from God. She must achieve that status before he would accept her presence, her assistance, once more on the crusade trail.

Incredible as the whole concept might be, to me as I read the account of it many years later, more incredible was the fact that Martha accepted the edict. Went into a more or less self-imposed period of isolation, meditation and prayer with the resolve that she would indeed stay with it until she obtained the proper "visitation." Somewhere along the desperate trail she even had to accept the assistance of "sisters" who had already been there.

May we believe it? The figure of a prostrate woman, Martha. Bent over her the "sisters of the Holy Ghost," shouting, gesticulating, pressing sharply with their hands upon the prostrate form, accompanied by an unintelligible torrent of Pentecostal utterings. It was so violent that the prostrate Martha was aware of salivary ejections spraying upon her.

"I have heard thy prayer. I have seen thy tears; behold I will heal thee."

The words, on a little prayer card that she had selected from a pack before the experience, she had accepted it as a sign that today would be the fateful day.

In the end - Martha said it herself - after the sisters of the Holy Ghost had become somewhat exhausted from their spiritual labors and had retreated a bit, she was able to detach herself, in spirit, from the hullabaloo.

"Exhausted and drained of energy, I became silent," she wrote. And then ...

"Then I felt it - a cool, refreshing breeze hitting the top of my head and passing, not over my body as I had expected, but through my being. It reached the pit of my stomach with a tickling sensation and I began to laugh for the pure joy of it. I had not sensed such spiritual joy since the time of my 'pasture concerts.'" (As a child she had paraded in the pasture alone, singing gospel hymns at the top of her voice, experiencing rapture.)

"When the laughter subsided, the Spirit broke forth in His own beautiful language, the language that only heaven can understand, now completely in His control - the complete surrender to God."

Well, that is the way she said it. Who am I to dispute it?

Jinks had come back to California in time to witness the episode and apparently was satisfied that his wife was now worthy as a consort to one of God's chosen ministers. But, tragically, if we may believe Martha herself, even this ultimate submission had not brought a change in his domineering and autocratic treatment of her.

But, on the other hand, neither did her new spiritual experience bring to his crusades the magic success he had dreamed about. So, now both of them continued to suffer.

Somewhere along that seemingly endless road Martha did summon enough courage to leave the man who dominated her life. She ended up in Portland, Oregon, supporting herself once more with needlework. But Jinks tracked her down, wheedled and promised once more as he had during those hectic days of their "courtship."

She returned. To more tyranny. The only promise he kept was to permit her to become pregnant. She had always wanted a child, children. Jinks had always practiced a strict system of birth control because, he had said, children would only interfere with his ministry.

It was after her only daughter, Jo Anne, was born that the tables turned. The man who had wanted no children suddenly became an adoring father. More conflict as they fought over the upbringing of the child.

One small part of the Jinks Harris dream did eventually come true - the airplane part. In my own mind I was never able to understand the connection between evangelism and flying an airplane.

Well, in the early days of his great "mission," he had used the gimmick of the "flying evangelist" as a lure to attract crowds. Along with the exploitation of his former sins. Airplanes had been more of a novelty then. The planes he had flown, or flew in, had been borrowed or rented. During the Great Depression the owning or flying of a plane was simply out of the question.

Later, as World War II approached and the economy revived a bit, he began working part time as a ferry pilot, delivering planes for the Piper Company. Saving his earnings, he eventually had enough to become the owner of a Piper Cruiser of his own. His plan was to use the plane to transport his wife and child on further evangelistic campaigns. It never really worked out.

One reason it didn't work out was because something else was about to intervene, his ultimate test of faith. His own death.

It all started with a little lump on his neck. No pain. No problem until it grew so big Martha had to make special shirts for him.

For the record, Jinks simply adopted the position that the whole thing was up to God. If God wanted the lump removed, He would remove it. One day, during a sermon, he had remarked, "Some 'o these days, I'm gonna have to get serious with God about this lump on my throat."

Several friends suggested seeing a doctor. Jinks refused. It was up to God, he said.

Until, in time, the lump began to provide pain and to affect the voice he must use to preach the messages of God. When Jinks' own prayers didn't help, his own congregation set aside three days for special prayers and fasting. Jinks eternally asserting his faith, joined in, shutting off not only food but water. On the third day he collapsed.

Somewhere along the line, the pain became so unbearable Jinks allowed himself to be hauled, by car, across the country to Oklahoma and a faith healer in whom he trusted. No help.

Finally, to other famed faith healers, even Oral Roberts. Still no help.

There was that "green light" factor. Along the trek to the faith healers, as Martha remembered it later, they would encounter it. The healers would take a look at that great, evil colored growth on Jinks' neck and hesitate. Sensing, somehow, that a case like this would be a tough one. For them and God.

With a case like this on their hands, wrote Martha, the healers would first ask God for that "green light" thing, giving them the signal to go on into the real healer routine, the big pray. In Jinks' case, as she put it, "they had not received the green light from God." Did it mean God wasn't able to handle a case like this?

And it was then, unable to bear the pain any longer, that Jinks finally surrendered to the suggestion of seeing a doctor. Diagnosis? One might have guessed it, cancer.

One thing the doctor did offer was pain killers.

"Amazingly, he took them," said Martha.

Jinks, the faith evangelist who had preached against medicines all his life. Jinks, the man who had risked going to jail to prevent doctors from giving medication to his own infant daughter on an occasion when, it seemed, she was dying of a fever. And when she recovered, gave the credit to God. Now he, Jinks, was taking the drugs.

The only way God could be given credit now was in making pain killer pills possible. "Thank God for pain pills," he said.

Somewhere along this road of pain Jinks finally agreed to surgery. If the medics could promise a "cure." They couldn't. He had waited until it was too late for surgery.

"I'm ready to die if God wants to take me. If he doesn't, He will heal me."

Jinks had sold his precious Piper Cruiser to pay for his travels to the faith healers. Now he took what was left and, for the first time since he had married my sister, bought what might be called a home, a house trailer. It would do to die in.

Martha's position during all this process of Jink's slow death had become a strange one. She simply determined to keep her hands off the case. It was easy to rationalize. Jinks had never permitted any interference in any of his affairs during all their married life, so she would not interfere now. Hers would be the passive role.

The psychologists might have a field day with that one. Were there subconscious thoughts on her part now, that God was about to liberate her from those long years of tyranny? The subconscious wish? A prayer, as well?

It was in that last "home," the trailer house, that Jinks offered Martha the first signs of a man's breaking spirit, of a man weeping in pain and frustration.

"It was the first sign that Jinks' spirit was breaking, something I had never expected to see," Martha would write of it.

And then Martha said it. God was indeed answering prayers now. But this time it was her prayers that were being answered, not Jinks'.

The rationale for that one - simply the fact that in his terminal illness Jinks Harris, for the first time since Martha had known him, was willing to soften his attitude towards his wife. For the first time he could accept her and regard her as an equal.

"It was something I had coveted for years," she said. Her own miracle in the face of death.

And then another step, perhaps the logical outgrowth of his change, "I reached the point where my heart responded to the suggestion of complete forgiveness for everything Jinks had done to me over the years."

But one more little God drama had to be played out before it all ended. Jinks suddenly confessed to Martha that God was letting him die, refusing to heal him, because of a vow he, Jinks, had made when Martha left him in 1941. He refused to reveal what the vow had been. Sufficient to confess that he had made it and that he had broken it.

On June 22, 1948, Jinks Harris went into his last coma. As for Martha, "I knelt and committed his soul to his Maker."

A few hours later the man was dead. Quietly he had gone. His faith, if not intact, at least viable.

It is odd. Whenever I have occasion to remember Jinks Harris now, so many years later, it is that airplane incident which always intrudes upon the mind.

He had told me that he must consult God about my request for the plane ride. Perhaps he had hoped I wouldn't bring it up again. But I wasn't ready to let him off the hook that easy. Besides, I was also curious about what God had to say about the matter. So I had waited a few days and asked again.

When I did, I found the matter had been decided. So simply.

"I asked God about it," said Jinks,
"God said no."

Chapter Nine – Born Again

The Glory Road, all posted with One Way signs.

And I, travelling on the holy highway -   in the wrong direction.

It was enough to send my Dad, if he had known, into a state of near terminal shock.

Oh, he discovered it soon enough. It was inevitable he would.   Then came the shock and more - anger.   Followed by thunder, lightning, shouts, threats and tears. And prayers. Loud ones, intended for me to overhear.

But my point of no return was already behind me. Already I had excommunicated myself from Dad's religion. He would have excommunicated me from his family except that times were tough and I was helping with the work that was feeding the family.   I was needed.

But to try to explain it all, you see I really was born again. That was what Dad had been praying for all those years. The only problem being that my soul, following Dad's map, had been headed in the wrong direction when I experienced my new birth.

But it was my soul I was fighting for, not his. If his soul suffered sore wounds in the head butting, so be it. I had tried it his way nearly 10 years. Now I had my own soul to save. My own life to live. My own way to follow.   I didn't intend to live it in his hell.

Dad would never be free. I would.

In fact, at that moment, I could summon no compassion for him for he was the one who had created my hell for me. He and his compatriot "soul savers."

An odyssey of the soul had brought me to this point.

115

The early awakenings of a child mind - beginning at age 4 or 5, perhaps - into a culture, a life style centered around a single, all-encompassing entity. God. The Holy Bible. The mystic Biblical figures caught in their constant turmoils. Conflict. Evil. Good. Wrath. Love. Commands. Blessings. Heaven. Hell.

Mostly hell. The threats of hell to strengthen the will to righteousness. The cow barn hells of my childish nightmares. My first confrontation with God in that same cow barn.

The refusal of God to show me his face. The desperate lie to escape a ritual of supplication that had become an ordeal of exhaustion The living hell of trying to live that lie - was it now the most unforgivable of sins?

But even that sin, if it had been one, did not save me from the return of my cow barn hell. Nor from the inevitable compulsion to continue the odyssey. I would have to go back to God again with my prayers, my pleas and my tears.

My cow barn hell? In time, it lost its clearly defined form, the measured dimensions. But never its reality. The midnight dreams may have even become somewhat changed in substance and form, or even less frequent, but that could only mean that my hells became more real by day. When the waking mind had to deal with them. Or lying awake in bed at night.

The boy mind was growing, now, expanding. Which could only mean I was entering my true "age of accountability." It would move me with relentless certainty into a new confrontation with God. One very big one.

But even before the big one, I would try it on my own. Dad and his evangelists loved to tell the stories about the people who "got saved" on their own. A one-on-one confrontation with God.

"You can do it in the privacy of your dark closet. You can do it out in the forest, alone with God," the preachers had said so many times.

In any case, as the compulsion began to drive me once more, I vowed for the present to leave Dad and his preachers out of it. That experience with Dad in the cow barn had left too many scars. I lived in fear that there might be another failure. The great flood of the spirit of God and his holy light might elude me once more and then I might have to lie once more to Dad.

Then be forced to live under Dad's constant scrutiny as he measured, day by day, the depth of my salvation. Face his questions. "Are you sure you are saved?" Or the worse one, "Are you backsliding?"

116

If I did it on my own, and if the spirit failed to come again, at least I wouldn't have to fake anything. For nobody would know but me. The dread secret would remain buried within me. If I failed on my first try, I could always try again.

So there I was, a kid of 10, on his knees out in the cottonwood grove on the south end of the farm, certain that I was out of earshot of anybody except God. Praying. Pleading for God to send the great holy light into my soul with the certainty that I was saved. Born again.

Oh, I was doing some confessing, too, for I was well aware that this was the key to the whole deal. I confessed to every sin I could remember, especially the ones that Dad had whipped me for. The whippings, more or less, confirmed their status as sins. I knew that the whippings fulfilled Dad's obligations to God in performing his duty as a father. As the son, I still had to satisfy my own obligations to God about those "sins" in the form of confession and prayers to God to forgive me.

So I asked God to forgive me for stealing the cherries from Uncle Bushman's orchard. For calling Cousin Irvin a goddamnsonofabitch when he tried to run over me with his horse. For wishing to kill Cousin Frank for stuffing a horse turd in my mouth. For fighting with my sister, Eva Mae. For bullying my brother, Ernie. All these and more.

Plus one.

I had to rip from my soul the sin of lying to Dad and God about the state of my salvation after that first prayer session in the cow barn.

I don't know how long I prayed there, on my knees in the shadows of the great cottonwoods on that Sunday afternoon. I just know that after that cow barn failure I was determined to make it work this time.

Oh, God, how I prayed. How I confessed. How I suffered. How I wept. And in the end, failure once more. The bitter realization that if God heard me - and how could he fail to hear me? - he had given me no sign.

At some time, a state of exhaustion in my knees and spirit had to bring to an end that session, too. As I had decided on that night in the cow barn, a boy could not stay on his knees forever.

Chore time would come. I would be missed. Dad would begin yelling and looking for me. That would be the one thing I would not be able to face.

I had hoped that when I walked back to the house I would be walking on a cloud - my legs, my heart and my soul afloat on a wave of holy salvation. Instead, I dragged home in dejection, tears drying on my cheeks. Above all, the sense of being rejected once more by God.

But why? Why would God reject the earnest, nay, soul wracking prayers of a boy of 10?

Oh, I had heard talk of something called the unpardonable sin. If a body committed this sin there would be no salvation. God would slam shut and bar the doors of heaven forever, irrevocably, to anyone who committed that sin. Had I, somehow, unknowingly, committed that sin? It was absurd but I had to think about it.

The preachers had never clearly defined that great cursed sin. Maybe they couldn't One preacher had suggested that it was the act of cursing God which would blight a man's soul beyond salvation.

But I had only lied to God, never cursed him. I had indeed cursed Cousin Irvin but the preachers had universally agreed that this was the type of sin which God would gladly forgive. If you asked him.

But somewhere, somehow, some way, a vital element seemed to be missing from my efforts to communicate with God. Certainly, and the certainty lived in my faith, God had heard me. He had to hear me. But for some reason which I could not comprehend, he had refused to answer.

Or, had he, indeed, heard me? Was God really up there?

The merest shadow of such a thought may have flitted through my mind. Are not such flitting, uninvited thoughts at times the impudent, irresistable intruders? I could only push them ruthlessly aside. I must never, but never, allow even the innermost reaches of the soul to allow the suggestion that God did not exist. Could not that, indeed, be an unpardonable sin?

At least three or four times during the next few months I made new "dark closet" approaches to God. Mostly in the cottonwood grove. It was the nearest thing to a forest one could find out there on the Oklahoma plains. And the spot most likely to be beyond the hearing of Dad. Or the kids.

In fact, one time I was surprised out there by the sudden appearance of brother Ernie and some of his buddies, out to play in the cottonwoods. We had always liked to play out there.

To their sudden demands, "What are you doing out here?" I could only shrug. "Sounded like he was praying," one of the kids snickered. Was it another sin to deny that I was trying to communicate with God? It could not have been called a communion since communion requires the presence of both parties and, up to this point, I had never seen God. Or heard his voice. Or felt his presence.

Unless it had been the fear, that gnawing presence of hell, that had been the manifestation of God's presence.

Then came the big confrontation. It was revival time again.

Oh, there had been other revivals since the big Schultz show of my childhood. Other big tent shows. Then there had been some that were simply special services in the regular church building but called revivals. Some had been put on by churches other than the Mennonites.

In fact, Mom and Dad by this time had left the Mennonite Church and were now offering their allegiance to something called the Church of God. A change brought on by my Dad's never ending search for a more valid truth, ever driven by a strange restlessness within his soul.

But this is my story and I was about to encounter the man who would bring me to my own new rendezvous with the sawdust trail - Evangelist J. H. Stuart.

He was one of the gifted ones. The great ones. I should know for I had been hearing preachers all my life. Even as a baby. Most of them left a kid itching and twitching with boredom. Wishing, somehow, you could sneak out and get away from it without incurring the wrath of your elders.

Even my Grandpa Friesen, who had been pastor of that little white Mennonite Church on the edge of Kroeker Farm, had never been a spellbinder. The church elders went to sleep on him, too.

My own Dad was probably the most boring preacher I ever heard - but that is another story. This guy Stuart, now, he could even keep the kids' eyes popping.

He could make you laugh. He could make you cry. He could make you twitch. Of course, he had his stories about young people who had died suddenly without meeting their "saviour," their souls eternally lost. He could make hell come alive until you could smell the coals scorching your pants. Smell the smoke. Hear the wails of the damned. He was famed for the great flocks of sinners he lured onto the sawdust of his tents. He would be the man of destiny to bring my own knees boring into his sawdust.

I guess I first heard Evangelist Stuart when he conducted a big revival at Clinton. That was the "big town" down the road 15 miles away. Clinton had a real Church of God. We drove to

Clinton every Sunday. It had been the Clinton church which had brought Stuart in for another of those big summer tent revivals.

I knew Dad was impressed. The man was a magician with words, luring people in by the hundreds, from other churchs as well as our own. That was one of the marks of the great evangelists, they could lure people across denominational boundry lines. Only a spellbinder could do that.

And, after all, you couldn't go to the vaudeville, to a circus or the movies. They were all on the sin lists, not only for the Mennonites but the Church of God as well. In such an entertainment vacuum, listening to a guy like Stuart could even be fun. Like a good show. If only he hadn't heated his hell fires quite so hot.

It worked, too. On his best night he would have 15 to 20 of those "sinners" down on their knees at the "big bench."

I didn't hit the sawdust trail at that revival. There was within me, still, too much of the humiliation from my barn experience with Dad. From my lonely sessions in the cottonwoods. What if I walked that sawdust trail in public, with all my family and friends watching, and have salvation elude me once more?

It took a lot of courage for a kid to make that "walk," even if he were nearly 13 years old, as I was. And even if a kid didn't have those humiliating experiences, such as I had, behind him.

I was terrified. I desperately wanted to go down to the "big bench" but the fear of another failure was simply too strong.

But Dad had a plan.

You see, Weatherford, our home town, didn't have a Church of God. Always that long drive to Clinton every Sunday. Plus evenings, too, if you made the evening service. Dad had always dreamed of a church of his own. He had stated publicly that he had the "call." If he could persuade Preacher Stuart to come put on one of his big "shows" at Weatherford, round up enough "born againers," he might be able to start a new church.

In the end, Dad pulled it off. The revival part, anyway. Stuart agreed to come and pull out all the stops. Dad managed to arrange for the use of a big vacant lot just a block from Main Street, right behind the Ford dealership. The big tent arrived. Dad and some of his friends got it all arranged just like in the old Evangelist Schultz days. They were going all out with a "four-weeker."

To tell the truth, they didn't get crowds as big as they had in Clinton. After all, Weatherford was a smaller town. But the thing went over pretty big. Before it was over, word got around town that a whiz-bang preacher was cutting the smoke down in the big tent. Even the Baptists and Methodists were sneaking in for a listen. Somebody saw a Baptist deacon put 10 dollars in the collection plate one night. Maybe he figured he was buying a bit of insurance, just in case this guy Stuart and his doctrine had a bit of truth the Baptists hadn't cornered.

But all this was beside the point. The big thing was what was happening to me. The status of my soul. For, under the spell of this master preacher, my "age of accountability" was coming alive again. Very fast. Maybe my dreams weren't leaving me dangling over the edge of the cow barn hell any more but hell was still there waiting.

How could a budding teenager escape it? Church was two or three times a week. Those long prayer and Bible sessions at home, five times a day, counting the full blown prayers at mealtimes. The periodic whippings from Dad, reminding me of at least some of my sins. The nights, lying awake and pondering the state of my soul, how deeply I would land in hell if "I should die before I wake."

Was it really strange how, at times, those things had a way of building up pressure, likes steam, inside a guy's mind, his soul? Becoming more intense by the moment until you would be tossing, turning, unable to go to sleep. Even the waking, conscious moments before sleep, almost as bad as the cow barn hell dreams that had awakened me at midnight.

I had been doing a lot of thinking, too, trying to find the reasons why God had not come to me. During that painful session in the cow barn, or in those "lone wolf" attempts out in the cottonwoods. Why, why, why? The question churned its way through my consciousness a million times.

In the end, at least for this period of my life, I never found the answer. But now this revival thing was playing its course before my eyes. I was a "captive" audience simply because Dad had decreed my presence every night. That much could not be avoided.

Maybe, just maybe, God would pay a bit more attention to my prayers, my pleas, if I did it formally from the mourner's bench. The "official" way. True, Dad and the other preachers had always assured us it could be done the lone wolf way but now I was beginning to wonder. I had witnessed so many of those seemingly successful "saves" at the revivals. The bursting smiles. The joyful shouts of triumph. Maybe there was something to it, doing it the way of the sawdust trail.

There was a bit of organization to it, as well. They had those consecrated, delegated "assisters" spotted around the audience at bench call time. Top grade "saved souls" who wandered through the audience, looking for the tell-tale signs of a wavering sinner with a look of trance on his face. Someone struggling with his soul, wanting to go but lacking the courage. These assisters would take you by the arm, tugging gently, and pleading. "Don't you want to give your soul to God tonight? I'll go with you and help you pray. I'll be by your side." It could be so seductive.

I had seen it all so many times. Felt the tug on my own arm. Watched them work on some of my buddies.

And now, somewhere along the way in that four week program, I made my decision. I was going. I vowed that I would do my kneeling and I would pray and pray, no matter how long it took, until that great heavenly light flooded into my soul.

"You will know it when it happens. There will be no mistaking it. It will be like a great flood of white light flowing through your body, bringing peace and love and joy. Freedom to your soul." Dad and all the preachers had been making those assurances for years. Now the great Preacher Stuart was promising it again, so eloquently, so persuasively. I would try again.

But even after my decision it wasn't easy. During the first two weeks Preacher Stuart gave sermons that laid out the doctrines of the church, the one church - the Church of God. Then, in the last half came the fire and brimstone sermons, followed by the mournful calls.

I had decided but my flesh was weak. "I'll do it tomorrow," I kept telling myself, night after night. Then tomorrow. Then tomorrow.

Apparently others were fighting the same battle and the harvest was meager. It was always that way. It would build up until the last two or three nights. Then they would come.

I waited until there were no tomorrows left. The final night.

"Softly and tenderly Jesus is calling," the haunting, entreating song that soul "harvesters" had been using for generations.

"Why not tonight?" I had no answer to that beseeching melody, except the fear in my heart.

"Almost persuaded." I was persuaded. I only needed a burst of strength to make my legs go and my knees bend.

"Jesus, I come." I finally went. Like a sleepwalker. Mechanically. Trancelike.

"Lord, I'm coming home." I was praying for it.

My knees - pressed into the yielding sawdust. My head - bowed over the rough wooden bench. My lips - trembling in desperate prayer. My soul - somewhere out there, searching, searching.

I had been the last to go. Perhaps as many as 10 or 15 "sinners" were already there, bowing, praying. The "assisters" busy with the other supplicants. So now, even in my public surrender, I suddenly found myself praying alone once more. The help I counted on to guide me was busy with other repenters. Even Dad was tied up on the other end of the bench with a stubborn "case."

"Just as I am." Another melody of entreaty floating out over our bowed heads. My troubled head. "Please, God, take me as I am."

One by one, some taking longer than others, the bowing supplicants reached their "blessed events." They would rise to their feet, tears of joy streaming down their faces. They would be embraced by parents, wives, husbands, "brothers" of the church. Welcomed into the blessed fold. The great moment of joy. Another soul gathered into the flock.

Still I prayed. But now no longer alone. The very act of reaching triumph for the others was freeing the God helpers to come to me. I felt their hands on my head. Their arms around me.

Had I confessed all my sins? Even the most secret ones? Had I offered my soul to God with no reservations? Was I ready to serve him?

Sobbing, trembling, from the heaving emotions I swore it.

"Yes, I did. I did."

They sent their own prayers to God. "Please, save this humble soul." Now there were two, three, or even more of the assisters clustered around me for I was the last. The time would come when I would be aware of my own father, kneeling beside me. He had found his moment of triumph with his own sinners and could now turn his attention to his own son. I felt his arm, once more, around my shoulder.

Once again, that strange, involuntary sense of revulsion at the feel of his arm. At the nearness of his voice. I was fighting now to resist this evil thought, for could it not also be considered a sin? But is the psyche ever in complete control of its own strange

surges? Even in such moments of intense rejection of that surge?
Must the subconscious be ever the unstopable intruder? Somewhere
a hint of anger, resentment. Why was God granting the prayers of
these other "sinners?" Giving them joyful moments of saving grace
but withholding it from me? No, I must not be angry and resentful
with God. Another sin.

I was once more becoming emotionally wrung out,
exhausted. I had prayed. I had wept. I had confessed until there
was nothing left. I had waited so long for the great holy flood of
light to engulf my soul. And it had not come.

Somewhere near the end, I was even aware of Evangelist
Stuart, the great man, kneeling beside me, his resonant voice adding
to the prayers.

For a moment, his presence gave me new hope. For the
others he had remained in the pulpit, lending only his presence from
that distance. But now he had given me, the last hold-out, his
attention. If the master saver of souls was at my side, sending his
prayers to God, surely God could not turn a deaf ear. But he did.

It was, in the end, sheer exhaustion of body and soul which
brought me to surrender once more. The surrender of lies. What
else could I do?

I had been on my knees for what seemed like hours. The
audience had long since gone home. The tent was nearly empty.
All the other supplicants with their own sense of triumph and glory,
had gone home to the restful comfort of their beds.

Even the assisters, despite their devotion to the soul harvest,
had also lost patience and drifted away. Dad, of course, had
remained. But in time, even Stuart gave up and left. His weary
body also crying for sleep. The meeting ended around 10 p.m. It
must be now, or so it seemed, long after midnight.

So, in the end, I faked it again. Knowing full well what it
would cost me. I did not have the courage or the strength to admit
the truth that the great moment of salvation had eluded me once
more.

Trembling I arose to my feet. I forced a smile of triumph. I
put my arms around Dad and told him, "I am saved." It was the
ritual that was required of me. I gave it.

I had given, once more, the lie.

And then I had to pay. The pure life. A baptism in
Leonard's Lake. Ordered by Dad to teach a tiny Sunday School
class - maybe six kids in it - in the little Church of God congregation
Dad had been able to establish after the Stuart revival.

The price was higher now, too, for I was a bit older - 13 or 14. Back in the cow barn days, folks hadn't taken a boy of 9 so seriously.

But I was trying to rationalize, too. Perhaps - I could hope - if God saw me trying to live the Christian life he might relent and grant me the great gift he had withheld from me. Maybe, if it didn't come in one grand burst of light, it might come gradually, as I earned it.

But it did not arrive in this manner either.

In the end, not only I knew but Dad knew, my Mom knew, everybody knew that it had been another lie. Or, at least, a failure. And if it had to be classified as a failure, it branded on my forehead, symbolically at least, the dread mark of the backslider. My scarlet letter.

But slowly now, all of it, the cow barn hell, the fruitless trips to the cottonwood grove, that horrible night on the sawdust, the monstrous horror of trying to live a lie for months and years on end, were doing something to me. Slowly but certainly I was moving towards an inevitable "high noon." Either my soul would be destroyed - can a soul be destroyed without destroying the being? - or I would somehow have to destroy that terrible shadow hanging over me.

Before I could reach that fateful "happening" I would spend one more of those crushing nights in hell. Again, not clearly defined as the cow barn hell had been, with the slippery poles, but a hell just as real. Perhaps, even more so.

Indeed I had, in a sense, been living my hell every day. But that night the literal gut ripping torment of the damned.

A doctor might have a psychological explanation for this one. Perhaps something I ate. A churning of the gut. Cold sweat. The refusal of sleep to bring the shroud of peace. The gripping fear that I might die. And go to hell for living that great lie. A hell that was suddenly upon me in all its livid fury.

Tossing, churning in bed. Even my brother Ernie, trying to sleep beside me, became aware that something was going on. "Why don't you lie still and sleep?" he demanded. If only I could.

Instead, the raging tumult within me was still growing, with an intensity that brought the feeling that I would explode. I would die. And then a compulsion which seemed to be hurling my being, my soul, into the vortex of a hurricane. A compulsion which suddenly sent me creeping into the bedroom where Dad and Mom were asleep.

I awakened Dad and with tears in my eyes pleaded, "I've got to get saved. Tonight. I can't take it any more."

It was the most humiliating of all the "sessions." For this time I had not wanted to go. I had been hurled into it. By a force I could not fathom.

Once again I scraped the last crumb of sin from the bottom of my consciousness, even the one I swore would never pass my lips. My secret passions with pictures of seductive girls.

If that were not humiliating enough, there was the fact that my relationship with Dad, at this period, had become bitter, ugly. Perhaps I even hated him. And here I was, grovelling on the floor beside his bed.Trying to forgive him. Asking for his forgiveness. Trying to love him. Above all, to ask once more for his help in seeking God.

Everybody in the family knew about my terrible relationship with Dad now. Quiet, but listening, everybody in the house was aware of what was going on.

Perhaps I knew, even before it began, that it would be another failure. Even Dad, no matter how much he longed for my salvation, somehow seemed to sense that something was not quite right. That I had been driven by a mad nightmare rather than by the cold and sober rationale of a daylight decision.

In fact, when I crept back into bed and before I finally went to sleep, I had already made up my mind that I would not fake it this time. I didn't. I believe Dad knew it immediately. The only residue I had left from it this time was that galling humiliation.

And from that grew a new facet to the whole picture. A borning resolve, nay a demand within my soul, that before I ever again would offer my soul to God, I must have a manifestation. I had gone to God. Now God would have to come to me.

Oh, it wasn't a full fledged unbelief. Or a denial of God. Not yet. It was simply that my being was becoming so utterly crushed by the endless failures that I simply could no longer bear it. I would settle for nothing less than Damascus.

Aye, Damascus. The trail of the sinful Saul, the cruel persecutor of the early Christians. Who had been struck down by the hand of God with a blinding light on the road to Damascus. And thus, having been given his "sign," he was led to pray to the God he had reviled and defied. To become the great apostle.

I had never reviled God. Nor defied him. I had only feared his wrath. But I had been the humble one, the beseecher, the soul in torment.   Now I wanted my sign of Damascus, clear and unmistakable, before I would pray again.

Oh, it didn't all happen that night. Nor in a matter of two or three days. I was older now, about 16. Growing up. The brain expanding, nearly exploding.   Perhaps the seeds had been germinating in the days, the weeks and months or even the years, before that last humiliating soul trip.

For one thing, I had become close to my cousin, Gordon Friesen. Our church folks spoke bitterly about Gordon. An infidel, an atheist, an unbeliever, they called him.

Perhaps true, in the sense of their own beliefs. But not completely true. Gordon spoke of another possible conception of God. Not the God of wrath. Not a God who constantly threatened hell. Never the God of my father, whose perception of the Divine Being had driven me to that hell behind the cow barn.

In fact, Gordon never clearly defined God at all. Perhaps he couldn't. And knew it. But wasn't God, perhaps, simply a part of the good in the soul of man? The embodiment of the eternal search for God? The very compulsion to search? Even the spirit of mankind itself.

Gordon had further opened my growing mind by giving me things to read, such as I had never read before. Philosophy. The history of mankind and the universe. He exposed me to the writing of men like H. L. Mencken, the forever rebel. By this time I had even been able to read Gordon's book, "Flamethrowers," a novel which explored the soul of a young man who might have been Gordon himself.   A story of rebellion, of sorts, against the entangling, stifling, Mennonite culture.

I probably never really understood it all. But I listened. I read.   I pondered.   And there grew within me a partial understanding, at least, of what had been happening to me.

Did I dare challenge the God of my father? And of my mother? Or my grandparents? The God of all my uncles and aunts. I wasn't quite sure.

No, not yet a total unbelief. Still, the fear. The awe. Still, the faith, even if a faith becoming more fragile with the passing of the days. But the stage was being set for the biggest soul drama of my life.

Evangelist J. H. Stuart, the great one, the spellbinder, was coming back into my life.

I was 17 now. Dad, and what was left at home of the family, had moved to Roger Mills County, truly one of the most desolate corners of Oklahoma. Where God, if he had indeed created this barren corner of the earth, had cursed it as well. A rocky, hilly soil which could sustain but the toughest of sparse grass. Mostly open cattle range with a few scraggly farms sandwiched in between, in spots where men had found a few acres of soil a bit more fertile and amenable to the plow than those bleak red hills.

Dad, still searching for his own niche in God's kingdom, a church of his own, had finally been offered a pastorship. To an almost non-suriving little congregation which had for a home a wind battered, aging and graying church building atop one of the bleakest of those red hills.

It was a widow, one of the survivors of that tiny group, who owned a farm nearby, who had offered the farm to Dad so that he could scratch out a meager existance while he tended the little flock in that battered church on Sundays.

Nothing so unusual about the arrangements. In the Mennonite church it had been the custom, if not the doctrine, that preachers must make their living as they served the needs of the flocks. With the Mennonites it had also seemed as if farming was the only honorable profession. Why should he not accept the same terms in the Church of God?

But Dad was simply not willing to accept the meager flock he inherited. He must build. He must increase the flock. It was the only measure by which God would judge the fullness of his performance. But in a reluctant realization of his own weakness of talent, he had dreamed the dream of bringing the great master, Preacher Stuart, to that lonely hilltop church for one more "great revival."

And now I made a deliberate decision. It was a decision which embodied, perhaps, even the element of that challenge which had been growing within my being. I would give God and his mighty servant, Preacher Stuart, one last chance.

They must show me God's face or make his presence known beyond any doubt. God must come to me. Or - was it indeed a threat? - I would turn my back on God forever.

This time I believed I was mature enough, that I had courage enough, to carry out my plan. I knew the revival format so well. In a "two-weeker," as this one would be, the first week would be the warm up. The last week, the soul harvest featuring the mourner's bench, that place of reckoning for the sinners.

I resolved that I would sit through every session. I would listen once more to the sonorous and eloquent voice of the master preacher. I would then, not on the last night as I had done before, but on the very first night of the "invitations", make my march to the bench. I would offer my soul to God and God must, this time without fail, make himself felt in my soul. Up to this time I had done all the travelling. This time, if God wanted me, he must meet me at least half way.

My road to Damascus either lay atop that bleak hill or there would be no road to Damascus.

I am sure that it must have been a shock to Preacher Stuart when he set eyes on that ravaged old church on that bare, rocky hill. Where he had been accustomed to audiences numbering into the hundreds, here he would be lucky to have 50. Or 75. But he had made his promises and he was the servant of God. He would go his mile.

I am sure that neither Dad nor Mom nor anyone else knew what was going on in my mind. My plan. I didn't want them to know. And as it turned out it was good that nobody knew for it was a plan which took a strange turn.

I had been so confident I would now have the courage to do it. But when the first night of the "calls" began, here came that old hesitation again. "I will do it tomorrow."

For one thing, somehow Preacher Stuart's messages were no longer moving me as they once had. Was I imagining it or had some of the fire indeed gone from his famed delivery? I no longer felt the shivers running down my spine.

Was it due to the process of growing up? My budding maturity? Looking back on it now I am certain that something of these factors were indeed at work. In fact, although I may not have realized it at the time, subconsciously the decision may have already been made.

And so I waited until, once more, there were no tomorrows. Only the last night. They had brought a beautiful soloist, a girl with a heavenly voice, from Elk City to lead the choir and to voice those haunting entreaties. If anybody was sending shivers down my spine it was this beautiful young creature with the voice of an angel.

"Softly and tenderly Jesus is calling, calling dear sinner, come home."

Something of the torment was back in my soul. Pulling me towards her, and the sinners bench. But then the battling doubt. The fear of another rejection. The soul patrol people were tugging at my sleeve. "Won't you come forward and give your heart to God tonight?"

But despite the pull, the lure, there was something new, a force I could not define, working within me that night. I simply stood there. They always asked the audience to stand during those plea sessions. Perhaps the psychology of making it easier for a wavering sinner to begin the journey if he were already on his feet.

Until the last chord of the last pleading song faded away, I waited. Until the last "sinner" had left the mourner's bench. Until Preacher Stuart and the lovely singer had vanished into the night. Until the sound of the last motor car had died away. So long I sat in that church.

Finally only Dad was left. Our house was only fifty yards away, the shabby little three room "pastorate". Dad was closing the door for the night. It was fall. The air was nippy, almost cold. They had built a coal fire in the huge, pot bellied stove and the embers still glowed.

"Are you coming?" Dad asked.

"No, I'm going to sit here by the stove for a while. I'll come later," I said.

He hesitated. He started to say something but stopped himself.

Our relationship had become a bitter one. Perhaps he also sensed that something was going on within me that night. But if he did indeed hope that I was working with a decision about God, the time had come to leave the matter to the greater powers of that God.

Then I was alone in that deserted church, alone with the dying embers of the coal fire and my dying faith.

It was a long, long time, that lonely session with my soul that night. Perhaps as much as two hours or more. Until after midnight. Until the glowing coals had become cold and black in lifelessness. My thought processes were working as they had never worked before. And somehow I knew I was making the most fateful decision of my life.

I could still have gotten down on my knees, alone in the darkness beside that stove, to pray and ask once more for God to come. In a sense I did it, asking God for the slightest sign. Truly that was all I wanted.

But God was gone. Somehow, it was beginning to seem, He had never been there.

I shivered and pulled my jacket around me against the growing chill. And still I sat. Until, eventually, the decision was born. Exactly how, or in what manner I reached that decision, I could never say. But during that night I had indeed decided that for me God was dead. At least the God of my father. That God of wrath, of anger, with the power to cast one's soul into hell. In the sense of my need, if He had ever been there, He had now ceased to exist.

And then, suddenly, inside that cold and deserted church atop the bleak hilltop, I felt and received the peace I had sought with so much pain and suffering for so many years. A peace which stilled the sound and fury of battle within my soul. The fires of hell, for first time in my life, were dead and cold - like the coals in that stove.

I stepped outside the door and looked up into the cold, clear skies. I saw the stars which, I had always been told, were the creations of God. Now they were only stars. Bright, cheery, but so utterly far away, so unreachable. As unreachable as their supposed maker I had sought so long.

On that night I had finally been saved. I was born again.

My soul had finally found its peace.

Chapter Ten - Quicksand

Sam and Pat were up to over their butts in quicksand.

And here I was, running away from them as fast as I could go.

The logic could only be tortured - if I was capable of any logic in that moment of panic. One part of my brain was telling me I couldn't have helped if I had stayed with them. I could only have watched them die - choking, gurgling, drowning in the waters of the Washita River.

On the other hand that furiously churning brain was also telling me that to run for help was useless. Where would I find help? How could any one help if they did come? God, at the rate those two had been going down when I left, they would drown long before I could bring help.

I had seen the brown water begin to trickle across Sam's back and Pat was in nearly as deep.

But running was action. Some kind of action.

People say that when a man, or a boy, faces death his whole life comes whirling back through his consciousness. Like a vast, madly whirling kaleidoscope.

It wasn't I who was near death that day, except that my lungs were about to explode from the frenzied running. I had run too fast and too far, driven by that desperate panic. The lungs, the legs, were leaded with pain. Perhaps I was even near collapse, unconsciousness. I had run and run for what seemed like miles across that sandy river flat and then down that lonely country road.

But what my brain was telling me, in that mad whirling of thoughts, was how much of my life, Dad's life, the whole family's life, I was destroying that day. Because I had been the one who had commanded Sam and Pat to enter that quicksand muck. And they, obedient to a voice they trusted, had gone in.

It wasn't as if they were ordinary horses and that we, perhaps, owned a whole stable of horses from which a pair could possibly be spared. These were the most magnificent horses Dad had ever owned. Most important, they were the only horses we owned at the moment.

They were virtually our entire means of a livelihood in a time of bitter economic depression when Dad couldn't possibly replace them. It was tragedy, pure and simple. A tragedy so vast, in terms of our marginal existance, that it might take weeks, months, merely to comprehend it all. How could I understand it all during those few torturing moments as I ran?

But I did. That was the rending hurt of it all. So overwhelming. So complete.

And if it was not my life that came plunging through my consciousness in those terrible moments, it was the lives of Pat and Sam. Theirs and mine, for they had been such an enormous part of my boyhood as I had grown up.

They were the sons of Reuben the terrible, the monster devil horse that had tried to kill me. No, they were not stallions as Reuben had been but had been properly gelded in their time. But still so big, so strong, so willing. And despite the gelding, horses which had inherited so much of that wild, unyielding spirit of their father.

I had been there when they were born, Pat a few months before Sam. I had watched, with stars in my eyes, as the two little black horse babies nuzzled and nursed at the sides of their mothers, those two broad hipped, strong and gentle mare mothers, Jane and May.

It was I who would grab them around the neck, out of sheer exuberance of youth, to wrestle with them, to glory in the vibrant rush of pulse and blood for boy and beast as they bolted to be free.

It was I who would sneak a handful of sugar out of Mom's kitchen, two handsful, to entice them into being my friends. To come nuzzling at my shirt in playful anger when the sugar had disappeared.

It was I who would stand and watch with exploding boy joy when the two of them, free in their paddock, would leap and plunge at each other in mock battle. Sometimes "attacking" while on their hind legs, their forelegs swinging as if in deadly intent.

In my boyish innocence I had even tried to "stunt their growth" by use of a sack of Bull Durham tobacco. To try to keep them small, as colts, eternal playmates for a happy farm boy.

For somewhere in that Bible influenced world in which I grew up, I had been warned about the evils of tobacco. It would stunt your growth, my Dad and his church people had told me. You never grew up to be a man if you used the stuff.

Could it have been sinful then for a boy to wish to stop the growth of these lovable young animals?

It was some farm hand who had lost a bag of "roll your own," and which I had found, which provided the thought and the means. If tobacco could stunt the growth of a boy, why not a colt?

Making sure that Dad didn't see it, I carefully divided the tobacco, half and half, into the feed boxes of the two colts, mixing it with their ration of oats. Then I waited, impatiently, for the dwarfing action. It didn't come. In fact it was soon apparent that Pat and Sam would be giants, like their father, Reuben.

Which brought joy, not sorrow, to my father who needed two more big strong horses for the farm. Knowing how huge and strong their father had been, and their gentle mare mothers, Dad somehow knew that these two just had to be something special. But I doubt even that Dad expected what he got. Horses so very big. So utterly strong. Such glorious horse flesh that a time would come when grown men, lovers of fine horses, would come for miles just to stand and watch the pair of them toil. Dad, his chest swelling with pride at what his two great black horses were doing.

But all that was in the future. These two young colts still had their "growing up" to do, as I did.

I would always remember that day when I had to forgive Sam after he had inflicted upon me the considerable ignomy, and pain, of flying through the barn door and landing on my "arse".

Dad, wise in the ways of horses, had warned me so many times about walking up behind horses, and horses in their stalls without speaking. A horse would need the gentle assurance of a familiar voice if he heard a sudden noise behind him.

Otherwise? Well, otherwise it happened.

I probably forgot to speak that day as I walked up behind young Pat and Sam as they stood in their stall. Possibly I didn't even believe it was necessary with "them." Weren't these young colt-horses my friends, my pals, my playmates, even though now half grown? Certainly they wouldn't harm me.

But Sam, undoubtedly startled, thought otherwise. As I approached to his rear, he simply planted his two hind hooves, already big enough for a yearling, into the pit of my stomach and cut loose with a mighty heave.

Some folks would call it simply being kicked by a horse. My sensation was of flying through the air with considerable pain in the mid-section. And, after I landed on my arse as well.

But no permanent damage. I gasped desperately for air for a few moments and then, when my lungs began pumping air again I was able to get up. Then as the pain subsided, a surge of anger struck me. I thought of grabbing a stick and beating that goddam horse. I'd kill him, that evil thought said. But I didn't. I even forgave him.

After all, I knew I was the one who had been guilty of the sin, unpardonable around horses, of walking up behind them without warning. Even if I told Dad he would only have told me it was my fault. So, I didn't kill Sam. But I learned to respect his feet. And we remained friends.

Perhaps the most tragic day in the life of any young male horse is his gelding day. A day avoided by the few chosen to be breeders. But Dad had had enough of stallions around his farm, with Reuben, and that fateful day would come for Pat and Sam.

I don't remember too much about Pat's. Dad had it done one day when I was in school and it had marginal effect on me. But for Sam a few months younger, I was home when this young horse faced his moment of utter truth. God, how could I ever forget that epic battle? The sheer drama of it, the pain and ignomy of a young horse named Sam.

Those ropes. The ugly, hooked knife. That great struggle. Those screams. Oh, those screams.

It seems that Dad had delayed it a bit too long for Sam.

I had overheard Dad and other horsemen discussing it - that you shouldn't geld too soon. True, it didn't hurt as much if you did it when they were younger. But, those horsemen agreed, if you did it too soon on a horse intended for work he never developed full strength, that great fullness of body so loved by the men of horses.

But I had also overheard Dad discussing the fact that Sam was overdue. Perhaps he was even tempted, just tempted, to allow Sam to become a stallion, a sire. He would have made a good one. But, if Dad was indeed tempted, the memories of Reuben eventually crowded it out. There was enough hell on the farm without having another devil horse around.

135

In any case, I know that the vet showed up one day, with his little black bag. And the ropes.

I called him a vet but Charlie Gunter wasn't really a veterinary surgeon as we know them today. No college degree. Vets in our time were simply men, usually farmers who had served time with an older man who trained them in the ills and hurts of animals. And, to do the gelding, the "denutting" if you please, of calves, pigs, the yearling colts. In fact Dad, like most farmers, did it himself on the calves and pigs. But when it came to a colt, well it was good to have a bit of help.

Funny, Dad didn't even chase me away from the corral that day when I showed up to see what was going on. Perhaps, he decided, I was old enough to learn about the birds and the bees and the gelding.

Sam seemed to sense the danger, almost as soon as he saw the stranger with the black bag and the ropes. Certainly he sensed danger if not the ultimate "dehorsing". He was penned in a one acre corral and galloped furiously as Gunter swung the lasso. At least a dozen times he escaped the loop, despite Gunter's skill, but in the end the results were inevitable. The loop settled on his neck.

Then Sam reared. He plunged. He bolted with the terror driven strength of a madman, or a fear maddened horse. It left both Gunter and Dad dragging in the dirt of the corral floor as they hung on and fought desperately to bring Sam to the snubbing post. Even at the snubber Sam continued to fight with the mad strength and fury of a true son of Reuben. I was watching goggle eyed and somehow I was hoping Sam would win this battle.

Eventually the two men did manage to get the young stallion horse snubbed and then, with loops on his legs, threw his struggling body to the ground. Sam was plunging and screaming in defiance but it could only be a losing battle.

The ropes they used to tie his legs, all four of them, seemed to be an inch thick and surely strong enough to hold him. Or even an elephant. I wouldn't have dared to predict what I was about to see.

There Sam lay, seemingly so helpless. Securely hog tied. Gunter approached to straddle the heaving horse body. The blade of that razor sharp knife was gleaming with menace. Gunter carefully fingered one of Sam's testicles from below, squeezing it taut against the enveloping skin.

I can see it today as if it happened only yesterday. That shiny black skin stretched taut over the egg shaped organ gripped in

136

Gunter's hand. In his other, the knife coming in to make its slit in the taut skin. A slit would allow the "egg" to pop out and become accessible to the crimping tool.

And then it happened. As the razor edge of the blade slid across the tight skin, bringing a little spurt of blood, that tensed body of the shackled young horse seemed to explode.

Even as a boy I had heard the stories of how a man, in a moment of terrored stress, might suddenly find the strength of 10 men. I had even heard the story they told in our town about the local townsman who had driven up on the scene of an auto crash, with the car overturned and the screams of a woman coming from beneath it. The man, folks said, simply grabbed the car and rolled it off the woman. Something he could not possibly have done without the stress factor. Adrenalin at work?

As that knife edge had touched his testicle, Sam had simply blasted loose with the most ungodly horse scream I had heard since the days of Reuben. The frenzied cry to the god of all horses to free him from this ignomy.

But it was his body that exploded. Those seemingly sturdy ropes which had shackled his feet seemed to shred like confetti. My eyes were unbelieving. I had seen the impossible. Sam was free. Back on his feet. Plunging, bolting with the terrored strength of the unbending spirit. Oh, God, how that young horse could fight.

If it had been a battle to get Sam down and shackled the first time, it was doubly so now. Young Sam fought with the fury and strength of an enraged Samson.

But men like Dad and Gunter didn't give up easily either. Somehow the men managed to rope the young horse and put him down once more. This time bigger and stronger ropes were used to tie those flailing feet.

And in the end the knife and the crimping tool did their work.

Then, when Dad and Gunter loosened the ropes and Sam stumbled back onto his feet, the fight was gone. It seemed to me that his spirit was broken. Forever.

The wound didn't bleed much. They never do. If any bleeding was taking place, it was from the spirit of this noble horse animal. Sam hung around the corral for several days, barely touching his food or water. But, somehow, in the ways of nature, even a wounded spirit can mend.

Eventually, after several weeks perhaps, Sam regained a bit of his spirit of youth, if not that of a young man horse, and went back to join Pat in a bit of horseplay. Or colt play. They were, after all just overgrown yearling colts.

Pat's wounds had long since healed and he had, perhaps, forgotten the surge of the mighty sex spirit which had just begun to course through his veins before his gelding day. Sam was in the process of forgetting his.

Or did they ever forget?

I lived with those two animals daily, as colts, as horses. There were times, I believe, when I almost loved them as brothers instead of horses. Eventually, I would travel with them into their valley of the shadow. And the evil.

But somehow the memory of it all, those years with Pat and Sam, have left me convinced that there is heritage in the matter of spirit, even in horses. Yes, they had both suffered their gelding days, that fateful submission to the knife which supposedly makes tractable work hourses out of stallions. And yet, in the end, I knew that the gelding had never deprived these two magnificent horses of the greater portion of that undying spirit which had made their father such an unforgettable beast.

True, they would never sire more colts. They would never know the plunging passion of a fight to possess a mare in heat. But, aside from that, so little of the fire and surge had gone from the life of these two great horses.

Dad knew, for Dad had owned many horses in his lifetime. Dad had worked with Grandpa, the breeder of fine work horses. Far more than a simple horseman, Dad was a horse's man. In spite of his stern sense of God's justice, I believe Dad, in his way, loved those two great horses, too.

As I grew up I was around hundreds of horses. On the annual summer threshing trek, 20 to 30 teams assembled to haul the bundled wagons serving Grandpa's huge power threshing rig. I listened as men, prideful of their horses, did their boasting. I was around the horses of our neighbors. Later, I even worked in a big riding stable at Akron, Ohio. Perhaps I cannot be objective and if not, so be it. But in all that time I never, but never encountered two other horses that could match, in all fullness, the beings embodied in "my" horses, Sam and Pat.

Oh, it was not all pride and joy. One of the real manifestations of that wild, inherited spirit in Sam and Pat was that, despite their gelding and despite the patient training of Dad, they came under the spell of that greatest of all curses from the equine gods - they became runaways.

138

To most horsemen, to own a "runaway" is the ultimate disgrace, the sorest wound to the pride. If such horses become incurable, as Sam and Pat were, there is only one solution. Get rid of them. A dishonorable horseman would simply take them into an area where they were not known and sell them at auction. The risk of living with a confirmed runaway is simply too great.

But Dad could never have done that. His sense of honesty and duty to his God would never have permitted him to lie about those horses. But Dad was also a stubborn man and I doubt if he ever seriously considered selling them. He did determine to conquer them. And live with them.

I am certain he prayed about them, asking God to somehow temper the spirit of these wild animals which were so magnificent in their calmer days. In the end, we would both know, Dad and I, that the magnificence was greater than the evil.

Perhaps no man knows what it is that makes a horse a confirmed runaway. What causes him to bolt suddenly at an unfamiliar sound. Or movement. Then to dash madly, uncontrollably, until all the animal energy pent up in a horse's body has simply blown itself into exhaustion.

In the case of Sam and Pat, I am sure it was not Dad's fault that they became runaways. Certainly not intentionally. Although, when it began, Dad may have compounded the terror. I would suggest that it is more of something in the genes which creates the nature of a horse. In the case of Sam and Pat, perhaps, their heritage from Reuben, the great devil horse. From where else?

But the runaway episodes with Sam and Pat would become almost epic. Costly in wrecked wagons and property. Dad did his best to conceal this black mark on his pride. And he determined to conquer.

Dad knew horses. He had "broken" Sam and Pat properly. As colts they were permitted to romp alongside while their mothers worked. Or even on trips to town with the wagon. A colt running free stayed close to "mom" and did not cause much trouble.

Later, as the colts grew a bit, Dad took the second step of haltering them to their mothers' sides, to the harness, so they would become accustomed to walking or trotting, alongside the work horses on the road. Or in the fields. They would learn the routine, the commands. Later, as they grew almost to maturity, Dad would even load a light harness upon them, so they would become accustomed to the feel.

With Dad, the slow and patient process was a must. He could see the makings of great horses in these two and he didn't propose to botch their training. He had plenty of time.

In the end, the patience paid off. At least, for the time. When the time came that they must be harnessed and hitched to a real load, you could hardly call it a "breaking" for these two. Oh, sure, they bolted and balked a bit. For a few days, or weeks, perhaps. But after that, they worked as if they had been born to it.

All of which was so deceptive, considering what was to come later. No hint that these beautiful and huge young horses were runaways.

It was a railway steam locomotive which set off the explosion the first time.

Perhaps Dad, lured into a sense of security by the ease and quickness of his mastery over them, had decided too early to take them to town. Hitched to a wagon. Perhaps, he had even succumbed to the prideful need to display to the town folks his magnificent young team.

All we knew then was that Dad came home walking that evening - behind the two horses. Still driving them by rein and bridle - but walking. The wagon had been wrecked.

Again, Dad didn't talk much about such defeats. I pieced it together later from bits of information he let drop to Mom or others. Some of it I learned from other people. Dad, together with his young horses, had been near the railroad tracks when the engineer on one of those giant freight locomotives let loose a "blow" of steam.

Anyone who has ever been close to such a steamer when it cut loose with that blast of steam from its giant boiler will know that it was a sound which, especially if unexpected, can frighten a half grown child into a panic. To the young horses it must have been the embodiment of total evil. Danger, sudden and complete. Perhaps, at that moment, the horses were even to be forgiven for what happened.

Dad, I am sure, explained it to himself that way. The horses were young, barely broken to work. Perhaps it wouldn't happen again. His fervent hope, at least.

Next day, Dad hitched up the mares, May and Jane, borrowed another wagon to go get the wrecked one. He repaired it and started out again. In time, he even bought a big Newton farm wagon, the heaviest and sturdiest of them all.

140

The trouble was, it did happen again. And again and again. Until it became clear that Sam and Pat were indeed marked with that age old curse.

Incurable runaways.

The second time, as I remember, a huge crate was dropped from a loading dock and slammed on the floor of the wagon. After that second episode, Dad went back to the fang toothed bicycle chain bridle bits, such as we had been forced to use on Reuben, the wild father. Dad was simply determined to conquer the wild devil spirit in these two otherwise magnificent young horses.

It may have been at this point that Dad made one of the few mistakes of his life in training horses. With the bridles equipped with those fanged bits, Dad drove the young team back to the scene of their first disgrace, the railroad yards. When another monster steam locomotive came snorting up to a cross, he deliberately drove Sam and Pat right up to the big steamer. Deliberately daring that giant machine to frighten his horses again.

It did. The two of them were rearing and screaming with terror, trying to bolt. In any direction but forward and Dad headed them into that monstrous black terror. Dad was adding to the terror with a whip, driving the horses up to within five or six feet of the big "loke." Meanwhile, to control their bolting terror he was sawing with those cruel bits. Foaming flecks of blood were beginning to drip from their mouths. It was cruel. It was terrible.

For the moment, Dad had conquered. Looking back on it now, it must have only added to the image of terror in the brains of those two horses. But Dad had hoped that the two would become accustomed to it and their fears would abate, especially when they would see that the big, black snorting monster had done them no harm.

It was all in vain. The psychical beings of these two horses, if horses indeed may have such, were marked forever with the vision of terror.

Perhaps the most epic of all their runaway episodes came on a day after Dad had taken on the job of mowing the grass on the campus of the Southwestern State College in Weatherford, with a regular hay mower. The mower borrowed.

His mowing had taken him near the athletic field on a day when the track coach was out practicing with his team. And using a starter's pistol to set off his sprinters. He chose the exact moment when Dad was turning the corner near the track field to pull the trigger on his pistol.

141

Sam and Pat made one giant leap of terror, throwing Dad backwards off the mower seat and then, with nobody to saw those cruel bits, they were gone.

Off the campus and onto the concrete pavement of North Broadway. The concrete added to the roaring clatter of the machine behind them. So fast were they running that the madly flying sickle, jumping back and forth within the sickle bar, exploded to bits. But that sickle bar, some five feet long and armed with sharp prongs, facing forward, was still there. A menacing danger to any person or beast that might stray into its path.

The horses and machine clattered past the schools, the primary school on the left and the high school on the right, moments before dismissal time. On and on, down the hill towards the spot where Broadway crossed Main Street which also bore the traffic of famed U. S. Highway 66.

People who witnessed it that day said it was a miracle that the horses managed to cross Main Street without becoming involved in a crash with a car or truck. Traffic was, as usual, quite heavy. A block and a half past Main Street it finally came to an end. That sickle bar, protruding as it did on the side of the machine, caught in the tires of a Model A Ford parked at the side of the street. The impact swung the horses slamming against the side of the car. And there they stood, foam flecked and panting, when Dad eventually arrived on foot. He had run the whole way, a tormenting physical trial for him as well.

By the time he arrived, a crowd of townspeople and an angry chief of police stood gaping at the wreckage. Eventually, they had to let Dad go when it had been determined that he had, after all, committed no crime.

But not before, once again, he had become obligated to pay damages - this time the slashed tires of the Ford. Not to speak of the wrecked mower. Even the heavy iron wheels were broken from the mad pounding on the pavement. Another bitter defeat for Dad, who had counted on those few dollars from the mowing job to pay the grocery bill.

On this particular day I believe Dad was so bitter he would have sold the horses if he could have. Except it was now clear to everyone that they were runaways. Especially after that front page story in the Weatherford News. No sensible farmer or horseman would buy runaways.

Plus the fact that at this particular stage of Sam and Pat's history, we were in the bottom of the cruel economic depression of the 1930's and those two horses were all the horses we had left. Virtually our entire means of a livelihood.

In any case, it was inevitable that as I grew older the time would come when I would be handed the reins of this pair and sent out to work with them. And to face my own moments of truth.

Dad knew that I knew all about those runaway episodes. How could I have escaped knowing? He also knew that I knew about those cruelly fanged bits and that I knew how to use them.

"Be gentle with those bits and don't saw them unless you have to," he admonished his oldest son. "You know how it cuts their mouths."

That "sawing?" You did it when the horses bolted, or tried to, by jerking first the left rein, then the right. A see-sawing motion which jerked the bits back and forth across the jaws, the teeth and the mouths.

Above all, Dad always warned me to be alert to any unusual or sudden noise which might frighten the horses. Beyond that, after that notorious episode of the mower on the college campus, after Dad had ignominiously been tossed backward off the mower and thus deprived of any chance to bring the devil horses under control, it became a rigid rule never to drive Sam and Pat without having the reins knotted behind your back. We had, at least, learned that much.

Armed with this precaution, Dad and I were able to control those animals. After a fashion, at least.

I remember the day when Sam, perhaps kicking at a stubborn fly, managed to kick one of his hind legs over the traces. It was enough to set him off. Pat, at his side, bolted with him.

I was cultivating corn with a riding cultivator. If it had not been for the reins, knotted behind my back, I would have been thrown off backwards just as Dad had been. As it was, I brought it under control.

By using my head, lowering the cultivator blades as deep as they would go, standing on the cultivator gangs to add my weight to the digging shovels and by "sawing" the bits. But not until we had gouged two huge furrows into the soil for perhaps 400 yards.

Dad saw it. The bloody abrasions on the inside of Sam's legs. The flecked lips. The mighty gashes in the earth. And then he knew. But he did not scold. How could he, after those defeats he had suffered at their hands - or hooves? He could only be thankful that I had been able to maintain a measure of control.

143

But there would come my day of defeat, too. It would be my fault - saved from disaster by the barest of margins.

It came on a day when we were moving from one farm to another, near Clinton. Somehow, it seems, we were forever moving. If not from Oklahoma to Oregon, as in the earlier years, from farm to farm now, from county to county. I would be tempted to blame it on that restless spirit of Dad. In truth that may have been a factor. But we were gripped in the jaws of a cruel economic depression that turned us into Pilgrims. Unable to pay the rent on one house or farm, we moved to another for a new try.

On the way, losing so much. The new tractor Dad bought in 1928. Our other horses. Farm implements. But always clinging to Sam and Pat.

As we entered the moving process, I had been entrusted with the most precious cargo of all. Those hundreds of glass jars containing my mother's hoard of home cooked food, each jar carefully wrapped with newspaper as a cushion of sorts. And all of it loaded in the farm wagon. A literal treasure in those depression ridden days.

Dad had given me his usual warnings about watching the horses. Perhaps a special warning because of the precious cargo I was transporting.

But somehow the beautiful warm spring day, the plodding peacefulness of the horses at the moment, and the hawk, were all so enticing to mischief.

My younger brother, Ernie, was with me. Otherwise I might not have done it. I believe he was the one who spotted the hawk first - and pointed up at it. In any case, I had a .22 caliber pistol hidden in my shirt. Even Dad didn't know I had it. I didn't need it, the necessity provided only by the macho spirit of teenager.

The prairie hawk which suddenly came sailing overhead, floating slowly across the brilliant blue sky. In a moment of complete forgetfulness of my responsibility, of any danger, I handed the reins to Ernie, not even noticing that he didn't slip them behind his back. I drew my pistol, aimed at the hawk and fired.

Oh, God, it had happened. That starter pistol thing again.

The worst part about it was that the sudden plunge of the fear maddened horses had jerked the reins out of Ernie's hands. They dangled down between the horses as they began their explosive dash. Without those reins, there wasn't a hope of bringing the startled horses under control.

My heart was pounding with fear but there was no choice. It might cost me my life but I had to climb down on the tongue pole between those plunging horses and retrieve those reins. To this day I don't know how I did it. I balanced myself by clinging to the harness of the leaping horses. It couldn't have added to their fright. I know when I grabbed at the reins I missed. Twice. Three times. I would have to get even lower down between the horses, desperately clinging to the harness and the pole. And then I made it. I had those reins in my hands.

Now I had to climb back up on the wagon seat and begin the battle.

The big wagon, with no springs, was jolting mercilessly against the glass jars. I could hear glass bouncing and breaking. But, once back on the seat of the wagon I slammed on the brake as hard as I could and began sawing the reins. The brake wouldn't help much. Even with the rear wheels locked, the smooth steel of the wheel tires would simply slide over the dusty earth like the runners of a sled in the snow. But the reins, and those fanged bits, they would work.

Despite the evil that had lured me into that mess I was lucky. Lucky that the stretch of road where it happened had been fairly smooth. If we had encountered one of those jolting gyp rock hills which dotted the Oklahoma prairie country, the glass breakage would have been horrendous. I "sawed" the horses to a halt after a run of perhaps a half a mile and just a few yards short of one of those menacing rock hills.

I tried to swear Ernie to secrecy but it didn't matter. Dad and Mom would find the broken jars - thankfully, not too many had broken. Dad would see the blood on the horses' mouths. The white foam on their sides. I would have to take his wrathful scolding. And the wounding of my pride.

That was the last time Sam and Pat ever ran away with me. Well, almost. They tried a few times. And with Dad. But if we had not learned our lessons by this time we never would. The wild spirit of those horses never left them but now we managed to control it. At the cost of the bloodied mouths.

Beyond that, those two great horses - so big, so strong, so willing - in their calmer moments did so much to compensate for all the hell they caused. Unlike their wild, plunging father, Reuben, they worked with the steadiness of a tractor. And nearly as strong. So utterly strong. So magnificent.

145

A man must be forgiven his lack of objectiveness if he insists, as I do, that he never saw two other horses do what Sam and Pat could do.

On those occasions when Dad would call upon the two of them to do the seemingly impossible, like pulling a tree stump, those huge horses would simply knot their big leg muscles, lean forward into their heavy collars and something would give.

If the stump didn't move, the hickory double-tree would break. Their ability to break those stout hickory double-trees became legend. I remember hearing Dad say, one time, that he didn't believe a hickory double-tree had been made that Sam and Pat couldn't break.

But the crowning glory to the long work career of these two great horses came in those days just prior to that fateful day of the quicksand.

It had all started with a flood. The biggest, most disastrous flood in the history of Roger Mills County, folks said. Some 34 people were drowned, along with thousands of cattle. The whole countryside stank for weeks as the ranchers and farmers buried or burned all the dead animals that had been caught in the wild rush of water on that dark night.

Depending on the source, some 7, 9 or 11 inches of rain fell that night. I heard some people swear they measured 17 inches of rain, if that were possible. I just know it was more rain in a few hours than I had ever seen in my life. It fell hard and fast. The fields around us, instead of being muddy, were beaten hard, almost like a concrete floor.

Wooden bridges around the county were simply gone. The newer concrete highway bridges that still stood were like islands in the middle of a half mile wide torrent of water. Earthen approach dikes just washed away. The big bridge over the Washita River where State Highway 34 crossed, about two miles from our house, was a good example.

It was still standing the next morning but several hundred yards of approach dike had been replaced by a roaring mass of wild and muddy water filled with debris. Even after the water went down, several days later, there was that huge gap filled with water. Our town, Strong City, completely without access from our side. It was several days before the water dropped low enough for farmers to ford the river with horses and wagons. Still too deep for cars.

But that left the State Highway Department stuck with the job of rebuilding that long approach dike. Even the bridge itself was

146

found to have been moved several inches. Engineers had to pull some fancy hydraulic engineering to stabilize it.

That washed out roadway was where Dad, Sam, Pat and I came into the picture. Instead of bringing in their own crews to repair that dike, the Department shipped in earth moving equipment with a few supervisors. They hired local farmers and mule skinners to man the equipment.

So, that was why Dad jumped at the chance to put Sam and Pat to work earning a few extra bucks to supplement our scratch-poor farm income. They simply joined a small army of horsedrawn earth movers who were slowly moving a big hill, a quarter of a mile south of the river, dragging its dirt in to fill the huge hole. I'm not sure exactly how long that job took but I know it was several weeks.

At first, Dad worked one of the long convoy of earth movers, a two horse job. But then one part of the equipment the Department had brought in was a big big earth breaker plow, usually drawn by four big horses or mules. It dug loose the dirt from the side of the hill so the earth movers could pick it up and cart it off.

A mule skinner with four mules had been on the plow for several days. His mules had proven to be unmanageable. One day when the mule driver failed to show up the boss walked up to Dad, looked at those big horses and said, "Man, do you think that team can handle this plow?"

"I think so," said Dad, and calmly hitched Sam and Pat to it. Part of the idea in making the change was that two horses, or two mules for that matter, would be easier to manage on a bucking plow of that type. Sam and Pat handled that plow as easily as the four mules that had been doing it. Old time horsemen stared at what they were doing. They were magnificent.

But the real challenge came a few days later, in the form of the Mormon Board. Gee, don't ask me where that name came from. All I know was that it was a substitute for a bulldozer in a day when we didn't even know what a bulldozer was.

A big, flat board structure made of oak, maybe 26 inches high and perhaps five feet wide. A steel scraper blade attached along the lower edge with two handles, like plow handles, sticking up from the upper edge.

Steel cables were fastened to both the lower corners of the contraption and joined in a vee about 12 to 15 feet ahead of the board. At the vee, another cable, much longer, was fastened. This cable led all the way out across that huge pool of muddy water to the bridge, where it was anchored through a roller sheave and then back to the earth bank.

Attached to the end, back on shore, was an "evener" with a hitch for four horses. The mule skinner had showed up after a one day of absence, and found his job taken over by Sam and Pat. The boss put him and his four mules on that Mormon Board.

The guys on the Mormon Board would dig the blade into the pile of dirt on the water's edge, deposited there by the convoy of earth movers. The mule skinner would call on his mules to heave. Like a bulldozer, the Mormon Board would shove a big load of dirt into the hole.

But again the mules turned out to be a bit unmanageable. Isn't the stubborness of mules, after all, legendary? The problem was stopping the mules with precision, at just the right point, to keep from pulling the Mormon Board out into the water. That did happen so often that they had fastened a "rescue rope" on the back of it to pull it back up the bank when it got dunked. The mule skinner was also having trouble making his four mules back up in unison for a new load after each heave.

After witnessing that Mormon Board taking one dunking after another and listening to the curses of the mule skinner fighting to control his crazy animals, the boss came walking up to Dad on the big plow and again asked the question.

"Do youth think that pair can handle that Mormon Board?"

"I think so," said Dad. They could. And they did.

Oh, but it was beautiful. At least to Dad, so prideful of his great horses. And to me, who somehow gloried in what all those magnificent horses stood for, even that wild spirit that had made them runaways.

One reason that Sam and Pat worked out so well on the Mormon Board was because they were not only strong, they had brains. It took them perhaps all of half an hour to master the routine.

Pull. Whoa. Back up. Pull. Whoa. Over and over, a thousand times a day. Those commands the horses had learned long ago, even in the days when they had been spindly legged colts, tethered to the sides of their hard working mothers. Now they worked with the precision of a machine. It was seldom that the man on the "rescue rope" every had any work to do after that. The Mormon Board just didn't get dunked any more.

When we started our team on that Mormon Board job, the board handlers, charged with digging the blade into the pile of dirt,

148

loaded it a little lighter than usual. They realized that there were only two horses on what had been a job for four horses. But after a time, when they saw the ease with which those big horses handled the load, they begn digging a bit deeper.

Those board handlers began to make a game out of it. They would dig that board in as deep as possible, shoving an unbelievable load. It seemed they were determined to find out just how strong those horses were. A few times they almost stalled the pair but not quite. Each time, when the two found they had an extra load on the board they simply made that familiar Sam and Pat heave which had broken so many double-trees. Leaning far forward into their collars with the muscles knotted, something moved. If the huge mound of dirt in front of the blade didn't move, it was the double-tree that snapped.

After a time, the guys gave it up and simply allowed the two great horses to work with normal loads. Dad's pride would not have allowed him to plead for mercy.

Somewhere along the line, it was bound to happen. Dad asked me to spell him on the job. I was, perhaps, 17 or 18 now, and well accustomed to working with "my" horses. Dad knew I could handle them and they hadn't run away for months. Or was it even longer?

I had spelled Dad on the earth carrier, on the big plow and now on the Mormon Board. There really wasn't anything to it. Sam and Pat were doing it all. We didn't even have to tell them when to back up any more. They just did it automatically. The man assigned to hauling the double-tree back after each heave, had to move fast to keep up with the horses' back-and-forth movements.

All those two horses wanted was the sound of a familiar voice, telling them to pull, and to shout "whoa" at exactly the right moment. So far as the reins were concerned, I could have thrown them away.

Now came the time when word of what Sam and Pat were doing spread through the countryside. Men of the land, horsemen all, came to look at the magnificent display of brute horse strength. They would come and make comments. "Man, those are some horses. They tell me that is supposed to be a four horse load. But look, they hardly sweat."

Dad or I, listening to such comments, could only choke with pride.

I remember one day, when a wealthy farmer and a lover of horse flesh who lived at Cheyenne, came out to watch. He stood there for long minutes, his eyes filled with yearning. In the end, he took Dad aside.

I'll give you $300 for those horses," he said. This was at a time when you could buy a good team of horses for $100. But Dad could only say no. Aside from the pride of ownership of such horses, he had to tell the man they were all the horses we had and we simply had to have them.

The man went up to $350. Still no. Up to $400 and Dad still said no. The man was gulping stubbornly now but he wanted those horses.

"I'll make it $400 and give you another good team. A good team," he said.

Now it was Dad's turn to gulp. That $400 would be a fortune to us. I believe he almost accepted. But in the end Dad still said no and we kept our horses.

And now - these were the two horses I had commanded to enter the quicksand, which I had left there in the muck as I fled in terror.

And it all happened because we had no water well at home. We had a cistern for drinking water. The water for the horses and the cows had to hauled in barrels from a neighbor's well. Working on this highway job, Dad came upon the idea of filling the barrels in the river. It was easier because we were already at the river It saved the extra trips to the neighbor.

I had helped Dad do it several times and had even done it myself on days when I worked afternoons. On that day, Dad had said, "The water barrels are empty. Fill them before you come home."

The easiest way was to drive the wagon in the river. You didn't have to lift the heavy buckets so far. We had never had any problems. On this particular day - how could I forget - I had gone into the small town to pick up a few items from the grocery store, then headed back to the river.

But this time, weeks after the flood, the water had dropped. Our usual place of crossing was so shallow it would have made dipping difficult. I looked for a deeper spot. When it seemed I had found it, I simply headed for the edge, clucked the horses and drove in.

Then it happened. The horses had scarcely stepped into the water when they began to go down. At first, they struggled and then their feet locked into the clutching sand. They just went down. And down.

150

My brain had been properly conditioned, from years of reading the western pulps, for the terror of that moment. In the stories, if it was the villain who slipped into the quicksand, he simply sank out of sight. Gurgling unto death. If the hero with his lasso arrived in time, the villain would be pulled to safety only after he confessed all his horrible crimes.

In any case, the writers had never left me an inch of room to doubt. If you stumbled into quicksand you were gone. Unless someone came galloping to the rescue - but quick. Down in the muck and that horrible, gurgling death.

And that was the way it was happening now, right before my frightened eyes. I was safe. Most of the wagon still perched on the edge of the river and only the front wheels were in. But the horses, my Sam and Pat, were down much further.

Sinking, sinking. Immobile. For once, their great strength had met its match. The powerful legs locked into a gigantic force from which they could never bolt in panic.

There hadn't been time to think. I just leaped off the wagon and started running. At my last backward look, the water had begun to trickle over Sam's back. Pat was in almost as deep. Please, somebody, help me. Oh, please, God.

My little side trip to Strong City had meant that by the time I got back to the river the whole work site was deserted. The work crew gone. As I ran across the sandy river flat towards the road, not a soul was in sight. It was not until I reached the road that I saw a single man, in a horsedrawn wagon, rattling down the road at least a quarter of a mile ahead of me. His horses trotting. There was no way I could overtake him. I began to scream. Or try to. My long run had exhausted me and screams were only hoarse screeches. My tortured lungs could barely make a sound.

I was frantic with frustration. Please, God, why doesn't he turn around and look? Please, please. Now anger was added to my panic and fear. If I had had a gun I believe I would have shot him.

On and on he went, refusing to turn his head. I know now that he could not hear me, over the rattling sound of his wagon. My screams were futile wasting of strength. This distance between me and the wagon growing by the moment.

And then, when it seemed I must collapse, he finally turned and saw me. Now I began waving my arms frantically. Come back. Come back.

The man did stop. He turned his wagon and came towards me. But instead of whipping his horses to a gallop, it was only that slow, shuffling trot as he approached. If only he could know the urgency in my heart.

I had finally collapsed and was lying there on the roadside, gasping for breath as he drove up.

"What's the matter, son? What's wrong, " he asked.

"The horses. The horses. In the quicksand," I croaked. "Please help me."

I believe he understood then but he was still so calm. So casual. Why didn't he whip his horses and go flying back to the river?

But he was trying to tell me something at a moment when my ears did not want to listen.

But suddenly I did begin to listen. And what I was hearing I couldn't believe. Oh, blessed Mother, if it could only be true.

"Take it easy, son. I don't believe you have anything to worry about," the man had the nerve to say.

"But they are gone. They are gone. The horses. Don't you understand" I was croaking at him.

"Yes, I know, son, but I live here on the river and my cows are getting into that quicksand all the time. I haven't lost one yet."

Did I dare believe such insanity?

He continued to explain. My brain was telling me I could only hope - not believe.

"You see, quicksand is only sand filled with water. Most of those quicksand pockets are not very big. When a big solid body like that of a cow, or horse, gets into it they go down until their body squeezes the water out of the sand and then it solidifies. They go down only so far and then they stop," he said.

"But they were almost gone when I left them," I insisted as I climbed into his wagon.

"We'll see," he said. "I believe your horses are all right."

Somehow the pounding of my heart had lost some of its urgency. But I was still impatient. Why didn't he go faster? As we approached the river my eyes were searching frantically for something to tell me whether the man had lied to me. Or, maybe, told me the truth.

First the wagon box came into sight, perched there on the edge of the river. An then, oh, glory, I could see the heads of the horses. My horses. Those beautiful, beautiful heads. Still above the water. Still alive. I wanted to scream with joy.

When we came near it was the wide, white rims of the eyes which told me they, my noble horses, were frightened, too. But so strangely quiet and still. So firmly locked in.

But even now, reassured that Dad's horses, my horses, were still alive, how could we possibly lift them out? They were so heavy.

My eyes looked imploringly to my new, suddenly found friend. I didn't even know his name. I had never seen him before.

Seeing the question in my eyes he spoke again, so calmly and reassuring. "I believe they can do it themselves," he said.

Then, after looking the situation over a moment he had a question.

"Will those horses mind you? Will they do what you tell them to?"

"Yes, yes," I assured him. They had always obeyed my orders, except when in the panic of a runaway. But those runaway episodes were so far, far away now.

The man squatted on the bank of the river and gave me directions. It was clear now the he wasn't even going to help. Not physically, at least. I and the horses would have to do it.

"You go out there and unhitch their harness from the wagon, and unsnap the reins between the horses,"he said.

"But the quicksand. It will get me, too," I protested.

"No, you don't have anything to worry about. It's solid now. It's not quicksand any more."

I hesitated but then I gingerly tried it. It was true, incredibly true. The water was only 8 to 10 inches deep and below that the sand was solid now, like a floor.

So I waded out and unhitched the horses. I had to dig into the sand to get to the traces.

"Now, go to the one that isn't down quite as far as the other, the one on the left," he said. "Go to his head, get hold of his bridle. Pull and speak to him. Tell him to come."

Lord, how could the horse move? Locked in so tight? But I was beginning to trust the man a bit now. I followed his directions.

"Come on, Pat, come on." You could see the big horse struggling but he barely moved.

My stranger friend had seen that slight movement, however, and encouraged me.

"He moved a bit. Keep trying," he said.

I spoke again and Pat struggled again. Had he moved? Just a bit more. Over and over I tugged on his bridle and kept talking.

"Come on, Pat, come." Four times. Five. Six. Seven. Maybe more.

Then suddenly, the horse's movement did indeed become apparent. He was moving. He was moving. My heart was pounding again, with an exciting prospect now. In a moment, Pat was free from that terrible grip, climbing out of the hole. And that was what it was now. A hole. The edges of the sand slowly crumbling into it.

"Bring him out here to me, " said the man. "Then go get the other one. It will be easier because of that hole beside him."

And thus, incredibly, it happened. It took Sam only a few moments to free himself when I spoke to him . Just as Pat had, he walked on sand that had been so treacherous an hour earlier.

Oh, joy. My horses were alive. Well, and standing on firm ground. I could hardly believe it but there they stood. I wanted to kiss them for sheer joy. The man, too. But he was preparing to leave, still telling me it was my job.

"I believe you can handle it from here," he said. "I see you've got a chain in the wagon. You can tie it to the rear axle, hitch the horses to it and pull the wagon out backwards. I've got to go now. I'm late for the milking."

And then he clucked to his horses and was gone. I never saw him again.

Now I tied the log chain to the rear of the wagon, hitched the horses with the double-tree retrieved from the wagon, and it was all over. It was child's play for the animals to pull the wagon free. And now I, too, was free from that terrible belief that I had killed Dad's horses. My horses. Our horses.

Like the stranger friend, the man late for his milking, I, too, was late with my chores. I still had to fill my barrels with water. Dad would be scolding again. But none of that mattered now.

My heart was singing with the joy of deliverance. I was alive again. I, Sam and Pat.

Chapter Eleven - Buck

Buck the terrible. Buck the ferocious. Buck the fearless. Buck the furious. Buck the gladiator. Buck the terrorist.

Buck the rabbit.

Yes, rabbit - that symbol of the timid, the shy and the fearful. Yet to be described as a ferocious and furious gladiator? Truthfully?

Perhaps nobody could ever say what a strange mixture of genes, what a weird accident of nature, conspired to create a rabbit like Buck.

All I knew was that there he was, the incredible rabbit who could, and would, accept the challenge of a very large and courageous dog, bent on slaying and eating him.

He would willfully and with somewhat malice aforethought, lay hidden in ambush to launch one of his terrorist attacks. Against even a human. A grown man.

A rabid rabbit? His courage enflamed by the ravages of a disease? No, that was not quite possible because it all took place over a period of months and maybe even years. Rabies would have killed him in a matter of days.

It must all be explained in context with the environment in which it took place.

J. H. Kendall - pioneer, trading post merchant, postmaster in Corn Colony around the turn of the century - moved in 1915 to the bustling railroad town of Weatherford in western Oklahoma, some 20 miles away, to start a new business venture.

It was the borning age of the new fangled motor car and when Kendall's oldest son, Charlie, began showing talent at fixing the sputtering chug buggies, Pop Kendall built him a shop. A huge tin roofed building that looked more like a warehouse than an auto repair shop but, folks said, at one time there had been a whole crew of mechanics kept busy there.

I know, this is supposed to be a rabbit story. We're getting there.

By the time I arrived on the scene as an apprentice in Charlie's shop, a red head of 14 who still gaped with wonder at the innards of a motor, things had changed a bit. There must have been some kind of a dust-up in the Kendall family.

Charlie had established squatters rights to a section of alley in the rear of the Kendall establishment and had set up an auto machine shop business of his own.

Up front, Pop Kendall, together with two of his other sons, Claude and Archie, were operating the Texaco station. Not a bad spot, considering that it fronted onto that famed transcontinental highway, Route 66.

In between stood that huge hunk of tin roofed building, nearly empty. Nobody ever tried to explain it to me.

If it had been some kind of a family feud it hadn't been a very bloody one. Charlie still spoke to his Dad and the brothers. If we needed gas we always bought it up front, at Texaco. Charlie still used a rear room of that big building for parts storage.

Charlie used to send me into that storage room for parts. Sort of dark in there, not many windows and only a single light bulb hanging from the ceiling.

We're getting closer to the rabbit business now.

One reason I liked to go into that room was because, stored in one corner was a dusty old Stoddard-Dayton racer. Charlie had raced it in his hot rod days. I liked to stand there gaping at that monster engine with the big rocker arms. I wanted to hear it roar.

"Maybe. Some day," Charlie would say. But the engine needed fixing and Charlie, most of the time, could barely pay his bills.

Stoddard-Dayton. Wow, what a hunk of glamor a name like that had for a kid.

The rabbit?

It was Charlie's brother, Claude, who started the rabbit business. Times were tough. Real tough. The worst years of the worst economic depression of all. Texaco wasn't paying off much, those days. Especially when you had to split the take three ways - Pop, Archie and Claude.

Claude eyed all that empty shed space between Charlie's territory and Texaco country. Room for some kind of a new enterprise.

From somewhere Claude got the idea he could set up a string of rabbit hutches in all that space and make a few bucks raising domestic rabbits for the market. I guess somebody sold him on the idea that there was a market for rabbit meat. Or furs.

Claude apparently got Pop's approval for the project and soon rabbit hutches were popping up all over the place. Claude built most of them. Along the walls. Out in the middle. Before it was over, he had hundreds, maybe thousands of rabbits in there. I never tried to count them.

Oh, there was a market for them. But not much. I doubt if Claude ever got his investment money back. I know he eventually gave it all up, went to Washington and got a government job.

But in the meantime, rabbit time.

It was all sort of fascinating to a teen-ager like me. When I got a chance I would sneak up and watch Claude feeding his rabbits. Breeding. Nursing the sick ones. Butchering some. Shipping away the meat. And the furs. I never caught on to all the details.

And then there was Buck.

The first time I saw Buck I became curious, for two reasons. First, he didn't look like the rest of Claude's rabbits. Something more like a wild rabbit. A jack rabbit, maybe? Not quite. The second thing was that he wasn't penned up like all the rest of Claude's rabbits. He was just wandering around loose.

How come he wasn't penned up like the others? I asked Claude.

"Oh, he doesn't need to be. He's not really one of the rabbits. He can take care of himself," Claude said.

I wasn't quite sure what he meant about "taking care of himself." That was the part I was about to find out about.

Where did Claude get him?

"A guy came by and gave him to me," said Claude. When I pressed the matter he gave me a half way explanation. The "guy" was a friend who raised a few rabbits in the country. One day one of the "guy's" mama rabbits came in heat, escaped from her pen and wandered off out in the fields. She apparently had met up with a boy jack rabbit and got herself pregnant. Then she came back "home" to have her babies. Buck was one of those babies.

Well, it was not so hard to believe when you saw the evidence. Half jack rabbit and half Belgian hare. That's why he looked so much like a wild jack. Big scoundrel, too. Belgian hares are no small rabbits so Buck was at least as big as a jack rabbit.

"Is he tame? Will he let you pet him ?" I asked.

"Better not try. He's sort of mean," said Charlie.

I wrinkled my nose at that one. A mean rabbit?

No way. I had grown up on a farm. I had plenty of experience with wild rabbits. In the spring I'd catch one or two of the new baby jack rabbits and try to raise them. I soon gave it up.

But aside from that, all rabbits always spooked when you got close to them. They'd run like hell. Even the babies. My dog, Pedro could chase the grown jack rabbits and sometimes catch them and eat them. I saw our neighbors hunting rabbits with guns. Dad wouldn't let me have a gun.

The only possible proof I ever had that a rabbit was mean came one day when Pedro was chasing a jack rabbit and the dumb beast, in a panic, came running straight at me. I hunched down and grabbed it but that was when I found out what a rabbit's main weapons were.

No biting. Or scratching. But wow, those feet. They had feet like hammers. That rabbit, that day, nearly kicked the stuffings out of me.

Felt like some crazy guy was hitting me with a hammer. Bang. Bang. Hard. Sharp. It hurt. Plenty. After a few seconds of that beating, to my arms, my chest, my head, I had had enough and was happy to turn that rabbit loose. My arms, my chest and face hurt for days.

But I never thought about all of that when I first talked to Claude about Buck. I suppose I had mostly forgotten it. I was about to get my reminder.

That day. My boss, Charlie, told me to go into the storage room, my Stoddard-Dayton dream room, and get some parts he needed.

I just went. No fear. No reason to be afraid. I had been in there many times.

But that day, after I opened the door, I was trying to adjust my eyes to the gloomy dimness when it happened. Wham. Like the blitz.

In the dim light I hadn't even seen what hit me. It just slammed into my legs like some sort of battering ram. In a split second a violent wave of terror gripped me. Fear, panic, at the unknown. It just never occurred to me that it was Buck. Couldn't possibly be.

But it was. By the time my eyes could get focused in the dim light I could see him and had to believe it. He apparently had been hiding in a corner and when I came groping through the door he had charged like a wild bull. Smaller, but like a bull. In fact it was so sudden, so unexpected, he almost knocked me down.

By the time I identified my assailant, at least a part of my courage returned. No rabbit was going to do this to me. I began kicking like mad at that crazy rabbit. Most of the time he was able to elude my kick. Like Pedro when the cows tried to kick him. But I finally got a few licks in. Simply because he hadn't been satisfied with one charge and kept coming back for more.

I got in one good kick that sent him flying like a football and I thought that would take care of him but it didn't. He scrambled to his feet and charged again. And every time he hit me those hind feet of his were going like hammers. Wammity wham.

But I kept kicking too. I had shoes on, of course, and should have been hurting him. Badly.

But somehow, he was landing a lot more blows than I was. Thump, thumpity thump. I was hurting, too. And maybe that was when I started remembering the rabbit Pedro had chased that day, and I had grabbed.

In the end, even though I had landed several good kicks it was I who retreated. My legs were bleeding. Hurting like hell. My khaki work pants were ripped.

Charlie Kendall wasn't the kind of boss who liked to be told by one of his employees, least of all a snot nosed apprentice, that he could not carry out his orders. But he, too, must have sensed that something was wrong. From the frightened, bewildered look on my face. The bloody scratches on my legs. The torn pants.

"It's that rabbit, Buck," I said, trying not to blubber. "He's crazy."

Now it was Charlie's turn to indicate he didn't believe a word of what I was saying.

"You mean a rabbit did that?" he demanded. "What's the matter, you afraid of a rabbit?"

I didn't know how to answer that one. I was and I wasn't. I never had been afraid of one before. Now I was. But I didn't want to admit it. All the rabbits I had ever seen had been afraid of me. Now, suddenly - an impossible situation.

The upshot of it was that Charlie said, "Come show me." He led the way to the storage room.

159

I was hoping, praying, that Buck would repeat his attack but he didn't. The stinker. When I needed him to keep me from being a liar he wouldn't come. Maybe I had indeed hurt him with my kicks and he was off somewhere nursing his hurts. Which didn't help for the moment. Charlie got the parts he wanted, gave me a dirty look and that was that. For that day, at least.

But several days later it happened again. And once more I was the one who was forced to retreat. Until I armed myself with lethal club and decided to kill that sonofabitch if he tried it again. I got a flashlight and approached the scene of battle cautiously. But Buck wouldn't attack when I had that stick. He apparently had some brains. He wanted to catch his enemy by surprise, unaware, unsuspecting and - unarmed.

After the first two or three episodes I complained to Claude about it and demanded that Buck be kept locked up, like his other rabbits were. He refused and said something along the same lines of what Charlie had said. "You're not afraid of a rabbit, are you?"

That challenge to my budding manhood made it a sort of a standoff. I couldn't admit I was afraid.

Buck continued to enjoy his freedom and I continued to go "armed" when I was sent into the storage room. I never stayed any longer than I had to and even the Stoddard-Dayton had lost its attraction for me.

I suppose things would have stayed that way and Charlie, plus Claude, probably never would have believed my story if Buck hadn't decided to attack old man Kendall, Claude's and Charlie's pop, one day. Pop Kendall went into the storage room that day and got the "Buck treatment."

Old man Kendall was in his 70's and when he emerged from that storage room he was roaring with rage. His trousers were torn too, just as mine had been, and his legs were bleeding from scratches.

Now it was Charlie's turn to become angry. He never said anything about believing my story now but he went to Claude and extracted from his brother the promise to keep Buck locked up.

Claude kept his promise during business hours but I believe he had been getting some sort of perverse joy out it all. He kept on letting Buck run free in the evenings and weekends when the shop was closed and Pop Kendall was at home.

The most incredible performance on the part of Buck came, however, on the day when I saw him take on a big German Shepherd dog. The dog belonged to the Marathon dealer down the street, two blocks from the Texaco station. Mr. Marathon was proud of his big dog, Buster. He had taught him all sorts of tricks and he swore the dog would bring him a quart of oil from the shelf when he needed it. Right brand and right weight. Buster could recognize the right can by sight.

But none of this higher education had stopped Buster's instincts for killing and eating rabbits. If anybody had told Buster that he would one day meet a rabbit which would not only refuse to retreat, but which would make a fight out of it, I'm sure his dog brain would have refused to believe. Well, I had suffered my share of wounding surprise, too.

I saw it all. The big German Shepherd had cornered Buck in the alley on the west side of the "rabbit factory" and was moving in for the kill. Buck made no move to escape. He just stood there, facing Buster.

When the big dog lunged in for the finish Buck simply flipped over on his back, quick like the blitz again, with hind quarters aimed at the dog. When the lunging dog's nose arrived within striking distance Buck cut loose with a double barreled whammy. I don't believe I ever saw a dog so surprised. He let out a yelp and backed off a moment. This was something new.

But Buster had guts, too. He wasn't ready to quit. He came back for more. And more.

Buster didn't take more than two or three of those slams to the nose until blood began trickling out of his nostrils. That crazy rabbit wasn't playing for fun. He knew if he lost that battle he would end up inside the dog's stomach. It was a deadly game.

When the big dog began changing tactics, coming from the side or front, he always found that the rabbit could move faster than he could and he was constantly facing its rear end. And those deadly, hammering feet. I remembered full well now how hard a rabbit could kick. Judo, rabbit style.

Several of Buck's kicks landed so solidly they brought howls of pain from the dog and in the end it was the dog, not the rabbit, who retreated. Buster went slinking back to Marathon country.

After a few months of this, Buck became a celebrity in town. Word got out about the dog-rabbit fights and some guys got to where they would purposely hunt up a dog and "sic" him onto the rabbit just to see the fight. Several guys in town lost bets when they bet on the dog, instead of the rabbit.

It was only a matter of time until folks were saying Buck could lick any dog in town. I found myself wondering what would happen if Pedro, my famed rabbit slayer, ran into Buck. I was glad, in a way, that we still lived three miles out in the country and wouldn't have to find out.

In the beginning, when Claude's famous rabbit roamed the streets, folks who knew about the "rabbit factory" but hadn't yet learned about Buck's special status, would spot him running loose and telephone the Texaco station. "Hey Claude," they would say, "One of your rabbits is loose. Better come get him."

Claude had only one reply. "Oh, that's Buck. He can take care of himself."

He could. And he did. Until . . ..

Trying to remember it now, I'm not sure exactly how long Buck's reign of terror in the town lasted. Three months. Six. Maybe more. But a time did come when Buck didn't come home to the rabbit factory.

After a day or two even Claude became concerned and began searching the town for his crazy devil rabbit. He never found him.

It was I who suggested to Claude one day that he shouldn't have allowed Buck to run free that way. He was bound to get killed, sooner or later.

"I'll bet a gang of dogs jumped him," I suggested. "You know he couldn't fight more than one or two dogs at a time."

Claude didn't answer so I tried another tack.

"Maybe Buck jumped some kid and the kid's Dad got mad," I suggested. "The Dad probably got his shotgun and shot Buck."

"Maybe so," said Claude. He wrinkled his nose a bit and I could see he was thinking.

After a moment he said, "Maybe Buck's wild instincts took over and he went back to the country."

Oh, I had hated that rabbit with a passion. There had been several occasions when I would have cheerfully killed him. But then you couldn't keep those other thoughts from crowding in, too. You had to admire the crazy animal. Especially the way he would fight a dog. The rabbit with guts.

I sort of preferred Claude's latter suggestion. The picture of Buck, the crazy mixed up half breed, roaming the Oklahoma prairie.

The Rabbit King.

Chapter Twelve - Plague

Uncle Joe Stalin would have chortled with glee, through that huge walrus mustache of his, if he had known about the fearful secret weapon that had been "smuggled" from Russia into the heartlands of America.

The only thing wrong with that picture is the fact that the "smuggling" took place long before Uncle Joe cranked up his Cold War against America. Even before the great hot war.

Even before the Russian Revolution of 1917, when nobody in Russia was mad at us.

But the poor dirt farmers of Mid-America still had to suffer for it in Uncle Joe's time. Since most country folks didn't know the true story, it gave them another excuse to hate the Russians.

For want of a better name for the beastly things, people just called them Russian Thistles. They could threaten your crops, rip down your fences and give your cows the GI's.

Sometimes, looking back on it, it seems that we were forever yanking the things out of the ground, piling them up and setting fire to them. Dad was constantly on our butts to help him get rid of the things. But it was impossible. We had no herbicides in that time and the damn things would grow faster than you could destroy them. At times, it seemed they grew so fast they just popped out of the ground. Whoosh.

And if the soil was really fertile they would grow to monstrous sizes. Out in the wheat fields they might be only about 30 to 40 inches in diameter, round like a ball.

When they got started near a manure pile, I've seen them grow so big a single thistle could fill your whole living room.

Seems that it was the Mennonites - honest, God fearing and peaceful as they were - who had to take the blame for bringing them to America. Oh, they didn't do it on purpose. In fact, most of them knew about the pesky things and tried to prevent it but somehow they got here.

Maybe that is why the Mennonites I grew up with didn't like to talk much about it. Might have had a bit of a guilt complex, despite the innocence of their intentions. But I was finally able to get the story out of Mom and Dad.

Folks who know the story of the Mennonites know that they were a Pilgrim folk, kicked around from one country to another in Europe, and persecuted because they believed in peace and refused to carry guns and serve in the military forces.

They had spent a couple of generations in western Russia before they got kicked out of that country and ended up in the "Great Land of Liberty." In my folks' case, that was Kansas and Oklahoma.

One of the things these resourcefull Mennonites had learned about, while they sojourned in Russia, was winter wheat, that you plant in the fall. It would sprout and live through the bitterest of winters, then give a bountiful harvest of the bread stuff the next spring or early summer.

When they made that last migration - to America - they all "smuggled" with them a few pounds of that winter wheat seed. They figured it would stand them in good stead in the promised land. It did. Except for those damnable thistles.

For, it seems, the Russian Steppes had been plagued by these thistles long before this and thistle seeds got mixed in with the wheat.

I believe it was Mom who told me the story, passed down from her Mom and Dad. About the time when the Mennonites were on the ship, en route from Russia to New York, and the folks would pour out their precious hoarde of winter wheat seeds on the tables, or perhaps even on the deck, and they would slowly, grain by grain, pick through it to make sure none of those Russian thistle seeds sneaked through. If they found some, I suppose, they dropped them into the vast, devouring sea.

But apparently some of the Mennonite immigrants were not so careful. Somehow, some of these dreaded seeds got through. They got planted into the soil of America along with the winter wheat seeds.

164

That winter wheat, incidentally, turned out to be one of the greatest blessings of all times for those pioneer farms on the plains of Oklahoma, Kansas, Nebraska and elsewhere. The thistles? A blessing they were not.

Funny, how those thistles and the wheat seemed to work together in a strange cycle of nature. You planted the wheat in the fall - September or October. If the earth was moist the wheat would quickly sprout, spreading a blessed blanket of green across the fields all winter long. It didn't grow much in the coldest weather but it didn't die, either. No sooner would the breath of spring begin a gentle warming of mother earth than the wheat would spring to life like magic.

In fact, if the weather was right and a farmer didn't overdo it, he could even graze his cows on the wheat in the spring without harming the coming harvest in June or July. As a kid I always marveled at what that green wheat did to the milk and butter in the spring, before the grass would green in the pasturelands.

In the winter months, as the cows would be forced to eat the dry hay stored in the winter, their milk would be white as snow and the butter a pale yellow. Then, the moment the cows got their first grabs on the burgeoning green wheat sprouts, the milk streaming into the buckets in the evening would turn a creamy yellow. The butter Mom made in those early spring months would begin to darken until it was more orange than yellow.

Well, we're talking about real butter. Not the corn oil stuff which never changes color.

Anyway, those plaguey thistles. When the wheat began to grow in those warming days of spring it would somehow choke the thistles down. You'd look out over the waving wands of wheat - filling your fields by the millions - and not a single thistle would you see.

But then in June or July would come the reapers, cutting the golden stalks of grain and leaving only a stubble, perhaps six inches high. No leaves or foliage now to block the rays of the hot sun from hitting the ground. And those waiting thistles.

That was when they popped out of the ground. To a youngster who knew he now would have to gird for battle with the plague to come, it was a literal explosion. One week, it seemed, you had the nice clean field of stubble after the wheat harvest. The next week, thistles would be popping out of the stubble. By the hundreds. Nay, thousands. To me it seemed in the millions.

165

Oh, they grew other places, too. Even in the pastures. In the corn fields. Any spot where they could stab roots into the earth. But most of all in the wheat fields. It even seemed that nature decreed that in the wheat-thistle cycle, the two strangely different plants were made for each other.

It really wouldn't have been so bad up to this point. It was what happened in the fall that caused the pain. For the thistle was a short cycle plant. They grew to maturity in a matter of weeks and then they died. From a brilliant green they would, at the first breath of chill in the fall, turn into a dead, mousy brown.

Then came those howling winds of the fall which would, in time, rip the dead thistles out of the ground and send them rolling and tumbling along. The Russian brand of tumble weeds.

You didn't have to be Mr. Smart to know that as the thistles went tumbling along they were performing the sex act nature had built into their pesky makeup. Scattering seeds for a new harvest of plague the next summer. Over and over, year after year.

And if that wasn't enough, there was that fearsome fence busting these nasty things did.

They'd go on that merry roll, bouncing along with the gusty winds until they hit an obstruction. Mostly fences. One thistle couldn't do much damage but when several hundred of the monster things, or maybe a few thousand, piled up against a fence and a mighty gust of wind hit it, blooey, there went your fence posts, barbed wire, all of it.

To a farmer in those plains countries, the fences were as precious as gold. Since everybody also raised a certain number of livestock, cows for milk, calves for meat, horses for the plow, it was an absolute must to keep crops and animals separated.

But, blam. Combine thistle and big wind - fences gone.

The secret of success in the endless battle against the thistles, if there was any, was to destroy the beastly things at just the right moment. You had to wait until they were dead and dry. Otherwise, they wouldn't burn.

But you couldn't wait until the wind ripped them loose from their precarious grip on the ground. So well I remember Dad, watching and testing for the right moment. Just right for burning but not quite ready for uprooting by the wind. Then, on D-Day, or Thistle Day, all hands were ordered into the fields for the attack.

You advanced against the enemy, armed with pitch forks. You had to learn how to scoot your fork under the thistle, with the tines straddling the root. Then you pried until the big ball came free. Rake them into piles and set them afire.

I was always amazed at how fast a pile of those thistles would burn. Almost like an explosion. One minute you had a pile of them stacked up, maybe 10 or 15 feet high. Next minute it was gone.

You couldn't just toss a match in the pile. The space between the thistle twigs was too gappy. The match would go out. The trick was to use your foot, press a mass of thistle into a tighter wad and then do your light up. Sometimes Dad, who handled the matches, would grab a handful of dry wheat stubble to get the pile started.

But once you got the pile started you could even hear that whoosh. Almost like a pool of gasoline going off.

Only one problem - don't launch your attack on a windy day. Otherwise, just about the time you got a bunch of them piled up, here came a gust of wind and took the whole damn pile tumbling away. Seeds spreading like one of the plagues of Egypt.

Somebody, by this time, might be suggesting that we could have saved ourselves a lot of work by waiting until the thistles all got stacked up against the fences and then burn them. Not a bad idea until you remember that, by this time, they had already scattered their seeds. And then, fence posts burn, too.

In any case, if all this wasn't plague enough, there was that nasty trick these thistles could pull on your cows. Normally, a cow wouldn't honor a Russian thistle by taking a bite. Scratchy and bitter.

Then came those drouth years in America's southwest when the crops didn't "make."

Even the grass in the pastures would dry up and die. I knew some folks who ran so short of feed, their cows got so hungry they'd begin nibbling on the Russian thistles. Ah, what ignomy for a cow. First , the disgrace of being forced to eat such uneatable food. Then disgrace number two which quickly followed.

How do we describe it? Those Russian thistles didn't really have barbs. Not like a briar patch which can rip your pants. The barbs on the thistles were tiny, perhaps not more than an eighth of an inch long. Or less. Sharp but not nearly as hard as a briar or blackberry barb.

If you plunged your bare hand into the middle of a Russian thistle it might scratch a bit. Irritate the skin. Sort of like an itch. But not severe enough, usually, to draw blood.

But if a cow got real hungry and overcame her reluctance to sample one of those thistles, imagine what the little barbs did to her insides. Old mama cow paid for her mistake with diarrhea. The stuff would come out in evil, smelly squirts of green liquid. Almost like water. The cows would lose weight. Stop giving milk. It was a "must" to keep them away from the thistles.

Oh, I suppose if I tried hard enough I could say something good about those Russian thistles. I do remember a few occasions when we'd see a big one scooting down an open road on a windy day, like when we walked home from school, and someone dreamed up the idea of tying a big thistle on the front end of a kid's scooter wagon. Make a sail out of it.

I remember we were too poor to own a scooter wagon but Uncle P. E. Friesen's kids, who lived down the road, had one. We got together and tried it. It would have worked pretty good if you could have, somehow, put guide reins on one of those huge thistles, like a horse, to keep it from dragging you into the ditch. Well, it worked a few times, anyway. And created a small measure of fun.

The only other thing I can remember they were any good for, was hiding jack rabbits. The long legged jacks were fond of creeping under a thistle to hide.

If you were old enough to own a shotgun and could sneak away from Dad long enough to go rabbit hunting, it was fun going around kicking Russian thistles for rabbits.

Of course, there wasn't a rabbit under every thistle but after you had kicked 30 or 40 thistles you were bound to find a rabbit. He'd come exploding out from under the thistles and take off like a streak.

If you were fast enough and could shoot straight enough, you could knock him down before he ducked behind some more thistles. I know because I bowled over many a jack rabbit with this kind of hunting after I grew older and was allowed to own a gun. On a day like that, you were sort of glad the thistles were around.

There was another way to do it, in the fall after the thistles had died. Almost any ravine or gully would get filled up with the rolling thistles in the fall. The wind drove them along until they dropped in. Then you could get a few of your buddies together, with shotguns, surround one of those gullies and set the thistles afire.

When the thing went whoosh and the rabbits came bursting out, you popped them. We thought it was fun.

168

But sometimes I didn't enjoy that trick so much. Sometimes when you had burned out one of those ravines and the fire went out, you found a dead rabbit or two in the ashes. They hadn't been fast enough getting out when the fire started.

I don't suppose it makes much difference whether the rabbit died from a fire or a shotgun blast but, somehow, when you found a half fried rabbit, it wasn't quite so much fun any more.

Anyway, when a man gets through talking about the Russian thistles, it's easy to think of a lot of things to say "damn" about and darned few you can say blessings over.

Wish they had kept the doggone things in Russia.

Chapter Thirteen - Ants

"Hey Amarillo, if you're out there somewhere, I believe you now. You hear me?"

I didn't believe him then. It was all too crazy.

It started when Amarillo jumped on top of Joe Ragalsky and started whacking the tar out of him. That's the way it looked. With that nutty story about the bracelet of ants.

It was a hot, dry, thresher sort of day but Grandpa Friesen's big threshing rig wasn't threshing. A shaker boxing had burned out. Uncle Dave and Uncle Jake were out there on the machine, working to fix it. As for the thresher crew, it was a time to goof off.

Lying in the shade of the machine - shooting the bull. A few of the guys dozed off. I was sitting there, 10 years old and listening to all that man talk. Stories about the strange things men did with women. About bottles of white lightning. Fist fight tales.

I was the "scoop man" on the grain wagons. Just a farm kid but when the machine was running it was my job to handle that man sized grain scoop - shovelling the grain to the front of the wagon. The spout dumped it in the rear. If you didn't work fast enough the wagon boxes would spill over, dropping all that precious bread stuff on the ground. And you'd catch the wrath of God from Dad.

When the sun got hot - it was always hot in the summer time in Oklahoma - muscles would ache and the sweat would pour. I committed the sin of praying for that darned threshing machine to break down so we could rest. Most of the time it didn't. Uncle Dave and Uncle Jake were pretty good at keeping it going but, well, once in a while it happened. How blessed those breakdown breaks when you could sit in the shade.

I'll swear I didn't pray for it to break down that day. But since it did, I was happy.

My ears, big as jugs, soaking up all the man talk.

Then, right in the middle of all that peaceful goofing off, one of the new hands, a guy from Amarillo, Texas, jumped up screaming - like a plains Commanche. He jumped right on top of Joe Ragalsky who was dozing lazily.

Amarillo started slapping like crazy at Joe's right leg. He jerked at Joe's pant leg up and started yelling.

"Get 'em off of you. Quick. They'll kill you."

As it turned out, those "things" were ants. The big red ants, about a half inch long, that infested the Oklahoma and Texas prairie country by the millions and billions, I guess.

Joe didn't even know what was going on but he jumped up out of his sleep to defend himself if this Amarillo nut wanted to fight.

"Hey, you crazy or something?" Joe hollered at Amarillo.

"No. These ants - they killed a man down at Amarillo."

That's a bunch of horse," somebody said.

Several others jumped into the argument. Most were home folks. All knew each other. Amarillo was an outsider, a stranger who had drifted through and asked for a job. He had to be outnumbered.

I could have added my three cents worth, too.

I grew up out there in that country and those ants were everywhere. I had suffered my share of bites. There was a big den of those ants right behind our granary and I had been zapped several times.

Sure it hurt. Made a red spot. But kill a man? That, in my mind, was a lot of horse manure. Wasn't even as bad as a bee sting.

But Amarillo didn't give up that easy. He had to defend himself now and there was a bit more to his story.

"You see, it wasn't one red ant that killed him," he said. "It was a whole ring of them around his leg. The guy went to sleep, just like Joe did, close to an ant den. While he was sleeping, the ants crawled up on his leg and formed a circle around his ankle. Like a bracelet.

"They didn't bite the guy until he woke up and started moving around - then they all cut loose on him at the same time. There was 40 or 50 of them. Maybe more. It was all that poison from them ants at the same time that killed him. I'll swear it. Even the doctor said so."

After Amarillo told it, a big argument got started among the guys. Most thought it was a lot of horse. A few said, maybe. If a whole gang of ants bit you all at once, it might make a guy sick. But dead? As I said, Amarillo was outnumbered.

But my kid brain kept asking how the ants got that much sense to climb up on a guy, form a nice round bracelet around a man's leg and then go bang, all together? Did they have a boss ant who said, " Now, fellows. All together. Wham."

It sounded sort of impossible to me but with all of my 10 years of wisdom I wasn't taking sides. It's not always too smart to butt in on grown folks. I had grown up in red ant country and all of us had been bitten once or twice. But I never heard that "bracelet" story and I had never heard of anybody getting killed.

One of our "Church Uncles" got bit by a rattlesnake and almost died. Not quite. He got over it. But a rattlesnake was something else.

Oh, those big "reds" were pesky enough. One of the worst things they did was kill off vegetation. They'd build a den and destroy every trace of grass, weeds, wheat, cotton, corn or anything growing within reach. There would be a bare circle maybe 15 or 20 feet across at each den.

If you had flown over one of those wheat fields in a helicopter - they didn't have helicopters then - you would have seen one of those bare circles every 50 yards or so.

In the winter time the ants just disappeared. Hibernated. But every spring, here they were again, with those hungry jaws chomping away at anything that grew. The farmers hated those pesky red creatures and sometimes tried to get rid of them. One of the favorite tricks was to pile up a big bunch of straw on top of one of those dens and set it afire. When the fire started getting warm the ants would just crawl down in their cool tunnels and wait for the ashes to cool. Then they just came out and went about their ant business as usual.

Another favorite trick in battling those ants was to bury a quart fruit jar, right up to its neck, near one of those dens and then pour a cupful of kerosene in the jar. The theory was that the ants would slip over the edge of the jar, fall into the kerosene and drown.

It worked, too, up to a point. I tried it on a big den near the watering trough and filled several jars full of ants and thought sure I was going to lick them. I didn't   They just kept on breeding and coming back. After a while, they even got smart enough to stay away from that hole in the ground. Maybe they got smarted up to the smell of the kerosene.

There was that time when we were living in town and had an ant den right behind the house. It was Mom who decided to do battle with that tribe, since they were in her domain. She started a campaign of burning her household trash right on top of the den, every time she had a pile of trash. Since we didn't have garbage pickups in those days, she had enough to burn maybe twice a week. She burned and she burned. Her campaign went on for months, a whole summer. But when it was all over, the ants were still there.

Then I fought my big battle with a den in the front yard. I was angry at the ants because it was the first house we ever lived in with a lawn in the front yard. And right in the middle of it was a big dead circle. I used a spade on that tribe. If I could dig down to the end of all their tunnels, kill every ant in sight, plus their eggs, I could lick them.

I dug on that den for weeks. Made such a big hole Mom and Dad complained somebody was going to fall in it and get hurt. I stayed with it until I was certain I had them all wiped out.

During the course of that battle I became the victim of several doses of "ants revenge." Ant bites. After that I began dunking my shoes in kerosene so they'd stay off. When I was certain every ant and her eggs were destroyed I filled the hole and waited. A week. Two weeks. I was certain I had won.

After about three weeks I went out one morning. There was a new ant tunnel entrance. Not more than a few inches from where the old one had been. My God, did they have compasses in their heads, too?

If you weren't angry it could almost be fun watching those ants at work. The way they would travel back and forth lugging grains of wheat, weed seeds, pieces of grasshopper, a leg maybe, when they killed one. If a cow or a horse happened to dump a load of their smelly stuff near an ant den, the ants were in ant heaven cleaning it up.

In any case, to get back to my bracelet story. I know we moved several times but we never got very far away from those pesky red ants.

I asked several old timers about that bracelet story but never found anybody who had ever heard of it. So, as the years went by, I forgot all about it. At least, if I remembered, it was way back in some corner of my mind that I didn't use much. Until it happened to me.

It was in the Roger Mills County chapter of our family odyssey. I suppose the ant bracelet story was at least seven or eight years in the past. But there was one of those red ant dens out on the shoulder of the country road that ran past our house

It was after dark one night when I heard Ray Leyerly, our neighbor, hollering for me. He had ridden up on that old mustang pony of his and was hollering at me from the road.

I walked out, stood on the shoulder of the road near his horse, jawing with him for 10 or 15 minutes. He was on his way to the Berryhills, about a mile down the road. He wanted me and Ernie to go along. Since three guys were too much of a load for the mustang he suggested we walk and he'd ride slow. We finally decided to go.

I took that first step, moving from the spot where I had been standing and there was that "zap" on my right ankle, a sharp, stinging pain. The first vision to pop into my mind was that of a rattlesnake but then, almost immediately, came the remembrance of that red ant den. I had been standing right on top of it in the darkness while we talked.

I yelped with anger and pain. Anger at my stupidity. "Those damned ants got me," I said to Ray.

I bent over and began slapping at the ankle to get rid of them. Ray, a Bull Durham man, lit a match and cupped the flickering flame in his hands as we took a look. There were 10 or 12 of the angry little creatures. All of them, it seemed, had bitten me around the ankle at the same time. As I took that first step.

And now, under the impetus of the pain, the memory of Amarillo's ant bracelet story came rushing back into my mind. But despite the pain, my brain continued to reject the story's validity. I refused to consider it a death threatening factor.

Oh, the pain was valid enough. Much worse than any ant bites had been before. But nothing I could not bear for the moment. So, after recovering from the first impact of the thing, we remembered our goal, the Berryhills. And we decided to go ahead.

After we began walking down the road, perhaps a hundred yards or so, the pain began increasing past the annoyance stage. Beyond that, it was now creeping up my leg toward my groin.

As it reached groin, it became so intense the sweat was pouring off my face and something very near paralysis was gripping my leg. I lay down on the ditch bank beside the road. At the moment, I was beyond caring whether I was lying next to another ant den or not.

The pain, if not the worst pain I had ever suffered in my lifetime, was very near it. I was groaning, rubbing my leg, perspiring. And now, frightened as well for Amarillo's ant bracelet story was becoming more real by the moment.

I began thinking about a doctor but it was a wasted thought. Strong City had no doctor and the nearest one would be at Cheyenne, more than 20 miles away. What would he do? I had heard of snake bite serum but who ever heard of such a measure against ant bites? The doc probably would laugh at the suggestion. Didn't all country folks suffer these ant bites and survive? Single bites, that it.

I may have lain there on that roadside bank 20 or 30 minutes when my senses began telling me that the pain was slowly subsiding. I was finally able to get back on my feet and walk. Hurting but up. By this time, all thought of going to the Berryhills was gone. I only wanted to go home.

It was after reaching the house and looking at the ankle in lamp light that the whole thing became so vividly clear. The red spots from the ant bites were in a perfect circle around the ankle.

The blessed truth was, however, that there had been only those 10 or 12 bites, with several big gaps in the circle. The fright of the whole thing, reinforced by the memory, so strong now, brought up the question. What if I had stood on that ant den long enough for Amarillo's "40 or 50 ants" to find my leg, crawl up and get themselves in place?

One thing was certain, it had been when I took my first step that the ants had all bitten, as if on a signal. Perhaps my motion itself was the signal. All of it just as Amarillo had told us on that day my Grandpa's thresher rig broke down. And he had to take his lumps for warning us. Yes, it is true, as I lay there on that roadside bank that night, the though of death became a living presence.

I was sorry that my reaction to Amarillo's story had been a sneer - even if not openly expressed - the super smart opinion of a boy of 10.

If only I could find Amarillo now I would at least apologize.

Chapter Fourteen – The Black "Thing"

A black hole burned in my memory.

From that spring day in 1934 when that fearsome, monstrous black "thing" came towards me out of the northern sky.

The wildest furies of the elements could have been no strangers to a boy of 17 who grew up on the western plains of Oklahoma, for I had known them all.

Hail storms which crushed the tender, growing shoots of wheat in the fields and smashed the roofs of our barns. Powerful bolts of lightning which exploded huge chunks of concrete from foundations of our houses while I huddled with fear in my mother's bedroom. Awesome thunder, shaking the earth with its fearsome but majestic explosions.

Killer tornadoes, one of which tore away half a barn while the horses whinnied in terror inside. A howling wind which started somewhere up in Canada, or the Dakotas, swept down through the corridors of Nebraska and Kansas, into Oklahoma with such unrelenting fury it could nearly sweep a youngster off his feet as he bowed into its teeth. Winds so unrelenting they would howl for days, until the mind grew numb from the incessancy.

The equally howling and frigid blizzards which sometimes piled drifts 20 feet high, or more, blocking the road to the plunging efforts of our strongest horses. Rain, often so lacking it sent devout farmers to their prayer chambers to beseech the heavens for it - yet it could, on occasion, come pouring down in such torrents as to sweep man and beast away into the darkened nights.

All this and yet - there had been nothing to prepare me for that eerie black "thing" in the northern sky that April day. So ominous. So utterly black. Something to awaken real tremors of fear in a questioning mind.

Some startled soul, rendered momentarily irreverant by the fearsomeness of that mysterious darkness, had said, "God, it's black as hell."

But to a youth like me, reared in the ever devout aura of Mennonite creeds, in the veritable shadow of hell, it was not a moment for blasphemy. Maybe this was indeed the end of the world that preachers had so often threatened. No time to talk of hell. In a moment, I might in it.

Still so strange, remembering it all today. A day so beautiful. The warming breath of springtime. The grass, the flowers, coming into life on the hillsides. The brilliant and cheery sun which hung in a blue sky, not cluttered by the whisps of cirrus clouds.

The fact that I was riding in a car when the "thing" appeared on the northern horizon had little relevance to what was happening. With a group of my fellow high school seniors, about to be graduated, we were returning home from Elk City where we had gone on that carefree Sunday afternoon, to have our class picture made. Home was Strong City, a Roger Mills County town so small it didn't even have a commercial photographer.

First, east a few miles on Highway 66, then north on State 34. We had been going north some eight or 10 miles when the black thing suddenly imposed itself upon our consciousness. Almost immediately the chattering voices which had been exploding with the exuberance of youth, suddenly became smothered in a choked hush.

After a moment, someone blurted, "My God, what is that?"

Indeed, what was it?

It is certain that no one in the car had ever seen anything like it. Nothing even remotely like this strange, ominous black presence. Even today, so clear in my memory, the blurred black hole of fear.

What really made the thing so fearsome was that even after the sighting, the air around us remained very clear. Sunlit. Visability unlimited - in any direction but north. This was no sudden spring thunderstorm out of the northern sky. It was simply so different.

How to describe it? Perhaps the only way would be to suggest that it was if the gods of the universe had somehow fashioned a huge, impenetrable black curtain in the form of a giant arc that perfectly fit the curve of the horizon. The upper reaches of the black arc reaching to the limits of man's eyesight. The lower edge of the curtain touched the floor of the earth before us. It as if these gods had chosen that bright, sunlit and cloudless day in which to suddenly lower a curtain across the sky.

Never before, nor since, have I seen the closing of a horizon, the sky and the hills, the road and the pasturelands, with such utter black finality. Could a boy of 17 be forgiven for a sudden, unknowing fear? With visions of death, the final ending, standing suddenly in the black unknown?

I can only guess what strange thoughts were going through the minds of the others in the car. Or the farmers and cattlemen living in that nearly barren countryside who might have been standing outdoors and looking toward the northern sky.

I would guess that at the moment of sighting, our car was moving about 45 or 50 miles an hour. But we were moving towards that black unknown "thing" and after a few moments the car began slowing down. Joe Sanders, our teacher, had slowed down almost unconsciously. A subconscious desire not to go forward to meet the dark. The car simply moved slower and slower.

And yet we continued to move northward into the face of that black unknown. And it seemed to be moving to meet us. Whatever threat, unknown and mysterious, that the black carried with it, would soon be upon us. Would we know then? Or would we simply be swallowed up into some sort of never, never void in which the consciousness would cease to exist?

When we had first spotted the "thing," it appeared to be at least two miles away. How could one say for certain how far it was when you didn't know what it was? Yet, even at that distance it had been so huge and imposing that it was impossible not to be aware of it.

Now, in a moment, it would meet our beings and then it must either reveal its nature or shut us off forever from the past, that which had been life.

Looking back on it from the perspective of today, I must realize that my dramatization may seem forced. At that moment, nothing could be forced. Nor could any description of our feelings be too wildly expressed.

I suppose by the time we met the "thing" Sanders had slowed the car to perhaps 10 miles an hour. Or even slower. We were barely moving. It would have taken the most reckless courage to have simply gone plunging into that mysterious blackness at 50 miles an hour. How could anyone know what the visibility would be? What solid force we might hit?

And then, the inevitable moment of fearsome truth. Sudden and complete. We met the black thing. We were engulfed by it. No crash. Not even the slightest sound. Only the sudden, clutching and engulfing hand of blackness.

In a matter of a second, certainly no longer than two or three, the unlimited visibility which had been granted by the brilliant sun was gone. So utterly gone. It was 3 o'clock in what had been a bright afternoon . In that sudden enveloping darkness I could not even see the radiator ornament on the hood of the car, no more than four feet in front of me.

By this time, the car had simply coasted to a stop. Teacher Sanders had even shut off the engine. We sat there in almost complete and silent darkness. Each brain struggling to comprehend. In those first ominous moments there was no sound. No wind. Only engulfing dark.

But inevitably we all had to comprehend. A choking dust began to seep through the cracks of the rolled up windows, the car body. And a few moments later the first sounds of the wind, not violent at first, only gentle enough to penetrate the consciousness.

I'm not sure how long we sat there before someone spoke. Minutes, perhaps, as our minds began telling us what the reality of that blackness contained. We suddenly knew that the "black hole" was nothing less than the worst dust storm that had ever struck the Dust Bowl of western Oklahoma. Or since. I can know because I lived in that country during those searing, dusty years.

There had been giant dust storms before. I knew what they were. But none had approached in such a manner - without sound and from a clear sky.

Not even accompanied by the whipping gales which appeared in advance of all such storms. And clouds of dust, identifiable as such, appearing in whipping gusts. Always before the build up had been gradual. The wind came. Then whisps of dust. It built into a howl with the dust growing thicker as time passed. Visibility slowly going away. But never the sudden blackness. Never before the silent darkness. Even so we would have understood and accepted, if only it had approached as they usually did.

A meterologist would have to explain how it was possible for this particular storm to begin so strangely, with such utter blackness. And in silent stillness. Without, at first, the winds. The only explanation I could venture would be that somewhere up north, miles away, this storm had begun. It had probably been picking up strength for many miles. And somehow, through some mysterious forces of nature, floating ahead of the storm, a gigantic balloon of vacuum. Floating in silence, and blackness, before the body of the storm. A balloon of dust.

It had become the custom of country folks living in the Dust Bowl area to measure the intensity of each dust storm by the amount of visbility. Or lack of it. In the manner of such folks, to exaggerate, they would say, "Visibility was down to 100 feet". Or 50 feet. Or 30 feet. With the need to top any previous story it was inevitable that someone would eventually bring it down to 10 feet. Or even such reckless assertion as, "You couldn't see your hand in front your face." The obvious expression of the excessive will to impress the listener.

But now we had seen it. And belief was imposed upon us.

After we had sat there, soaking in the reality, for perhaps 10 minutes, visibility began to improve. Just a bit. With the headlights turned on we could see perhaps 10 feet in front of the car.

"What shall we do?" The question came from Teacher Sanders.

Then, when nobody answered for a few seconds, "Shall we turn around and go back to Elk city? Or shall we try to make it home?"

Eventually we all voted to try to make it home. Out here on the road we felt somehow alone, assaulted by the elements of nature. Home, after all, even a home enveloped in dust, was better than this suddenly hostile environment of the open road so many miles away.

After all, we had grown up in this cruel country. We had lived through the worst of the plagues, the worst curses that the gods of weather had inflicted upon the land. Now we must learn to endure one more. And if it were not to be endured, then we must perish. But not on a country highway, huddled in a car that would still run. Even in this black stuff.

For a long time Teacher Sanders was forced to keep his speed down to 10 miles per hour. Or less. Otherwise it would have been a mad plunge into an unknown. We could barely see the drainage ditches beside the road although the clocks would tell us it was still afternoon, not night.

Normally we would have been home by 4 p.m., less than an hour after that blackness had struck. As it was we did not approach

Strong City until long after true night had fallen. Perhaps 8 or 9 o'clock. So slow we had been forced to drive. Sanders had to exercise extreme caution because when we did meet occasional cars you did not see the headlights until they were almost upon us. And so often a driver would be straddling the center of the road, for safety.

In time, along those remaining miles, the wind did grow in strength, and intensity, until it was indeed a gale. The dust was whipping now, in whirling clouds as in a normal dust storm. Tumble weeds, those damnable Russian thistles, were also tumbling about in the darkness like strange, fleeing ghosts, also trying to escape this maddening blackness. Some of them would come crashing, harmlessly, into the front of our car as we met them.

Our house lay perhaps a half mile off the highway and normally Teacher Sanders would have simply swung off and delivered me to our door. The others, my classmates, all lived in the town, two miles away.

"Do you think you can make it by foot from here?" asked Sanders as he stopped at our cross road.

Then he added, at the questioning look in my eyes, "It is so late and I need to get these other kids home. I know their parents are worried."

So I got out and headed my way through the storm. The temperature had also been dropping and I had been dressed for a warm, spring day. I clutched my thin jacket around me and struggled that half mile home. Several times, in the double darkness, I stumbled into the ditches beside the road. It was only at the last moment, when only a few feet away, that I finally was able to make out the dim light of the kerosene lamp through the window.

When I stumbled up to the door I was met by both Mom and Dad. They had indeed been worried. I was four or five hours behind schedule. But they didn't say much. They knew. There was a visable relief in their eyes at the sight of their eldest son. Beyond that, what could one say about the terrible curse of nature that had caused it. They couldn't blame me and they were not willing to blame God.

My brother, Ernie, and I slept in a tiny lean-to room which Dad and I had built onto the side of the little two room house we had been forced to move into. It wasn't the best of rooms. No insulation. Not even an inner wall. Only the pine outside siding, with its inevitable cracks.

It hadn't been that Dad or I had been lousy carpenters. There simply hadn't been any money to buy materials to finish it. If you could see a crack you stuffed a rag into it. If you couldn't see it, the dust and the wind would find it.

Even the tightest of houses, in that time, were invaded by the microscopic particles of dust. So tiny that when the winds stopped the dust might hang in the air for days before settling gently to earth. Unless, on the most merciful of occasions, you got a rain which would wash the air clean. In the first minutes of the rain, raindrops were stained with dust.

Without a rain you suffered. Choking, sneezing, sometimes wrapping a handkerchief around your face, your nose. The horses, the cows, they simply had to take it.

On that night, after I made it home and Mom had warmed something to eat, I crawled, shivering, into bed. You didn't have to sniff the air to detect the presence of the dust coming through the walls. The only protection available was to pull the covers up over your face. What else could one do?

And when the morrow did come, and Mother called for breakfast, we peeped out and became aware that our bed covers had become the color of the dust. Perhaps an eighth of an inch thick, at least. When we threw the covers back it filled the air with a cloud of dust.

One became aware of a crust of dust that had built up around the rims of the nostrils. God knows what was in our lungs. You could peel the nose crust off with your fingernails.

With Mom's help we took the quilts off the bed, took them outside and shook of the offending plague.

When we ate breakfast, even the food was gritty with the cursed evil. But we were alive and for that Dad would give thanks. But also pray for relief. For living, in those dust enveloped days, was not for happiness.

Even in the main part of the house, much better built and with proper inner walls, Mom had to fight the dust. She must have filled a pail with the sweepings of her broom. But the stuff was so fine it even defied the broom and remained with us almost constantly. There were still traces of it between storms, when the air was clear.

So, for the next few years we simply had to learn to live with that dirty, mousey brown stuff. Giving silent thanks for the days which were clear. Praying for rain when the air shut out your sight.

In that time we would wonder how long a wrathful God, or the evil forces of nature, would continue to invent new plagues to hurl against the feeble struggles of man to survive. Who could know? Each new storm brought the question anew. What evil sins had man committed to deserve the fates of Job?

For at least several more years, the dust storm plague continued in the heartland of America - Oklahoma, Kansas, Texas, Nebraska and other states.

In time, as men took measures to halt the erosion of the soil, and in years blessed with a bit more rain, the dust storms faded. Mostly into memory. True, a few times in later years of drouth they would occasionally return but never with the quick succession or that dark intensity of the storms of the 1930's.

For never again would I see another dust storm that could compare to that utter blackness which descended upon us on that spring day in 1934.

In my memory, the black hole.

Chapter Fifteen – Yellow Eyes

Old Yellow Eyes shouldn't have thumbed his nose at me the way he did.

It made my boiler steam. I swore I'd catch him if it took forever. And there's a pretty big Dutch stubborn streak in me.

The itch to catch him had been there for a long time. Ever since I was a kid. A luring challenge because coyotes were supposed to be smart. It took a lot of doing, everyone said, to outsmart one of those critters.

All those books in the school library were partly to blame. Tales of Teddy Roosevelt out west. The Indian yarns. The buffalo herds. The trapper stories. And then those wild west pulp magazines I borrowed from Cousin Ike and sneaked into the house. Dad whopped me when he caught me reading those things but I read them anyway.

The fur buyer companies were also partly to blame. They kept sending me those trapper guide books, for free, with price lists telling how much they paid for furs. The more furs you sent them, the more money they made, which explains the free trapper guide books. Those price lists, dangling all that green stuff in front of the eyes of a scratch poor farm kid who might get a nickel from Dad on Saturday for a candy bar.

Made a farm kid do crazy things. Like trapping skunks.

But the wily coyote, now he was in a special class all by himself. Those trapper guides made that pretty clear. How smart you had to be, how super smart to catch one. The instructions ran for pages, all about how to hide the human odor, how to hide your trap so a coyote couldn't see it or smell it. Until he got caught.

Even the prices they offered for a coyote skin gave you the wild itches. Three or four times as much as for a skunk fur. Maybe even up to 12 or 15 dollars. Like a grab at Ft. Knox.

I knew we had coyotes around, out there on Oklahoma's western prairie, even if I seldom saw one. You just knew they were there. At night they'd be sitting out there on those gyp hills and they'd be howling.

The moon would come out, full circle, on a clear night and you could bet it would set the coyotes to howling. Sometimes they sounded so close. Made a kid shiver, even in the summer time.

My dog, Pedro, would hear it, too. He'd start getting restless. He'd pace back and forth, looking out into the night. After a while, he'd howl back. Crazy, the way those howls would affect a dog.

I sometimes wondered if Pedro ever met up with a coyote. If he ever had a fight with one. Pedro would sometimes disappear at night and not show up until morning. But he never looked as if he had been in a fight so I guess he never tangled with one of those wild, half dog creatures.

I tried, a few times, to follow the instructions in the trapper books and set traps for the coyotes but never had any luck. In the first place, my traps were not big enough. To hold a coyote you needed those big No. 3 double spring traps. I couldn't afford to buy any. All I had was a few of the small, single spring traps. Only big enough for a skunk or a possum.

It really didn't matter because no coyote ever walked into one of my traps. But I'd tell myself, some day, some time, when I grew up a bit, I'd get me some of those big traps and I'd get me a coyote.

But then everything began to go around in a circle. That horrible depression hit. Dad couldn't make a living in town, not even by hiring out with the tractor to do plowing. Or hauling, with the horses. Eventually, Dad even had to sell the tractor to pay bills. When we couldn't even pay the rent, Dad started looking for a farm again.

We ended up way out on the prairie, farther than ever. Roger Mills County, where most of the land was open range grazing country with only a few dirt farmers sandwiched in between, like intruders.

Through church connections Dad was able to rent a scraggly farm which belonged to a widow. Dry, desolate hill country. We had just about hit bottom.

And here I was, trying to finish high school with no money for a decent pair of pants. Or books. Or for graduation. That's when I got out my traps again and started roaming those red prairie hills, looking for signs of possums and skunks.

It really didn't make much sense. After the depression hit, the bottom dropped out of the fur market, too. You were lucky to get 15 or 20 cents for a possum hide. Maybe 50 cents for a skunk pelt. Beyond that, skunks and possums were not as plentiful as back in Custer County. Their dens were few and far between.

By the time I located enough signs and dens and trails to make it worthwhile, I had a trap line laid out that took me on a five to six mile hike every day. With the cold winds howling across those dreary hills.

Worthwhile? It was almost a joke. I hate to remember how many miles I trekked for a single pelt. And how many days or weeks before I had enough furs to make a small package to ship to fur buyers. When the check came back, maybe two or three dollars.

I simply would have revolted against the whole idea except there wasn't anything else I could do. So I walked and walked and walked. Sometimes days on end without a single animal in my traps.

But that circle I travelled took me back to coyote country. Those quavering howls were echoing through the nights again. Pedro was making his mournful replies. The old dream of trapping coyotes was coming back. Oh, sure, the bottom had dropped out of the coyote fur market but , at least, one would bring in a buck or two, maybe even three.

If I only had some traps. Those big No. 3's. And could somehow sharpen my skills until I could nab them.

That was when Ray Leyerly came into the picture. Ray, a leathery old bachelor, lived with his sister and their aged mother in a weatherbeaten old house across the road from us. He had lived in this desolate country all his life and bore the marks of all the defeats it had inflicted upon him over the years.

A few scraggly beef cows. A skinny team of horses. Mustang pony. All they had. Ray could plunk out a pretty tune on his mandolin. It was a way to spend an evening in those lean years. We'd "sing along."

No radio. Television hadn't been invented yet. Even if it had we wouldn't have the money to buy one. No telephone. No money for movies. Strong City didn't have a movie house, anyway. For that you had to go all the way to Cheyenne, the county seat.

It was after that horrible flash flood which had killed so many people and washed away all those cows - perhaps half of Ray's herd was drowned that night - that I had been able to do my little Good Samaritan deed for Ray and his womenfolks.

Down near the bottom of a gully behind their house they had an old one lung gas engine to pump drinking water for their cattle. The flood buried that engine under tons of mud. It was a forlorn sort of effort but Ray dug it out. Not much use, it seemed. It wouldn't run. Cylinder full of mud. Bearings full of sandy grit. Magneto full of mud and water soaked.

I suppose Ray knew I had worked in a machine shop several years and had a bent for fixing things. He wasn't the kind to ask a man for a favor but under the pressure of things, he brought it up one day.

"You reckon it's possible to make this engine run again?" he asked.

I took a look. And shuddered. It looked impossible. Nothing but a big hunk of rusty iron. Lots of mud.

But I suppose it was knowing how badly they needed it that made me tell Ray I'd try. Lord, I don't know how many hours I spent on that thing. Even after the mud was dug out, the piston was stuck solid in the cylinder. It took hours of patient work just to budge it.

Then, though I was trying to be careful, one of the piston rings broke. It needed new rings anyway but nobody had any money to buy them. I smoothed up the rusty cylinder as best I could with some scraps of emery cloth. We'd have to make do with two piston rings and leave the middle goove empty. Then hope and pray we would be able to crank up a bit of compression. The valves had to be ground in by hand.

When all these problems were taken care of, at least partly, it was the magneto which turned out to be the toughie. Not a sign of a spark.

Oh, I know, this is supposed to be a coyote story but the engine comes first. It is part of the coyote story.

I finally took the coil wiring out of the mag and laid them under the hot sun for a few days, to give them a chance to bake out all the moisture. Then put it back together and tried again. I jumped with joy when the mag made enough spark to tingle my finger. Oh, boy. That old engine had started being some kind of a challenge to me.

Compression was weak. Spark was weak. But after cranking and cranking I could hardly believe it, the old engine gave out a few chuffs. And died. Crank, crank, crank. Maybe all that spinning was seating the rings in a bit. Crank, crank, crank. I don't know how many times we tried before it really made with the chuff, chuffs and ran.

It didn't have as much power as it had before - but it ran. It began to pump water again for the cattle.

It was after that when Ray sort of sheepishly brought up the matter of paying me.

"I might be able to pay you when I sell some calves in the fall," he said. Heck, I knew he owed more at the bank than his calves were worth. A lot more. But Ray had his pride, too, and it took a bit of doing to convince him I wouldn't be taking any pay.

When his old mother heard that the engine was running again she said, "God will bless you for it."

Maybe God did but he sure took a long time about it.

Oh, yes, that coyote business. Somewhere in the middle of one of our conversations I must have brought up the coyote business.

"I used to trap coyotes," Ray said, suddenly. "Caught a few of them but I gave it up. Too much work for nothing. Coyote hides won't bring anything these days. Besides, there's too much work around the place for one man anyway. No time."

Oh, wow. My brain was going clickety click. Maybe Ray could teach me how to do it. That haunting challenge was coming back to me.

Yes, I agreed, the hides would hardly bring anything. But I wanted to try. If I only had some of the right traps. I almost jumped with glee when Ray answered that lead.

"I've still got a few of my traps hanging in the barn," he said. "You can take them and try it if you want." He was trying hard to repay me for my engine work.

But he had that age old warning.

"You probably won't have much luck. Awful smart, those critters. Hard to get 'em in a trap. Some of them were smarter than I was." But every word was just firing up my dander. The challenge of it. I was going to try. That was certain.

But first I wanted to pump out of Ray all the trapping lore he had accumulated. And that was when I found out that Ray

Leyerly's methods were quite different from the ones I had read about in the trapping books. Mostly his cow shit hang up.

Some of the trapping guides had talked of smearing fresh chicken blood on your gloves and boots to hide the human odor.

"That's not good enough," Ray said. "The best thing to use is cow shit. Fresh cow shit. Lots of it. Coyotes are used to that odor out on the range. They are around cows all the time. They aren't afraid of cow smell. Smear the crap all over your boots. Then get a pair of old leather gloves and smear them, too."

The trapping guides had said to drive hefty stakes into the ground with the trap chain fastened to them.

"That's no good, either," Ray said. "The coyotes have such fast reflexes you wouldn't believe it. They can feel it when they step on the trigger of your trap and sometimes they are so quick they can jerk their foot out . The jaws of the trap might just catch the end of their foot. A few toes, maybe. If you have the trap staked down, they'll jerk and pull until they pull their foot out. Even if they lose a toe or two. My traps have long chains with hooks. I'll show you."

He disappeared into his ramshackled old barn and came out carrying three No. 3 coyote traps, all he had. I noticed he wasn't carrying them in his hands or touching them. He had them dangling from a wire hook and held them far out from his body.

"Don't touch them with your bare hands," he warned again. "You'll never make a catch if you do. That human odor stays on for days. Carry the traps on this wire. When you take them off, do it with your gloves. And don't forget, put cow shit on your gloves first."

Gosh, this was becoming unbelievable. Were coyotes really smart? Were their smellers really that super?

Ray carried the traps by the wire to a corner of the yard and carefully laid them on the ground. I asked him why he carried them so far. He said he didn't want to lay them on the ground where folks had been walking. They'd pick up some of that human odor, he said.

The thing was becoming more fantastic, more entrancing and more challenging by the minute.

But even here, Ray wouldn't touch the traps. He picked up a stick and poked at them to show me about their chain system.

"You see the traps, when they come from the factory, only have a chain about two feet long. I added on more chain until they are about eight feet long. And then you see I don't have stakes. I have hooks."

I couldn't quite understand it, at first. What I saw was double barbed hooks, with a shank about 10 inches long, and then two sharpened steel hooks. Like small anchor hooks. One extended in a curve from each side of the shank. One of the hooks was pointing down towards the earth. The other slanted upward.

Ray took his stick and flipped the hook over.

"See, the way they are made, one hook is always pointed down, towards the ground, to dig in and drag. No matter how much the coyote jerks and flips the thing, he's always got one hook pointed down."

It was diabolically clever. I was in trapper college.

"The hooks make just enough drag to give the jaws of the trap a chance to set, to bite into his foot and get a good grip. Then, by the time he gets hung up, the trap is gripping so well he can't get out."

Then the next lesson.

"Always make sure you don't set your trap too near a clump of bushes because, after the coyote gets over his first excitement from being caught, he's going to head for the closest clump of bushes to try to get rid of that thing dragging behind him. He'll get it tangled up in the bushes and that's where you're going to find him. But you want at least 50 yards, better a hundred or more, to the closest bushes. To give the trap jaws time to set while he's dragging that hook."

What if the coyote went further than that? I asked.

"You'll just have to trail him. He'll get hung up sooner or later. That hook, dragging in the ground, will leave a trail."

By this time, I was shaking my head with the complexity of it all. All this I would have to do to catch a measly old coyote worth about two or three dollars? I was beginning to understand why Ray had given it up.

But he wasn't through. The best place to set the trap? I asked him.

"Use the cow trails," he said. "Coyotes like to trot down the cow trails. You can see their tracks. But you can't set your traps in the trail because cows will step in them. You have to set it just about 12 inches to one side of the cow trail, between the trail and a clump of prairie grass."

I was beginning to see the picture. Except, what would make the coyote step out of the trail to put his foot on the trap? I should have known the answer to that one, especially after my experience with dogs.

"A coyote is just like a dog," Ray said. "They like to stop and sniff a clump of grass beside the trail to see if another coyote has been there. A nice little bitch, maybe. Then, just like a dog, they pee on the grass and leave their own message for the next coyote. They step off the trail to sniff, or pee on the grass clump, and they step right into your trap."

Oh, wow! I was anxious to get at it. But Ray wasn't quite through.

"You might need something else. Got a big piece of old cow hide?"

I shook my head and Ray disappeared into his old barn again. He came out with an old moldy sheet of cowhide. He had it draped over his stick to keep from touching it.

"You'll need this," he said. "When you dig your hole to bury the chain and the trap, you put every scrap of dirt you dig on this cowhide. Then, when you have finished your set, carry the dirt at least 200 or 300 yards from your set to dump it. Never leave any fresh dirt laying around your set. It's a dead give away. I told you, coyotes are smart. Oh, by the way, smear some fresh shit on that cowhide, too."

I was ready to grab the traps and take off. Ray still had a bit more.

"You dig your hole with a hunting knife, very carefully," he said. "You have to dig it big enough to coil up the chain under the trap and then set the trap on top of that coil of chain. Make sure your knife is smeared with cow shit, too. First, cook it in boiling water. Then pick it up with your shit gloves and smear some of the crap on it, too. Never bring that knife into the house. Leave it out in the cow shed. The same with your boots and gloves. Leave them out in the cow barn to soak up cow smell."

Then there was the matter of hiding the trap after it was set.

"You sprinkle dry grass over it until it is completely hidden," said Ray. That I had learned from the trapper books but Ray added a warning.

"After you think you have your trap well hidden, step back a yard or two and look at the set. If you can see it, the coyote can. It's got to look natural. You'll just have to practice until you get it right."

One more trick - about cold rain and traps freezing solid in winter.

"If you find some leaves from a tree out on the range, or from some bushes, you can put a thin layer of leaves over the trap before sprinkling the grass on. The leaves will sort of protect the trap from the water if it rains. And it keeps the trap from freezing solid if it turns cold after a rain."

Finally, Ray was ready to let me go take a try at it. I left, carefully carrying the traps at arms length, by the wire, and a cow hide draped over the stick. Since it was a bit awkward, carrying them that way, when I got home I rigged up a pole to carry over my shoulder with the traps and cowhide dangling from the pole. No touch.

In that daily trek over my possum and skunk trap line on the Miller Ranch, I had learned every cow trail. It was one of the marks of those frontier prairies, the way cows would make trails that crisscrossed the hills. The range cows would walk those trails in single file, going to and from their feeding grounds or watering holes. Anyplace. I had never been in an airplane but I sometimes wondered what those crazy patterns of cow trails would look like from the air. I had read in magazines about coyote bounty hunters shooting coyotes from low flying planes, with shotguns loaded with buckshot. Somehow, that always sounded a bit like cheating to me. It didn't give the coyotes a chance. But if you were trapping, you matched your wits against the wits of a coyote. It was a bit more fair. A coyote had a chance, at least. I was to find out he had a lot of chances.

For example, Ray had his system down pat, all right. I believed folks when they said Ray had caught his share of coyotes in his lifetime. But, as he warned, it took practice and so much care, to do it all right.

You'd dig your trap hole too shallow and have to start over. Always with the danger of leaving your man odor around. Then you'd dig some more. Maybe a bit too deep and you'd have to fill some of the dirt back in. After a while, I learned.

Then that business of hiding a trap. Time and again, when I stepped back to look, it was easy to see the place had been disturbed. In time, I learned how to mix a bit of dry dust with my sprinkled grass. In time, I was satisfied nobody would know if they looked. Not even a coyote.

I knew where to set my traps. I had seen plenty of coyote tracks in those cow trails. They were always fresh because the cows, coming along later, would stomp out the old traces. A few times, I had caught glimpses of the ghostlike creatures, flitting over a hill, maybe half a mile away.

Only once, on a stormy, windy day, bucking homeward into the wind, did I stumble onto a coyote close enough to shoot. But he was too fast for me. Before I could swing the barrel of my shotgun up, he was gone. Just a gray shadow in the bushes.

Then Ray told me one other thing about locating the right grass clumps beside the cow trails.

"If you'll look real close," he said, "you will be able to find the clumps they are using. It will always be a nice little clump of grass, almost always about two feet off the trail. If you keep your eyes sharp you may see from their tracks where they have stopped to sniff and pee."

That made it so much easier. I'd just follow one of those cow trails, looking for the grass humps at the right distance. Then, sometimes crouching down to get a good look, I would study the tracks. Sure enough, I finally began spotting places where the coyotes had been making those fateful pauses.

Tracks suddenly close together. Tracks heading, perhaps, at an angle off the trail. I couldn't sniff, like a dog, to see if a coyote had peed on the grass but I eventually found some of those "hot" clumps.

Ray warned me about not walking in cow trails and leaving my own tracks and smell.

"Coyotes know what man tracks are," he said. "When you follow one of those trails, always walk parallel to it, at least three feet to one side, in the grass. It will help."

But even armed with all of Ray's intimate knowledge of trapping coyotes, somehow I must not have been quite careful enough. It was at least a month, maybe six weeks, before I caught my first coyote.

She was a young bitch, just reaching maturity. Maybe not quite as wise as the older coyotes. She had done just as Ray had predicted. The signs showed a burst of activity, marks on the ground, where she had fought and tried to get rid of that "thing" hanging to her foot.

Then she had taken off, heading for the nearest clump of bushes, perhaps a hundred yards away. That was where I found her, the trap and chain tangled into the bushes as she had fought to free herself. Also, just as Ray had predicted, she had only three toes in the trap but the jaws were set tight. If the trap had been staked down, as the book suggested, she probably would have pulled herself free.

Oh, but was I happy? My first coyote. Even if it wasn't be biggest marauder of the prairie it was a coyote. I had done it. I had done it. My big dream. I had caught a coyote.

I was a full fledged coyote trapper.

Well, not quite. I got an inkling of that when I rushed home, carrying my prey, and hurried over to show it to Ray.

"I got one," I said, proudly. He grinned and shook my hand.

Then he scratched his stubbly chin a bit and made that remark which deflated my joy.

"A nice young bitch," he said. "But it is the old ones, the big ones, that are the smartest. Especially, the old dogs."

By that, of course, he meant the "he" coyotes.

In time, I caught a few of the "dogs," too, but only one or two. Mostly the younger ones. Meantime, one day, I lost one of those precious No. 3 traps.

I had obtained permission from the Miller Brothers, owners of the biggest ranch in the neighborhood, to trap on their ranch. They had about 6,000 acres. It was big enough for me. I had ranged far and wide, looking for those cow trails with a "hot" grass bush beside it. One day I made a successful set, only about 200 yards from the boundry of the neighboring ranch. I didn't know the owner but the Miller Brothers had warned me about not crossing the line onto his place.

"He's sort of mean and doesn't like trespassers," they said.

Well, I caught myself a coyote and the beast headed for the border. I trailed him until he crossed it. Should I follow? After a moment's hesitation, I did.

And when I came to the nearest clump of bushes, there it was, all laid out in ground signs. The coyote had gone into the bushes to try to get rid of the trap. He got hung up. But then I saw the spot of blood. And the horse tracks. Even boot tracks, where a man had dismounted from a horse, that led towards the bushes - and that spot of blood. He apparently had been armed with a gun, shot my coyote, picked it up and took it with him. Together with my trap.

A wave of anger welled up in me. "That sonofabitch," I muttered. "He stole my trap."

I looked towards that ranch house, within sight about half a mile across the prairie. I could see a man standing in the yard and looking towards me.

A moment later he disappeared towards the barn. Then he was on a horse, coming towards me. Should I confront him? Demand my coyote and trap back? After all, I caught him fair and square on Miller property.

I could see the man was carrying a long gun. Rifle or shotgun. My only weapon was a tiny .22 caliber pistol I used to kill my coyotes and skunks, shooting them in the ear to keep from making a hole in their hides.

It was a tough decision. I wanted to stay. Surely the man wouldn't shoot me. Even this wild prairie country was supposed to be at least half civilized. But how could I know? I had been warned that the guy was "tough" and hated trespassers. I didn't have much time to make a decision. Much as my anger wanted me to confront this "thief," I decided I'd better get back across that boundry line, but quick. I went just over the fence and stopped. It was anger that gave me courage.

"Hey, you," he shouted. "You keep your goddam ass off my property or I'll blow you off."

"I want my trap and my coyote. I caught him on this side of the fence, " I said defiantly, watching the shotgun in his hand.

"I don't know nothing about a trap or a coyote," he said. "If he was on my side of the line, it's mine anyway. Get going. Stay off my land."

So I did, bitterly swallowing a big hunk of anger. The guy was lying. I had seen the horse tracks heading back to his ranch house. But what could I do? Get my ass shot off?

Now I had only two traps. Damn.

I went back to my trapping, with two traps. I needed two dozen.

When I told Ray what had happened he bristled a bit, too. "That dirty sonofabitch," he muttered.

But then he said that I had done the right thing.

"Your coyote was on his property when he found it," he said. He paused a moment. Then, "He's a mean bastard. Somebody ought to shoot his ass off." I decided to keep my traps a half mile from that boundry.

But now something else was stirring. Out there in one of the far corners of the Miller Ranch I had started seeing some big coyote tracks. The biggest I had ever seen. It had to be one of those "big old dogs" Ray had been talking about. That old challenge thing started boiling inside of me again. Man, if I could only get that beast in my trap. I'd be as good a trapper as Ray.

And I was going to try. To use every smidgen of skill I had been able to pick up from Ray and from practice.

Funny, he didn't use cow trails as much as the other coyotes. But on a hillside, near a fence, I found a spot where he seemed to be crossing a lot. There were even a few clumps of grass he might have been peeing on.

I chose my spot carefully. I guess I never did spend as much time making sure everything was perfect as I did on that one. Fresh cow shit on my boots and gloves. So careful, digging my hole and concealing the trap. Sprinkling the grass. I was even proud when I stepped back to inspect. I defied anyone, man or beast, to detect that I had been there.

I had even learned another little precautionary trick Ray hadn't told me about. Out there on those prairie hills the cold wind would sometimes cause my nose to drip. So when I was making one of my sets I always wore a handkerchief tied around my face. Ray would have approved of that. In any case, I had my perfect "set." And exciting hopes for my biggest trophy of them all.

Then it happened. That sonofabitch. He thumbed his nose at me.

This was something the trapper books never told you about. Even Ray had never mentioned anything like this. Incredible. Unbelievable.

I had long ago learned that it was mostly a waste of time to expect a "catch" on a fresh set. It had to age a day or two, at least, before you could expect action. This time, I had action the first night. But not the kind I wanted. Or had hoped for.

I had learned never to walk up to your set when you come back to look but to stay at least 50 yards away. You could always see if anything had happened to your trap. If nothing had happened, you backed away.

But I always took a look on the first day, anyway. Long before I got there, that first day, I could see that Old Yellow Eyes had been there.

Oh, I didn't call him Old Yellow Eyes then. I hadn't even seen his eyes. I guess it was a name I dreamed up later.

In any case, nobody had to tell me what that super coyote had done to me. It was all laid out there on the ground, in signs so clear he might just as well have written it all down with a pencil.

The "happening" was a big ring, a circle, around my trap. My "perfect" set. Deep scratches clawed into the earth by the hind paws of a big coyote. Violent claw marks, throwing the dirt for 10 feet or more. A circle of claw marks, perhaps 20 feet in circumference and with my trap like a bullseye in the center. He had clawed furiously until a clod of the flying dirt had hit the trigger of my trap and had sprung it. Then he had gone.

As I read the sign I was almost shaking with anger. I could almost see him sitting on a hillside somewhere, perhaps half a mile away, laughing at me. Thumbing his nose. What else could you call it? The cleverness. The impudence. It was bitter medicine I swallowed that day. How could an animal, any animal, be that smart?

But I was angry now. I swallowed and tried again. And at least three more times within the next few weeks he did it to me again. No matter how hard I tried, slaved, over my set. He found it while it was still fresh. I would have to figure out some way to make a set where he might not find it the first day.

I told Ray what had happened. He allowed a faint smile to play over his lips. He wished me no ill but it amused him, nonetheless.

"I told you they were smart, didn't I?"

After a few minutes he had something else to say. "I know an old time trapper over at Cheyenne. He's an old codger but he has caught more coyotes than anybody I know. He used to make some kind of bait from the piss of a female coyote. Mixed something else in with it. Never would tell me what it was. Next time I get to Cheyenne, I'll go by and see him. Maybe he'll give me a little of that stuff."

This really wasn't something new to me. I had read about some of that "Sure Fire" lure stuff. The trapper supply catalogue had it listed and they mentioned that one of the ingredients was the urine of a female coyote. That stuff old Cheyenne was making was probably nearly the same thing. But it was worth a try, anyway. Anything to catch Old Yellow Eyes.

Sure enough, a few days later, Ray came over with a little bottle.

"The old man's not trapping much any more. Getting old and there's not as many coyotes as there used to be. He didn't want to give me any of the stuff but when I told him your story he gave me a little. Said that happened to him a few times, too." Ray was still trying hard to repay me for fixing his pump engine.

Now I began searching for a new spot to make a set for Old Yellow Eyes. I had seen his big tracks on a cow trail not far from where he had thumbed his nose at me. Not every day but often enough. If he only came by every two or three days, maybe that would give my set a chance to age.

That cow trail led through an arroyo with a flat bottom, maybe 30 or 40 yards wide. The cows had tromped their trail down one bank of that gully, across the flat bottom and then up the other side. And down on that flat bottom, beside the cow trail and in a perfect spot, was a nice clump of prairie grass. Just perfect.

If I had labored hard for a perfect set before, I labored twice as hard now. I had no way of knowing whether that clump of grass was "hot" or not but if it wasn't hot, I was going to make it hot. For, after I completed my set and made sure it passed inspection I sprinkled a few drops of Cheyenne's lure on the clump.

The trap, exactly half way between the cow trail and that hump of grass. Now, if that sonofabitch pulled that "thumb the nose" trick on me again I'd probably throw my traps in the creek. And jump in after them.

The next morning, I approached carefully and from a distance peered cautiously over the rim of that arroyo. No sign of Old Yellow Eyes. Hooray. At least part of my plan had succeeded. He hadn't found my trap while the set was fresh. It meant I had a chance. He would be back. I was almost certain.

And then it worked. On the second day, as I came once more and peered over that rim, nobody had to tell me what had happened. My heart lunged in a wild joy. The signs were everywhere. So incredibly clear. The ground once more ripped and torn but with a terribly important difference. Now it was all the signs of mad battle as the fear crazed beast had fought to try to free himself from my trap. I had caught him.

That battle scene was awesome. No 20 foot circle now. A hundred feet or more of the earth was ripped and torn. Incredible, once more, the way he had fought. Plunging, leaping, clawing to rid himelf of that evil "thing" clinging to his paw. Whipping that chain in wild, furied circles.

Oh, he wasn't there. I never even expected that. But he was in my trap. Somewhere, perhaps within half a mile, he was out there waiting for me.

But first I would have to trail him. To do that I would have to go over that scene of battle to sort out the spot where he had made his last assault on the walls of the gully for his final bid for escape.

I found it. Traces of the "hook," gouging into the earth in jumps across the plain and headed right for the nearest clump of bushes.

I didn't find him in that clump of bushes. Or the next. But in each of those clumps I found once more a scene of battle as he had tried to use those bushes to scrape off that clinging trap.

I believe I must have trailed him at least a mile. Several times I lost the trail in areas of thicker grass where the hook did not leave its telltale signs. Each time I would ram a stick into the ground to mark my last "sign," then circle for a new sign. I had learned how to trail them by now.

Then I could pick up his trail again. Over another hill. And another hill. Then that last hill. Another clump of bushes, perhaps 200 yards ahead. And there was Old Yellow Eyes.

He was indeed a big old dog of a coyote. The biggest I had ever seen. Perhaps twice as big as the first young bitch I had caught. And the big clump of bushes offered dramatic evidence once more of his last desperate battle to free himself. Now the hook and the chain were hopelessly snarled in those bushes. He had less than a foot of chain to move.

He lay quietly on the earth, crouched as if to spring, staring at me. I knew, of course, that he could not. But I was wary. I had my little pistol in my hand, cocked and aimed, in case he did manage to lunge free. For the first time, I looked into those yellow eyes.

I had always anticipated this moment of triumph when I would have this monster in my trap. I had been stalking him for months now. So carefully. I had been so angry on those days when I had found his impudent challenge to my skill. When he had found my trap and decided a certain young upstart trapper needed a lesson. Perhaps, in a sense, in my dreams I had been stalking this big coyote for years.

Now he was mine. All I had to do was take careful aim at the hollow of his ear, pull the trigger and those great yellow eyes would cease to see me. That startling cunning of his brain would be destroyed.

But then, somehow, I became aware of the fact that I wasn't as happy as I had thought I would be.

I found a sudden reluctance to pull that trigger. Now that he was mine, at my mercy, I felt something close to a sense of sorrow at what I had finally done to this magnificent king of the prairie.

Chapter Sixteen - Hoax

May I be permitted the use of a small potato as a symbol, please?

It is a little round potato. Smelling of kerosene. With a series of little overlapping circles indented on its surface in random style.

It is the symbol of a monstrous hoax.

Listen. A story in several newspapers said I was the president of the Brotherhood of Electrical, Chemical and Spiritual Treasure Restorers of America. I had called a national convention for July 11, 1936, at Weatherford, Oklahoma. As the inventor of a gold sniffing machine, I had been beaten, robbed of a treasure find and left for dead in the steaming jungles of Guatemala.

The only problem with the story was that I knew nothing about it.

Where did it come from? It was incredible. Insane.

Even today, nearly half a century after it all happened, a reading of that faded old newspaper clipping awakens a new shiver of unbelief. Did it really happen?

To begin to explain it, we must return to the symbol - the little potato with those strange markings.

Most Americans today would not even recognize it. They would have to be old enough to have lived in rural America a half century ago - when darkness came with the night and when the only light at night came from a kerosene lamp.

Most folks called the lamp fuel "coal oil." It really was kerosene. The lamps, or the lanterns hanging in the barn, carefeully tended by father. Trimming the wicks, polishing the glass globes with a wad of newspaper. The fuel bowl was refilled from a round gallon can from which protruded a pouring spout in the shape of a pipe stem.

There, jammed down on the spout, to prevent spilling, was our little round potato.

Perhaps nobody remembers who invented the custom of jamming a potato onto the spout to seal it. The practice was nearly universal. Farmers who had their own potatoes could always select one from their own potato bin in the cellar.

But I also remember that one winter I worked after school in the grocery store where one of my chores was filling the kerosene cans as farm folks brought them in for refills at six, may eight cents per gallon.

Ir was unthinkable to hand the can back to the farmer or his wife without a potato on the mouth of the spout. If the can came in with a potato in place, it was your responsibility to make sure it hadn't become too mushy to be used again. If you saw it was going bad, you went to the store's potato bin, selected a nice, round and firm potato and jammed it onto the spout. The ritual of the kerosene refill was then complete.

The next duty becomes that of connecting the little potato symbol with my cousin, Gordon Friesen, who dreamed up that news story about a "brotherhood" of treasure seekers.

Oh, I knew Gordon well. In fact, for a long time I considered him my best friend. Otherwise, he would not have dared to create that incredible hoax around my name.

Gordon was several years older, so I had never known him well during school years. I had gone to school with his younger brother, Oliver, also a bit older than I was. Oliver had a propensity for growling at younger kids - and that included me. It gave me the impression that he didn't like me so I didn't like him very much, either. It left me with an uncomfortable feeling every time I found myself in his presence and I would try to shuffle out of sight without being growled at.

I knew that Gordon had been attending high school in town and had been hurt while playing football. The injury had forced him to drop out of school. He was lying around in that shabby little hilltop farm house, developing a rather vigorous case of agoraphobia.

By the time I got to know Gordon, he had pretty well recovered from that football injury but he seldom ventured more than a hundred yards from home. He hadn't been into town, three miles away, for years. Or even out of his his own front yard.

I must have been about 17 when I became Gordon's friend. The books and magazines attracted me in the beginning. His room was stacked full of them. Strange books and magazines such as I had never seen before. Books on politics, philosophy, science, anthropology, religion. With a certain scandalized air, folks even said Gordon was an atheist. He had a book about Albert Einstein's theory of relativity. And books about the communist revolution in Russia.

He had magazines, like Time, which were a true rarity in a Mennonite community in western Oklahoma. He would lend me books and old copies of Time which I devoured hungrily. I had always been a book nut but before I met Gordon my reading had been somewhere on the Zane Grey level. I was now, suddenly, graduating into something else. They didn't have stuff like this in the high school library.

I found it fun, talking to Gordon. Politics. Science. Literature. Sociology. Geopolitics. For the first time in my life I heard symphonic music although the quality of the sound coming from his battery powered radio left a good deal to be desired. Sunday afternoons, it would be NBC with Arturo Toscanini and the New York Philharmonic.

The encounter with Gordon was causing my mind, my consciousness, to expand with explosive rapidity. I never did learn to comprehend the Einstein book. I felt better when Gordon told me he didn't understand it either.

In any case, almost every Sunday found me hiking the three miles over the gyp hills to Gordon's house. Sometimes during the week.

I would have to confess there was some truth to the suspicions of his neighbors and relatives that Gordon didn't have much faith left in the old Adam and Even fundamentalism that pervaded our God fearing Mennonite community.

In time, I would even come to recognize the fact that he was in the process of becoming a communist.

He felt forced into it by the crushing poverty that had been brought upon him, his family and his neighbors by the cruel economic depression of the 1930's. I never said much about that communism business. Folks were already scandalized enough at Gordon's eccentric life style. Mom and Dad had made it quite clear they didn't like my associating with him.

God, if we were poor, so poor that sometimes I didn't even have a pair of socks to wear in my battered shoes, Gordon and his family were even poorer - if that was possible and still allow life to remain in the body.

The little potato is coming closer now. And the gold sniffer tale.

Gordon's dad, Uncle Jake, was the epitome of the defeated man. Folks said that in Uncle Jake's younger years when times were better, he had been a successful real estate dealer. Somewhere, somehow, he had met his ultimate defeat. He had retreated to his 80 acres of barren and unproductive red hills and slowly withdrew into a shell which enshrouded his crushed soul.

His conversation also had retreated into the realms of his childhood. And with it, perhaps, his mind. The impression became forced, at times, that he had become little more than an empty human shell. At times, a considerably animated one. He would laugh. Jabber something one could never quite understand. Most of the time he just sat there in the shade of the back porch. Silent and unwanted.

Occasionally, in the springtime, under the urging from people like my father, or his compartively wealthy brother, Uncle Pete, he would make a feeble assault upon those barren hills of his farm.

By this time he was so poor he didn't even have a team of horses. So my Dad, or Uncle Pete, would lend him a team, a plow and the implements with which to place seed in the ground. He would stir haphazardly into action for a few weeks. I would see him out there on those hills, scratching the earth with the plow, harrow and seeder. Somehow, nothing ever really came of it.

If he planted cotton, the stalks would be scrawny and virtually barren of cotton bolls. If it was wheat, he scarecely ever made enough to warrant the expense of bringing in a harvester to reap the grain.

The most unfortunate farmer I ever knew. Almost as if that poverty of will which had come to live in his soul was somehow imparted into the steel of the plow and into the seeds he entrusted into the stubborn earth.

If it hadn't been for Aunt Mary, the mother of his children and my father's sister, and for Gordon, plus a portion of charity from his brother, Pete, I suppose that family would have simply withered to breathlessness atop that dry, dusty and windswept hill.

Folks might have found them all, weeks later, skeletal, desicated and perhaps a bit mumified by the dry and pitiless wind which eternally moaned across the Oklahoma prairie.

It was Aunt Mary who somehow retained her faith in God which sustained her in her hours, her years, of trial. She became a scrounger who managed from the least to make the most. She worked a garden. Raised a few scrawny chickens. A wonderful cook when there was something to cook. A miracle worker when there wasn't.

And then there was Gordon and his footman brother, Oliver.

For Gordon, despite his phobias, was a writer. In fact, he had written a splendid novel, Flamethrowers, a rustic chronicle of his Mennonite heritage which had impressed editors enough to get it published in those lean years. Even the critics saw merit in it. But the book never sold well enough to put much by way of potatoes or kerosene in the family pantry.

Somehow, Gordon had managed to become the Weatherford correspondent for both the major news agencies, Associated Press and United Press. Oliver did the leg work. Gordon did the writing. Weatherford just happened to be the home of Southwestern State College so, during the school year, the Gordon-Oliver team could scrabble up a few dollars, damned few, by covering the football, basketball and baseball games. Plus what other dribbles of news that might be gleaned from such barren land.

Of course Gordon had to guard well the secret that he was working for both competing news agencies. Otherwise, his services would have been terminated fast.

But now, because his family's need for income was so urgent - and because he was paid according to the number of inches of his stuff that got in the papers - Gordon was about to become one of the most prolific news agency writers in the history of southwest Oklahoma. If real news did not exist, he would invent it.

In the beginning he merely dressed up his true stories a little. Then, suddenly, strange sounding stories under the Associated Press logo, date-line Weatherford, began appearing in the papers across the state. For example, "a grizzled old Indian chief" became the subject of several amazing interviews about the old days in Oklahoma. This "chief" recalled colorful tales about the last of the Indian wars. He remembered all the pitiful travails of the tribes.

Good reading - but it sounded suspicious. I was certain that neither Gordon nor Oliver had ever seen a "Chief Antelope." One thing for certain, Gordon's phobia had not permitted him to leave his hilltop refuge for years. Which left Oliver, his legman. I knew Oliver well enough to know that he had never seen such a chief.

There was also a wild story about a great panther attacking cattle, threatening people and, according to each succeeding "panther bulletin," drawing ever closer to Weatherford itself.

And then came the time when even I became grist for Gordon's fiction mill. Unknown to me.

Perhaps, in retrospect, I have tried to rationalize. Somehow, to bring myself to forgive Gordon this abomination which, in the end, forced me to flee and go into hiding until the storm was over. At the moment, I was frightened, bewildered and angry. My temporary absence did not allow me to escape the wrath of the townspeople and the Weatherford News. When I returned they screamed for my scalp.

Painfully I must confess that, in a sense, I may have planted the first small seeds of the crazy story in Gordon's mind. Charlie Kendall, my boss at the machine shop, had planted a few of those seeds in my mind. But such tiny seeds. Could such a monstrous hoax have grown from such small seeds?

I, too, had dreamed of becoming a writer, a newspaperman. But in those depression ridden days, it was not to be. Then, because I had been born with that mysterious "knack" for mechanical things, it was inevitable that I end up working with tools, machinery and motors.

That job was an apprenticeship in Charlie Kendall's shop. In the beginning, I worked for $1 a week.

My brother, Ernie, and several of his buddies had been playing in a gully washer ravine in a pasture out west of Clinton. They stumbled onto a pair of bones and discovered that they were human. Almost the complete skeleton except for the foot bones. Those bones had been swept away in a torrent of water through the gully.

A corroded canteen with the remnants of a leather cover came to light with the bones. A brass buckle. Several brass covered buttons. From these we deduced that the man, buried some 40 inches under the pasture surface and lying on his side in a fetal position, had been a frontier soldier. How and from what cause he had died, we would never know.

Since I was a bit older, the kids brought the skeleton to me. I called the sheriff. He came, asked a few questions and decided it was no murder and he drove away. He didn't even take the bones with him. So we asked an elderly farm couple who lived about 500 yards from the gully if they knew of anybody being buried in the pasture during the 60 years they had lived there. They knew of no one.

Since nobody wanted the bones and they sort of fascinated me, I kept them. The skull, in particular, intrigued me. One would catch himself wondering what kind of spirit had once lived in that cranial cavity. What thoughts, what yearnings, what fears and longings, had once inhabited that mind.

I carefully cleaned all the dirt out of the skull, attached the jawbone with wires and a spring, varnished the skull and in the manner of impish youth, placed it on a shelf. Once I even wrote a poem about it.

One day, I told Charlie Kendall about the skeleton and the skull. He asked me to describe the site where it was found. Then he had a story of his own to tell. That one had come from his father, Henry Kendall, one of the true pioneers of this territory, the first postmaster at a little trading post which later became Corn, Oklahoma.

While the elder Kendall had been a country store keeper and postmaster at Corn, Charlie related, two travelers stopped to buy provisions. The strangers had questions about the topography of the land.

The two were relatives of still another pair of men, a father and son, who had been to California for the gold rush. They struck it rich in the gold fields, loaded their gold on a burro and headed home.

Somewhere in western Oklahoma, near the Washita River, the father and son had been attacked by Indians who killed the father. The son hurriedly buried the gold in what, it was said, was a sand bank that faced a sandstone cliff. He had then escaped down a gully which led to the Washita River, perhaps a mile or two away. Finally, nearly starved and exhausted, he had found people and made his way back home to Missouri.

This son, it was told, had made several trips back to Oklahoma before he died, trying to find the gold. He never found it. He died without finding his lost riches. But he had drawn a crude map that showed where, to the best of his memory, it had been buried. He left the map to relatives when he died.

Now, those two men buying food and asking questions at the Kendall store, were those same relatives. With the map. Kendall had claimed he once saw the map.

It was probably only a quirk of circumstances which determined that about 200 yards from where my brother, Ernie, and his friends found the skeleton, there was a sandstone cliff. The cliff was about 20 feet high and on a turn in the gully where, during a heavy rain, the water whirled. In front of the cliff - a sand bank.

It had been Charlie Kendall, my boss, who had mused idly that it was a coincidence that the skeleton had been found near that sandstone cliff. And the cliff was on a gully that led to the Washita River, only a mile or two away.

It was an interesting story and an interesting set of circumstances. But it had never been enough to set me off with pick and shovel on a gold hunt. It had been this story which, on a Sunday afternoon, I had told my cousin, Gordon.

I attached virtually no credence to the story. I certainly hadn't the slightest idea about what mad machinery it was setting to whirl in Gordon's fertile mind.

In fact, with good conscience I could take my oath that the first inkling I had of anything in the nature of skulduggery was when, one day, I got a letter with a Missouri postmark.

"I read about your gold seeker group and your convention," the letter stated. "I'd like to come. Please, send me more information."

I hadn't the slightest notion of what the man was writing about. I put it down as some sort of a nut letter and went about my business.

I wasn't allowed to forget it. The next day brought more letters.

And the next day more and more and more. From Missouri, Kansas, Arkansas, Nebraska, Illinois. God knows where they all came from, not to speak of other towns in Oklahoma. All I knew was that something strange was going on and I didn't like it.

Eventually I had to connect Gordon with it. I jumped in my old Chevy and headed for his house. I dumped the pile of letters in front of him. I wasn't very friendly.

"Are you responsible for this?" I demanded.

He picked up a couple of the letters, skimmed through them. Reading his face, I knew,

Gordon had nothing to say. He only shrugged.

"Good God, Gordon, what in the hell got into you, anyway? What am I going to do? I don't know what to tell these people. It's crazy. You've got to do something to stop it," I yelled.

Gordon may have been the victim of his phobias but he seldom allowed his emotions to hang out and didn't now. I didn't know whether he, like me, was frightened. Or embarrassed. Or what. He certainly had no right to be angry. That, at this moment, was my prerogative. And I was on the verge of caving in his skull.

Friend? Hell, a friend wouldn't pull a trick like this one on me.

"Why in the hell, if you had to cook up another of your phoney stories, couldn't you use a phoney name instead of mine? I can't face these people," I said.

Gordon wasn't talking, so eventually I left, angry as I had come. And even then I wasn't aware of how crazy his AP story had been. All the wild stuff about my gold hunting trip to Central America. Being beaten and left for dead. The gold sniffing machine. The spirits of Ghost Mound.

The story bore almost no resemblance at all to the skeleton Ernie had found, or the sandstone cliff story.

I just know I went home. And the letters kept coming. As the pile grew I faced Gordon again.

"Damn it, what am I supposed to do? Some of these people say they are coming to Weatherford on July 11. Just tell me what the hell I'm supposed to tell them? It's your baby. You'd better come up with something."

He didn't. Finally I just blurted it out, "I'm not going to face it. I'm leaving town."

I must have yelled and cussed a long time. Several times. And Gordon's reaction to it all was something in the nature of what folks would call, in a later time, stonewalling. Having created the whirlwind he couldn't stuff it back into a bag. All I was able to get out of him was a feeble, "I'm sorry."

A couple of days before July 11, I carried out my threat and simply left town. I hadn't created the hoax and I'd be damned if I'd stay around to face the storm.

But I still caught hell when I returned. Mom and Dad were mad. Charlie Kendall was mad. The chief of police was mad. The editor of the Weatherford News was mad. The citizens of the town thought I was a kook.

People, would-be treasure seekers, had indeed come flocking into town on July 11, asking for that guy Duerksen and his convention headquarters. When somebody finally told them where Mom and Dad lived they stormed out and made life miserable for them. Poor Mom, she didn't know what it was all about. I hadn't warned her.

She and Dad were even threatened by some of those crazy people. Angry people now.

208

Those that didn't hound Mom and Dad, hounded poor Charlie Kendall, who also had no warning. They hung around his shop all day, growling, cursing, threatening.

"Where in the hell is this guy Duerksen?" they demanded. Charlie didn't know. But they disrupted work around the shop all day. Charlie was fit to be tied.

I doubt if anybody in the town that day ever really knew exactly what had taken place. In fact, Gordon, who should have borne the brunt of it didn't even get involved. I was the only person who knew he was the perpetrator. And I was gone.

Looking back on it now, I realize I should have left Gordon's address with someone, with word on how to find him out there on his barren hilltop. At least he could have caught his portion of the hell.

Charlie Kendall was so angry he almost fired me. He probably would have except for the fact that, other than for an absence caused by a crazy hoax, I was a fairly dependable slavey. I had simply not had the guts to face what I knew was coming.

Charlie said that if those people who descended upon Weatherford that day had been able to get their hands on me they probably would have strung me up on a telephone pole. Charlie almost threatened to do it himself. It was days before he stopped cussing me about that one.

Even when I tried to explain, he only transferred a bit of his anger to Gordon, and me by association.

"That's what you get for associating with a crackpot atheist like him," he said. I didn't argue with that one. At the moment I was almost angry enough myself to join a lynch mob if someone had decided to lynch Gordon.

When Bruce Rainey, the police chief, heard I was back in town he also came around and made growling, threatening noises.

It was only when I told him the truth, and who was really responsible, that he calmed down a bit. Nobody ever saw Gordon in town but most folks knew who he was. I don't know whether Rainey ever went out to see him or not.

The Weatherford News, a weekly, ran a front page story about the whole mess. I was the villian all over again. Gordon was still escaping.

I was so bewildered, so young and inexperienced, so frightened by the sudden publicity, I didn't have sense enough, or possibly not enough nerve, to go to the editor and explain what had happened. As a result, I spent weeks explaining to people who confronted me about it. And when I would explain about Gordon, they would just sort of shrug their shoulders. A lot of them already knew about that queer eccentric on his hilltop. "Oh, him," they would shrug.

I guess some of the people never got over the idea that I was a bit of a crackpot, too.

Folks told me that on July 11, those out of town gold seekers milled around town all day. When they couldn't find me and got no satisfaction from my parents, or from Charlie, they just sat on the street curbs, trying to decide what to do. Sitting on Main Street like a bunch of Indians, somebody said.

The town probably harvested a few dollars from the Pilgrams, for food and meals and gas to get home on. So the town merchants should not have been too angry at me.

I never did find out exactly how many Pilgrams came. Folks told me they never really got together but assembled in small groups all over town. There was nobody to bring them together, to organize anything. I had made sure of that. The "seekers" finally just gave up, the thing petered out and they went home. Disgruntled and unhappy but, perhaps, a bit wiser. No gold.

I guess that I was so angry that it took months before I would even speak to Gordon again. I made it very clear that if he ever tried a stunt like that again, with me as the victim, somebody was going to get his skull busted. If he wanted to write phoney stories and risk getting into trouble, fine, but leave me out.

Actually, although we became friends again, I don't believe I ever completely forgave him. Every time I'd have occasion to remember that incredible hoax I would feel, welling up in my throat, the urge to plant one of my 10 1/2 boots in Gordon's rear.

I suppose it was simply time that eventually softened my anger. Or it could have been the memory of some of those Sunday afternoons and evenings spent on that Friesen hilltop.

Days of unfinished symphonies when the radio batteries went dead and there was no money for fresh ones. Days when the evening meal was little more than some of Aunt Mary's flour dumplings. Or even less. It had always been taken for granted that I sat at the table with them.

And the evenings, after dark, when the kerosene lamp had been lit. When its flame would flicker and begin to smoke - the "coal oil" all gone. No more in the spouted can on the porch.

As the lamp flickered and the black smoke began whisping out, from the burning of a dry wick, conversation would become meager. Everybody knew. Aunt Mary, in a voice that was little more than a whisper, said, "There's no more coal oil left in the can."

Gordon grabbed the lamp, shook it violently to slosh the last drops of kerosene at the bottom of the lamp bowl up onto the wick. The lamp would flare up for a few minutes and then, once more, the whisping smoke.

Although Aunt Mary had already said the can was empty, Gordon got up and went to the porch where the spouted can stood. A little round potato was stuck on the spout, as if still on duty to prevent a spillage of that which was no longer inside.

Gordon removed the potato, turned the can up and tried to drain a few drops of kerosene from the can into the lamp. Nothing came. Only a few drops.

He was still holding the little potato in his hand. He looked at it and I heard a subdued curse come from his lips.

His hand curled around the little potato and squeezed, perhaps more in anger and frustration than for anything else. But somehow it seemed to me an almost subconscious effort to squeeze that little vegetable like a sponge. As if, perhaps, he could squeeze a quart or a pint of "coal oil" out of it.

Perhaps he did, indeed, squeeze a few drops out. Enough to moisten his hand. Nothing more.

Another half suppressed curse. He hurled the little potato to the floor of the porch and stomped it with his foot. His anger, nearly silent, said so much.

It was, perhaps, moments like these that created a desperation which drove Gordon Friesen to write an impudent story about gold seekers. An act of defiance, perhaps, at fates which had been so unkind to his father, his mother, his siblings and to him.

It was an act of fraud, we would insist. But fraud perpetrated in desperation, to wring from the cruel "system" a few dollars with which to buy a few quarts of kerosene for the lamp. A few potatoes for the table.

I suppose I could not remain angry at his hoax forever.

Chapter Seventeen - Woody

Woody was woozy and Woody was woozy.

Two Woodys. Two woozies.

The only way to make any sense out of a silly little equation like that is for me to confess that there might have been some transposition of identity. I was the one who did it . I have to accept the responsibility.

I won't try to justify it, unless justification abides within the confines of the crazy story itself.

True, some folks might argue that it is doing injustice to an honorable man, now dead. But since nobody can tell me who the dead man was, or give me a true account of his honorableness, the question is more or less moot.

All that remains of that dead man now is his polished and varnished skull resting quietly on a shelf in my closet. I once had him perched on top of a cabinet in my den. It was the tender sensibilities of my wife which dictated that he be banished to the darkness of the closet.

I could also blame the real Woody who was indeed woozy to a considerable degree, for getting me involved in all this. If I somehow make the transfer of wooziness to the second Woody, I can always suggest that it was the real Woody who motivated it. Or was it the "Colonel?" I had to take my revenge on somebody and an unidentified dead man cannot fight back.

That polished and varnished skull is all the tangible evidence that remains from that wacky incident when my cousin, Gordon Friesen, concocted his wild hoax.

Inventing that brotherhood of gold seekers, making me president, announcing a national convention and almost getting me lynched.

It had been the discovery of that skull, together with most of the skeletal bones, by my brother and some of his buddies, that had made the whole crazy thing begin to jell.

And then, added to that, the story of two gold miners who buried their gold near a sandstone cliff - and the coincidence that the bones were found near a sandstone cliff. The story began to knit itself together. But I explained all that. The big hoax.

Several months had passed. After a flurry of newspaper publicity, the whole thing had somehow died down. My town folks in Weatherford probably still harbored a residual suspicion that I was a bit on the nutty side. I was trying to forget the whole thing. Hopefully, other folks would, in time, forget it, too. Especially if I comported myself in the manner of sane men.

Then, one day, the "Colonel" drove up in front of Charlie Kendall's shop. In a nice, reasonably new Buick. Tall, portly, well dressed. All evidence to indicate he had a few bucks salted away in those bitter depression years.

In the rear seat of his Buick I could see another person, wearing a little round black derby hat. Even in those days, the sight of a derby hat was rare enough to warrant a second look.

Peering out from under the brim of that hat were two beady little eyes. At least I prefer to remember them as beady. It fits the story better. Besides, I got a good look at them later.

The Colonel came in, introduced himself and asked for me. By name. Oh, God, here we go again.

It seemed the Colonel knew all about the big hoax story, although he chose to suggest that he considered it more than a hoax. Otherwise, why would he have driven 200 miles from Tulsa, with his passenger, just to consult me?

"Woody, out there, seems to receive messages from supernatural sources," he said, gesturing towards the back seat of the car.

He was suggesting that, if I would accompany them to that sandstone cliff area, Woody might be able to locate the pile of gold, employing his gifts from the "supernatural."

I glanced hesitantly at my boss, Charlie Kendall. Who could know? He might take advantage of the provocation of the moment to brain me with a ball peen hammer. God knows he had threatened to, when I came back to town after the big hoax. Strangely enough, he didn't get fired up at all. He even suggested that it was a slow day in the shop and if I wished to accompany the gentlemen, I was free to do so.

The sudden sweetness and light on the part of my boss cued up a bit of hesitation on my part. Was this some sort of special Charlie Kendall revenge?

And the truth is, I really didn't want to go. I, for one, had never believed the crazy story. I considered myself at least reasonably sane, despite what some of my neighbors thought. I was just at the point of putting the big hoax behind me. So why should I lend myself to any more of this idiotic nonsense?

But the Colonel turned out to be a persuasive talker. A smoothie. It was about 20 miles to the cliff site. He would buy me a good lunch, he said. We could have a nice, quiet ride into the country in his big, shiny Buick and watch Woody call on the supernatural spirits to guide him to the gold.

I took off my greasy overalls and went.

Even today I'm not sure whether the Colonel really believed any of that baloney. Somehow he seemed too worldly wise to be sucked into that kind of madness. Obviously, he had been successful at some kind of businesss or enterprise. He just seemed so darned sensible.

Maybe he simply had a lot of time on his hands and was having a bit of a lark. I'm not sure.

In any case, as we got into the car I sneaked a couple of glances at that beady eyed character in the rear seat. I couldn't help thinking about Charlie Chaplin. The little black derby hat. A long, black, moth eaten wool coat that reached nearly to his ankles - on a hot day.

He was just a little, skinny guy. Not more than five feet and five inches. I'll bet he didn't weight more than 125 pounds, hat, coat and all. It was that face like a mole that got me. Real moley, squeezed down to a point by his pointed little nose. Jugged out ears. Tight, thin lips and those dark, beady eyes.

Woody hardly said a word, just squeaked a word or two, all the way to Clinton. The Colonel more or less ignored him. He kept his word, though, bought me a 50 cent lunch at the Clinton Hotel, which was a pretty good lunch in those days. You could buy a pretty good plate lunch for a quarter. The Colonel ordered one for Woody, too.

I noticed the other people in the hotel apparently saw something moley about Woody, too. They kept sneaking glances at him. Woody didn't even take off his hat or that long black coat, to eat. He just gobbled his food down without saying hardly a word. It was becoming a bit weird by now.

After lunch we drove to the cliff.

It wasn't much of a cliff. Not more than 15 or 20 feet high. The little gully, which ran full of water when it rained hard, made a sharp bend right in front of the cliff. I had always assumed from Boss Charlie Kendall's story that, if there was any gold buried around here, it would be in that sand bank.

In fact, my brother and I had already gone out there with shovels and had dug into that sand bank a bit. We discovered there was hard rock beneath a bit of sand and we gave that up without spending too much sweat on it. Somehow, I believe we always knew the whole story was a lot of baloney. The bones Ernie dug up were from a uniformed soldier, no gold miner.

But in any case, here I was back again and I led the way to the cliff that was about 200 yards from the road. I sort of explained the lay of the land, where the bones were found, and the cliff.

The Colonel had been leading Woody by the arm, almost as if the guy couldn't walk by himself. The long heavy coat flapping around his ankles.

"Woody, you remember there is supposed to be some gold buried around here," said the Colonel. "I want you to find it."

It seemed more like a circus animal trainer giving orders to a chimpanzee rather than speaking to a man.

Woody stood there for a few minutes, sort of blinking those beady black eyes and peering around. He seemed to be looking for something. He was. He was looking for a place to take a pee.

He found that immediate necessity behind a clump of bushes. And then, when he had finished, he started peering around again. This time, however, he clamped those eyes shut so tight it made squint wrinkles all the way down his moley face.

He then stretched his hands out in front of him, sleep walker style, and stood still as a pillar of stone for a few minutes. At first, completely silent. Then he began to mutter something.

I couldn't make it all out but it sounded something like, "Golly, Jesus Lord, show me. Show me." Over and over he repeated this - at least a dozen times. "Show me. Show me."

Several times I was certain I heard that "Golly, Jesus."

Oh, wow. I didn't like this at all. Trying to get Jesus involved in it, too. If it was only some sort of unidentified unnatural spirits he was trying to talk to, that was O.K. with me since I didn't believe in them anyway. And while I wasn't so hooked on Jesus stuff any more, the whole thing was making me a bit uncomfortable.

The Colonel just stood there and watched. Really, he seemed more or less indifferent to the whole show and I still suspected he wasn't really sold on that supernatural power business, either.

After a few minutes, Woody stopped, opened his eyes and just sort of went limp. His arms dropped to his sides like pieces of string.

"I don't think it is working," said the Colonel. "I don't believe he made contact."

Woody had already made that quite clear.

In any case, after a few minutes, Woody started looking around again. This time, beyond the immediate cliff area. Back beyond the cliff and out into the pasture land behind it. He started walking, his eyes open now and not in a sleep walking posture. Just walking.

It was about 150 yards behind the cliff where he stopped, started looking around again. The land was pasture. On the scrawny side. The grass not very lush. A few bushes. A few stones.

I was even more uncomfortable now. What was he doing out there in the pasture? So far from the cliff?

I said to the Colonel, "I didn't think anything was supposed to be out here."

"Well, you never know," said the Colonel. "Maybe your story is not completely accurate anyway, after all this time, going from mouth to mouth. Who knows where the stuff is? Woody might be getting a message now."

From the appearance of things, it could have been true.

The little guy was becoming more animated. His mumbled pleas were more urgent. With his eyes tightly closed and the arms extended, he suddenly began moving again. Faster now, back and forth in a crisscross.

"Show me, Jesus God. Show me. Golly, Jesus."

That "golly" thing really had me bugged. Was it some sort of a key word? Or only some sort of an appendage he had snagged onto somewhere, to include in his act?

In any case, Woody was suddenly going wild. Rushing back and forth, stumbling over bushes and things, but somehow remaining on his feet.

216

That mumbling plea came out in a rushing torrent now. "Show me. Show me." All mixed up with that Jesus and golly stuff.

All at once, in the midst of his trancing rush, Woody plowed into one very big and stubborn bush and fell flat on his face, cushioned only by the bush. The little derby hat rolled onto the ground, the first time it had been off his head that day. It revealed a real mouse tousle of black hair. A moment of compassion welled up inside of me.

Why did he have to go through all this? Why was the Colonel doing this to him?

I started to rush towards him, to help him back on his feet but the little guy managed it by himself, even with the heavy coat flapping around his ankles. Strangely enough, he had kept his eyes clamped tightly shut even when he fell. He scrambled to his feet. As he stood, his arms were once more in that sleep walking position. It was the Colonel who jammed the derby hat back on his head and guided him around the bush.

Somehow, it seemed, the tumble and the fall had not even knocked him out of his trance, or whatever it was. He was rushing wildly again, pleading, praying. Whatever.

Gosh, was this for real?

Was it possible that some sort of unearthly power was guiding and propelling him? Sending him into this frenzy of activity?

I didn't want to believe any of it, refused to believe it, but I was becoming entranced, too. Just by the spectacle of the thing. It was all so real. Something was certainly driving the moley little guy.

I'm not sure exactly how long it went on. Perhaps five minutes. Maybe 10 or 15. Fifteen minutes would be a long time for such intense activity. Sweat was pouring down the little guy's face. My compassion machine was in high gear now. I was truly feeling sorry for the little moley and wanted it all to stop.

But somehow I was helpless, too, caught up in the intensity of the thing. I believe if I had indeed rushed in and tried to stop Woody, the Colonel would in turn have tried to stop me. So, I just stood there in a bit of a trance myself.

Then, suddenly, the whole thing was over. Woody just stopped, opened his eyes and dropped the arms once more in that limp, rag-like motion. He was limp. Wrung out. Whatever driving force had sent him into the frenzy was gone. Pooped out.

Perspiration pouring down his face. That monstrous black coat on such a hot day.

The Colonel walked up to Woody.

"Tell me, Woody, did you get the message? Did you see the gold?" he demanded.

Woody looked at him, so strangely for a moment. As if not comprehending. His eyes almost a blank. As if he did not even recognize the Colonel, his friend.

After a moment or two, Woody's face began to relax. He shook his head. No. No message. No vision. No gold.

I looked at the Colonel, trying to decide if he was disappointed or not. Hard to tell. You couldn't read the Colonel's face too well.

The Colonel waited a few minutes, then sat on a big stone. Woody was recovering his breath after the mad rush but he did not sit down. He just stood there, trying perhaps to remember where he had been in those trancelike moments.

I suppose it would have been futile to try to understand what the litttle guy was thinking. I only know he looked more and more like a pathetic little Charlie Chaplin figure each moment. A rag doll hanging on a string. Chaplain had been such a genius at creating those effects.

After a while, the Colonel got up and walked over to Woody.

"Want to try again?" he asked.

Woody never really replied. He squinted up his eyes a few more times. He would close them momentarily but without clamping them shut as before. A bit later he walked around and made a few more feeble attempts. The sleep walker stance. Eyes closed. "Show me. Show me."

But the intensity was gone and never again during that afternoon was he animated by forces which seemed to be coming from somewhere outside his own soul. After a few such half-hearted tries he simply quit. Gave up. He was physically and mentally exhausted.

I began looking around in that area where Woody had been so excited. Was it possible that gold was buried around here somewhere? I looked for a likely spot. There was none. All spots in that pastureland looked alike to me. Grass. Rocks. Bushes. Where would a man dig?

It would have taken a bulldozer to rip up that whole hill and bulldozers had hardly been invented yet. A steam shovel, perhaps, to gouge and rip at the pasture turf?

The Colonel must have read my thoughts.

"It would take a lot of digging to dig up this whole area," he said. Considering his age and the size of his paunch, he didn't sound as if he were seriously suggesting that he was up to much digging. I knew he couldn't ask Woody to do it. As for me, I was still too skeptical to be allowed to be bullied into any voluntary hard labor.

I couldn't see any gold lying under that pasture sod.

Or at that sand bank near the cliff, for that matter. And Woody had virtually ignored that site.

I doubt if the Colonel had even enough faith to bring a shovel along. Unless he had it hidden in the trunk of his car. I didn't ask him.

After some moments of seeming to ponder the situation, the Colonel said, "Let's go." That was all.

We went. The Colonel was once more leading Woody by the hand. His rag doll puppet.

The little guy neitheir protested nor showed any motivation of his own now, other than to move his feet enough to stay on them at the side of the Colonel. A listless little bundle of disturbed humanity, except for those few moments of flashing fire out on the pasture hillside.

And even that, when I began to examine it in the face of cold logic, was nothing more intense than some of the frenzies I had seen in the tents of the Holly Roller revivalists. Something self imposed, drawing upon some dormant, inner fire which might bring savage intensity to the soul for a few wild moments.

Doesn't the soul sometimes stir mightily at the sound of a rousing marching song? The crash of a mighty Beethoven symphony? Even the frenzy of a tense football games?

As we drove back to Weatherford, the Colonel had little to say. Woody, huddled in the rear seat, was completely silent. Spent. Like a wind-up puppet whose spring had run down.

I wandered what his track record was in that "supernatural" field. What had he done to convince the Colonel it was worth all that trip, the time and expense of driving to Weatherford and Clinton? Maybe some third party had sold the Colonel on Woody's ability. Maybe there was indeed nothing. Maybe the Colonel had only used it all as an excuse for a bit of a trip into the country. A strange search for adventure.

Back in Weatherford, the Colonel let me out of the car and, as a matter of courtesy, went into the shop to speak to Charlie. The proper thing. To say goodbye.

"Well, what happened?" Charlie asked.

"Not much, really," said the Colonel. "I don't believe Woody got a real message. We gave it up."

I permitted myself the luxury of toying with an idea - that the Colonel might only be saying that for our benefit. Maybe later, without Woody, without me, he might return to the site and do some digging. Bring in machines.

But it was only silly mind play. The whole idea was a bit too absurd for that. It couldn't be done in secret anyway. He would have to get permission from the land owner. No, I decided, the episode was really over.

I did feel sorry for that pathetic little moley in the rear seat of the Colonel's car. It couldn't have been a Charlie Chaplin act. Woody was only Woody - and Woody was woozy.

Later, after the Colonel and his little puppet had left, Charlie grilled me about what had really happened out there at the cliff site. I told him.

"The little guy, Woody, is crazy," I said. "He's woozy."

I told him about everything except that strange fire which had seemed to animate the little guy for a few trancing minutes. I sort of wanted to keep that to myself. After all, as I said, I considered myself sane and I wanted to keep it that way.

In any case, when I told people about the incident later, I started referring to the little guy as Woozy Woody. The lilt of the words caught my fancy. The name would do.

And later, when I put the skull up in the cabinet in the den, I started using the same term in reference to the skull. "Woozy Woody."

That momentary spell of Woody's trance that I had seen and shared, out there on the pasture hillside, was mostly gone. Had I transferred the identity of the little mole guy to my empty and varnished skull so that now there were two Woodys? Perhaps each was a bit symbolic of the other - forming the web that knit the story together.

Subconsciously, perhaps, it was even a form of revenge for being subjected to Gordon's crazy hoax. I didn't like being pushed around, having folks suggest I was a bit on the nutty side.

Chapter Eighteen – Wildcat Bus

I guess my career as a wildcat bus driver began cracking up on that day in Bakersfield when I fell in love.

Honey blonde hair. And those alluring, pleading smiles that could have melted the heart of a polar bear.

"Mama went to heaven," said the tyke of only three years.

"We didn't have money for the doctor," said the boy of four.

It was the chapter of the Grapes of Wrath story John Steinbeck never wrote. Perhaps because it didn't happen in time. But it did happen and was part of the story.

In some ways it was probably even more tragic than the original "wrath" story. In Steinbeck's story, his people, the "Oakies," hit bottom. In the wildcat bus phase of the story the bottom dropped out. And I became involved.

The "wrath" story was the uprooting of a people. People like my father and mother, whose parents pioneered in the opening of the vast prairie land of Oklahoma, what had been Indian Territory.

Perhaps it would have been expecting too much of these early day farmers for them to have known that in the very act of plowing that vast expanse of prairie they would eventually bring tragedy to themselves or at least their children.

For the native prairie grass had not only fed the buffalo and the Indian ponies for centuries but had provided that vital protective covering for the soil underneath. The plow would lay bare the soil to eroding force of the great winds which swept down through central America, across Nebraska, Kansas and Oklahoma. On into the flatland of Texas.

To the people, it would be a double blow of tragedy. First would come, in the 1930's, the most cruel and devastating economic

221

depression of all time, destroying the economic existence of workers and farmers.

Then it was as if the gods of nature, or perhaps the gods of the once resident Indians, had finally turned their wrath upon the palefaces who had driven the Indians out of this land.

For now it was the curse of drouth, marching in unison with that economic depression, which would turn the soil into dust and the dust into clouds as the rains departed and the winds came. They always came, those winds.

They had been a hardy breed, those settlers and their children. Used to hard times and hard work. But now, under the triple blows of the deppression, the drouth and the dust storms, they had reached the limits of their endurance. Hunger, stark and fearful, rode the land. It was blowing away. The mortgage holders, the banks, were taking what was left of it.

And so the "wrath" story. Of a people pulling their meager stakes and heading for California - the Promised Land. There, they were told, a small trickle of milk and honey still flowed. All chimera, of course. Overwhelmed by the coming of so many poor, with nothing really to offer them, California simply became a staging point for more hunger, suffering and despair. California did not even have jobs for its "own," much less for the horde of hungry Oakies that swept in over their border.

All this, Steinbeck knew and wrote. His epic for our time.

But then came that phase of the story which did not get into the books: The Return. As those people, the ones who survived, gathered the last remnants of their strength and tried to go back home again.

To what? They had left the dust bowl because it had become a frying pan in which they - body and soul - had been in the process of being slowly destroyed. If California had now revealed itself as nothing more than another frying pan, perhaps even hotter and more destructive, what now would they find if they went home again?

They had seemingly severed their ties to Oklahom, Arkansas, Kansas and Texas. They had sold, for a pittance, their last meager possessions to finance the trip west. A few dollars for tires, piston rings and gas for the battered old cars they might own. What tie could now lure them back?

It was a tenuous one, that last remaining tie. It was the relatives they had left behind. For the dust bowl had not completely emptied itself.

There had been those a bit tougher, perhaps. Or more stubborn. Or a bit more fortunate in having some pittance of an existence. These had been the ones to stay. Perhaps some had stayed because they lacked even the means of leaving.

My Dad and his family had been among those who stayed. Dad's restlessness had taken him to California and Oregon in an earlier time when things had not been so desperate. But even then we had suffered the rolling stone existence that sentenced our family eternally to the life of the "have nots."

Perhaps it was exactly for this reason, because Dad had already been there and had learned a lesson of sorts, that he now clung to his fragile roots in Oklahoma. Roots which seemed to have less and less grasp on the eroding soil, year by year. But we stayed, somehow surviving.

Amid all that - a growing boy. Seemingly born with the gift of making broken things whole, making things, repairing mechanical things which broke down.

But even when I did obtain my first job in Charlie Kendall's motor machine shop, I was there to learn and not to earn. Apprentices were not paid, I was told. My salary, $1 a week. Of course, I was in high school and worked only afternoons and Saturdays. But it was an exciting adventure, there among the lathes, drill presses and cylinder grinders. Fingers and brain reaching out for a new existence.

But also doomed - because tough times remained tough - doomed to a sort of fringe existence for the next 10 years, even when I found other jobs. Money? There wasn't any. Skilled mechanics worked for $12 to $18 a week. The lucky ones who found jobs, that is.

Grease monkey. Mechanic. Blacksmith. Machinist. Painter. Auto body man. All these were the arts I grasped into my eager hands in that time. At $1 a day. A few times it was $10 a week.

Until one grand splurge of work brought on by still another freak of nature, the worst hailstorm in our history, which sent small boulders of ice hurtling earthward.

The frozen chunks damaged so many cars, hundreds of them, that our body shop was buried with work for months. It was insurance money, for the lucky ones who had insurance, that financed that splurge.

In the midst of all this, I presented my bosses with a surprise by "inventing" a machine to smooth the hail dents out of the steel tops of cars. It cut the work time in half. My salary was suddenly $25 a week. I was rich.

So rich, in fact, I bought a Packard. Which, in turn, became the propelling force which pushed me towards that wildcat bus thing. Bakersfield, California and the honey blonde hair were closer now.

First those cars - mine and those of the Okies.

My Packard wasn't a new one. Even my "riches" couldn't possibly have managed that. It was a year old. A dismal sight. A clunker. It had belonged to a building contractor from Oklahoma City who had used the brand new car more as a truck than as a car. Made an unholy mess out of it in one year and traded it in.

"You can have it for $175 if you'll take it like it is," the dealer said. I took it .

The machine was a natural for a young guy who liked to fix things. Straighten the banged up fenders. Give it a paint job. New upholstery. Rework the engine a bit. In a few weeks, one of the slickest and best running cars in town. Go 70 all day long, like a breeze.

Now about the Okie cars - they weren't.

Steinbeck knew about that, too. Those old clunkers the Okies had spent some of their last dollars on to make them fit for travel, but barely, for the trip west.

Many of the old cars never made it. Expired on the side of the road. Most of them that made it to California got sold out there for peanuts in a market glutted with junkers. Brought maybe the cash value of their tires and batteries. Enough, maybe, for another week or two of groceries.

Perhaps a few of the cars even survived unto the day when their owners reached that stage of despair in which they yearned to go back home. But then, faced with the reality that the old clunker wasn't up to another trek across the country, the owner would sell it to help finance the trip by other means.

And thus, born from that need for some "other means," emerged the wildcat bus. To bring the Okies back to where it all started. To where, in a sense, it would all end.

The only desperate hope that remained for them was that their relatives back home who had stuck it out, tragically poor and living on the fringe of existence, would at least be a bit less hostile than Californians fighting to keep what little they had. The hope that somewhere would be a bit of biscuit dough and flour gravy for the returning Pilgrims. Enough to keep life in hungry bodies.

But in the midst of all this struggle to return was another happening so incredible it was nearly impossible to believe it could happen - for that westward trek had not ceased. Still some, drawn like the moth to the flame, came westward.

Was it possible that word had not yet reached the Dust Bowl that the milk and honey fountains had dried up? But completely. Word that should have prevented any new Pilgrims from attempting a westward trek. But, somewhow, without logical explanation, some still headed west.

A tragic, purposeless shuffling of human souls back and forth across the continent. The endless search for a grail which had ceased to exist, east or west.

Certainly the westward migration had slowed from a flood to something less but it continued. Now, those heading west were less often families and more often the young who insisted on believing the dream. Refusing to believe the tales of shattered dreams and despair of those who had gone before. Insisting on believing that their luck, somewhow, would be much better. The eternal optimism of youth.

Being young in a time of depression meant they didn't even possess the battered jalopies that had wheeled the first tide westward. Their purses, if they had any, were about empty.

The regular bus companies, Greyhound and such, would take you through Oklahoma City to Los Angeles for $23. Most of the returning Pilgrims could only dream of that kind of money.

So, in such a picture, the wildcatters were probably inevitable. There simply had to be a few people out there, lucky enough to own a car of some kind, sturdy enough to make the trip. Individuals who would offer to haul this desperate human cargo for less than the price of a bus ticket. Most of the wildcatters were victims themselves, perhaps, without jobs and hungry for the slimmest buck.

At first, they would offer to carry a "body" for half price - say $12 to $14. Since they were not insured or licensed as public carriers, they could make a buck on the deal. They were willing, as illegal operators of carriers, to dodge the lawmen.

Later, as more of the drivers got into the act, the very nature of competition would insure that even those low prices would be cut. Somebody would offer to take you through for $11 or even $10. Not many bucks left for profit but still the wildcatters rolled.

Then that other amazing adjunct to the wildcat picture, the equally wildcat travel agencies. Also ignored by the historians of that tragic time. But it was common knowledge that at one time, at the peak of the wildcat activity, Los Angeles had as many as 350 wildcat travel agencies to serve the wildcat buses.

Their operators, again victims of the depression themselves, out of work and trying to grab a buck of their own out of this sordid traffic in human bodies. They would set up shop in a tiny store front with a splashy sign in the window, "Need To Go Home? Oklahoma City For $12." Sometimes only $10. They lured and rounded up the "bodies" for the wildcat bus men - for a small cut of the "take."

Most of the travel agency men operated them as adjuncts to another small business, a hamburger grille or a hock shop. A used clothing store, perhaps.

Technically, these operations were illegal. But despite an occasional protest from legitimate bus companies, California lawmen chose to ignore the open existence of these "bootleg" operations. Both the wildcatters and the body finders. Simply because it was more important to rid California of this horde of unwanted job seekers in a time when there were no jobs. Enforcing the law could only bring more woe to the enforcers, filling their jails with more mouths to feed.

It was inevitable, of course, that these agency operators were well aware of all this. How else could they dare to flaunt their illegal body commerce with the bold and gaudy painted signs in the store fronts?

Back in Oklahoma City, and in other centers of the Dust Bowl, the agencies were neither so numerous nor so flauntingly open. The badge men at least made a semblance of enforcement there. On the other hand, just as with the whiskey bootleggers, if a man needed an illegal agency he could always find one.

It was in New Mexico, the wildcatters said, where the enforcement was the toughest. No one seemed to know exactly why. The state was neither a major source nor a major recipient of the human floods. Only a stretch of miles that had to be crossed. But there it was, the danger zone. Perhaps the state government of this commonwealth had determined that there was indeed a bit of revenue in fines, or in confiscation of automobiles. The jails in New Mexico, the "catters" said, were the toughest..

Somewhere, sometime, it was inevitable that I, hanging around the automobile crowd, should become aware of the wildcatter story. Even in our small town we had a few of the "catters." Pudge, for one, who operated a small hamburger grille, together with his wife. There would come times when he would simply disappear for a few days, running the wildcat trail in his Ford V-8, while Mrs. P. continued slinging hotcakes and hamburgers.

"If you're careful you can make a few extra bucks," he said.

With hungry ears I listened to his tales of brushes with the law in New Mexico, the long rides through the night, a few non-scheduled adventures in Los Angeles. I was young. I had the itch for adventure. I had my Packard.

Of course, I also still had my job at the body shop but there came times, expecially after the big hail splurge subsided, when business was slow. My bosses didn't mind if I disappeared for a few days.

It started before I intended for it to.

Pudge simply showed up at the shop on one of those quiet days, said he had a load for the "west" but he couldn't get away. "You want to take them?" he asked. "You can have 'em. I won't even charge you a cut.

"I can even give you the names of some Los Angeles agents who can get you a load coming back."

There stood my shiny, eager Packard, ready to roll. What adventure minded young buck wouldn't have gone?

First, I had to learn a few tricks of the trade from Pudge.

"Don't carry any luggage tied to the outside of your car. You either get it inside or make your passengers leave it at home. The outside stuff is a tip off to the troopers," Pudge said.

Then, "Be sure to memorize the name and home town of each passenger. And be sure to explain it all to them. If you get stopped, your are just a bunch of friends out for a vacation trip, sharing expenses. Nothing illegal to that. Warn your riders that if they don't stick to that story they'll land in jail, just the same as you."

I briefed my riders but my sleek, shiny Packard must have thrown the lawmen off for I never had a challenge.

You had to carry at least five passengers, making six "bodies" in your car, to make your buck out of it. And you rolled all the way through, no stops except to gas up and grab a hamburger. If you stopped for a sleep, even at $1 a night, that and the extra food would eat up all your profits. Besides, your passengers didn't have the money for stops anyway. It was 26 hours from Oklahoma City to Los Angeles, if things went smoothly.

Somehow, none of us ever considered it an outlaw occupation, running the wildcat trails. You were just trying to make an "honest buck" in hard times. If you didn't carry the "bodies," somebody else would You didn't even consider it cheating on the lawful bus companies because you knew the kind of people you were carrying didn't have the fares for Greyhound anyway. If they couldn't ride a wildcatter, they didn't ride.

In fact, I never even became a regular. Just a load now and then when the work in the shop was slow. Maybe Pudge would come up with that extra load he couldn't carry. He seemed to have a way of finding them and his hamburger grille was known as a sort of unofficial travel agency in our town.

Nobody was getting rich at the wildcatting business anyway. There were times when, considering the wear and tear on my shiny Packard, I wondered if I was really making any money at all.

Competition among the "catters" was getting rougher, too. Some drivers had cut the price down as low as $9 a body. I even heard of $8. That was a lot of traveling for nickles. Even if you didn't have insurance or permits. What if you wrecked your car?

In fact, I did have one small wreck in, of all places, New Mexico. The lady driving the other car insisted on calling the troopers. I sweated mightily on that one until my nervous brain came up with the idea of suggesting to my "bodies" that they take a stroll and stay out of sight until the trooper left.

No sweat. The trooper turned out to be one of the friendly ones. No questions about the passengers. Home free.

On one trip when the passengers' luggage turned out to be a bit on the bulky side, I left the spare tire at home so I'd have more luggage space inside. 1 regretted that decision, too, after I hit a detour where they were using chopped rocks as roadfill and split a tire. Had to walk four miles to the nearest service station for a tire. After that I even stuffed bits of luggage under the hood. Anything to make room for that precious spare tire.

It didn't take long for the glamour of the thing to wear off. I even began to suspect that Pudge wasn't really being so generous. He was probably getting fed up, just as I was. The lean pickings and the tough grind on a good car.

These 26 or 27 hour runs with no sleep. Roll. Roll. Roll. Coffee by the gallon to try to stay awake. No-Doz pills. And still the eyes would droop. Until you got that warning rumble of a tire hitting the shoulder of the road.

A wave of sheer terror would jerk you back into wakefulness. For 15 or 20 minutes at least. Fight, fight to keep the eyes open. The senses functioning. You could, for example, occupy your thoughts with visions of your shiny Packard lying smashed up in a ditch. Perhaps a bit of blood mixed in.

On one trip, when it seemed impossible to stay awake a moment longer, I turned the wheel over to one of the passengers while I tried to take a snooze. It had been raining and water washed a sheet of slick mud across a low place in the highway. It was the rocking of the car that jarred me awake that time, the Packard in a spinning slide. I then had to make the decision that if anybody were to be allowed to privilege of wrecking that Packard, it would have to be me. I never surrendered the wheel again.

The impetus for one of my runs was a cry for help from one of my own aunts who had allowed herself to be lured to California by a son-in-law. Somewhere in the vineyards near Lodi, they had also hit their bottomless bottom. Two of her older sons left behind in Oklahoma managed to raise a part of my "fee" to bring them home. The remainder was a promise. I never got that "balance" so that trip ended up in the loss column.

The tragedy of the senseless migration and second migration was coming closer to home now. Perhaps what I had seen was becoming a sufficiency.

If all that was not enough, some of the agency people turned out to be blood suckers, too. On the make for the last buck. Even if they had to lie a bit.

First, they promise you that they had a load. Then, when you show up, ready to roll, the sad stories. "This rider only got $10. I'll give you $9 of it." Always the suspicion that the story wasn't true and Mr. Agent had pocketed the difference. I had sworn I wouldn't run for less than $12. But in the end I did. One never really knew the truth.

But something was becoming inevitable. The day when I would make my decision that I was making my last run.

That honey blonde hair.

My westward bound passengers wanted to go to Bakersfield, that trip, instead of to Los Angeles. Bakersfield was no hot spot for picking up a return load. But to avoid the 100 extra miles of driving to Los Angeles, I would give it a try.

Yup, slim pickings. Not more than half a dozen agencies in town and I was a complete stranger to them. Even Pudge hadn't been there.

"No luck, friend. Not much moving this week." I made all the travel agencies. Maybe they wanted a bit of palm greasing. I wouldn't

"Maybe tomorrow," said one or two of the agents. To stay over another night would eat up more of the slim profits. Hamburgers and bed, even if the beds were only $1 a night. But I stayed.

Next day, still no load. I was about to head for Los Angeles when one of the agents spoke his piece.

"I know you've got to make expenses but all I've got is two good riders. Then I've got three more on my hands who are really broke. Only $21 between them. I've had several drivers turn them down. Nobody could make a nickel off of them. But I'll let you look at 'em if you like. They're in bad shape. Need help. If you can take 'em I wouldn't charge you a nickel. You can have it all."

Normally, I would have walked out and headed the Packard towards Los Angeles. No use burning up your car for nothing. It would cost a few gallons of gas to get to Los Angeles but at least I knew some agents there.

But there had been a note of urgency in the agent's voice, too. As if he had been pleading for someone. I suppose he was. It was that crazy impulse which led me to say. "Where are they?"

"Right here in the back room" he said, taking a step towards a door. Again that crazy impulse which led me to follow him as he flung the door open.

And then I saw them. On the floor on an old blanket, a man and two kids. The girl perhaps three and the boy about four. At first I only glanced at the man. Small. Humble. Crouching in defeat. I did notice that he was clean. It was the sight of the children which grabbed my attention. God, that beautiful golden hair. And those little angel faces.

As they looked at me they both managed to smile. Entreating, questioning smiles, somehow pleading for something they weren't old enough to understand. So utterly beautiful, both of them. Little angels with golden crowns. The beauty so vivid as to be almost shocking. I had not expected anything like this.

They had a battered little suitcase and a "bindle" beside them, their total possessions. The man took a comb from his pocket and began combing that golden hair. The little ones had been lying on the blanket and their hair had become just a bit on the tousled side. It was, somehow, as if the father was aware of that golden treasure as the only treasure he had. He must tend to it with his comb.

Then the defeated father got to his feet and offered me a hand. As the agent had said, several drivers had already been there and turned their backs. Now I stood there, an awkward young red head. A stranger. Would I turn my back, too?

"Their mother is dead," the man said. "Died a couple of months ago. We're finished. I've got to get back. I've got some kinfolks at Fort Smith, Arkansas. If we can just get back there we will manage some way."

"I only go as far as Oklahoma City," I said. "And the agent tells me you don't even have enough money to get that far."

"If I could get to the railroad station at Oklahoma City," he said, "I could get my kinfolks to come pick us up there. The little ones can sit on my lap. They won't take full spaces. I've got $21. I'll give it all to you." His eyes were doing most of the pleading.

Perhaps, if it had only been the man asking, I could have turned my back and walked out on him. It was when I looked at those golden children that I could feel something creeping up in my throat. Such singular beauty. Or, were all children golden and precious?

I didn't give the man his answer at that moment. We walked out of the back room, the agent and I, closing the door.

"How long have they been here?" I asked.

"Three days. I been giving them a bite of food."

Maybe all those agents weren't crooks, with hearts of flint.

And I, at that moment, was becoming aware of the fact that I wasn't going to be making any money this trip.

I went back into the back room. "O. K. I'll take you to Oklahoma City," I said.

It was in the man's eyes that I read the prayer of thanks. And then it was the little boy who spoke. "Are we going home?"

"Yes, you're going home," I told him.

Going home? What did this child know about home? Something he had heard his father speak of, perhaps?

Could a child of four understand what was going on? The utter defeat in his father's life? His own? Knowing only that anything was home if it was better than this faded blanket lying on a stranger's floor.

As for the little girl, that tiny bit of shimmering, golden haired beauty, her offering at that moment was another of those pleading smiles. At that moment I believe it would have melted the engine block in my Packard.

231

It was late that night before the agent had the other passengers rounded up and we were ready to roll. It was going to be another of those long nights. It would be morning before we stopped for gas and a bit of breakfast.

I, and the other passengers, headed for a hamburger joint near the service station. The father, leaving the children in the car, headed for a grocery store that was just opening. He came back with a nickel box of soda crackers and a tiny sliver of cheese. He proceeded to divide the food for the children.

Somehow I had forgotten to think about how they would eat on the journey if he gave me all his money.

"How much money did you have left when you gave me the $21?" I said.

"I had 47 cents left," he said. "We'll get by." It was not a plea. It was only a statement. That was when I walked back to the hamburger grille and spent some money. I was trying very hard to feel tough, emotionless, but it wasn't working very well.

Next time we stopped for lunch I simply told the father to bring the children and come with me. I no longer gave a damn what the other passengers thought.

It was fall time. Somewhere in New Mexico it began to rain and it never stopped. All the way through the Texas panhandle and into Oklahoma it rained steady. Rain. Rain. Rain. It was still raining when we hit Oklahoma City and I let the other passengers out of the car.

Then, as I began to head for the railroad station, my big mouth got me into trouble again. I began asking questions about those "arrangements" for his kinfolks to pick him up.

It was easy now to see that the man had been lying. Yes, he had those kinfolks at Forth Smith but they lived far out in the country. He had never been able to contact them.

He simply knew he was heading in the direction of the only "home" he knew. Carrying with him the hope that somewhere was a bed and a bit of food for him and those golden angels. From kinfolk nearly as poor as he.

I had been watching the children on the whole trip. God, how could a man keep his eyes away from such beauty? The boy, bright as a chrome button, had talked about when his mother had died, after she had been ill for months.

"We couldn't take her to the doctor because we didn't have any money," he said. The father tried to hush him. But the little girl angel was talking a bit, too. "Mama went to heaven," she said.

DEAR GOD, I'M ONLY A BOY

They had been such good children on that trip. Never cried. Not even the little one. So quiet most of the time, as if tragedy had somehow made them older. More sober. As if it had robbed them of their childhood.

A few times, the father, apologetically had quietly asked if I could stop a moment so the little ones could "go." And that was it.

We found the railroad station. I stopped the car and they got out, the father and the two golden children.

I started to say something but the father, sensing what I was about to say, interrupted me. "Just leave us here. There is a waiting room with benches. We'll manage. You've already done so much. God will bless you."

For a moment I considered doing exactly as the man said. My eyes were once more leaden for lack of sleep. My bones ached from the long drive in the endless rain. My bed at home was only 75 miles away.

But it was not to be. Not now.

I almost barked it, like a command when I spoke, to cover what I was feeling inside. "Get back in the car. We're going to Fort Smith."

What a night. The torture of the damned. It was still raining and we had gone barely a dozen miles east of Oklahoma City when we found the road under construction. A detour.

That detour route, battered by hours of pouring rain and the pounding of cars and heavy trucks, had virtually disintegrated. It was no longer a road, only a gravel track gutted by a million potholes. Potholes filled with water so you couldn't even see them in the darkness, only hit them.

Now I truly had reason to regret my decision. But I had made it and I would keep my promise.

Fort Smith was 200 miles to the east and if my poor Packard, seemingly being pounded to bits, held together we were going to make it. That car must have hit at least 90 per cent of those million potholes between Oklahoma City and Fort Smith. Bang. Bang. Bang. Hour after hour. it was impossible to travel more than 15 or 20 miles an hour. Any faster would only invited disaster - on a night when nobody could afford it.

My three "passengers" just huddled there as if afraid to speak. Feaing, perhaps, that I might yet put them out on the road and head for home. I am sure they could hear my whispered curses at this bedeviled road and knew the hell I was going through. My soul, that of a mechanic, was the kind that could feel an affinity for a thing like a motor car, as if it were something alive and precious to me. The hurt being transmitted to this vehicle of iron and steel beneath me was being transmitted to my gut as well.

If I had never had reason to respect the quality that the Packard people built into their cars, I did now. It was magnificent. Indestructible. But at the rate we were going, it was going to take forever. It almost did.

I don't know what time it was when we finally arrived in Fort Smith. Perhaps I had lost all sense of time. My brain, my bones, an aching mass. From the endless pounding, the endless strain of watching that road of horror, hour upon hour upon hour. The lack of sleep for two nights.

This time, in Fort Smith, I didn't argue when the man insisted that I leave them at the train station and not try to drive into the country to find his kinfolks. I was so numb my brain was no longer functioning normally. My only thought and longing was for sleep. Sleep. Sleep. Sleep.

"I have a friend here in Fort Smith. He will take me to my kinfolks," the man said. "God will bless you for what you have done."

At that moment I felt no blessings. Only pain. And numbness. So I left them, the father and those two golden angels. Forever.

And I still had that return trip over that seemingly endless and heartless road. Only now it would be impossible to face it until I had parked beside the road and slept for several hours.

Back home, I took a day off to catch up with my sleep before heading back to the shop and work. It was perhaps some 10 days later when Pudge dropped by again.

"I've got another load. Want to take them?" he said.

It took me all of a half second to say no.

It wasn't that I was only weary of those long, dreary night hours of fighting sleep. The uncertain and meager profits. The pounding of my precious Packard.

The real fear in my heart was that once again, somewhere, sometime, I would meet another angel with dimpled cheeks and honey blonde hair.

Chapter Nineteen - Chien

After I met Chien, one of the first things I discovered about him was that he had bed teeth. From a crazy habit of carrying rocks around in his mouth.

Then I discovered that he was somewhat of a philospher - if a dog can be a philospher.

Chien's philosophy had to do with those rocks that the carried in his mouth, coupled with a strange and fatalistic attitude toward people. There was a certain internationalism tied in with it all, forced on him, perhaps, by the inescapable instinct for survival.

We discussed it all, as thoroughly as one can discuss things with a dog and he convinced me that there was indeed a connection between the rocks and his philosophy. I must admit that when it all started I thought Chien was a bit balmy.

It was not exactly incidental that Chien, the French word meaning "dog," had no real name. Or if he had, it had long ago been swept away by the mad whirl of international history which had engulfed the animal. So I used the simple expedient of calling him Chien. It was in France, near Granville, that I met him during the dying stages of World War II.

Chien was about the size of a wire haired fox terrier and in some ways reminded me of one but it was impossible to escape the fact that the exact nature of his ancestry was questionable. But he made up for any lack of patrician ancestry with mysterious power of penetrating a man's reserve. Even after you realized he did not have the slightest intention of surrendering any of his own.

I had never met a dog quite like Chien. His short, wiry coat, partly black and partly white, the white spots brindled by black specks, was worn with a complete air of indifference. In this respect he was much like any other dog. It was his singular and stubborn mode of behavior, that deep pool of melancholy wisdom peering out from his dark eyes, which set him apart. These things - and his insistence on carrying rocks in his mouth.

This peculiar dog lacked the normal dog enthusiasm for mankind. Oh, he was willing, by necessity, to accomodate the humans around him. He was never hostile. But missing were the bursts of frenzied joy with which most dogs greet the slightest act or gesture of kindness. The wagging of the tail, the happy yipping of the voice, those spontaneous reactions which most happy dogs normally display after being given food, a few words of praise, a stroke on the head, a scratch behind the ear.

In this lack of such qualities, Chien reminded me of the French people among whom he lived. Especially the older ones who had lived through two tragic wars.

Oh, these people did not lack all the signs of animation that mark humans. It was their souls which were so sorely wounded by having seen too much, of having lived too much, in a diseased atmosphere that can destroy the soul. Does a dog have a soul, too?

These people had lived through one devastating war from which they had tried to recover. Then they had been plunged into a still more devastating war in which the issues and consequences had been an enemy occupation lasting five dreadful years and forcing them to bend into an accomodation with bitter reality. The enemy.

They had then lived through a liberation which could only be a source of more disillusionment because of the vast devastation it dragged along in its wake. A devastation which lay around them like a huge sea of despond. A liberation which, after a few heady days of joy, could only tell them now that they must draw upon their own moral resources to create a new existance. Somehow, for the moment, they did not have those needed resources.

It was inevitable that I saw so much of this mood reflected in Chien. For his character - if a dog is not allowed to have a soul - had been warped and shaped by the same tragic events. Only in a place like this could you find a dog so changed from the normal doglike qualities one considers inherent in the canine being.

Someone might suggest that Chien's strange and passive spirit was simply due to old age, that the juices of life were ebbing. They might point to my revelation about the bad teeth as proof of age. But it would not have been true. Any true lover of dogs has long ago learned to recognize that peculiar grizzling and greying which betrays old age in a dog. Chien did not possess these signs.

It was those stones which had worn down his teeth.

Chien and I had several arguments about those stones and I tried to convince him that while I respected his dog given rights to carry inanimate objects around in his mouth, it would do much to improve his physical welfare if he would agree to a nice, smooth stick of wood. A rubber ball was not available. But to carry those rough, gritty stones!

I would take his stone away from his mouth and throw it as far as I could into a thicket of bushes. Then I would place a nice, smooth stick in his mouth and pat his head encouragingly.

It was an argument I could only lose. He would quickly discard the stick with disgust and then go scrambling into the thicket looking for his stone. If he couldn't find it he would return with a gentle whine of disappointment and contemplate me with so much sadness in his face. He would then go searching for another stone. In time, I simply had to give up.

Chien's memory may not have been too clear on the point of who taught him that trick about carrying rocks in his mouth instead of a stick or a ball. It was one of the things he preferred to hide behind that inscrutable mein he carried about with him so stubbornly. It may even have been that by this time he understood more about the Germans and wanted to deny that it was the Germans who taught him about stones. It was a time in which it was easy for the Americans and the French to blame anything bad on the Germans.

Carrying things is a very simple trick in the dog world. A human merely throws an object and the dog runs off to recover it. In orthodox dog circles it is appropriate to wag one's tail and show signs of enthusiasm when one brings back the object and lays it at the feet of the "master." This, Chien would not do.

There is the human side of this equation, too, for in the normal course of things, if the dog performs his part of the trick, the expectation is that there should be some kind of reward. At least a pat on the head and a friendly word of encouragement. Food, of course, would be preferable. The Germans probably gave him food. At least, at times.

Any dog of normal intelligence soon learns the next step in the little act of play. He learns that it is often profitable, expecially if one is hungry, to initiate the action on his own. He simply picks up an object, for Chien it was a stone, brings it to the feet of his human master, lays it down and whines gently.

It would be reasonable to guess, in the case of Chien, that he had lost some measure of spontaneous enthusiasm because of the countless times he had been disappointed. It wasn't because people were reluctant to reward a properly performing dog, it was simply because unusally they had no food. If the dog insisted, however, upon bringing his offering of a stone and whining for attention, it was easy to toss a stone a few times with the full knowledge that this would be the extent of his participation.

But Chien persisted in the routine because he was often hungry and the memory that in the past, such a performance had earned him a few morsels of food. If the food episodes were becoming less frequent now, it was still a routine to which a dog must be committed through successful past experience. Even if he had forgotten how to wag his tail and yip with joy.

Chien's internationalism was not a matter of choice. It had probably been forced upon him. I had inquired in the village about Chien's past and the French villagers had confirmed that Chien had been properly born a French dog in the nearby town of Jullouville. When German troops invaded France in 1940 and chose the dormitories of the big, rambling school for boys on the lake at Granville, for their use as a barracks, they picked up Chien and took him along.

When I asked if Chien had a name before the Germans took him, all I got was a shrug. "Only a dog," they said. "Chien."

Chien might have objected to this "kidnapping" by the Germans if he had been a bit older and had understood more about loyalty to the motherland, patriotism, love of countrymen and not fraternizing with the enemy. The fact that he had, at the time, been so young and his little belly so often empty probably became one of the reasons for his decision to stay at the Germans' barracks. The invaders had undoubtedly fed him quite well, at least at the beginning when there were ample rations.

The disillusionment may well have begun during those last months of the German occupations, after the Yanks and the Tommies landed on the opposite side of the Cherbourg peninsula and began raining such a torrent of bombs and shells upon the Germans that it soon became apparent they would have to leave those comfortable dormitories and hike their posteriors closer to Festung Deutschland. Under such circumstances, the Germans must have become a bit forgetful about a little brindle dog in their midst. The hail of bombs and shells upon their supply lines certainly were not conducive to an increase in the supply of food. It would be quite understandable that these Germans would lose any great interest in tossing stones and rewarding the fetching of them with morsels of food. One thing is certain, when they decamped they did not take Chien along.

And then one might contemplate the lean days of the interval between the time the Germans retreated and the arrival of the Yanks to take their turn at sleeping in the boys school dormitories. In that interval, which lasted for weeks, it not months, it need not stretch the imagination to picture a little dog with his lean ribs showing as he wanders aimlessly about the bomb pocked area surrounding the old school. Sniffing now and again at former garbage dumps which had become barren of even the smell of food. On occasion, approaching some of the French villagers or farmers still in the area with the faintly whining hope of a bit of food.

It is certain that the French, at this period, did not have enough food for themselves, not to speak of a dog. And those French may not have forgotten that for years Chien was a German dog.

It would not increase their charity.

It may have been a bit difficult at first for Chien to appreciate the Yanks when they arrived. They were a boisterous, fun loving lot for the most part and should have known all about the rock trick. Except, perhaps, like me, they couldn't understand why this strange little dog insisted on carrying rocks instead of sticks. They may also have tried to change his habits but, as I would also learn, Chien had learned how to deal with that problem.

It meant that he simply had to take matters into his own hands, or mouth, when it came to choosing the object to be tossed. He would simply pick up a nice sized rock, carry it with his teeth to the feet of the nearest Yank, deposit it on the ground and sound that gentle little whine. If hunger was indeed the mother of this procedure, it was a part of Yank nature to forgive that, too. In any case, by the time I met Chien, it was obvious that he had been successful enough at his little extortion game with the Yanks to have carved a survival out of it.

If Chien hadn't begun to learn about internationalism from the French, the Germans and now the Americans, he certainly had to make that final adjustment when the Yanks reached their time to vacate the boys school and chase the Germans toward Berlin. For now it was a contingent of United Nations Relief and Rehabilitation Administration personnel who moved in to occupy the boys school dormitories. The school had now become a staging area for the

UNRRA people being moved into Germany to care for the horde of refugees left over from the war.

UNRRA, as any school boy of that time would have been able to tell you, was a truly polyglot and international organization. Its people came from as many as 44 nations. If members of the organization often found it a bit confusing or frustrating, trying to work smoothly with all the others of foreign tongues milling about them, was it any less perplexing for a dog like Chien to decide whose world he was living in now? Only a dog which could adopt an international philosophy would ever be able to survive in this shifting tangle of human beings.

It was certain that Chien would now have very little time to devote to the finer points of nationality, race and religion. If you saw him at the boys school now, carrying his rock and seeking anyone's attention, it was clear that he would seek out a Greek as quickly as an American. Or a Latvian, Belgian, Brazilian or Pole.

If Chien's philosophy of life had been taking a beating lately, if disillusionment had become one of his facts of life, that was all multiplied now as he faced a fantastic mix of UNRRA humanity.

Most of them had long ago forgotten about the joys of owning a pet. Many had suffered so severely during the war that any thought of tossing food to a dog was somewhat in the nature of sin. Not to speak of the fact that even now, as they drew their rations from American military stores, these rations were often on the short side. There was still somewhat of a hunger in their bellies.

Oh, it is true that occasionally someone would reward Chien's rock lugging trick with a bit of food. But for the most part, one would have to label Chien's efforts as devotion to a lost cause. It was habit, more than food, that sent him on his eternal rounds with the rocks. From person to person, nation to nation.

He would drop his rock at their feet, sound his gentle whine and wait. Even Chien was smart enough to sense almost immediately if the trick was not going to be rewarded. His wait would be short and then he would pick up the stone and drop it at someone else's feet. It mattered not. Chien was a stone carrier. His duty to perform was eternal.

Oh, there were Yanks among this polyglot crew, too. Although Chien was such a vastly different kind of dog, I was reminded of the faithful boyhood companion, Pedro, back in Oklahoma. So I began saving little bits of food for Chien, watching

240

him perform his rock trick and studying the strange philosophies that controlled him. Oh, there we go with that soul business again.

I learned about the tail that didn't wag. The inscrutable and passive face. That deep pool of mystery peering out from his dark eyes. The stubborn insistance upon carrying a rock in his mouth. I was getting to know the Chien that evolved after seeing so much of this world and its people.

I probably spent too much of my time with Chien. We talked a lot. In the ways that a man can talk to a dog - and a dog with a man. Even if Chien refused to surrender that stubborn and abiding reserve. I was a bit stubborn, too, and somehow I determined to penetrate the wall this little dog had set between himself and people. Such a strange wall since he was willing to accomodate himself to the necessities of a routine which called for the presence of a willing human. And yet he refused to give of himself.

Somehow, I would waken in this dog those long dormant memories of just being a dog. A normal pet. Persuade that tail to wag once more. Feel a rough tongue across the back of my hand. Create the will to sound a bit of a yip. During the short time I would be stationed here, before my name would be posted for the motor convoy trip to Germany, perhaps Chien would become "my dog."

In truth, it was a bit of cruelty on my part, for even if I had succeeded I would not have been able to keep him and take him with me. The rules were rigid and the practicalities made it impossible.

I even allowed myself the luxury of hoping that even at this late date Chien's philosophy could still be broadened a bit. Perhaps by a real home. That he could be morally rehabilitated. Perhaps he would respond again to human love. His eyes might sparkle once more. The tail might wag a bit.

I spoke to several French farmers in the area, suggesting that they might give Chien a home. The answer was always, "Non." No extra food for a dog. Of what use was a little brindle dog? Besides, even if it was unspoken, they all knew that Chien had been the dog of the hated Germans.

In the end, it didn't really matter. Chien himself took care of that. He had learned his lessons well. Whether people tossed his stone or not. Whether they rewarded him or not. Chien knew that everyone he came to know would move on and leave him behind. He refused to give what I asked of him. Perhaps he was now unable to give it. I would never know.

In time, my name was posted for my convoy trip. As I packed to leave, I thought once more of Chien. Perhaps with a bit of sorrow at the thought of leaving this strange and baffling little dog behind.

The dog with the wounded soul. Now I have said it.

But I did save from my last rations a hunk of bread. I scrounged a couple of bones for him from the kitchen. The gesture, at least, would have to be made.

I knew full well his habit of attending each convoy "departure." I made it a special point to look him up that morning as I was scheduled to leave. I tossed his stone for him a few times and made my little "presentation" of my bread and bones. Somehow, I still nursed the forlorn hope that in a farewell, Chien would wag his tail or lick my hand. It was a hope Chien would never allow to be fulfilled.

Nevertheless, I stroked his passive head. "Goodbye, Chien." Was there anything more a man could say to such a strange little canine victim of the war?

As our truck pulled out of the school yard, I looked back and saw Chien depositing his stone at the feet of another "prospect." He sat there in front of his new person, looking up with that air of passive but querulous anticipation so peculiar to a dog I called Chien with his unforgettable philosophy about stones and humans.

Somehow, within me, I must find a sufficiency of grace to forgive him.

242

Chapter Twenty – The Brown Hand

The captain of the ship had warned us about that porthole.

We must keep that porthole closed, he had said, or something "bad" would happen at Naples.

I'm afraid I didn't take his warning very seriously. He might have been trying to have his little joke with the "Americano" passenger. And then we were having a bit of a language problem too. I didn't speak more than six words of Italian. His English or German, the only languages I knew, served him little better.

To make sure it wasn't some kind of a joke I waited until I was certain the captain wasn't looking, then sneaked out on deck to take a look over the sides of the Cavallo Marino, down towards "our" porthole.

No way, I decided, that "something bad" could get to us through that porthole. It was at least 10 to 15 feet above the water line, from below, and almost that far from the deck above. Nothing but the slippery sides of the ship.

Besides, that porthole wasn't big enough for a human body to squeeze through, even if some sort of "bad thing" could manage to crawl up or down the straight sides of the ship. Nothing to cling to. Even if a guy dangled from a rope from the top, no way to get in.

Besides, it was too hot to sleep in that cabin with the porthole closed. No air conditioning. Nothing but a feeble little electric fan that didn't stir much air.

The captain had emphasized that if the "bad thing" did impose itself upon us it would be at Naples. We had hoisted anchor at Genoa and, from what I could learn, we were scheduled to make harbor at Naples some time in the middle of the night.

The Cavallo Marino was really not much of a ship. A little 900 tonner, and slow. The thumping diesel engines pounding away down there in the guts of the ship were making enough noise and vibration to prevent sleep from coming easily. But we would try.

I told Ruth to take the top bunk. That way she would get a bit of fresh air from the open porthole. I'd take the lower. Not much air down below but, well, she was my bride of a week. Love was generous.

Young and in love, the two of us. But it was going to one heckuva honeymoon cruise aboard this dumpy little Italian freighter, headed for Istanbul, with lots of stops in between. Naples. Catania on the Sicilian coast. Malta. Athens.

All I knew was that my bosses in our London heaquarters for United Press operations, Europe, wanted me down in Turkey to cover the new Truman Doctrine military aid program being cranked up for Turkey. Or any other nation in that part of the world in 1947, willing to thumb a nose at the Russian communists. But I had refused to leave either my girl, or my car, in Frankfurt, so there had been some hurrried nuptials with the blessings of General Lucius Clay.

Only a day after the wedding, what there had been of a wedding, we had driven my battered little Opel down through Switzerland into Italy - to Genoa, where my boss, Pat Conger, had arranged for us to be loaded, body, baggage and car, onto the Cavallo Marino making a run to Istanbul. It was the only ship available that would agree to take my precious car and even then it had to be lashed to the open deck up top.

And now this porthole matter.

I guess we had somehow managed to doze off, despite the heat, the meager ventilation and the thumping of the diesels.

But then, suddenly, that sleep was sharply shattered by a scream such as I had never heard, coming from my bride. We had left the lights on. I leaped out of my bunk and tried to shift my sleep fogged brain into gear, to focus my eyes on whatever had brought such a horrible fright to my little girl.

At first I could think only of a mouse, or a rat, which might have crept out of the hold to terrify my bride. But it required only two or three seconds for my eyes to tell me how wrong that guess had been.

A dirty brown hand, attached to a human arm, was groping its way across her face. It was still dark outside.

The owner of that hand apparently was courageous enough to persist in the groping, despite her screaming. Ruth had tucked her purse under the edge of her pillow, but fortunately on the inboard side of her bunk. Otherwise, on the porthole side, it would have been easy prey for the groping hand and it might have been stolen even without waking her.

Located there on the far side of the berth, it meant that the hand had to grope its way across her sleeping face to reach the hand bag. Her terror would have to be forgiven.

In any case, no sooner had my eyes focused on the cause of the terror than I leaped into action.

If I hadn't been willing to close that porthole before. I was now. I slammed it shut against the flesh and bone of that groping arm and held it tight.

Now the tables had turned, very quickly. I had captured the brown hand. The sharp edges of the porthole cover had trapped the hand, and the arm, into a vise-like grip which would cost its owner the arm and hand if he succeeded in jerking himself free.

Now it was the turn of the owner of that hand to begin screaming in a terror and pain of his own. And I didn't give a damn.

Ruth had managed to slip out from under that arm, and mine, as I pressed the porthole cover shut. She was standing there now, wide eyed, staring at the brown arm and hand, the source of her terror. I made sure there would be no escape. I was willing, at the moment, to hold that brown hand forever. There was the wish of vengeance in my anger.

I screamed for help but nobody came. Ruth cautiously opened the cabin door and also cried for help. Still nobody came.

I don't know how long I braced myself there and held the arm but it was inevitable that there would come a moment of another kind of truth. Blood was beginning to trickle down the wall from that trapped arm as its owner struggled to free himself and the sharp edge of that metal cover began biting into the flesh.

I wasn't certain but it seemed as if I could also hear bone breaking.

It was the realization, on my part, of the pain and hurt I was inflicting on the unseen man which began to turn the tables once more. In a symbolic sense, at least, it was now I who was the victorious gladiator, standing over my vanquished foe, watching the pleading look in his eyes as I prepared to plunge the blade of my sword into his throat. And such an act would require courage of yet another kind.

My first surge of courage had been born of anger and excitemen in that first moment I saw danger threatening my beloved. Now it was fading fast at the sight of the blood trickling down the wall. And the sound of the soul shattering screams from a man I could not even see. Only that hand and arm.

How long could I do this? How many moments of pain must the man suffer to pay for the terror he had brought to the eyes of my girl? Or for the attempt to steal her purse?

My resolve to hold that arm "forever" was fading fast. My anger was cooled by compassion for another human in pain. Besides nobody had come to my assistance. No policeman stood by to take a prisoner off my hands. It would eventually become a question of how long I could hold out, physically, to keep the capture a reality. Even my strong young muscles would not endure forever.

And then somehow, amidst all that surging drama of the moment, the urgency of what I had seemingly been forced to do, a crazy, nagging question was creeping into my consciousness. It went back to that warning from the captain about that porthole. How in the devil had that robber managed to reach my porthole? Was he aboard another ship or boat, swinging alongside the Cavallo Marino? Or what? Or how?

Crazy, but even in the midst of what I had been doing I found myself wanting to know. Very badly. And in the end, torn between a growing compassion for my "fallen gladiator," the knowledge that I could not hold him there forever, the tiring of my muscles, the fact that nobody was answering my cries for help, was bringing closer the hesitant decision to let him go.

So it was, faced with the knowledge that I could not hold him forever, I let him go. I simply eased up the pressure on that sharp edged porthole cover and watched the bloody arm slip away. And with it the screams of pain.

Now I could at last slam that porthole cover shut and latch it.

But then I had to satisfy my curiosity. I had told Ruth to close the cabin door behind me as I left and to open it to nobody, except me. Then I was gone, my pounding legs carrying me towards the gangway and the upper deck. There was probably no way I could have been prepared for the incredible scene I was about to see.

First, as my eyes came to the level of the upper deck I could see why nobody had answered the cries for help. The entire crew, including the captain, the mates, engine crew and even the cook, was on that upper deck, facing outward, into the darkness away from the ship. Their attention, on all sides, drawn to something in the sea around them. And from that sea around us a torrent of babbling sound. The captain and his crew were also shouting, swinging long boat hooks out toward that sound. The captain and at least three or four others of the crew had pistols rammed into the belts, boldly displayed. As if they wished the guns to be seen. This was the beginning of the drama.

But as I reached the deck and could see beyond the ship itself, I was suddenly aware of a vast, teeming motion in the water around us. Almost like an undulating floor, with a sea of faces turned up toward us. These were people in boats, completely surrounding the Cavallo Marino. Dozens of the little row boats, in a swarm so close together you could have walked all the way around the ship, from boat to boat.

For a distance of at least 50 yards, maybe more, the dark water was simply blanketed by this teeming mass of boats and men. The harbor lights, a quarter of a mile away on the shore, cast an eerie illumination across this panorama.

There must have been at least 200 of the little boats. Maybe 300. Or even more. Too many to count. The face of the sea was a vast tumult of boats and men, of upturned faces and babbling voices. The sound in that Latin tongue so foreign to me.

As this strange scene began to register on my mind I became frightened. There was something so menacing, so threatening about it. The boathooks with which the crewmen were jabbing, spearlike, at the boat men below, the pistols so visible in the belts of the ship officers, could only lend credence to the fright.

It was when I approached the railing and could look down at the sides of the ship that I found my answer to the nagging question - how they could they reach those portholes. Many of the boatmen were equipped with long, sturdy poles to the end of which were fastened big, wide throated hooks. Bigger than the hook on a normal boathook. They had obviously been fashioned for a purpose. The poles were as much as 20 feet long.

If a man in the boat spotted an open porthole he would reach up, insert the hook over the edge of the hole, then scramble up the pole like a monkey. Even as I looked, several of the pole climbers were perched on the side of the ship, clinging to their poles and attempting to reach inside the ship. For anything their fingers could grasp and pull out. Most of the portholes were closed.

But despite the fact that it seemed all the crew members were on deck, there must have been a few persons below in the bowels of the ship who had opened their portholes willingly. Once or twice I was certain I could see a hand from inside the ship, reaching out to hand something to the pole climber outside. A bit of food, perhaps, to a hungry countryman.

It was when I confronted the captain and demanded to know what the tumult was all about that he tried to tell me, in a broken mixture of Italian, German and English.

"They want food. They want trade," he replied. "They still hungry from the war. Their bellies empty." He patted his own lean stomach to emphasize his words.

Meanwhile, it was clear, from the skill with which the boatmen manipulated and climbed their poles, that it had become a routine, a ritual of begging, bartering and pilfering. The captain had not called it robbery. After all, he had warned me.

But it was also becoming clear why the captain and his crew were stationed along the railing. Some of the boatmen were trying to hang their hooks over the edge of the deck and board the ship.

For the most part, a crewman would kick the hook away before it could secure a hold. Where a boatman managed to make a "hang" and scramble up the pole, he was ruthlessly jabbed away with a boat hook. If he stubbornly insisted on coming aboard he was simply thrown off. Either to fall into the sea or back in his boat. Some of them were obviously bruised and injured as they landed in the boats. At times, a comrade below might try to cushion the fall at the risk of upsetting the boat or for the waiting man to be injured himself.

Then, when this happened, the fallen climber or his comrade below would turn their faces upward to the deck and cut loose with a torrent of anger. Obviously obscene.

The whole picture a scene of madness. One might have thought the captain and his crew would have had a bit more compassion for these other men who were, after all, their own countrymen. Brother Italians. But then, one needed only to contemplate for a moment what would have happened if they had indeed allowed the swarm of hungry boatmen to come aboard. The wild pilferage, even piracy, that might have taken place.

In the midst of all this madness, it became apparent that something else was taking place, too. A few of the boatmen below had fish, or other objects which they seemed to be offering for sale or trade. Still others had wads of Italian paper money, those grotesquely huge bills which made it seem so much. They wanted to buy. Food. Cigarettes. Anything they could trade on the black market. I had seen the black market in operation in Germany after the war but I had seen nothing like this.

The longer I stood and watched, the more details of this crazy drama were sinking into my consciousness. For it became apparent that the captain and some of the crewmen did, indeed, know at least a few of the boatmen down there. When the tumult had died down a bit, it was they who pushed their boats through the throng to the side of the ship.

It then became obvious that some sort of trading, bartering or selling was taking place with a few selected boatmen. Packages and boxes were being hoisted aboard and other boxes and packages were being lowered to the boatmen. Sometimes wads of those huge bills changed hands but, for the most part, it seemed to be barter. I had already learned that nobody really wanted money. It was largely worthless. Even at the official exchange rate, it took 600 Italian lira to equal a dollar. On the black market, much more.

Later in the voyage before we reached Sicily, I happened by mistake to open the door of the wrong cabin. It stood empty, the door sometimes ajar. But later I had seen packages inside. Cartons which bore the trademarks "Lucky Strike," "Camel," "Chesterfield." Cigarettes in that crazy economy after the war had virtually become the legal tender of the ravaged countries.

I didn't ask questions. The captain would only have shrugged and pleaded, "No compre."

But back to that crazy harbor night scene and the tumult surrounding it. At some point, my mind flashed back to Ruth, locked in the cabin below. Wondering, perhaps, about what was going on. Was she, perhaps, in some sort of danger?

No sooner the thought than I turned and headed back towards the gangway. Then I saw her face. She had acquired enough curiosity and courage to disobey my orders. She stood there at the head of the gangway, peering out cautiously to see what was going on.

I ran towards her, gesturing fiercely for her to get down. Below. Back to our cabin. I could see vividly in my mind what might have happened if that mad mob had managed to overcome the crew and come tumbling aboard. The word "rape" flashed into my thoughts. She had no business up there on deck. She was young, beautiful, and I didn't want these crazy people down below to even catch a glimpse of her. She had set me mad with love and desire. I wanted to take no chances with crazy boat people.

Now I simply took her by the hand, led her back to the cabin and tried to explain what had been going on out there. I made it clear she had no business on deck.

There was only one other woman on board, a somewhat older and buxom personage who had identified herself as a war refugee from Rumania. It also became clear, as the voyage proceeded, that she had come aboard for a purpose. She would wink and smile at the crew members, disappear with them into her cabin. She let it be known that she was available. At a price. The captain let me know she was a woman for sale.

But in that mad, tumultuous drama in that night at Naples, even she had remained locked in her cabin and had not showed herself. She might be available but not to a mob.

Later, as things became a bit more calm, I ventured up on deck once more, still warning Ruth not to open the door. Many of the little boats were gone now. Only a straggly ring of them surrounding the ship. Some of the boatmen you could see rowing their way back towards the harbor lights, the city, perhaps a quarter of a mile away. For most of them, their mission had been a failure, their hands empty. To face hunger, perhaps, at home. Even the hunger of their children.

As the boats slowly left, peeling off from the circle, one by one, the excitement and the fear I had felt when it all began, my struggle with that brown hand, the wild scene I had witnessed from the deck, those menacing hooks, all began fading back into a calmer awareness.

And it was inevitable, somewhere in my mind the question came back as to what might have happened to my man of the brown arm and hand. In those first moments when I came on deck, the scene had been too wild, too incredible for me to try to see the man and identify him. I had been too surprised and terrified to even try.

But later, as I searched my memory, I could somehow remember a glimpse of one of the boats where a man lay on the bottom of the boat with two other men bending over him. It seemed they were trying to comfort him, to wrap a bandage of sorts, a piece of shirt perhaps, around his arm. and then the boat had detached itself from the tumult as its rowers pulled towards the harbor lights. It had probably been my "brown arm."

I also remembered, later, seeing perhaps two more boats a bit larger and equipped with motors, hovering around the outer fringes of the horde. I had seen uniforms and the word, "Polizia," painted on the boats. But the crews of these boats had made no effort to become involved.

They probably knew what was going on, that it was a forlorn and desperate attempt by countrymen to obtain food. Why should they interfere? At least so long as there was no desperate danger to the ship and its crew. They probably had orders to interfere only in case of dire emergency.

It had only been in the later stages of the wild scene that I had even been aware of those police boats and perhaps they had only come later on. But somehow it calmed the fear just a bit to know they had been there.

Later, after most of the boats were gone, one of the police boats came chugging alongside for a few moments. The lawmen in the boats shouted up at the captain and he replied. I could not, of course, know what was being said but, from the tone, it seemed a cordial conversation. The captain tossed a small package down. It was grabbed eagerly and a moment later the police boat chugged away. There had been some sort of an understanding. A communication of countrymen.

Next day, around 8 in the morning, a tender with a barge came chugging alongside and made fast. Bigger crates of cargo were now being unloaded, by use of the electric crane aboard the Cavallo Marino. This was obviously the legitimate cargo for which this voyage was being made. A few crates came aboard.

This transfer of cargo scene would be one that would be repeated at Catania, Malta and Athens. Probably also at Istanbul after we had left the ship. But nowhere did we again experience another tumultuous scene such as I had seen at Naples. In this, Naples seemed unique and special. Something having to do with the nature of that world port which had somehow acquired a special means of dealing with the outside world in those desperate years immediately after the war.

At Catania a few boats had come out to meet the ship. It had been a daytime arrival. But later that night, when we departed, I was aware that the Cavallo Marino was towing a small boat as she left the harbor, the boat lashed to the dark side of the ship.

It was after we had passed the entrance to the harbor that I saw boxes being passed down to the boat. The two men aboard it then cast off and drifted away into the darkness. More commerce, perhaps, of the black market.

When my thoughts drifted back to that picture of the wounded man in the boat, I could never be sure. There had been too much going on. I had never been able to concentrate my attention on a single boat among so many. The owner of that brown hand and arm would remain a man without a face for I had never seen his face. I would never see him again.

There would come a time when it would all come tumbling back into my memory. I would remember the screams, the blood trickling down the cabin wall.

But that desperate pulse of anger from the moment when I had slammed the porthole cover shut against the brown arm, would never return.

The sword was stilled. In my hand. In my heart.

Chapter Twenty one - Green Frog

If it had not been for that strange cacophony of sound which hung like a blanket of audible smog over the city of Istanbul, and that weird Turkish philosophy which created it, I and my Green Frog might have been in serious trouble.

Istanbul itself had been a glorious sight that morning in September 1947. As the Cavallo Marino glided into the harbor we stood on the deck watching that fantastic skyline, the ancient city of Byzantine antiquity, come into view. Etched against the sky, the hillsides, that unbelievable panorama of mosques and towering minarets.

But nothing had prepared us for that eerie sound. It could never have been the call of the muezzins from the minarets.

It was only later, in the taxi, climbing up the hillside towards the Ayas Pasha and our hotel, that the mystery began unfolding itself. Our taxi driver was helping out with the understanding by tooting his horn every few seconds.

What was now becoming so piercingly clear was that all that noise was made by the honking of motor car horns. Not one. Or two. Or three. But dozens of them sounding together. Maybe even hundreds of them all sounding at once. That strange cacophony of sound which somehow would not cease.

No, it was not some sort of celebration. Nor even some kind of emergency which required it. Nothing more, I soon discovered, than the end results of a crazy Turkish philosophy about driving motor cars.

The Turkish cab driver - most of the cars on the streets of Istanbul in 1947 were taxis - had somehow acquired a creed which

253

declared that it was a betrayal of your status to drive more than 50 to 75 yards at a time without tooting your horn.

It mattered not that nobody was in front of you, in need of being warned. In fact, it almost seemed, in watching them, that when a pedestrian did dare to cross the street in front of one of those crazy drivers, he would suddenly stop blowing his horn and take aim with his machine. But those Turkish "footers" were pretty good at their game, too, and seldom got hit. Just a game - taxi driver versus footman.

But that noise. It somehow reminded me of that time, long ago in Oregon, when Mom and Dad had taken me along to those meetings of the Apostolic Faith Mission people. Those Faithers believed in praying. Lots of praying. And loud. But the important thing was that everyone was loudly praying at the same time. Each supplicant prayed their own individual prayer. That Babel of voices.

Now, the Babel of horns in Istanbul so many years later.

During your first days in Istanbul that noise could blow the fuses in your nerve box. How could the Turks stand it? Why didn't the police do something about it?

The noise may have grated with extras harshness upon my ears because, for the last several years before coming to Europe, I had been living in Memphis, Tennessee, a city proud of a national award for being "The Nation's Quietest City." In Memphis it had not only been a sin, but also illegal, to blow a horn.

Actually, although Istanbul was a city of some million Moslem souls, they only had about 6,000 cars. Mostly French, British, German, Italian - and most of them taxis. What made it seem as if they had millions of cars was the fact that the city had only a half dozen streets wide enough to accomodate motor traffic. All of the 6,000 cars were packed into those few streets. That noise helped with the illusion, too.

During the day, when people thronged the street, I believe that at least a fourth, maybe a third, of those taxi horns would be going at the same time. Is that possible? A moaning, undulating sound which never stopped.

Oh, it would slow down a bit in the evening and then, late at night, it would dwindle away until there would actually be moments of silence. How blessed the quiet. You could at least recognize the sound of a single horn. And perhaps by 1 or 2 in the morning the horn tooting might cease altogether. But next morning, when you got up, there it was again. It didn't make it easy to fall asleep in the evening, not in the heat and with no air conditioning.

Perhaps the only blessing emanating from the whole thing was the fact that most European cars were never equipped with real horns, such as the Americans had. Mostly beepers. It wouldn't have been so bad if they had not all been beeping at the same time.

It was true that there were a few old American cars in the city. But very few. The Turkish owner of a taxi garage down the street had an old Chrysler. Oh, how the Turks envied the healthy sound of that Chrysler horn, even though it was not a true blaster such as some drivers had in America. When my Chrysler Turk would sound his horn, every other driver within hearing distance would stop tooting, for a moment at least. Out of respect, perhaps? Or envy? Or was it to savor the sound?

I really couldn't know. Nor could I know, when it all began, how important that noise - and the strange philosphy which produced it - would be to me and my Green Frog.

Oh, yes. The Green Frog. That was my precious car. That battered 1936 two-liter Opel with a 2.5 liter engine.

In those first moments, or days, as I was getting my baptism of sound, that car was still in captivity, lashed to the upper deck of the Cavallo Marino. Later, hidden away in some remote storage place by the customs people. In fact, we didn't even call her the Green Frog then. That would come later.

There was a bit of a story behind the car. In the first place, in those first years after the war in Europe, any kind of car, even the most clattering clunker, was precious property. I had gone through a lot of crazy antics and a lot of trouble to acquire legal possession of her in Germany. Now I had brought her all the way to Turkey to help me cover the Truman Doctrine.

Where do we start a crazy story like this? For one thing, as the war ground to a halt in May of 1945, every GI in Germany who could find any kind of a motor vehicle running on the streets, grabbed it.

It mattered not that a German might be driving it and owned it. The Germans were the bad guys and you grabbed. Even if you had to hold a .45 automatic to his head.

The DP's, those liberated slave laborers in Germany, did a bit of the grabbing, too. I suppose some of the cars the GI's were grabbing were snatched from the hands of the DP's. But they didn't know the difference. If a guy spoke Polish or Russian it was the same as German to them.

Somebody had grabbed that old Opel.

After the Army had been in Germany a few months and things began to settle down, somebody in high place remembered all those "liberated" motor cars. A Military Government decree came down, stating that any officer, GI or civilian found in the possession of a motor vehicle on which they did not have documents to show they had acquired it legally, would have to give it up. Go back to walking.

"It's tough, guys, but that's the way it is."

The Military Government people skimmed off a few of the best cars, stencilled MG on them and kept them in their motor pools, especially the Mercedes. The rest of the cars, the worst of the clunkers, they turned back over to the Germans. No, not the original owners. Only a few special priority Germans got to drive cars, people like government officials rated essential, the police and a few doctors. They didn't own one. The cars were only assigned to them.

And there I was, in the middle of all that, a public relations officer for UNRRA, an agency assigned to running all those camps that housed liberated folks from all over Europe.

Our operation needed wheels, too. The Army gave us a few Jeeps and ambulances. I wheeled a Dodge ambulance around like crazy for several months. Somewhere, UNRRA got a fleet of 50 new British Austin Sevens. They weren't worth a damn. Our motor pool boss who happened to be British said they averaged about 4,000 miles per car before they pooped out.

The first time I stuck one of them in a snow bank the thing expired on the spot. Engine gone. No clutch. Nice body. Nice upholstery.

Seems we never had enough wheels to keep rolling. It must have been right after my Austin Seven pooped, when my boss came up with an idea. Peter Ball was a former Army captain who had been transferred to UNRRA because he had acquired a lot of experience in the last days of the war rounding up DP's.

Peter and I got to be pretty good friends. We both liked cars. I helped him acquire a streamlined custom sports job some rich German had hidden under a hay stack. Oh, we did that one legally. But, after a while, Peter revealed that he knew about another car, that old Opel, hidden in a shed, way down in Bavaria. I never dug too deeply into how he knew about it.

"If we could get that car up here we could slap some UNRRA stencils on it and get it assigned to our motor pool," he said. "It would give us an extra car. It would at least be better than those Austins."

His plan unwound something like this. He had talked our motor pool boss out of some UNRRA stencils, a bit of white paint, serveral Jerry cans full of gasoline and some travel orders to a certain little town in Bavaria. Nobody went any place in those days without valid travel orders. This was 1945 and the Army had roadblocks all over the country to check your papers.

We would drive down in an UNRRA Jeep. I had to take someone along to drive one vehicle back. Peter introduced me to a Pole-Russian he trusted. Seems Konstantin was one of the DP's Peter had liberated and Peter had helped him escape from the Russians when they tried to grab him. Nice guy, Konstantin. Educated at the University of Moscow. He spoke Russian, Polish, French and German. So we did our "sprachen" in German.

Turned out that Konstantin knew all about that car, too. Led me right to it. We had to slip out a few packs of Camel cigarettes to liberate the car from the shed.

Then the damned thing didn't want to run. Cold winter. Had to get my hands dirty getting the ignition and fuel feed working. Then the battery was dead. Had to do some pushing with the Jeep before it finally sputtered into life.

So we finally took off over the snowy roads. Konstantin driving the Opel with me following in the Jeep in case the Opel conked out. It conked several times.

But we finally made it. Those brand new white UNRRA letters stencilled on the old car looked real nice. The MP's thought so, too. They glanced at our travel orders and waved us through.

Back at Arolsen, the motor pool boss wrinkled his nose a bit but he agreed to "accept" the offering. With the understanding that he tune up the engine, give it a lube job and then assign it to the Public Relations crew. Me, to be exact.

During the next few months, I wheeled that old Opel all over west Germany. Not much of a car but, as Peter said, better than those wheezy Austins. My job specs called for me to roam around from one DP camp to another, interviewing the UNRRA crew folks and to send some nice, syrupy feature stories back to their hometown newspapers. Let the folks back home know how well their tax dollars were being spent.

Sometimes, when Congressmen or Senators showed up, checking up on the flow of tax monies, we escorted them around. Once we even wheeled Eleanor Roosevelt around.

I know, this is supposed to be the story of the Green Frog. Well, one day, I wrecked the car. I'll swear it wasn't my fault. Never is. Some nutty DP, driving an Army garbage truck, ran a stop sign right in front of me. It was raining and when I slammed on the brakes, old Opel started spinning on the wet pavement. I hit the truck going backwards. When the Opel stopped, she was teetering on the edge of a canal full of water. I had to crawl out the rear to keep from tipping it over into the drink.

No trouble climbing out the rear because that old car was a soft top, a cabriolet they called it. The crash had simply ripped the cloth top to shreds. To look at, it was a holy mess. Plenty of open air crawl room.

But nobody was hurt. When I managed to get the UNRRA on the phone they sent one of those Dodge amublances to pick me up. I didn't need an ambulance. I needed wheels.

As for the smashed Opel, I got a German to haul it to a garage nearby, for storage. Cost a few more packs of Camel cigarettes.

Next day, I made my report to the motor pool boss.

"How badly is it smashed?" he asked.

"Pretty bad," I said with emphasis. It had indeed looked pretty bad.

But the next thing the man said started the wheels to rolling in my head. And eventually to rolling under my butt, as well.

"If it's busted up that bad, I don't believe I'll go get it," he said. "It wasn't much of a car anyway. The engine is almost worn out. We'll just write it off."

Woweee. I had me a car. Wheels for private use in those days were almost so scarce a guy whould hock his soul - and throw in his best pair of shoes - to get a set. Any kind, so long as they would roll. And I knew I could make 'em roll. I hadn't slaved all those years in a motor machine shop in Oklahoma for nothing. And two years in a body shop.

First chance I got, I sneaked down to Giessen to take another look. Still a sorry mess to look at. But mostly because of that shredded cloth top. The bent top bows. But that part would be easy to fix. I could straighten the bows and get a German to make me a new top. Cost me a few packs of cigarettes, maybe.

As for the bent fenders and things, I could straighten them out. First, to make sure the car would still run, I got the thing out of the shed and pried the bent fenders off the wheels. Cranked her up and took off. Just like that. No damage to the running gear at all. Hooray.

I really needed that car. By this time I had a girlfriend down at Frankfurt. The love bug thing. Had to go. Besides, I was in the process of negotiating for a job with United Press in Frankfurt - leaving UNRRA. I happened to know that UP was short of wheels, too. A Jeep or two, that was all they had.

But there was a big fly in my soup. If I couldn't get him out, the whole idea would blow up. That decree from MG, that you had to have legal papers on a car to keep it.

Well, I was going to take a try on that one, too.

For the moment, I would just leave the car in the shed at Giessen while I worked on it. Maybe, just maybe, if I could trace the car through the motor number and the German motor car registration office, I might find the legal owner and buy the papers from him.

I enlisted the help of a German character I had met, Faemel, who seemed to know all about cars. We ran into trouble immediately. Seems the motor car registration records in Frankfurt had been blown all to hell by all those buster bombs the B-17's dropped on the town during the war. Wiped out half the town.

Faemel knew his ropes, though. We ended up at Wiesbaden where they had some duplicate reocrds. And then we struck gold. We had the name and address of the owner, a widow running a little butcher shop in a tiny village near Kassel. On the way.

When I walked into that little meat shop and introduced myself, the gal had suspicion oozing out all over. All Americans, even civilians, were required to wear uniforms in those days and maybe I was an "Ami" officer coming to give her a hard time. She wouldn't know the difference. But after I told her who I was, she calmed down a bit.

Then I sprang it on her. "Madame, I have your car. The Opel."

Now her eyes were all smiles. In fact, I thought I might have to defend myself against hugs and kisses. "Where is it?" she demanded eagerly.

That was when I had to slip the knife into her. I had it all carefully planned, with the help of Faemel. And I didn't have to lie a darned bit. The sad story was all true.

"Madame Schmidt," I said, "you know that all German cars are now assigned by the Military Government, by priority. As a butcher shop operator, you do not qualify to own a car. If I bring it back to you they will take it away. And you might not get paid for five or 10 years. But if you sign the papers over to me I will pay you, like buying the car. I'll give you two thousand marks."

At first she wanted no part of the deal. Wanted her car back. But Faemel backed me up. She still wouldn't sign and I had only one more card to play.

"Why don't we go visit the local Burgermeister. He will tell you," I suggested.

She bought that idea. I was gambling that the Burgermeister was a decent guy and would confirm my story. He did. She signed and I had my car.

Well, as the motor pool boss had said, it wasn't much of a car. The engine was about to poop. The running gear was getting the rattles. But it would run.

In fact, that engine was closer to pooping than I knew. A few weeks later I took my girlfriend up into the Taunus Mountains for a picnic - well, we called it a picnic so her mom wouldn't object - and were climbing uphill when smoke began pouring out from under the hood and the engine began to clatter. Ooomph all gone.

I started downshifting - into third, second, the bottom. Still no go. We finally made it back home by putting it in reverse, turning around and limping home. It would run downhill all right. And on the level, just barely. Engine gone.

Now I had to start searching all over again for an engine. I had already perked the old one up several times. It was past perking. So it was Faemel who came to my help again. Somewhere he had located a character who had a brand new motor in a crate. He had thought he was pretty smart by stashing a spare engine to his car through the war. But then, after the shooting stopped, the GI's had liberated his car and he was left with the spare engine. A 2.5 liter Opel engine but for a later model car than mine.

A few cartons of cigarettes - I didn't smoke anyway - and the engine was mine.

That was when my two-liter Opel became the 2.5 liter Opel.

Took a bit of doing. The engine wouldn't fit. But that didn't stop me. In fact, I liked the idea of a bigger engine. It might make the old clunker move.

Back in my shop days in Oklahoma, we had put a Buick engine in a Stutz chassis. A Pontiac engine in a Viking. Who was going to stop me now? I talked a German garage man into renting me work space - a few more cartons of cigarettes - and by sneaking a few hours out there, away from my job, I spooned that 2.5 liter engine into the two-liter space.

Exhaust pipe on the wrong side. Engine too long. But with a bit of cutting, sawing and welding, we made it. Wowee. I had a car that would really go. That new engine was a pip. Overhead valves and all - after that sick flathead engine.

The next episode in my Opel story was going to bring me closer to that rendezvous with the horn thing. In Istanbul.

Now that I had a car that would go, I found the biggest bugaboo was a combination of those narrow German roads and the big diesel trucks moving slowly and hogging the lanes.

Those German truck wranglers drove as if they thought they were King of Prussia. Straddle the center of the road, belch black smoke out the exhaust and to hell with anyone who wanted to pass. I would beep my horn until I almost wore out the beep finger. They'd act as if they didn't even hear me. Just kept on trucking, the creeps. I'd cuss. I'd boil. What could a guy do?

Maybe they didn't hear me. For my little car, like all European cars, wasn't equipped with a real horn. More of a beeper. A very sick joke of a horn. I remembered with longing those big twin throated Klaxons the horn companies began making in the United States just before the war. Those big blasters used so much juice from the battery you had to install a special relay to make sure they got the soup. But when you had it, you had it. A blast that could almost lift a guy off the seat. I would have given almost a quarter of my soul for a pair of those horns.

Well, I got them. A "Dear Dad" letter to Dad back home. "Dad," I wrote, "I want you to buy me a pair of the loudest horns you can buy. I don't care what they cost. I want them. Ship them to me. The loudest, remember."

I guess it was nearly six weeks before the APO package arrived. Ah, what beautiful trumpets. I was so anxious to get them on the car I didn't even wait to go to a shop. Got out my tool kit and bolted them on, right there at the office.

It was when I pushed that horn button for the first time that I almost started World War II all over again. Folks came dashing out of the building like they were heading for the bomb shelters. And there I was, grinning like a silly Buddha.

My girl, Ruth, the first time she heard them, thought I was crazy.

"They'll put you in jail," she said.

Who was going to put me in jail? I'd give them a try, anyway.

It was sheer magic, the way those horns worked on the roads. Almost like a snow plow. Even those Diesel wranglers who didn't care much for Amis, started giving me room to pass. Somehow it must have put the fear of Hitler back in their boots. A blast from my trumpets sounded like an order from on high. Gabriel, blow your horn.

I'm certain that at that moment I had the loudest horns in Germany. Most folks hadn't heard anything like them. Short of an air raid siren.

The car didn't look like much. Sort of banged up and needing a paint job but now I had an engine that would go and I had the super horns. What more could a crazy Amercan in Germany in 1946 and 1947 want? Oh, yes, the loving girlfriend. I had her, too.

It was 1947 when President Harry Truman announced the Truman Doctrine, the idea of giving military aid to any nation that was being pushed around by Russia but had enough guts to thumb their nose at the Russians.

That picture fit Turkey just fine. The Soviets, about this time, fat and sassy from winning the war, were making threatening noises at Turkey concerning two of the eastern Turkish provinces the Russians had lost in a long ago war. They now wanted them back. They also wanted free passage from the Black Sea out through the Bosphorus, the Dardenelles and the Mediterranean.

The gutsy Turks were thumbing away but Truman thought it might help if they had a few American tanks and shooting irons.

UP, that was United Press, where my pay check came from, wanted an American in Turkey to cover the Truman Doctrine program from the news end. Our competition, the Associated Press, had a Yank in Instanbul but all we had was a couple of local "stringers," part time Turkish reporters. Not much good.

So came the day when my boss, Pat Conger, called me in. "The London office wants you to get your butt down to Turkey."

I didn't want to go. I hardly knew where Turkey was. I was having fun in Germany. I had my loving girlfriend. I could speak German but no "Turkee."

But they put a lot of pressure on until the only excuse I had left was, "I don't want to go without Ruth." In love.

Well, I didn't believe what happened next because Military Government still had a flat ban again GI's - or any American - marrying a German. But Pat could pull strings, too. In a few days, came a letter signed by Lucius Clay, top general in the Army, giving one UP reporter named Menno Duerksen permission to marry his German sweetie.

It all happened so fast it almost seemed like a shotgun wedding but there I was, on the way to Turkey aboard the Cavallo Marino. My Ruth girl at my side and my two liter Opel with the 2.5 liter engine lashed to the upper deck.

It took me all of two weeks, maybe longer, to get my car out of hock from the Turkish customs people. In the meantime, on instruction from London, I fired the two Turkish stringers and hired two young Turkish newspaper reporters who were able to speak English, to help with the translating and the legwork. One in Ankara, the capital, and one in Istanbul. London suspected that the old stringers were intelligence agents, anway.

One of the first jobs I gave Zeyyat, my Istanbul man, was that of getting my Opel out of hock.

When I saw the beloved Opel, I was sick. She had ridden that open deck as the Cavallo Marino plowed its way through the worst Mediterranean storm in years. At least, that was what my stomach told me. It went on for days. One day, it was so bad that even the captain and the cook were sick. Those huge waves plunging over the decks and drowning my poor car.

With so little paint remaining on her, those salt waves had just about turned the Opel into one big hulk of rust. Beyond that, somebody had smashed the top again while unloading the car. Or else, they had set a big packing crate on top of her. I was ready to cry.

But with the help of my new friend, Zeyyat, I managed to push the top bows up enough so you could sit in it. And then, after a bit of cranking, my two 2.5 liter engine came to life. At least, I could move.

Next blow, friend Zeyyat informs me that before I can drive on the soverign streets of Istanbul I must have my car inspected by the police.

That meant making an appointment with the proper inspection officer and on the appointed day the drive downtown. My poor little mess of a car. It looked more like a rusty tin can than a respectable automobile. But I had brought her this far and I was determined to use her.

Mr. Turkish Auto Inspector turned out to be a dour old timer who looked more like Joe Stalin than a Turk. A long, droopy mustache on a face which appeared to have been eternally forbidden to smile.

At the sight of my Opel he blinked, almost cringed. He probably didn't even believe it would run.

Through Zeyyat he asked me, "Are you an American?" A bit sheepishly, I nodded.

"How come an American has such a shabby car?" he asked. "I thought America was a rich land." I tried to explain that I had come from Germany and this was the only car I could get my hands on.

He tried the brakes. They worked. He tried the lights. They worked. He check the steering. It also worked.

But none of this brought the slightest change of expression to that dour face. I could already see myself and my car being banned to Siberia. Here in Turkey, the Russians were not far away.

But then, suddenly, he touched the horn button and almost jumped out from behind the walrush bush. People all over the nearby street suddenly came alive. Mr. Mustache Car Inspector had his back turned to me when the horn blasted. I was certain that I'd at least spend the next night in jail.

But no. The miracle. When he turned around to look at me, there on that walrus face was the biggest smile I had ever seen on any Turk.

Now he could not resist. He pushed that horn button again. And then again. He must have awakened half the city for the sound of those glorious trumpets was echoing through the minarets. And Mr. Walrus Inspector was grinning happily, lika a Pasha full of joy.

Meanwhile, passing taxi drivers halted on the streets at the sound. They stared unbelievingly at the rusty old car with the great voice. Oh, Allah, grant me something like that.

As for Mr. Inspector, he was busy, happily and furiously stamping my inspection sheet, "Approved."

I was free to roam the streets of Istanbul and toot my glorious horn.

But now, doubly aware of my special status, there was a necessity to rescue the rusty part of my American image. I wrote another Dear Dad letter. "Please, send some paint."

I asked for a sort of bluish green, which was about the best judgement I could make of the remnants of paint still left on the rusting hulk.

I almost shed tears once more when the package came. I opened it and found several cans of John Deere Green. So dire the need, I had little choice but to use it. I ended up with the greenest car in town.

And that was how the Green Frog was born.

Oh, that name wasn't my idea. It was Zeyyat who told me, after I had been in Istanbul several months, that my car was known to every policeman in town. They all called it the Green Frog.

I never was quite sure if that name was a complimentary one in the Turkish language or not.

All I knew for sure was that as I cruised the streets of ancient Byzantium and approached a crossing guarded by a Turkish policeman waving his arms to direct traffic, if I made the slightest sound with my booming horns, the policeman frantically waved me through as if I were Kemal Ataturk.

Far from being offended by the blast, Zeyyat told me, they felt they were being honored. It was a salute.

Long live the King of Istanbul, I and my Green Frog.

Chapter Twenty two - Easter

First there were the buckets. And the heads.

Otherwise it seemed to be such a peaceful Easter morning in Jerusalem. The sun, without malice, in the crystal blue sky.

I had already worked the Easter story in Jerusalem. Gethsemane. The Way of the Cross. But someone had suggested that I go to Bethlehem to see special services commemorating the resurrection of Christ, at his birthplace. Somehow it all seemed so utterly out of focus - with all the bullets and blood and terror of that 1948 spring in Palestine. Nevertheless, I had more or less decided to go.

But then I saw those Arabs scurrying about the Jaffa Gate area of the Jerusalem wall with all those buckets. When someone would approach, the bucket carriers would stop. Folks would peer into the buckets, a little knot of people would gather and begin chattering excitedly. There would be that torrent of Arabic in which I could detect that contempt word, "Jehudi."

Some of the men waved their rifles threateningly. It made me want to duck for cover. I was well aware by this time of how wild those Arabs could be with guns. There had been so many times when I had seen them simply firing off their guns. At nothing. Aimed, often as not, skyward. As if Allah would somehow bend the flight of their bullets and make them strike the hearts of the hated Jews - the Jehudi.

As bullets had indeed struck the hearts of Jews out on Hebron Road the day before. Only I didn't know that - not yet.

I tried to walk up to see for myself what was in the buckets but at first each Arab with a bucket would scurry away as I approached. They seemed to sense that I was a foreigner. Perhaps even a Jew, although I had learned to go bareheaded so people could see my red hair.

One of the Arabs, perhaps a bit bolder than the others, finally did allow me to approach and peer into his bucket. He was watching me carefully to see my reaction. Perhaps he didn't even care if I was a Jew. He would display his contempt. For in the bucket, smeared with blood, was the head of a Jew.

Someone in the crowd spoke a bit of English.

"We kill Jews. On Hebron Road. We cut off their heads." He drew his finger across his throat in that ancient gesture of ultimate obscenity. It was the picture I bore in my mind as I went towards Bethlehem, the birthplace of the Man of Peace.

At Bethlehem the services we had come to see were somehow disappointing. There was something in the air that was distracting the people and the priests in the ceremony. Men with guns were everywhere. Excited talk. Cars and trucks loaded with armed men were moving southward along that Hebron Road.

I asked Artin, my driver-interpreter, what was going on. That battle out on Hebron Road was still going on and getting bigggger by the minute.

How could people focus their attention on a religious procession in Bethlehem? We headed south.

A few miles down the road our car was stopped by armed men. "You can't go any further," they said. "The road is blocked." By this time we could hear the gunfire. We got out and walked towards the "happening." Whatever it was.

Around a bend the whole panorama came into view. A Hollywood director could never have staged it with a better setting. With more drama. The incomparable "wagon train" scene from a movie. Only this was real.

The rocky hills formed an almost perfect amphitheater. Down in the center, "on stage," was the big stone house, Nebi Daniel. Rectangular, with a flat roof and a parapet. A fortress.

Parked in a semi-circle on the road in front of the Nebi Daniel was a double row of armored trucks, pocked with bullets, their tires shot flat.

Behind those "covered wagons" and in the house, the beleaguered Jews. Outside, on the sloping hillsides of the "amphitheater" surrounding the Nebi Daniel, the attacking Arabs. The only thing missing from a perfect Hollywood set was the Indian ponies. Instead there were the Arabs, their vari-colored kaffiyehs sitting like war bonnets on their heads. Hundreds of them. Perhaps even thousands. They had been coming since Saturday morning and were still coming. Many had come, as we had come, down Hebron Road from Bethlehem and Jerusalem. But others had come on foot across the hills from surrounding villages.

From scattered points on those rocky slopes, gun fire directed at Nebi Daniel could be heard constantly. Virtually all of the bullets striking the stone walls harmlessly. Or clanging off the sides of those armored trucks.

No shots were coming from the "fortress." The Jews did their fighting in a different fashion, counting every shot and shooting when a target was near. And certain. The Arabs seemed to be well aware of this and kept cover behind the huge boulders scattered on the hillsides. Most of them so far were out of effective range. So long as they kept that distance, the Jews would hold their fire. From various sources, then and later, we learned what had happened.

It really all centered around Kfar Etzion, an important Jewish settlement further up that Hebron Road. Inside what was Arab territory then, in that strangely divided land before it became Israel.

For weeks settlers at Kfar Etzion had been under siege from the Arabs and had been pleading by radio for help. In the end, unable to continue turning a deaf ear to the desperate plight of their fellow compatriots, the Jews in Jerusalem had assembled almost every available armored truck and car to run the blockade and bring food and ammunition to the besieged villagers.

Starting in the early hours of the Jewish Sabbath, the blockade runners counted on surprise to give them success. On the outward run it had worked. A handful of Arabs manning a roadblock had fled in terror at the size and strength of the armored convoy. But there would be no surprise on the way back. Word of the passing convoy flashed from village to village, to Bethlehem and even the Arab section of Jerusalem, calling for men to quickly erect roadblocks and to create an ambush for the Jews when they would return towards Jerusalem.

The roadblocks were mostly boulders from the hillsides, rolled into the roadway and stacked in heaps by sheer mass muscle power.

The Jews, always short of arms, ammunition and proper equipment, had devised a makeshift means for dealing with those roadblocks. They had equipped a few of their armored trucks with ram booms to clear the roads of the boulders. It worked, if the boulders were not too big, nor stacked too high.

On this fateful return journey from Etzion, the convoy had been led by one of those "barricade busters." It had dutifully rammed its way through two or three of the roadblocks, then it reached the "big one," an enormous pile of boulders heaped at a strategic spot on a sharp bend. Here the barricade buster had stalled and partly capsized. A hail of Arab bullets began pouring in from the hillsides.

That initial ambush had been a victory for the Arabs. Jews had indeed died on that Hebron Road that Saturday. Others had been wounded. Many of the armored trucks and cars were disabled, blood seeping from the doors.

A few of the vehicles on the tail end of the convoy, still able to move, turned around and fled back to Kfar Etzion. The battered remnants of the convoy, if their motors and wheels would still turn at all, even if the tires were shot out, limped to the front of Nebi Daniel and formed that half-circle. The siege was on. Something like 180 Jews, men and women, the dead, the wounded and the terrified, were now holed up in the stone fortress.

More Jews had been left lying there on the asphalt road, or dead inside their bullet-sprayed vehicles. Arabs had died, too, but the attacking forces had so greatly outnumbered the Jew.

All afternoon and all night the battle had raged. Once, during the night, the Arabs had tried a frontal assault, covering an attempt to carry in a huge explosive charge to blow up the fortress. But it had been driven back by the deadly and accurate fire of the Jews. More Arabs had died.

But all through the night and into the early hours of Easter morning, more Arab reinforcements had been streaming in to join the battle, anticipating a great "kill" of the hated Jehudis. It was to this scene, on a sunlit Easter day and on that Biblical site near the ancient Pools of Solomon, that I now arrived. I would be involved in far more drama than I had reckoned for.

I couldn't know it, sitting out there on a hillside overlooking the dramatic setting, but the besieged Jews and their commanders in Jerusalem were now well aware that escape was impossible. Their situation hopeless, unless they got help.

The British Army was still exercising its League of Nations mandate, dating all the way back to the end of World War I. But that mandate would be ending in a few more days. The British were still encamped in that hate-torn and divided land of Palestine. They would soon be free of any responsibility to take action to prevent bloodshed. At this late hour they would move only in the most dire circumstances. The situation at Nebi Daniel was dire.

Desparate negotiations were taking place in Jerusalem as Jewish leaders pleaded with the British to go out and rescue those otherwise doomed Jews. The British could hardly have cared less. They had warned the Jews not to try that convoy run. So now those Jew could just cook in the hot stew they had boiled themselves into.

When the British did finally consent to becoming involved, after being convinced that otherwise they would have the blood of those hapless Jews on their hands, it was only to the extent of attempting to arrange a cease fire. All those hundreds of angry Arabs sitting on the hillsides, firing their guns, would somehow have to be persuaded to stop shooting while a contingent of British soldiers would come down that road and make the rescue. The British officers made it abundantly clear that they would not, on the eve of their own evacuation and only a few days before wiping their hands of all responsibility, commit British soldiers to battle to save those Jews.

Only, but only, if the Arabs stopped shooting would the British go in and make the rescue. But then how, just how, do you tell hundreds of wild-eyed Arab irregulars, scattered over so many acres of stony hillside, to stop shooting? With no means of communication except the shouted human voice? And against the will of men who could smell victory, and a "kill"?

Somebody could only try.

And that was what was going on as I crouched behind my boulder, peering down at the "wagon train" scene, bearing witness to my own end of the desperate drama. One seldom caught a glimpse of a Jew. A few times I thought I barely caught a glimpse of the tip of a head over the rim of the stone roof parapet. Mostly nothing.

Once a single Jew made a dive from his position behind the parapet to a trap door opening in the roof and was visible for half a second. A hail or rifle bullets slammed towards him but he made it. The bullets were too late, or too wide.

Shots, from somewhere among those scattered points on the hillsides were being fired almost constantly. An enormous waste of ammunition but it almost seemed as if the Arabs needed the sound of the gunfire to sustain their spirit. I wondered why, with such a mass of manpower in the hills, someone did not attempt an advance, an attack. It might have been possible, by jumping from boulder to boulder, Indian style. But their courage did not seem up to it. They had a tremendous respect for Jewish marksmanship and were content to wait and starve the Jews out.

Even my constant shadow, Artin, said as much, repeating what he was hearing from the men around him. "When the Jews shoot, they shoot to kill," he said.

I asked him why his Arab friends kept shooting when there were no targets visible. He shrugged his shoulders. It was something about the temperament and character of these untrained, irregular warriors. I really needn't have asked. I had seen it so many times. Sometimes they hardly aimed when they fired.

Several times the drama even took on aspects of the comical when several of the Arab irregulars, now aware of my identity as an American newsman, offered to lend me their rifles to take a few shots of my own.

They would reach their weapons towards me and point down to the Jews.

"You shoot Jehudi," they would say with a grin.

I had to explain, through Artin, that a foreign newsman, by the rules of the game, was forbidden to become involved in the warfare. We only watched. To take a shot would be the big sin.

The gun profferers shrugged at that explanation, too. Obviously they would have enjoyed seeing me take a few shots. Maybe they had heard that Americans could shoot. I could, but I didn't.

Since no bullets were coming our way, there wasn't much for me to be frightened of. At least at the beginning. But then came that droning sound in the sky and a little Auster airplane came into sight. Now the Jews suddenly had a terror weapon of their own. The men in the plane began dropping bombs on the Arabs. Or, it seemed, directly at me.

I learned later that the bombs were nothing more than iron pipe stuffed with dynamite and a fuse. For some reason, the pilot of that plane seemed to have singled out the hillside where I perched, for his bombing run.

I could see the little bombs plummeting out of the plane and coming so straight towards me. Now it was time for me to experience my own moment of panic. With the juices of terror pounding through my veins I clawed, with nothing but my bare hands, at the stubborn earth to try to make shelter under a boulder. It was terror induced by futility.

Then the bombs began exploding. It was with relief that I saw the puffs of smoke, high in the sky. The bombs were exploding far short of their targets. Apparently the fuses were too short. But even that did not still my terror, for how could we know they didn't have more bombs with longer fuses?

The Arabs, who had been doing their acts of warfare with such an air of a picnic, were suddenly frightened now and began ducking for cover. Any cover they could find. Nobody had foxhole shovels. Or time to use them, for that matter. Those heavy boulders of stone which had been so reassuring in protecting us from possible gunfire from the ground were now suddenly so useless as protection from the new danger from above.

But then, in a few moments, everything returned to "normal" after the pilot had expended his pitiful little supply of pipe bombs and turned away. His efforts would have no effect on the fate of his "brothers" in the besieged fortress. But he also had been unscathed by the hail of bullets directed at him from those Arabs with enough courage to stand and shoot.

It was perhaps an hour later when we suddenly became aware that something else was happening. Messengers were scurrying around the hillsides, darting from boulder to boulder and bringing messages to anyone who qualified as any sort of "commander" of any group of irregulars.

The message - I had to rely on Artin once more - was that a cease fire had been ordered by the Arab command in Jerusalem. By Kamal Ireket, their commander who had ordered and arranged the ambush. At 4 in the afternoon, everybody must stop shooting. The Bristish Army was coming in, with men and trucks, to take out the Jews.

It was clear that the men were less than happy with the order. Some were muttering angrily. A few smashed their guns on the ground in anger. Others began firing their last flurries of shots towards the Jews as if hoping for a miracle from Allah that would suddenly endow their bullets with power to penetrate the stone walls and the steel sides of the armored trucks.

They had been so certain of victory, that the Jews had no hope for escape. They wanted blood. Or heads. Some, who had been wasteful of ammunition, now began scrounging around among their buddies to borrow a handful of cartridges for a last go at the hated Jews before 4 o'clock.

In any case, we now waited for sight of the first British troops. Nothing. At 4 o'clock the shooting did taper off and stop.

Almost. Some of the Arabs in the more remote corners of the hills may not have heard the word and a few scattered shots continued to sound through the Easter air.

The Tommies were late. Several times during the next half hour a flurry of shots would announce their coming. But each time, it was a false alarm. Until, at last, they did come.

The familiar British half-tracks. The troop carrier trucks and ambulances to carry the wounded and the dead.

It was a tense moment. Those few scattered shots were still sounding through the air. Would the excitable and angry Arabs now fire at the British? If so, would the Tommies shoot back? Would it turn into a three-way fight?

For the moment, nothing more than the sight of the British men-at-arms calmly making their way down the Hebron Road towards Nebi Daniel. The British Tommies were too well disciplined to panic at the sound of a few scattered shots. Many were veterans of World War II.

As the British reached that crucial roadblock, where the tragedy had all begun, the column was forced to halt while the remains of disabled Jewish vehicles and the rocks of the barricade itself were removed from the road.

Then, slowly, those last few hundred yards to the besieged fortress and the embattled "wagon train." Now the scene of action would be quickly transferred to the Nebi Daniel.

Obviously, I wished I were down there. As a newsman I needed to be. And yet I was aware of the danger of switching sides so suddenly. I had learned of the dangers of this on several occasions before. I might be shot in the back by Arabs made angry by the sight of me going down to join the hated Jews. A few single gunshots were still sounding through the valley. What were they aimed at?

Then it was a British newsman, also near me on the hillside, who made my decision for me. Suddenly we could see him running towards the fortress, dodging from one boulder to another in the "Indian style" I had thought the Arabs might have used in an attack.

If the British Tommies saw him coming, would they fire at him? Surely they would not wish to shoot one of their own but how could they know? The newsman was wearing civilian clothes, just as I was. Even as most of the Arab irregulars were, aside from the inevitable keffiyeh. The most obvious asset my British friend had at the moment was simply his lack of any weapon.

273

But his move had created my moment of decision. If this British correspondent had the courage to make that dash, why was I, the American, lacking in courage to follow? The challenge had been flung. With a pounding pulse I jumped up and followed.

I jumped from boulder to boulder but, at every sound of a shot, I would instinctively duck and listen for the whine of a bullet bouncing off a boulder nearby.

It would be the signal that someone was indeed shooting at me. If I didn't hear it and a jacketed bullet slugged its way into my back, well...

I never heard the whine. Nor felt a plunging impact. For all I knew, the Arabs were simply shooting. At nothing. Ever the impetuous, uncertain warriors.

It was, perhaps, some 400 to 500 yards, that trip down the hillside. My heart was pounding furiously. Even if I made it, what would happen after I got there? I didn't even know what kind of negotiations had taken place, what terms had been set. What arrangement had been made to take the Jews out. I wasn't even sure they would get the Jews out. I just knew that I needed to know those things.

I was about to learn that Kamal Ireket had driven a hard bargain. In return for ordering the cease fire, and giving the British permission to take out the beleaguered Jews, the Jews had to agree to surrender all their weapons and vehicles. Not to the British but to the Arabs.

It would be a costly bargain at best. Those weapons and vehicles had indeed represented nearly the total reserves the Jews had been able to scrape up for the convoy in those days before the British mandate ended. The Jews, at that moment, did not even have any legal authority to acquire weapons.

But even more, the Jews inside that besieged fortress did not yet know of that hard bargain. It would be up to Colonel G. W. Harper, the commander of the British contingent, to give them this news and make the bargain stick.

This very element was to make it a disputed surrender. It would provide for me, for several moments at least, the certainty that I was about to die.

As I arrived at the door of the blockhouse, the British sergeant on guard refused to allow me to enter. Thankfully, since I had been forced to leave Artin up on the hillside, I could at least communicate with this man in English. They had allowed the British newsman to enter and I quickly flashed my press card issued

274

by the British. It was then that the soldier allowed me that passage into hell.

The inside of that blockhouse was ghastly. Gruesome.

The floor was slippery with blood. On that floor lay 13 dead and 40 wounded Jews. It was dark. The stench in the air filled my nostrils. The windows were all shuttered. The unwounded walked around in that eerie darkness almost as zombies. Their eyes bloodshot. They trembled with exhaustion. From thirst and hunger. With fear. With despair.

And yet, some kind of a stubborn, undying spirit lived in these seemingly defeated young men and women. For there were girls among them, too. When Colonel Harper informed these people, these "walking dead," that they would have to surrender their weapons before they could be rescued, he was met with a torrent of curses.

"Never," shouted a young, blood smeared Jew, as he clutched his Bren gun. "Never will I give my gun to the Arabs. We will continue fighting, even if we die. You may go back to Jerusalem."

The British officer led the young Jew, apparently one of the commanders, to the door and flung it open. The exhausted warrior blinked in the sudden sunlight, for he had been in that murky and bloody darkness for nearly two days and a night. But the officer had led him to the door for a purpose. It was to show him his only alternative.

There, coming down the hillsides in a tumultuous rush, was the horde of bloodthirsty Arabs, waving their weapons above their heads. They were screaming wildly as they came. Their momentum would make their charge, perhaps, unstoppable.

The British would try to stop it. Harper had ordered his infantry men, perhaps 150 men, to form a circle around the "wagon train" and the blockhouse to hold back that onrushing mob. The Tommies were outnumbered by at least 20 to 1. And the young British soldiers were to use only their bayonets on the muzzles of their rifles. To fire no shots but to hold that mob until the Jews could be evacuated. With only that cold steel.

"Do not allow anyone to cross your line," went the orders from the young lieutenants out there with their men.

At the door, the officer was speaking to the defiant young Jew. "See that?" He pointed to the onrushing horde, pressing against the thin British line and with more hundreds of Arabs still rushing up from behind. Shoving.

"My men won't be able to hold them for long. They are coming in here. I'll give you three minutes to make your decision. Maybe we can hold them that long."

The young Jew gave up at last. He had been speaking English to the British officer but now he shouted in Hebrew to his people. And now it was his exhausted fighters who, in turn, became defiant. They would not surrender their weapons.

Several of them were then escorted to the door to take their own look at that tense scene outside. And still, incredibly, they summoned the spirit to be defiant in the face of death that was now so close.

The original line the British had set up had been in a circle perhaps 100 yards from that blockhouse cauldron of hell. But that line of Tommies was so very, very thin. There were, inevitably, places in the line where several yards would separate the shoulders of each man from his buddies. Some of the Arabs were attempting to rush those gaps.

But the Tommies were magnificent. Perhaps the most magnificent display of courage and training I would ever see. That thin circle of British soldiers holding back a mob that certainly numbered into the thousands. Inch by inch, they were being forced back, buying precious minutes, never breaking.

These men had been beautifully trained in the use of the bayonet. I would remember how, in the preceding weeks, I had sometimes looked out the window of my Jerusalem hotel, overlooking a British training field, and had seen the hours of grueling drill to which the sergeants had subjected their men. I had thought, on several occasions, those sergeants were a bit too tough, drilling these men for hours under a hot sun. Now I could only be grateful.

When several of the Arabs would attempt to bolt through a gap in the line, a Tommy would leap like a cat, his steel blade set. At least several of those wild eyed Arabs learned at the cost of a gash in his thigh, or his belly, that these Tommies obeyed orders. If the colonel said nobody would be allowed to pass that line, nobody would.

One advantage of the fact that the Tommies were being pushed back, inch by inch, was that as the circle became smaller, the shoulders of the men were coming closer together. Just a bit more dense, that thin circle of steel blades.

A captain and several lieutenants were out there with their men, watching for the slightest sign of a break. Offering words of encouragement, quiet orders. I did not know then, nor do I know today, what orders those lieutenants had been authorized to give in case the line broke. It didn't.

Meanwhile, back inside that chamber of hell, the furious argument continued.

Several of the combatant Jews, perhaps with senses and judgement dulled from the long hours of the seige, continued their defiance. At one point it almost seemed as if they would forcibly eject the British officers who had come to rescue them. Even at the point of a gun, perhaps. Incredible. Insane.

Even their girls and young women who certainly had spent the night manning a porthole or nursing the wounded, were equally defiant. One, who spoke English, shouted at the officers, "We will fight. We will never give up our guns. Never."

Those who did not speak English were shouting, too. I could only guess what they were saying.

The colonel had given them three minutes. I know the furious argument lasted longer than that. Maybe even 10 minute.

If these mad Jews were not afraid of that wild eyed mob of Arabs out there, I was. If there is any register of measurable fear in a man's soul, mine had just reached that level of the "exquisite" that medics use to describe the ultimate pain. Beyond that? There is no more.

As the shouting argument between the British officers and the Jews continued, I could feel within me the growing certainty that I was going to die on this day. There was no longer any question in my mind as to whether that thin line of bayonets would break - only when. Seconds, perhaps.

I would be slashed to bits by the onrushing horde. For there was also no question but that I would be taken for one of the hated Jews. I did not even wear a uniform as I had while with the United States Army in Germany. Only civilian clothes. The Arabs might spare the uniformed British but they would never spare me, caught up in that maddening whirl.

I did not even have Artin with me now to tell them I was not a combatant. Hadn't I refused to fire a gun, up there on the hill?

It was my fear that was sending me, every few seconds, to look out the door. The sight was chilling. Screaming and lunging. Pressing. Waving their weapons. The Arabs continued to push. The line of British bayonets was perhaps only 50 yards away now. Or less.

Why didn't those Tommies shoot some of those crazy people? It was one of the wild thoughts that flashed through my mind. But even in the borning of that thought, the inevitable answer came. Hell would really break loose for certain then. And I would be dead.

Oh, God, why did I have to follow the British correspondent down that hill? I had been so safe up there. Now, in a few minutes, I would be dead. I didn't want to die.

Somewhere, somehow, in that parade of racing minutes, a moment of reason must have finally prevailed and the Jews agreed to go. To give up the precious guns. They must - or die. The choice so limited.

First they carried the wounded out. Then the dead. At last, as the unwounded were allowed to pass through the door, each man or woman was forced to hand over their weapons. Rifles. Pistols. Hand grenades A few machine guns.

As the British sergeant took each weapon from the hands of each Jew, the weapon was tossed onto a growing pile in the roadway in sight of the maddened Arabs. It may have been a near fatal error. The guns should have been stacked inside, out of sight, at least for the moment. For the sight of those guns was adding to the fury in the eyes of the Arabs. Now it was greed. A gun. A gun.

There would be only a couple of hundred Jewish weapons. The mob numbered into the thousands. Which Arabs would get the weapons? That question was adding frenzy to the moment. Almost as if a new charge of adrenalin was surging into their blood. How could that wavering line of British Tommies hold? How had it held so long?

Hurry. Hurry. Get those Jews out of here. Onto the trucks. Move. Move. Faster. My mind was racing in a tumult of fear crazed thoughts.

It was in one of those last moments, with the British line of bayonets not more than 20 yards away, when it was certain that it would not hold more than a few more seconds, when I found that the British had not, after all, forgotten me.

One of the British lieutenants grabbed me, literally by the seat of the trousers, and pitched me like a bundle of hay into the back of one of the troop trucks.

"You'll have to go with us, old chap. Can't leave you to that mob out there," he grunted. He knew. I was glad he did. And glad that he had remembered.

The driver of the truck threw the machine into gear and we began to move. I could look back at that instant and see the mob of Arabs, surging like an angry tide, sweeping through and past that line of magnificent British infantrymen. It was a line no longer.

But the Tommies, their discipline intact in the midst of the madness, were forming lines for the march back to Jerusalem. The Arabs did not want their blood. All they wanted was that pile of weapons. And those armored cars and trucks the Jews had been forced to leave behind. One Arab had actually gotten the engine of one of the trucks started and went lurching away on flat tires.

As for that pile of weapons in the road, it had simply disappeared under the maddened horde of scrambling men. Fighting, screaming and slugging each other. Every man trying to get his hands on one of the guns. Wrestling with his neighbor for possession. Willing to slug his compatriot in the belly, in the eye, in the groin, anywhere, in order to maintain a grip on one of those instruments of death. Every vestige of Arab brotherhood had seemingly vanished.

A tragic convoy of British ambulances and trucks, grinding up the road, was now outside the boundaries of their collective awareness. We could go in peace. I would not, after all, die on that Easter Sunday.

As our vehicles reached the spot in the road where the original ambush had taken place, the convoy made its last stop. To pick up the bodies of those young Jews who had been killed there when it all started. In a time that now seemed long, long ago.

As the British medical corpsmen loaded the bodies, the most striking and chilling feature of the grisly sight was the fact that each of the dead young Jews lacked a head.

Theirs were the heads in those buckets at Jaffa Gate.

Chapter Twenty three - Lynch

Terror, divided by two? Nay, better multiplied by two.

It was real, the terror that ripped twice through my gut during that insane Kastel "happening".

Once when I went charging up the hill of that ancient citadel in the midst of an infantry attack, bullets whistling past my ears. Reluctantly, I insist.

And then when those crazy Arabs tried to lynch me after the battle was all over.

One thing is certain, it was Artin Kamegsisian, that unpredictable little Armenian interpreter, who got me into both of those absurd hot spots and, praise be to Allah, the one who got me out of the last one.

One minute, the guy was all mouse. The next - well, a lion.

That crazy springtime in Palestine of 1948 when nobody could know for sure what was going to happen to that once holy land.

It had been after World War I ended in 1918 when the British had been given mandate powers to govern Palestine. Now it was after World War II. The Jews, fresh from their holocaust experience in Europe, were trying mightily to get their hands on the little country as their "Promised Land."

The Arabs, who had claimed the same hunk of territory as their own homeland for centuries, were trying just as mightily to hang onto it.

It was a bloody mess. A three way bloody mess. Jews being shot and blown up by bombs. Arabs being shot and blown up by bombs. And in between the British, trying to keep the two warring sides apart - and in the process shedding their own share of blood.

DEAR GOD, I'M ONLY A BOY

By 1948 the British were fed up with the mess and had publicly announced that on May 15 they were calling it quits. Who killed who after that, well that would be somebody else's neck.

The Jews and Arabs, with the knowledge that it would be open warfare after May 15, were jockeying for position. And there was that little Arab village of Kastel, sitting high on a hill overlooking the Tel Aviv road to Jerusalem. Whoever had that hill, controlled the road.

The Jews, considering it a priority matter to keep that road open in order to supply their people in Jerusalem, sent a contingent of armed men in one night to blast the Arabs out of Kastel and hold it.

The Arabs, who had not reinforced the village, were taken by surprise. They howled with anger and began organizing a counter attack to regain that strategic village. Arab troops, mostly irregulars, were pouring in from all sides.

And there I was, sitting in Jerusalem, as a United Press newsman and trying to make arrangements to get to the scene. It seemed to be a matter of honor among these press folks that you weren't just supposed to write about battles, you were supposed to go out and look at them while they were going on.

"How about it, Artin, do you think we can get out there?"

He shrugged. He was in his mouse role. I could see he wasn't too anxious to get out there in range of flying bullets. But he agreed to try.

We started out by going to the headquarters of Abdul Khader Husseini, the Arab general who seemed to be in charge.

Omigosh, that was the guy they were going to accuse me in his death - of putting the finger on, to get him killed. That lynch thing.

Well, for now he was alive and well. This war was a sort of informal thing and we didn't have much trouble getting in to see him in his little headquarters. Nice looking guy, sitting there at his desk with a bunch of aides.

But when we told him we wanted to go out and see the war at Kastel, he said no.

"It's too dangerous. We don't want the responsibility for getting you killed," he said. I had the feeling he just didn't trust us foreign newsmen very much and didn't want us around when the rough stuff started.

He had just returned from a trip to Syria to consult with the Arab League. He was in a hurry, too. Now he was getting ready to go out there and take charge of the battle in person. Three counter attacks had been made. All had failed under the withering fire of the Jewish occupiers.

Abdul Khader was almost a legend among the Arabs. Dashing. Brave. Dynamic. A member of the royal Husseini family. If the Arabs would follow anybody into battle, it was Abdul Khader.

Abdul Khader made his attack that night, leading 300 men against a force of about 70 exhausted Jewish defenders who were awaiting reinforctments which failed to show up.

It was a brave attempt. Under the cover of rifle and machine gun fire, Arab sappers attempted to sneak in with bundles of explosives to blow up the buildings in which the Jews had taken cover. It was an attack which very nearly succeeded. Somehow, at the last moment, it had failed.

Nobody seemed to know it then but in that attack, Abdul Khader Husseini, the great Arab hero, died from a Jewish bullet. In fact, even after the attackers had retreated, given up and stumbled back, they were not aware that they had lost their leader.

Even as late as the next morning, when the Arab forces took stock of the situation, nobody seemed to know what had happened to Abdul Khader. Nobody had seen him fall.

Nobody had found his body. Some thought he had simply returned to Jerusalem.

Even the Jewish defenders, when they reconnoitered in the morning light, did not know what had happened. One of the Jewish soldiers stumbled across a body, turned it over and removed the papers from the man's pockets - and failed to recognize the dead Abdul Khader.

Later in the day, as word got around that Abdul Khader was missing, that he had not returned to Jerusalem, panic and anger whirled through the Arab ranks. Where is Abdul Khader? Where? He was an unidentified body lying on the slopes of the hillside at Kastel.

Word of the missing leader, of the possibility that something dreadful had happened to him in the night, flashed through the Arab villages and Jerusalem. The mightiest anger arose.

"We must find our leader. If he is dead we must find his body."

All through the morning, armed Arab irregulars streamed towards Kastel. If he indeed was dead, he must be avenged. Kastel must be retaken. Before the day turned into afternoon, at least 2,000 armed men had surrounded Kastel. I was among them.

Yes, I had finally made it. Once again Artin had come up with a solution after I kept badgering him to find a way to Kastel.

Our method bore a certain element of risk. Artin had contacted the captain of a company of Iraqi irregulars who had announced they would join the trek towards Kastel. The captain, without consulting anybody, had given us permission to accompany him and his men on the march.

But it would be a foot march, some 15 miles over the rocky hills and through equally stony ravines. A handful of donkeys to carry ammunition and water. Those donkeys would play another role on the trip back to Jerusalem.

One condition of the Iraqi captain had imposed was that "foreigners must wear a kaffiyeh." That ancient Arab headdress which came in such a variety of colors and patterns.

Somewhere a kaffiyeh was borrowed and Artin came to wind it around my head. Such an odd feeling, wearing that thing. As if, suddenly, I had lost my identity as an American neutral observer. Now I wasn't an American. Well, if it must be.

We must have stumbled over the rocky path, over the hills and into the gullies for at least four hours before we approached the scene of the battle. It was the sound of gunfire which told us we were getting near.

The closer we came to the firing, the more of Artin's mouse character was showing. No, I refuse to criticise. Not after what he did later.

"I think we are close enough," he suggested timidly.

But I was a reporter and wanted to see the battle, damn it. From where we were, safely behind the hills, I couldn't see a damn thing. Not even Kastel, the objective of all this weary marching. Only the popping sound of guns.

When I kept urging Artin to move up closer, he kept hanging back. The truly reluctant warrior at this point. Finally, when I kept needling him, he consulted with some of the soldiers and then indicated a high hill in front of us.

"They tell me that if you climb that hill you can see Kastel," he said. "And the battle." I climbed. Alone. Artin waited for me below.

I really didn't feel all that brave. However, I didn't hear any bullets whistling around my ears or bouncing off the rocks. Not yet.

From the crown of that hill I could see it all. Kastel, that ancient high hill that had been fortified as long ago as the days of the ancient Romans. It stood 2,500 feet high. Legend had it that during the days of the ancient crusades, Richard the Lionhearted had caught his first glimpse of Jerusalem from near this point and had wept with joy.

I was still half a mile from the beseiged village. Spread out below me in a panorama of color, the kaffiyehs of so many hues, on the heads of hundreds and hundreds of Arab attackers. At the moment they were all lying behind a series of rock fences as protection from gunfire coming from the besieged Jews. Except that, as usual, with the ammunition low, the Jews were seldom firing a shot unless they truly had a target.

At the top of the hill I found a small shell crater. The Jews, I was told, had a few two inch mortars and they made these little craters.

It was just about the right size for a man's body to lie in, offering a bit of protection as one peered over the rim of the hilltop. But the crater offered also just a hint of the danger. I assured myself that there was very little chance that a second shell would strike the exact same spot twice - but it did.

Oh, I was lucky. I had been in that little crater perhaps some 15 minutes when I decided I wanted to go still closer. I began scrambling back down the hill to make a circle to the next hill. I had gone about 50 to 75 feet when it came. The "blam" of another mortar shell blast, back up there on the hill top from which I had just scrambled. From what I could see, it had landed right smack in the same little crater I had vacated less than 30 seconds before.

Well, that one shook me for a moment. But I was stubborn, too, and told Artin I wanted to make my way around the hills to get out there where those hundreds of "besiegers" were lying behind those rock fences.

"Aren't we close enough?" he pleaded. Only after I insisted did we skirt the hill, on the sheltered side away from Kastel, and pick our way carefully up to the battle area.

At first, there was little going on except sporadic gunfire aimed at Kastel from behind the stone fences. Not a sign of the Jews inside the village. But that didn't mean they weren't there, nor that there was no danger.

One tall Arab, not five yards away from me, raised his head over the wall to aim his rifle, uttered a gagging sound and collapsed. When the first aid men reached him they found a neat little bullet hole right in the center of his chin. In two minutes he was dead, in a gurgle of blood. It was indeed a time to keep heads down.

Still no word as to what had happened to Abdul Khader. Only that he was missing and the Arabs wanted revenge.

It was in the early hours of the afternoon when the Arab leaders decided to obtain that revenge. Officers and leaders began creeping back and forth among the ranks, keeping what cover they could but now shouting excitedly. They were planning an attack, a charge to take Kastel.

All that frenzied shouting and haranguing was for the purpose of stirring up the fighting spirit of all these men hunched down behind the stone fences, to send them leaping over those walls behind which they had been cringing. "Nashamdi." Forward. Attack.

At the beginning, it seemed the haranguing was having little effect. Few of the men seemed eager to charge, in the face of that deadly Jewish fire. But as the shouting continued, the men, one by one, picked up the refrain, echoing the shouts. The psychology was working. Moment by moment, the frenzied courage they would need for an attack was coming alive in their souls.

In a sense, it almost seemed like an old time "Holy Roller" revival back in Oklahoma, with a fired up preacher shouting words of challenge in the name of the Lord and the spirits of the listeners aroused by shouts of "Amen. Praise the Lord." Now the lord was called Allah.

"Allah Akbar." God is great. God will send our bullets plunging into the hearts of the Jews. Of course, I couldn't understand a word but anyone could see the spirit of courage rising in the souls of these men. An attack was indeed coming.

Most strange of all was the effect all this "spirit rousing" was having on Artin. Suddenly he was joining in, his spirit also coming alive. My God, was he going to go charging off, too? Allah forbid.

Both he and the Iraqi captain had warned me over and over not to leave his side. Without him, dressed as I was in street clothes and speaking hardly a word of Arabic, I would revert to being an utter stranger. A foreigner. The danger would be real. I could easily be shot, perhaps as a Jewish spy.

In my sector, at the moment, a stocky Arab commander, armed with an American .45 caliber Colt automatic pistol, was doing the spirit rousing. The pistol was in his hand, the hammer back, his finger on the trigger and I was certain it was loaded. But he was waving the gun violently, almost as if it were a baton, to orchestrate a symphony of violence which was about to explode in these rocky hills of Judea.

And it was Artin, he of the mouse character, he who had protested each time I tried to get closer to the battle, who was now shouting with the loudest of them. That countenance of the mouse was suddenly being transformed into the face of a lion.

He had no weapon. Nor did I. Up until this moment, I am sure he would have cringed at the suggestion of bearing one. Now it was almost as if he were eager for the coming attack to start. Brave like the boldest of the Arabs now.

And then it came, that wild, strange moment of truth which I had never anticipated and certainly did not desire. True, I had wanted to come close enough to truly look into the eyes of the battle but I had never contemplated taking part in an attack. I didn't have that kind of courage, even if I had wanted it.

But then, that moment, the fateful instant when, amidst the frenzied shouting, there came that final order for the charge.

The stocky commander with his big pistol was firing. Behind the men he was firing into the ground near their feet. "Charge. Charge. Charge."

And they went. They first got to their feet with a bit of reluctance but then the frenzy of the moment, all the fire and courage these commanders had been pumping into the men for more than 20 minutes, began to assert itself. In a matter of seconds, the thing had indeed become a massive charge, the men running now, leaping over the rock fences behind which they had cowered so long. "Allah Ahkbar."

The shouts, the screeches, the yells, the madding rush. Was I at Gettysburg - or Kastel?

Yes, I had sensed that somehow a strange transformation had been taking place in Artin. That he, too, had been swept up in the frenzy of the moment but I certainly did not expect him to join the charge. He did - the crazy nut.

Suddenly, without the slightest regard for me, the man he had been hired to accompany and to guard, Artin was gone. Rushing along in the wild charge towards Kastel.

And then the chilling implication of it burst in upon my consciousness as well, for I must, I simply must, stay with him. Without him, in that screaming mob I was lost. So, willingly or not, I suddenly found myself dashing along with the charging men at arms, leaping over one of those stone fences after another.

Trying to keep sight of my mousy little guide who had suddenly gone crazy.

The Jews were firing with deadly accuracy. I saw more than one of the charging men stumble and fall. A gush of blood. Those ghastly sounds that men make when hit by a bullet.

But none of the gunfire was stopping, or slowing, that mad rush forward now. The spirit of it all, the momentum, was too great. The numbers, too many. At least 2,000 Arabs took part in that wild attack that day against Jewish defenders that numbered less than 100. Two thousand Arabs and one crazy American news correspondent who didn't want to go.

The results were inevitable. The Jews knew it, too, and it was one time when they allowed wisdom to take the place of valour. As we came dashing into the village from three sides we could see the Jews, far down the hillside, retreating as madly as we had been rushing towards them.

One angry Arab with a Bren gun caught sight of the fleeing Jews and from a spot almost directly behind me cut loose with a chatter of gunfire so close I could feel the impact of wind bursts from the gun at my back. Fearful he would be swinging that gun barrel further, I flopped face down on the mother earth.

And then it was over. Most of the Jews had managed to flee. A few bodies were found in the streets and buildings of the village. An Arab would walk up and kick one with frustration. For some strange reason, despite the fact that it was 2,000 Arabs to fewer than 100 Jews, Kastel had never been completely surrounded. On three sides only, leaving that one vital direction open for the Jewish escape. It was something only the untrained Arab irregulars could do.

But peering down that hillside at the fleeing Jews brought one more strange and tragic sight. Several of the Jews seemed to be kicking bodies, sending them rolling and tumbling down the steep slope.

I learned only later, from Jewish reports, that these had been their wounded. It had been the only way they could get those men down the hill fast enough to escape the attacking Arabs. To have tried to carry them, by litter or otherwise, would have been too slow. God, what a hell that must have been for men already wounded.

In any case, there remained one more tragic event, for the Arabs at least. Wandering around the scene of the battle, looking for guns, bodies, what have you, one of the Arabs stumbled upon a body of one of their own. He recognized it. Abdul Khader Husseini, their great leader.

He had been dead since the night before, struck by a bullet as he had led that bitter attack to regain for Arab hands the ancient citadel. His angry followers had the hill now, and the village, but they had lost their beloved leader.

At this moment a mournful wail of sorrow arose from the victorious warriors. Tenderly they wrapped his body, placed it upon a litter and carried it, in relays, all the way back to Jerusalem. "Allah Akhabar, Allah Akhbar." But the victory had turned to bitter tragedy.

It was time for the sad Arabs to gather up the remaining bodies of their dead, and the wounded, and carry them back to Jerusalem. And now those donkeys that had brought ammunition to the scene of battle would carry back the dead and the wounded. The dead were simply draped like bags across the backs of the little animals. For the seriously wounded, at least one or two men were assigned to walk on each side of the donkeys to keep the wounded from falling off. A few were carried on litters, the burden bearers changing about in shifts every quarter of a mile or so.

Somehow I sensed little elation as we slowly trudged those miles back to Jerusalem. My bones and my muscles were so weary I could barely lift one foot after another but once more, so long as the column moved, I must keep up with them. To become separated from Artin, and the Iraqis, who were now accustomed to the sight of me, would again have been too dangerous for an American in the land of these wild and angry Arabs. Especially now, with the new anger at their leader's death.

The thoughts were profane but they came. The weakness of man. As I stumbled over the rocky hills and through the ravines on that return trip I could see the wounded on the donkeys and somehow found myself wishing I could change places with them so I could ride. No, I wanted no wound but so weary was the flesh.

And when I did finally stumble, long after dark, into the press room at British headquarters in Jerusalem I still could not lie down, or go to sleep. I still had a story to write of the scenes I had just witnessed at the ancient village of Kastel.

My bones were aching and my eyelids falling like lead but somehow I managed to pound out some sort of a story, get it on the wire, then fell into my bed.

It seemed I had barely closed my eyes and had fallen asleep when someone was shaking me violently to awaken me. It was one

288

of my colleagues and in his hand he had a message from United Press headquarters in London.

"They said you filed a good story but you didn't put enough color into it. They want more description of the battle. That Arab who was shot in the chin, right beside you. They want more details of how he died."

Oh, God, and I had always dreamed of being a news correspondent in far lands. Right now I wanted to tell London and everybody else ot go to hell.

And the lynch attempt on me was still to come.

Somehow I must have managed to make London satisfied, if not happy, and caught up on my sleep. When I finally awoke, came back to life and was able to resurrect an interest in what was going on, I found that the Arabs had been so grief stricken over the discovery of Abdul Khader's death they simply lost interest, for the moment at least, in Kastel. More or less abandoned it.

Results, the Jews sneaked back and retook it on the very night after the "great Arab victory." Perhaps nobody had expected the Jews to come back so soon but mostly a grief stricken people had lost, for the moment, the will to fight.

Now, it seemed, everybody wanted only to go to their hero's funeral. From high places had come the edict that Abdul Khader would be, as a member of the royal Husseini family, and in view of his great sacrifice for his homeland, entombed in the Dome of the Rock in Jerusalem, that holy spot from which Mohammed had ascended to heaven. The holiest of shrines for the Islam world. Symbolically, something in the nature of a British hero being enshrined in Westminster Abbey.

It was Artin, my faithful mouse-lion interpreter, who came to tell me.

"Do you want to go the funeral?" he asked. "The crowd, it is enormous. It will be the greatest funeral."

So, with no more villages like Kastels to charge, no more crazy demands from London, I decided I would go. How could I know that even a funeral could turn so suddenly into a dangerous evil?

From the hills, from the villages, from the stone and dung houses of Jerusalem they came, the mourners, to pay their last respects, to wail their last prayers for the soul of their beloved but fallen Abdul Khader.

As Artin and I attempted to approach the area of the great Moslem shrine we were engulfed by the hordes. A sea of Arab humanity. Many of the men toting rifles, or knives, for in those troubled times, much as in the frontier tradition of America, men bore arms wherever they went. To the holy Dome. To a funeral.

To the eye it seemed as if a million Arabs had come. I could see that we had arrived late and would never be able to reach the Dome. But we were in that pressing horde, indeed a part of it. And now, as I saw the sea of bobbing kaffiyehs around me I suddenly felt naked, a foreigner again. My head was bare. I had learned as soon as I arrived in Palestine not to wear a hat in the Arab sectors, the mark of the hated Jews. Better to show my red hair - few Jews had red hair.

And now indeed something strange was going on around me. Artin had suddenly become nervous and began pushing me through the crowd. Faster, faster. I was becoming aware of an angry jabbering about me and fingers were pointed - at me. Some of the Arabs were attempting to push their way through the mob towards me. Menacingly. There were those guns, and those long knives.

"We've got to get out of here," said Artin in English. "They are trying to get you." He was pushing madly now, his elbows swinging wildly to plow a path through the mob and pushing me ahead of him.

At first I had resisted him, unable to understand what was going on but now, at his warning words, and those pointing fingers, the angry shouts, I joined in the frenzied attempt to escape. Once more those icy fingers of fear gripping at my gut.

It may have been only some sort of a miracle that, suddenly, the little Fiat taxicab was there. For me at least. But there it was, in the midst of that mob, its driver had discharged a passenger and was now trying to force his way out of the mob.

Somehow Artin managed to push his way, dragging me along, to the side of the little car and without the slightest sign to the driver simply yanked the door open and literally hurled me inside. Then he leaped in, slammed the door and quickly closed the locks.

We had reached that tenuous sanctuary not a second too soon. The mob was closing in on us now. They were grabbing at the little car. The tiny machine was rocking. I was afraid that any moment they would smash the windows with the butts of their rifles.

But Artin was shouting hysterically at the driver, "Go, go, go. Hurry."

And somehow the driver managed to do it. Roaring his engine and beeping his horn madly, he was ramming his way through what appeared to be a solid wall of human flesh. I know the car bounced off, if not actually ramming, some of the bodies. But we made it. The mob thinned and then, we were free.

But even now Artin, as if fearing pursuit - was there another taxi back there somewhere? - was shouting, "Go, go, go." Oh, I had suddenly realized the danger, too. It had been apparent enough in the faces of those angry men. The pointed fingers. The shouts. But I didn't have the slightest idea why.

I kept asking Artin what the hell was going on and he refused to tell me so long as we were in the taxi. Most Jerusalem taxi drivers understood at least some English.

Only after we were truly free, across the borders of the British control zone and out of the taxi did he find the breath to tell me.

"They wanted to kill you," he said. "They were saying that you were a Jewish spy and were responsible for the death of Abdul Khader Husseini."

It was then that the real fear I should have felt back in that mob, flooded in upon me. My hands were trembling.

"But, God, man, how could I have anything to do with Abdul Khader's death?" I demanded. "I didn't even know he was dead until it was all over."

Even Artin couldn't tell me more then. He didn't know more. It was later, with a warning to me to stay inside the British military enclave, he went back to do some checking. He came back with more details.

"Some of those Arab soldiers at the funeral recognized you," he said. "They had also seen you at Kastel.

"You were the only foreigner at Kastel. Some of them had also seen you at Abdul Khader's headquarters just before he went to Kastel. They heard him tell you he was going to Kastel. They also heard you ask for permission to go along and Khader refusing. They know you went against Abdul Khader's orders.

"Now they have the story going around the Arab quarters of Jerusalem that you sent a message to the Jews and they set up an ambush for Abdul Khader. They want revenge. They want to kill you."

After that rush of words Artin was silent for a moment. Then, "We were lucky that taxi came along."

Yes, we were lucky that taxi had come along.

291

Later he had more to say. "They will still try to get you. You'd better get out of Jerusalem."

Somehow I didn't like the idea of running out but then another kind of "taxi" came along. A wire from London, telling me to go to Haifa to cover the final departure of Sir Alan Cunningham and the last of his British soldiers.

Before I went I had to say goodbye to Artin, the little guy who had been such a mouse, and such a lion. When I took his hand for the last time I guess I almost blubbered a bit.

He had been paid only to be my interpreter and my guide. But I like to remember him as - when the occasion demanded it - Artin the lionhearted.

Chapter Twenty four – The Gallows Caper

Hermann Goering - the fatso crown prince of Adolph Hitler's Nazi Germany - most certainly did not even consider, when he popped that poison pill into his mouth, that he was messing up one of the neatest news scoops of my life.

The pill was costing Herr Goering his life. All it was costing me was chance at my own bright little moment in the sun.

But I had done all that skulking around inside the clock tower, dodged the MP's who had orders to shoot first and talk about it later. I had perched in that dangerous, cold, wet and bombed out tower attic, peering out through my field glasses so many hours - and all for nothing. Well, almost nothing.

Oh, Herr Hermann had no reason to be concerned about me and my elaborate plans. Heck, the guy didn't even know me. How could he? We hadn't even been introduced. But as he sat there in the prisoner's dock of the International Military Tribunal, his eyes must have wandered over the courtroom and the press section - and seen me sitting there, one of several dozen newsmen reporting the greatest court trial in history. His roving eyes must have caught my red hair and lingered for a moment. But he would never even wonder who I was.

But I knew him. How well I knew him. I had been reading about him for years. All that strutting around in his fancy uniforms. Playing the role of an Aryan Mussolini. Showing off his mighty Luftwaffe, touted as the greatest military air force in the world. Posing for the news cameras with the striking woman, Emmy, hanging on his arm.

Now, sitting in that prisoner's dock with his 20 fellow prisoners, he remained the Number One attraction. The prosecutors

293

had openly described him as Number One. He was second only to Hitler himself but Hitler had decided to end his life in his bunker suicide before the Allies could get their claws on him.

Rudolph Hess was getting his share of the attention, too, with his spectacular insanity act. The others were bigwigs, too. Hjalmer Schacht, Hitler's finance minister who was credited with raising the money to arm Germany. Joachim Von Ribbentrop, the foreign minister who engineered that treaty that double crossed Russia.

There were men like Keitel, Doenitz, Jodl and Raeder, top military commanders who fought off the armed forces of the world for years. Even Julius Streicher, that swaggering Jew baiter. And all the other Nazi big shots.

But Hermann Goering had always managed to grab more than his share of world headlines over the years, as the world hung breathlessly on every act, every word and every gesture of these Nazi strutters. Who, in all the world at that time, could say they didn't know him?

Now, with the world following their trial in Nurnberg, Goering remained the star attraction. Even when all the accusations about broken treaties, aggressive warfare, crimes against humanity, the mass slaughter of the Jews, came showering down on his head, Goering had managed to shrug it all off. Either he had not been in on the big decisions, he insisted, or else it was all something that world leaders and politicians had been doing since the very beginning of history.

A master showman, the guy. Should have been on the stage with Emmy, his actress wife. Even the judges and prosecutors agreed he turned in a brilliant performance under cross examination. But in the end, it really hadn't helped him a lot. The prosecutors had too many "goods" on him. He was sentenced to death, along with 11 of his buddies. One was Martin Borman, in absentia. Borman, like Hitler, had managed to make himself absent by death.

It was a day a young newsman would never forget, the day they brought in the verdicts. October 1, 1946. It was my boss, Pat Conger, in charge of United Press operations in Germany, who managed his own sort of scoop.

Working with American, German, French and British teletype technicians, Pat had managed something they said couldn't be done. By linking up teletype machines in all these nations he produced a straight circuit from Nurnberg - site of the trials - to London. The link went via Frankfurt and Paris.

Pat's "patch together" system worked so well that we were able to beat the competition on each verdict by one to three minutes. Working in relay with other messengers, I had lined up in the courtroom. As each verdict was announced, one of us dashed to the press room.

There, in the press room, sat a German girl who was our best and fastest teletype girl. Tears streaming down her face, she slammed out the messages. "Herman Goering, death by hanging." "Joachim Von Ribbentrop, death by hanging." "Wilhelm Keitel, death by hanging."

Her tears? Well, she was German and the leaders of her motherland were being sentenced to death. Even Goering's plea to be allowed to die before a firing squad, as soldiers die, had been denied.

The next scoop would be tougher to bring off - the executions.

It was all done in the name of security. Colonel Marcus Andrus, the rod stiff American Army man who was charged with seeing that nothing happened to disturb the peace of the trial, took his job very seriously. Even if there was a bit of vanity allowed in it, too, such as wanting to impress the parade ground British, the proud French and the stubborn Russkies that Americans could produce a bit of spit and polish as well as anyone. Like the helmets Andrus had chrome plated. I was to remember those helmets.

Well, the Werewolves had something to do with it. It had been those same Nazi big wigs, sitting in the dock there, who cranked up the Werewolf idea near the end of the war. Faced with military defeat on the battleground, the Nazi high command urged German soldiers to evade capture and go underground, organize guerrilla Werewolves and hide in the mountains. They would sweep down and strike at the conquerers when opportunity allowed it.

The Americans and their allies had taken the Werewolf plan seriously and prepared for guerrilla warfare. But the surrender of the Germans had quickly demonstrated that they were sick of the war. The Werewolves had simply not materialized.

Now, here at Nurnberg, as the trials of the accused war criminals had neared the end and it was apparent that the Allies were going to hang a bunch of Nazis, the old Werewolf stories began cropping up again. The Werewolves had indeed been in hiding, said the rumors. Since the end of the war they had been gathering their forces to rescue those big wheels from the Nurnberg prison.

295

So, this was one of the reasons Colonel Andrus and his men were keeping security so tight.

The trials were over but they hadn't announced the date of the executions. Deep, dark secret. Word was put out that no newsman would be allowed to witness the executions. That brought such a mighty protest that trial officials finally agreed to let two reporters each from the United States, Britain, France and Russia come in as witnesses. Their reports would be made available immediately to all the other reporters. No reporter, not even the eight chosen to witness the hangings, would have any advantage over the others. It was the only way to be fair about it. The names of the eight reporters would be drawn by lot.

The date and time of the hangings was to remain a dark secret.

When Pat, my boss, heard about this, he said it could hold up the story by at least four hours. Maybe more. We served newspapers around the world. At least one of our newspaper clients was going to press, somewhere in the world, every minute of the day.

He had his think cap on, trying to come up with some way to get the story sooner.

That would take a bit of doing. You had to consider the layout. The trials had been held in a great, ornate building, the "Palace of Justice." There was the prison at the rear of the palace but it was separated from the palace by about 30 to 40 feet. The only connection was a covered passage, like a tunnel.

The prison was surrounded by a huge brick wall that was some 15 to 20 feet high and about four feet wide. It was wide enough for MP's carrying "Tommy guns" to walk along on top.

The huge, triple winged prison building dominated the walled prison yard. Off to one side, separated from the main prison by about 50 to 60 feet, was a "gymnasium" for exercising prisoners in the winter time.

To maintain contact with the German side of the picture, Pat hired some local reporters to work part time, to pick up information an American reporter might miss, even if he spoke fluent German. It was one of these stringers who had picked up the report that the "Amis" had brought in some German carpenters to build something in that gymnasium That "something" could only be gallows.

Pat's brain was churning full time. If gallows were being erected in the gymnasium and the condemned Nazis were being held in the prison, it meant that the prisoners would have to make their last walk across an exposed area of 50 to 60 feet. If only a guy could figure out some way to see over the high wall that surrounded the prison behind the Palace.

That was when Pat roped me into the picture.

"You know," he began, "there is a clock tower on top of that Palace of Justice. Do you think you might just sneak up into that tower and see if there is any way to hide up there - and see what's going on inside that yard?"

Ah, a bit of adventure. I had always liked things like that. I was ready to go.

"Watch out for the MP's," said Pat. Colonel Andrus had assigned several MP's to patrol the Palace, just in case anybody got cute ideas. I suppose snooping from the clock tower would come under that category.

In any case, I started prowling the halls and corridors of the big Palace, searching for the stairways or catwalks that might lead to the tower. Finding the right door, or opening, would lead to the tower. It wasn't too tough getting up to the fourth floor. The scattered MP's couldn't be everywhere.

Somehow I found it. At first, there were stairways. Then only some ladders that led up to the tower. Up near the top, there was only some scaffolding and huge wooden beams to walk on.

There were no windows. How could you see out into the prison yard? Then I discovered that each of the four faces on the clock had a little latched opening, barely big enough for a man to crawl through. Apparently for repairmen and painters to work on the faces of the clock. Those four faces needed lots of attention now because the clock had stopped running during the war. The Germans had found more urgent business than fixing an historic old clock that was now more ornamental than useful.

Those little doors were not even hinged. You undid the latches and lifted them out, carefully. One of those doors could kill a man below if a clock repairman - or a nosy reporter who wasn't supposed to be up in the tower - let one slip.

I knew which one of the hatch oppenings I needed to look out of. Now, if I could only open it a bit without alarming one of those MP's down on the wall below. I did have sense enough to know I couldn't open it all the way. Just a crack.

Very carefully, I undid the latches, stiff and creaky from lack of use for years. Then, my heart pounding a bit more thumpily than usual, I began easing that door upward just a crack.

Ah, success. As I peered carefully out through the slit, the whole panorama of the prison yard lay below me. I was peeking over the wall. At least 30 to 40 feet above the wall, in fact. If the trial officials were building a gallows inside the gymnasium, off to my right, and walked the condemned men there from the main prison, I would be able to see them on that last death walk.

Pat might get his scoop. If we could determine the time set for the hangings, we would be able report to the world what had taken place, hours before the other reporters would be permitted to release their story. It would be a prtty good sized scoop. With the whole world watching. It was the kind of assignment that a young reporter dreams about.

I eased the door back in place, closed the latches and carefully sneaked back down the tower to report to Pat.

Next day, I crawled back into my tower again. This time I wanted to spend a bit more time at the peeping job. That was when I found my arms tiring of holding the weight of the clock door. I scouted around until I found a bit of wire in the tower. I made hooks to hold the door in position, with a cracked opening slit of about an inch. Just enough for me to peer out.

Now I could sit and peek to my heart's content. I could watch the MP's, each heavily armed, striding back and forth on top of his assigned part of the wall. Back and forth. They hardly ever looked up. I am sure they expected no skullduggery from above. Only occasionally did one of them happen to glance up.

The first time it happened, I instinctively ducked, fearing he might see me and maybe even shoot. He didn't see me. Then I persuaded myself that an MP down below would not be likely to spot that slit in the face of the dead clock. Nor would he be able to see my eyes, for I was in darkness while he was outside in the light. Reassured by such reasoning, I became bolder and when an MP did happen to look up I stared right back at him. It was true, they didn't see me.

After that, I climbed up into my clock tower every day. On some days, I climbed up more than once. Now I could even hear the hammering inside the gymnasium building. Something was indeed being constructed in there. German workers, citizens of the defeated nation, being required to build the gallows upon which would be hung the former leaders of their nation.

On one trip to the tower I was caught. One of the MP's on patrol inside the Palace spotted me coming down a stairway. At least I wasn't caught in the tower.

But I was on an upper floor, off limits to unauthorized persons.

"What the hell are you doing up here?" he demanded.

I had to think fast. What excuse would keep him from marching me off to MP headquarters? I knew he didn't take me for a Werewolf. I was in the Army uniform that newsmen were required to wear. Without insignia.

"I'm just interested in historic old buildings," I said. "I was taking a look."

He wasn't too tough. "Well, get your ass back downstairs and stay down there," he said. "You know the orders."

"Yes, sir," I said and trotted down the stairs. I promised myself to be a bit more careful. If only they didn't wear those rubber heels on their boots. Sometimes you couldn't hear them coming.

Now it was Pat who had the big news. He had a tip from one of his "inside sources" that the executions would take place on the night of October 14-15. They would start at midnight. It was only a couple of days away.

Oh, wow. We had our date and the time. The only problem now was that even if I were in position in the old clock tower, how much would I be able to see at night? How much light would there be in the prison yard?

"I've got a pair of field glasses with night lenses," Pat said. "Do you think you can sneak them up in the tower?"

What was making it all so urgent was that Pat, wise in the ways of competitive newsmen, knew that the Associated Press, Reuters, International News Services and all the other new agencies were doing their own scheming on how to get a scoop. If they weren't working on the clock tower, then it would be something else. We couldn't afford to fail. At least, we had to try.

Pat had more instructions. It all made sense.

"You're going to have to get up there in the day time and wait it out," he said. "It will be a long wait. You can put a sandwich or something in your pocket. You'll need a flashlight, too. We'll fix one that shows just a slit of light. Any place to take a pee, up there?"

That last question I shrugged off. If necessary, I'd simply pee on the floor. Just one time, maybe, that old Palace of Justice could take that. The long wait part didn't bother me, either. If the whole thing worked, it would be worth it all. We'd have our big scoop. Unless, of course, the competition had some kind of a "clock tower" that was better than ours.

The plan had gone too smoothly. No hitches, except that one little encounter with the MP on the stairway. Maybe on the last day they would be alert and more careful.

Indeed, they were. For now came a bitter disappointment. Not only were they more alert but they were heavily reinforced. When we entered the Palace on the morning of October 14 we were immediately met at the door by MP's checking our press cards. "You will be allowed to go only to the press room. All the rest of the building is off limits," they said.

There they were, MP's stationed at the bottom of each stairway, barring the way to those upper floors. Our entire clock tower plan was down the drain. All that climbing and peeping, the wiring of latches, was for nothing. Absolutely nothing. What would we do now?

Pat had to put his brain in high gear. He spent several hours consulting with his German stringers and a few other contacts. Then came the new emergency plan.

"On the other side of the prison courtyard is a four story building," Pat said. "It has been damaged by bombs. Most of the roof has been blown away. Nobody can live in it. I don't even know if there is enough structure left in it for you to climb to the top. But you've got to try."

The only part of the building still habitable was the basement. A German family lived in it. We would have to ease their worries and suspicions. All Germans were shivering in their boots, fearful of the occupying Army men in those days.

We would also have to run the gauntlet of another set of MP's now. They were in Jeeps, patrolling all the streets surrounding the prison yard. By timing them with our watch we were able to determine that a Jeep came by every five minutes. If I were to slip into that bombed building I'd have to make a dash between Jeep patrols. But what if the door on that lower level were locked and the Germans inside it refused to let me in? Probably, they had already been warned by the MP's not to let anbody in.

After an hour or so, Pat had the answer to that. Or, at least, we believed he did. From somewhere he had snitched a sheet of International Military Tribunal stationary which had an official letterhead on it. On that sheet he had written a letter in German, addressed to the occpuants of that basement. The letter, quite short, stated that I, Menno Duerksen, had been assigned to act as an "observer" on top of the building. He had stamped all sorts of rubber stamping over it. The Germans liked those things.

"If you can sneak in there between MP patrols and get them to open the door, show them this letter," Pat said. "Then see if you can climb up into the attic. See what you can see from there. If it works, stay there. If you can see them lead the prisoners from the prison to the gym, and if you can hear anything, make sure you count 11 of them. After you count 11, come back down and get over here as fast as you can. Be careful."

My boss' instructions. Pat had it all planned out. A hurried plan but maybe it would work. If I could keep from getting caught by the MP's on street patrol. If I could get the German folks inside to open their door. If there was enough of that bombed building remaining to enable me to climb to the top. High enough to look over the wall.

Well, we were going to give it an honest try. A bit on the hairy side, perhaps, but I was young and full of juice.

It was already dark when the try was made. I got into position as close as possible outside the MP patrol area. Then, as a Jeep passed, I made my dash. I didn't time that dash, maybe 150 yards, but I knew I'd have to hurry. I'd look very funny if the sweep of the headlights of the next MP patrol caught me out there, outlined against the building.

Not only did I have to worry about the Jeep patrol but those MP's patrolling on the wall with their Tommy guns, only a few yards away. If I banged too loudly or shouted to loudly to the folks inside, the MP's would hear me. I didn't want any .45 caliber bullets whistling past my ears. The MP's were still taking things pretty seriously. Especially on this night.

But nobody was answering my knocks. I kept knocking louder and louder, holding my breath, hoping the MP's on the wall wouldn't hear. Would nobody open up? We had not been able to plan for this kind of an emergency.

Bang, bang, bang. God, please, somebody open the door. The urgency was shouting at me now, in my mind. The heart pounding. The door remained shut. Locked.

Somewhere behind me I could hear the motor of the returning Jeep. The flash of its headlights. Was I caught? Even if they didn't shoot, I would be in trouble. And our Number Two plan would also be down the drain. For one thing, I didn't dare be caught with that phony International Military Tribunal letter on my person.

I was certain the Jeep had rounded the last corner and the sweep of its headlights was picking me up when, at the very last instant, the door did creak open. Just a crack as a man peered out.

It was all I needed. No time for reading letters. I simply rammed my shoulder against the door and slammed it open, almost knocking the man down. In a fraction of a second I was inside. But wait, before I could try to explain to my new German "friends," I must pause a moment to see if the Jeep stopped. That they hadn't seen me. For once, my luck held. The patrol droned on. I was inside.

Now it was time to flash my light upon the letter and try to explain who I was and what I wanted. It was reassuring that I spoke German, even if I did wear the uniform of an "Ami." The Americans, I said, wanted an observer up in the top of the building, in case of trouble. I must climb their stairs to the attic. Or what was left of the attic.

"But the stairs, they are kaput," the man said. "I don't think you can get up there. It is dangerous. The building has been inspected and it is forbidden to go up there."

Well, maybe so. But I would try.

I clamped the palm of my hand over the head of the flashlight, allowing only a tiny slit of light to escape between the fingers and began climbing the stairway. At first it was not too bad, except for the rubble piled on everything. But then, the higher I got the less remained of the stairway.

At times there was no stairs at all. Just blown away. Folks said I was "part monkey," the way I could climb a tree when I was a kid. Now I called on my "monkey" skill to cling to the joists, the rafters and studs, whatever was available, to make my way past the gaping holes in the stairway.

I did try to be careful. Before putting my whole weight on a piece of timber I would test it. When one was loose, I groped some more. This monkey climbing took both hands and now I couldn't even use my flashlight. I rammed it into a pocket. The field glasses dangled over a shoulder. I knew I also had to be careful not to make noise that would be heard by the MP's on the nearby wall.

Once or twice I held my breath when my foot would slip. Or dislodge a bit of rubble that would go clattering down below. How much noise would it take to alert those trigger happy MP's?

Somehow I made it, all the way to the top. That much of the framework was still standing, although most of the walls had been blown away. Only the shaky skeleton of a building still stood.

Looking upwards, toward the sky, there were gaping holes in the roof. I tried to grope my way to a spot in that attic that would support my weight and where I would be able to look out.

Success, success. For the moment, at least. While I wasn't as high as I had been in the old clock tower, I could still look over that forbidding wall. And when I carefully swept the forbidden area with the night glasses, I found that in some ways I had a better view than from the tower.

There were trees obscuring part of the area between the prison and the gymnasium but there were a few feeble lights strung over the area.

What was really important was that I could see that fateful door from which the condemned men would have to emerge. Would they be brought out as a group? Or one by one? I would have to wait and see. It was near 11 o'clock - one hour to hanging time unless our tip had been wrong.

It was reasonable to assume that it had been correct, that the hanging would be at midnight tonight. We had the same tip from several sources. The eight special reporters, chosen to witness the execution, had been taken into custody. The rest of us had been told we must wait. Pat and I had not been willing to do that.

As the slow minutes passed, I sneaked very careful glimpses at my watch, using only the tiniest of slits of light from the flashlight. I must not allow those MP's to notice anything suspicious in the night. I was "on station" and everything was looking so rosy I didn't want another foul-up.

It was a chill October night. A misting drizzle of a rain began to fall. I tried to maneuver into a spot where there was still a bit of roof over me. Every minute or so I had to wipe the lenses of my field glasses.

The minute hand on my watch was creeping towards midnight. Fifteen minutes. Ten minutes. Five minutes. My heart was pounding with expectancy. Would the door open at midnight and Herman Goering step out? It was reasonable to expect that he would be first, as he had been through the long trial of 10 months. He had been so brilliant in that sparring match with prosecutor Robert Jackson. In a few minutes that brilliant brain would be dead.

My watch told me it was midnight. No sign from the door. Nothing stirred down there in the courtyard.

Pat had warned me about some possible delay.

"I'm sure we have the right tip," he said. "But you know how these things never start on time. Be patient. If they're late, just wait."

I could wait. I was not going to botch things up by being impatient.

Actually, Herman Goering had already botched it up.

Waiting there in the darkness and the drizzle, how could I possibly know that he had popped a poison pill in his mouth at 10:40 and was now dead? Such a thought never entered my mind. Colonel Andrus had been so certain he had taken all the precautions. Didn't the colonel have a guard stationed at the peep hole of each cell, 24 hours a day, and with the cell lights on constantly?

The prisoners, those accused Nazis, had complained bitterly about those bright lights in their cells. How could anyone be expected to sleep with those bright lights shining on them. And with men standing there, in shifts, staring through the peep hole at them 24 hours a day?

Colonel Andrus had been adamant. Nobody, but nobody, was going to escape that rope around their neck while he was in charge.

But Goering had his boast, too. "They'll never hang me," he confided to one of the German defense attorneys.

So the end had come at 10:40, not at the end of a noose, but while PFC Harold F. Johnson was standing there watching him. That big fat man, not so fat as he once was , made a motion with his hand across his face, stirred a bit and was dead. He and his cell had been searched a hundred times but the cyanide capsule had been there. Somewhere.

All of that is history. The newspapers and magazines blared it all. The books have been written. But who would write about the red headed young reporter perched up in the attic of a shaky old building, shivering from the cold and the damp, peering through his field glasses and trying to figure out what had happened?

The minutes ticked by. No sign of activity in the prison yard. I sneaked another peek at the watch and waited. Fifteen minutes past midnight. Then 20. Finally it was half an hour past midnight.

The suspicion was growing in my mind that something had gone wrong. That our "tip" had been phony. What else could I believe, up there in the cold attic? No way to communicate with my boss. Had he learned something more during those hours since I had left him?

304

Oh, how close I came to seeing that final action, the fateful walks from the prison to the gallows steps.

My patience lasted until nearly 1 o'clock in the morning. I waited and waited, growing colder and wetter by the minute. My teeth were chattering. How long must I wait to make sure our tip had been false? At last, with only a couple of minutes to go before 1 o'clock, I decided to give it up and climb back down. Once more that careful climb down the rickety wooden skeleton and what was left of the stairs.

Down below, the German family had not gone to bed. My coming had disturbed them and they also sensed that something was going on. Something so important to their shattered homeland. The man was waiting when I got down.

To the question in his eyes, I could only say, "Nichts ist los." Nothing is going on.

Seeing my chattering teeth and the wet on my coat, it was his turn, the defeated enemy, to be concerned about my welfare.

"Come down. We will fix you some hot tea."

And they did. His wife stirred into action. I felt the hot liquid flowing down into my body and I was grateful to them. It wasn't real tea - but it was hot. We sat for perhaps 20 minutes. As I had arrived at the ground floor, cold and wet, I had been prepared to give it up. Dash past the MP's and head back to the press room to make my dismal report.

But the "tea" had warmed me and I felt a new thought creeping back into my mind. Maybe I should make that risky climb one more time and take another look.

And I did. Just in time to salvage a bit of the glorious scoop I had hoped for. For this time, when I reached the attic and swung the field glasses out towards the door, there was action.

It was the glittering chrome helmets, those "vanity" shiners of Colonel Andrus, that told me things were indeed happening. The door of the prison opened. A shiny chrome helmet appeared. Then, following, two more, side by side. Was that a dark figure of a man between them? I strained for a better glimpse and sure enough, when they passed a better lighted spot, I could see it. Two MP's with a shackled man between them, making their way towards the gym - and that gallows.

Now I was caught in the dilemna. The tough one. I was happy, in the sense that I had indeed caught some action. But at the same moment, the sinking realization that while I had sat and warmed myself, the fateful action had begun. I had missed the beginning. Pat had been so explicit. There could be no real scoop unless we could count the full number. All 11 of them.

Now it had begun and there was no way to know how many had already made their fateful trip before I reached that attic lookout for the second time.

Oh, there was drama, all right. As the uninvited "guest," perched in that rickety old attic, I was witnessing history being enacted before my eyes.

As the prisoner reached the door of the gym it swung open and there was a bright flash of light from inside the building. Then the door slammed shut. Darkness. Another wait. A few minutes, perhaps.

And then that shout, defiant unto death, of a man condemned to die for what the world had judged to be unspeakable crimes. A few seconds of silence and then - the sound I would remember forever - that thud.

So loud. So clear. Such a fateful sound. I had never before heard the thudding crash of a gallows trapdoor but nobody had to tell me what it was as I perched in that cold, wet attic.

A few minutes later, the prison door opened again. Those glittering helmets. And between them, another man, condemned to be dead in a few minutes, making his last trudging walk on the mother earth.

Other people, including Colonel Andrus, would doubt how much I had seen that night. But I did, indeed, see it. The fateful walk of each prisoner between that prison door and the house of the gallows.

Perhaps even more significant than what I saw was what I heard. Those defiant cries ringing through the night air. Those ominous thuds.

"I greet thee, oh, my beloved Germany." The voice, I would learn later, of Colonel-General Alfred Jodl, commander of the German armed forces when they surrendered.

Only one of the condemned men would dare shout, in that last dreadful moment, the name of the man whose life had been the cause of it all. "Heil, Hitler," the voice boomed out through the chill night air. The voice of Julius Streicher, the Jew baiting strutter. Even most of the Nazis had found it hard to be prideful of him. He had been a thug. Little more.

And then, after each of those defiant cries, that chilling thud of the death trap, vibrating in the night. That sound I heard so clearly.

After I had counted seven - or was it eight? - it all came to an end. Now they carried out the body of Goering, on a stretcher, and into the gymnasium so that the official witnesses could see him and verify that he, too, had died that night.

Once again, as it ended, I was trapped. In a sense, at least. I had not been able to make the full count so now I would have to wait again to make sure it had indeed ended. It would cost me another 20 minutes before I would be sure enough to creep down from my perch, make my way back to the press room and report to the boss that the executions had been completed.

Only later would I learn that it had been Herman Goering and his neat little suicide trick that had caused the delay of the start of the executions. The hour's wait for the executions to begin and my decision to retreat into the warmth downstairs had cost me much.

The only consoling thought now was that even if I had still been on watch at 1 o'clock, when it finally started, I would still have been trapped by the asbence of the Number One man. I would have lost the same amount of time in waiting, waiting, waiting for Number 11.

My sudden appearance back in the press room and my report to Pat set off a round of furious soul searching. Not that Pat doubted my story. He was certain I was telling the truth. In the end, he was even convinced that I had seen the end of the executions. It was then, with some hesitation, that he flashed the message to the world. "Executions completed." London and New York pleaded for more. Pat could give no more. There were too many unanswerable question.

I was pounding away on my typewriter, putting down on paper exactly what I had seen and heard.

The executions ended at 2:45 in the morning. It was 6:18 before International Military Tribunal press officers released their big surprise - Herman Goering had cheated the gallows. They did not release the stories produced by the eight reporters chosen to witness the executions, until even later in the morning.

It was during the time between 3:15 and 6:18 in the morning that we, a young red headed reporter and United Press, owned a sort of scoop. We had been able to assure the waiting world that the fateful decrees had been carried out. Anyone who read my desciption would have to know the accused war criminals had made their last walk. Even though the count was flawed.

307

One factor which robbed us of at least a part of our "glory" was the fact that at around the time of our bulletin - 3 to 4 in the morning - few newspapers in the United States, England or France, were still going to press. In the United States, morning papers already had been "put to bed," as newsmen say. The Goering suicide and the stories put out by the eight selected reporters would be available for the afternoon papers.

I would have to be satisfied with the knowledge that some odd-hour publication deadlines around the world had used Pat's "Executions Completed" bulletin, along with my description of that thudding trap. There was a bit of satisfaction in a note on the front page of the New York Times on October 16 that a reporter perched in a high building behind the prison yard at Nurnberg, had heard those last defiant cries of the condemned and heard the thuds of the gallows.

Herman Goering had popped his pill and kept his boast.

He also robbed me of my bright moment.

Chapter Twenty five - Oxenius

It is a story which must have two heroes.

One of the names would be recognized immediately by anyone familiar with World War II, General Walter Bedell Smith. Wartime chief of staff to General Dwight D. Eisenhower, commander of allied forces in Europe. After the war, the first director of the new Central Intelligence Agency and, later, our ambassador to Moscow.

Not even many Germans would recognize the second, Friedrich Wilhelm Oxenius. He was German by birth, a university student in England. Under the Nazis he had been an officer on the German General Staff.

Two men whom fate pulled together in the vortex of a drama much bigger than themselves - the end of the most devastating war that mankind has ever fought. With it came the personal drama of the two men themselves in that historic episode, a drama lost to the world, part of which has never been told.

I must explain because I may well be the only person who can do it. First, about this singular man, Oxenius, whom I came to know in that uncertain period after the war in Germany. I was in Germany as a newsman for United Press, on the prowl for news stories at a time when the American Army occupied most of West Germany.

One of my news sources was a captain in the United States Army's Historical Section.

"I don't know if you are aware of this or not," he said one day. "There is only one German alive who witnessed the German surrender at Rheims on May 7, 1945. He's living in Urach. Down south. Going to school at Tuebingen University. His name is

309

Wilhelm Oxenius. Here's his address. He may give you a good story."

It sounded great. The only living German who was at the surrender that ended the war.

Only three Germans had been present, we had been told. General Alfred Jodl, chief of staff of the German armed forces. He had been hanged at Nurnberg for war crimes. Admiral Hans von Friedeburg, commander of what had been left of the German navy - who committed suicide shortly after the surrender ceremony. Last, a man named Oxenius, a major who spoke English and came to Rheims as Jodl's aide and interpreter.

Did the captain at the Army Historical Section know something about Oxenius that he was not telling me? Somehow, I suspected that he did. But he obviously wanted Oxenius to tell me.

It didn't take much to convince my boss, Walter Rundell, to send me to Urach. He could smell a news story as fast as anybody.

It was early afternoon when I found my way up the stairs to the little apartment where, I had been told, Oxenius lived.

A young woman with a baby in her arms opened the door. Yes, this was where Mr. Oxenius lived. She would call him. Oxenius had married since the war and this was his wife, Lore, with their son, Matthias.

Then I was facing Oxenius himself. Perhaps I had expected a more imposing figure. Small, slender and balding in front. I explained quickly who I was and what I wanted. I pointed out that an officer at the Army Historical Section had sent me. Perhaps that would help.

It didn't help. I was met with a soft spoken but very firm no.

"I'm sorry but I do not wish to talk to the press about my experiences at Rheims," he said.

Perhaps I had even anticipated that. Many Germans were reluctant to talk to American reporters. I had, after all, been one of the enemy. Oxenius had been on the German General Staff.

"I promise to be fair and make no distortions in your story," I said.

I expected him to slam the door in my face. Perhaps it was his good breeding which forbade that. He made it clear that he would not discuss Rheims at this time. I was about to concede defeat and leave when he did a strange and unpredictable thing.

He made a motion to close the door, half closing it. Then he opened it . "You may come in. Have a cup of tea with us. If you promise not to ask any questions about Rheims."

It was a strange invitation but I quickly accepted. My ticking mind was telling me that if I could get to know this man and gain his confidence he might yet tell me the story of Rheims. If not now, then later.

We sat for an hour, chatting about inconsequential things. It was then that he told me about his marriage since the war, about their baby. He had decided to go back and complete his education that had been interrupted by the war, to obtain a doctoral in English literature.

The English literature thing was a surprise. Yet it shouldn't have been. My captain friend had told me of Oxenius' college stint in England. That explained his command of the English language although now we spoke at times in German.

In that first visit, I didn't ask him about his politics or philosophy. I didn't want to frighten him off. Yet there was something about this soft spoken German which drew my liking, my respect. Right from the start. Maybe one cannot explain things like that. They just happen. I would hesitate to suggest it was a personal magnetism. He never thrust himself into my perception. I simply felt strangely attracted to him.

In any case, I finally got up to leave. It was my turn to keep the door open. Could I drop by again some day when I was in that part of Germany?

"Sure," he said with a little smile. "So long as you don't ask about Rheims."Thus began our acquaintanceship which, in time, grew into friendship. It was simply impossible not to like him. Cultured. Polite. Articulate. Soft spoken and always friendly.

Yes, in later visits we did talk about those other things. Economic problems facing a wrecked Germany. Whether the German people could absorb a truly democratic system after the autocratic rule of the Nazis.

I quickly learned that this man had a much deeper understanding of democratic philosophy than one might have expected of a man who had been an officer on the German General Staff. His family, I learned, had been "academics," with interests ranging far beyond the narrow confines of a national socialist dictatorship in Germany. It explained why he had studied in England. I learned that his great passion in life was literature, centered on the English literature he was studying at Tuebingen.

One day, as we talked about literature, he mentioned that he planned on doing his doctoral thesis on the works of the famed English author and poet, Matthew Arnold. He was having a bit of trouble getting some of the books he needed for his research.

"They are probably available in London but I have no contacts in London now," he said. He did not directly ask me to get them for him but perhaps he thought I might make the offer to help. To ask would have placed him in "debt" to me. I might try to collect by asking him about Rheims. Oh, that factor would be there anyway. We both knew it.

Perhaps he thought he knew me well enough to know that I would not try to collect on such a "debt" but he was testing me. We had made a bargain. I decided to play it straight.

"I'll see if I can get them for you," I volunteered. He accepted, with the proviso that he would pay for the books.

It was a little game but I trusted him, too. I knew that he knew that Rheims had never left my mind, even though I never spoke of it. I could feel it, deep down in my gut, that if he ever felt free to talk about it, he would be the one to bring it up.

Meantime, I tried to help him with his doctoral project. I sent off a teletype message to London, asking if anyone in our London office could try to find the books on Oxenius' list. I explained, simply, that I was doing a favor to a news source. In a few days a package came with two of the three books Oxenius had asked for. The third book, the message said, could not be found outside a library.

This time, I made it a special occasion to drive to Urach with the two books. Oxenius' eyes lighted up when he saw them. I didn't have to be told that I had made him happy. He gripped my hand. "This means a lot to me," he said. I allowed him to pay our costs for the books and that was it. Not a word about Rheims.

It was months later, in the spring of 1951, when I decided to give up my job with United Press and return to the United States. I, too, was newly married, in Germany. There was a small son who needed to be acclimated in the United States for school there. I had a job waiting. But part of my preparation for going home was a last visit to Urach to say goodbye to a man I now considered a friend.

I knew he meant it when he said he was sorry to see me go. "I'm going to miss you," he said. And I knew I was going to miss him.

Suddenly, he said, "Do you mind taking a little walk with me to the park?" I quickly agreed. I sensed that something was coming.

"I've come to know you pretty well," he said. "I've come to trust you. Since you are going back to America I have decided to tell you my story of Rheims and why I didn't want the story published. I still don't want it published. But I will tell you the story with the proviso that you promise never to publish it without my permission."

I agreed to that. It was not only curiosity on my part. It was wanting to know merely for my personal satisfaction, even if I could publish it. Now I knew that if Oxenius had a valid reason for not wanting to see the story published, that reason would be valid for me, too.

So he began the tale.

"I guess the place to start would be when Hitler killed himself in Berlin on April 5, 1945," Oxenius began as we strolled in the park. "Hitler left a document that appointed Admiral Karl Doenitz, the wartime commander in chief of the German Navy, as the new head of the German nation.

"Doenitz knew the war was over. He knew that any further resistance by Germany was senseless. But he wanted to delay the surrender as long as possible, in order to allow as many German soldiers as possible to get away from the eastern front so they could surrender to the Americans or British, rather than to the Russians. We knew that being taken prisoner by the Russians was a death sentence to many, if not most, of these men.

"The roads were choked with civilian refugees, trying to escape from the Russians. We had already learned, after the Russians captured some of our eastern towns, that they were slaughtering old men, women and children. The women were victims of mass rapes.

"So Doenitz decided to surrender piecemeal, one army group at a time, buying time. Of course, the Russians were opposed to this. They protested."

(At an Allied conference at Yalta shortly before the end of the war the Allies agreed to a total, unconditional surrender formula which divided Germany into zones of occupation and it was agreed that German armies would not be allowed to cross zone boundries to surrender.)

"Our armies in northern Italy and southern Germany were allowed to surrender to the west. The army in Czechoslovakia was ordered to disengage and march to the west. On the east we had to make a sacrifice, ordering our troops facing the Russians to hold as long as possible, covering the escape of the refugees and army groups in central Germany.

"Doenitz then sent a delegation, under Admiral Friedeburg, the new commander of the German Navy, to the northwest to meet with Field Marshal Montgomery and offer to surrender on that front if Montgomery would keep his lines open to refugees and fleeing German soldiers.

"On May 4, Montgomery accepted our surrender and said he would continue accepting prisoners. Then Doenitz ordered Friedeburg to fly to Rheims, General Eisenhower's headquarters, to attempt to obtain the same terms.

"At Rheims, our luck ran out. Eisenhower refused to agree to hold his lines open after the surrender so that German soldiers and refugees could cross to the west. We were told that Eisenhower would order his troops to fire on any of our people trying to cross the zone boundries after the surrender.

"That was when Doenitz decided to send General Alfred Jodl, chief of the German General Staff, to Rheims to make one last try. Jodl took me along as his aide. Since I spoke English, I could act as his interpreter. But we met with the same answer.

"We conducted our negotiations through General Bedell Smith. Eisenhower refused to see us. General Smith was in sympathy with our position and realized that a cease fire delay, keeping the lines open for refugees and escaping soldiers, would save the lives of thousands of people. Eisenhower vetoed the idea. We pleaded with Smith to make one more try. He agreed.

"When he came back with his answer we could see that he was highly agitated. It was clear that his argument with Eisenhower had been a sharp one. He shook his head, sadly. He told us Eisenhower had flatly refused. We were told that we had 24 hours to communicate with our provisional government in Flensburg - and surrender unconditionally or the shooting would commence once more.

"Most men, faced with such a situation, would have given up but I have to say that General Jodl had great presence of mind and courage to fight to the last ditch. He tried one more angle. He explained to General Smith that in those last days of the war, our communication system was in chaos. There was almost complete breakdown in communications with some units. General Jodl said it would be impossible to reach all our military units in 24 hours and that 48 hours would be the minimum required.

"I'll have to give General Smith credit for being a courageous man. He agreed to go back to Eisenhower to plead for this last proposal. He did. This time it was apparent that he had convinced Eisenhower that it was the only practical thing to do. We had 48 hours.

"But on one point, Eisenhower was adamant. We must sign the surrender document immediately, that night, May 6-7.

"We got off a message to Doenitz as quickly as possible, outlining what we had achieved. It was not what Doenitz had hoped for but he realized that our situation was hopeless. Unless we signed immediately, the Americans and British would start shooting again. The bombers would return to our cities. We received permission to sign. At 2:41 in the morning, May 7, in the presence of the assembled allied officers, General Jodl signed the surrender document.

"General Eisenhower met with us for only a few minutes, after the surrender. His only remark was to ask General Jodl if he understood the surrender terms. Jodl nodded his head and that was it."

Actually, the Germans ended up with a bit less than the 48 hours promised them. The surrender ceremony took 2 hours and 41minutes out of the 48. The deadline remained at midnight, May 8-9.

In any case, I now had the story of Rheims which Oxenius had refused to tell me for so long. He added a word of warm regards for Bedell Smith.

"He was one of the most compassionate and understanding men I ever met," said Oxenius. He did not elaborate. That part would have to wait for years for a clarification.

But Oxenius did give me his explanation as to why he did not want me to publish the story.

"As you know, General Eisenhower has just been appointed chief of the North Atlantic Treaty Organization. The political situation has changed. You are no longer allied with Russia. You are now engaged in the Cold War. Your NATO was set up to prevent Russia from taking over the rest of Europe and that includes us in West Germany. We fear the Russians.

"There is talk of arming West Germany again. Of West Germany entering NATO. Many Germans are against it. They have had enough of militarism. Then you have to remember that thousands of our soldiers were taken prisoner of war by Russia and are still there. They were never allowed to come home. Our people still pray for those who may still be alive.

"There are many factors resting on the mood and termperament of the German people - my people. If you wrote and published my story about Rheims you would have to include General Eisenhower's denial of a period of grace. Mothers and wives would feel that Eisenhower was responsible for the deaths of their sons and husbands, for thousands of women falling into the hands of Russians to be raped and murdered.

"Yes, I know. It has been said that Eisenhower's hands were tied by the allied agreement at Yalta that no separate surrender must take place. That is hard to explain to German mothers, fathers, wives. Especially after General Montgomery made an exception. And we were allowed to surrender in the south. Eisenhower could have done more than he did. Apparently, he didn't try. It would be hard for the Germans to forgive him."

He paused here and I could see that his emotions were becoming involved. When he spoke again I could detect a slight trembling in his voice.

"At this moment Germany needs General Eisenhower and NATO - but you need Germany's help in return. We must cooperate. But I feel we would have serious difficulty working together if the German people heard about what Eisenhower did that night at Rheims."

I could see Oxenius biting his lips as he tried to formulate his next statement.

"I simply refuse," he finally said, "to say or do anything that would harm our relationship with Eisenhower or the western alliance. For that would also harm my own people. That's why I can't give you permission to publish my memory of what happened at Rheims."

My own emotions were getting slightly involved. Yes, I was beginning to understand why I would not be writing the Oxenius version of the Rheims story. Not then.

Today it has to be told and put into perspective.

On that spring day when I walked with Oxenius in the park at Urach and talked about Rheims, it was the beginning of 1951. The blockade of Berlin by the Russians had begun three years before, bringing the sharpest clash of the cold war between the United States and Russia. Confrontation was sharp - the cold war at its hottest.

DEAR GOD, I'M ONLY A BOY

Eisenhower would be elected President the following year. Oxenius' reason for refusing to allow his Rheims story to be published was as valid with Eisenhower in the White House as at the head of NATO.

I would not see Oxenius again for 20 years. We exchanged post cards at Christmas and a few letters in between. One of Oxenius' letters to me would have a fateful bearing on his own future.

I had sent him a clipping from an American news magazine, an article suggesting that West Germany and all of western Europe might become communist. The gist of it was that the communists had formed one of the strongest political parties in Germany in the early 1930's to oppose the rise of Adolph Hitler.

Many of those communists, of course, landed in Nazi concentration camps. Some survived the war. Now, after being liberated, they were demanding a place in the sun as payment for their opposition to Hitler. They were also playing on their relationship with the Russians who sat astride the eastern half of Germany which the Russians were rapidly turning into a communist satellite. Playing on the strong wish most Germans had for unification, communists said the best chance for this lay in cooperating with the Russians.

The writers of the article suggested that efforts by the Americans to punish war criminals and former Nazis, was alienating the German people from their western allies. Meanwhile, in the Soviet Zone, the Russians were using many former Nazis as officials in their new puppet government.

I sent a note with the magazine article, asking Oxenius for his opinion. In his reply he lashed out sharply at the theme of the article.

"It is the pessimists who say that Germany and western Europe will go communist," he wrote. "It is nonsense. It is also, perhaps, an intentional extortionist threat. I can speak for my people. They have experienced too many horrors from the East. For at least a generation, they are immune to any bolshevik enticements."

On the theme of democracy and the need to counter the communist propaganda, he wrote, "The western powers must support those forces of good will now existing in Germany. I realize, of course, that they must first have faith in the sincerity of the real democrats of our land. For a second thing, they must have patience for we are still so young for a democratic society. We will make many mistakes and have much to learn before we master the rules of the game.

"For a third point, it would seem that the time has come (it was seven years since the end of the war) to draw a line across the past and to remove all factors that would tend to continue bad blood between us. Especially when one considers that continued friction between us merely delivers more fuel into the hands of those opposed to our present political system. They would use it as propaganda to prove the western powers do not have honorable intentions towards us.

"Of course, the principal task lies with us. Please, be assured, friend Duerksen, that there are many people in Germany who are firmly determined to resist any brand of political philosophy other than the one that will win for us a place in the ranks of the free people of the world. You know from my family background, my upbringing and my character, that I belong to the western world. I am too much of an individualist to fall under the influence of any collective philosophy.

"I have a great deal of faith in your country. I always had a great deal of respect for your country because, in so many areas, it has broken trails and has set an example to the world. Now I have come to love your country, especially since I have become acquainted with two personalities of that land. One of them, as I have told you, is Walter Bedell Smith. The other, if I may dare say so, is you."

I was flattered. I was also touched. But I was willing to accept it because I knew he meant it.

But there was a bit more, that fateful message at the end of his letter.

"If you ever have the opportunity to contact General Smith, I wish you would give him a message for me. I want you to tell him that I will always remember him as a man of compassion and humanity.

"I would like to thank him for what he did for us at Rheims, in trying to help save our people from the Russians. I am sure that without his efforts we would never have obtained even that 48 hour period of grace which did so much to save so many lives. Please, tell him this."

Well, if I didn't have a ready opportunity, then I would make one.

When I returned to the United States I found that General Smith had been appointed director of the newly created Central

Intelligence Agency. The new agency had been created largely because of the cold war between the United States and Russia - a "war" that was being fought largely on the battle field of Germany. The nation was split down the middle, with Russian troops occupying the eastern half and the Americans, together with the British and French, occupying the western part. The divided nation shared a single language. An artificial barrier separated its families, friends and relatives. It was a perfect hot bed for political intrigue and intelligence work.

The Russians were sending their agents across their zone border to gather military information and to stir up communist political activity. In defense, we urgently needed a counter intelligence force to tell us what was going on and how to counter it. Much of the efforts of the new CIA were centered in that split nation.

In any case, I wrote a letter to General Smith, giving him Oxenius' message. I also took the liberty of going a bit further. I included most of the remaining part of Oxenius' letter, about communism and democracy.

If only I had known what I was doing.

For the moment, all I got in reply was a short but friendly letter from General Smith, thanking me for relaying Oxenius' message and his letter.

"Yes, I remember Oxenius very well," General Smith wrote back. "He seemed to be a very fine man." That made two of us with that opinion.

What began happening behind the scenes was something I would learn about much later. My letter to General Smith, including Oxenius' letter and his comments on communism and democracy, had kicked off a reaction with the new CIA director. A man like Oxenius, he decided, was needed by the agency's West German intelligence operation.

Smith sent orders for his agency people in Germany to contact Oxenius and try to persuade him to join their team.

I never learned just what thought process this proposal may have set off in Oxenius' mind. I did know he had planned an entirely different kind of career. He had meant to be a teacher. Now came a completely different suggestion.

Did he accept because he felt an obligation to me? No. More likely, if he did feel any obligation, it would have been to General Smith. Or, just as likely, to the suggestion that he would be serving his people and the cause of democracy. I only know that he

319

did accept. The strange world of intelligence became his new career.

Later, when the West German government set up its own intelligence service, Oxenius was transferred to that group. His last official assignment was as Counsellor to the West German Embassy in London. Near the end of 1970, he retired with the rank of colonel in the West German Army.

I repeat, I knew nothing about all this at the time, except there was a strong hint in a letter Oxenius wrote me a short time after he accepted his new position. The hint was enough. I knew what had happened, especially after a few more tips and hints. For one thing, Oxenius warned me that he would be unable to discuss his new work in any way. He didn't. In fact, letters between us after that became few and far between. An occasional greeting with a Christmas card. Little more.

Something else happened. In 1958, Admiral Karl Doenitz, the man whom Adolph Hitler had appointed to succeed him as wartime Germany's last chancellor, just before Hitler had committed suicide, published his memoirs.

Doenitz had been sentenced by the International War Crimes Tribunal to 10 years in prison for his part in German war crimes. He had served his time and was free to write about his career.

And there it was, the story of Rheims and Eisenhower's refusal to grant the Germans that grace period needed to save their people from the onrushing Russians.

By the time Doenitz' book was published, West Germany was firmly in the western alliance, a thriving Democracy and a part of NATO. The German prisoners in Russia, the few that survived, finally were released and allowed to go home. If the West Germans still had any feelings about what happened at Rheims, such feelings had now begun to fade. The big issue still remaining was the need to protect Europe from the constantly grasping Russian bear.

I had not pushed Oxenius again about his decision not to allow the publication of his Rheim memories. If he still did not wish it, the reason now must be his need for anonymity as a member of the intelligence community. Doenitz' memoirs made the question moot.

I finally saw Oxenius one more time - in 1971, shortly after his retirement. It was at his comfortable and picturesque retirement home in the village of Dorfen, south of Munich. Sitting on the veranda of his home, one had a breathtaking view of the Bavarian Alps.

My 1971 trip to Germany was my second honeymoon. My first wife, whom I had met in Germany after the war, had died. I had remarried - again to a lady of German birth. We were visiting her old homeland.

As we sat and talked, it was almost as if nothing had changed from the days when I had dropped in on him at Urach. He was a bit older and grayer, perhaps, but still the same man I had known before. Quiet. Friendly. Literate and cultured. His years in intelligence work had certainly not changed his character or his interests.

At times, over the years, I wondered if he resented my intrusion into his life. His letter to me in 1952 and my use of it, had changed the whole direction of his life. Away from the dream of a quiet, academic life with his first love, literature. If there was, indeed, any resentment he would never let me know.

We spent the day talking, having a leisurely lunch on that outdoor veranda, taking a drive through the beautiful Bavarian countryside to the old but beautiful village of Bad Tolz. There, if one could close his eyes to the presence of the ever intruding motor car, one could imagine himself set back in time for a hundred years or more.

Inevitably, at some point, our conversation would turn to literature. He jumped up and went into the house. He came back with a small gift for me, a small volume containing a play by Berthold Brecht, the famed expatriate German poet and writer. It was a little allegory in which Adolph Hitler is portrayed as playing the part of a petty Chicago gangster leader.

Someone might wish to smile at that one. So utterly impudent. Something only a man like Brecht could manage.

We said nothing at all about Rheims. The passing of time, the publication of Admiral Doenitz' memoirs, the coming of age of West German democracy, all had long ago lifted the urgency of Rheims from my mind.

I did ask Oxenius if he had given any thought to writing his memoirs.

There would have been so much to write. His early exposure to English culture and tradition at. His service with the German General Staff during World War II. Then, if permissable, something of his work in intelligence. That might not be so difficult - General Reinhard Gehlen, once chief of West German intelligence, had published a book.

"Yes, I've thought about it," he said. "Perhaps. I would like to..." The sentence drifted away, unfinished. I did not pursue it.

That was the last time I saw Oxenius and it should, perhaps, be the end of his story. But it isn't.

For the moment, I went back home to my own work and career. We continued to exchange a few letters, the Christmas cards. Then, in the fall of 1979, that black rimmed envelope that landed in my mailbox. By instinct, I knew what it would contain.

Friedrich Wilhelm Oxenius, doctor of letters, retired colonel in the West German armed forces, had died on August 13.

The note from Lore, "We had been working in the garden and after lunch he lay down on the couch to rest while I took the dog for a walk. When I returned he was gone. He had not been ill even an hour."

Someone will be asking, "Why are you telling the story of Wilhelm Oxenius now, so late?"

The answer? I'm not quite sure. I had given it so much thought over the years, especially in those early years when I had hoped I would someday be able to publish the story of Rheims. But that story lost much of its urgency after Doenitz' memoirs in 1958.

Perhaps, if I wished to pay some sort of tribute to Oxenius the man, the most important thing would be the revelation of his reasons for not wanting the Rheims story made known.

There's something else I learned about only some time after his death, a little story he called a "historical miniature," the story that has yet to be told.

Another reason for writing about Oxenius now is the fact that Louise, widow of Alfred Jodl who had taken Oxenius to Rheims, published her memoirs in 1979. It was published only in German.

Louise Jodl had been a secretary to the German chief of staff. When Jodl's wife died he had married Louise. She stood by him during his last ordeal at Nurnberg. Better than anyone else, perhaps, she knew Alfred Jodl and she had kept the personal papers he left behind.

In that book is the copy of a letter Jodl wrote to her in 1945, only a few days after the war had ended. In that letter is an account of what Oxenius had told me, their desperate efforts to obtain at Rheims that period of grace to save the lives of fleeing Germans. It details, just as Oxenius had told it to me, the story of their negotiations through General Bedell Smith. The final wresting, with Smith's help, of that fateful 48 hour reprieve.

It is the last line of Jodl's letter that becomes so significant when one considers it was written only a day or two after the event itself, dramatic   proof of the impact of Bedell Smith's character on Alfred Jodl, the hardened man of war.

That last line, "It is General Bedell Smith who has earned our thanks."

All that needs to be added now is that "historical miniature" from Wilhelm Oxenius.

It was some time after his death when I wrote to Lore, asking if he had ever begun work on his memoirs or written anything about Rheims.

Lore replied that she had searched through all his papers. All she had been able to find was a sketchy little outline scribbled by hand and a single sheet of paper on which he had typed an account of his own final visit to Rheims in 1974, some 29 years after the surrender and only five years before his death.

Here he had written, "Return to Rheims, 1974, after so many years. I drove to the technical high school which had served in the last months of the war as Allied Headquarters, under Eisenhower, and in which the signing of the capitulation of the German Military Forces, before the opposing Americans, British, French and Russians, took place. Suddenly everything was coming back to life: our arrival, formal, almost ice cold, the briefest of greetings, no handshakes, waiting in a bare room, a hot cup of coffee. And then, after the signing, our return to the bare, unfriendly and almost hostile room, something unexpected happened. Something almost beyond comprehension.

"The door opened and General Eisenhower's chief of staff, General Walter Bedell Smith, strode into the room. He was having difficulty holding himself erect - we would learn later that he was suffering from a severe illness which some years later, while he was ambassador to Moscow, but while in the service of his country, would take his life.

"Silently but visibly shaken with emotion, if not fighting tears, he walked up to each of us four German officers and gripped us by the hand - Jodl, Friedeburg, Poleck and then mine, the youngest. (Poleck was Friedeburg's aide but did not attend the signing ceremony.)

"With this hand grip Smith was giving expression to his respect but, even more, his emotional involvement. It was more than a formal gallantry. It was the gesture of a man able to balance the bad with the good. Silently, as he had come, he then left the room. I have thought of this incident as a "historical miniature," if such an expression is apt. But in that hour it was basically more. It was the peace negotiator consciously placing himself in a position at odds with that of his commander in chief as well as, perhaps, with his allies for whom hatred was the understandable feeling of the moment. Over the years I have followed the body of writing about Rheims but have never seen a mention of this little incident. Only five persons witnessed it and of these only Poleck and I are alive. (Both are now dead.)

"But with this little report I wish to pay my debt of thankfulness. To the memory of a towering eminence of character, I would place a small and humble monument, 'De mortui nihil nisi bene.' (One shall speak only good of the dead.) To say this of General Smith is not a burdensome task."

So now, even if so late, and since nobody else can do it, it becomes my duty, nay, my privilege, to do for Friedrich Wilhelm Oxenius, scholar and soldier, what he did for General Walter Bedell Smith.

"De mortui nihil nisi bene."

And to repeat, to do this for him is not a burdensome task.

Chapter Twenty six – The Bitch

They called her the bitch of Buchenwald. If one considered all the evidence, it was true. Perhaps.

The good burgers of Augsburg, Germany who heard her the night she screamed all those lurid obscenities out the window of her jail cell, must have concluded that she was indeed somewhat of a crazy bitch.

Professor Rudolf Englert was assigned to her last trial, as a sort of psycho-medico expert, to pass judgement on any bizarre behavior. He suggested the jail window episode may have been part of an act she used to make the trial judges think she was a bit on the nutty side. That act, suggested the good professor, may have been the only defense mechanism she had left.

Nutty bitch? What a combination.

If she had been guilty of half the things they accused the woman of, she would have to be considered a top flight, certified bitch.   They said she ordered the murder of prisoners from Buchenwald concentration camp who had tattoos - so she could have their skins made into lamp shades. Lamps for which leg bones served as the stand, with one of the victim's toe bones as an electrical switch to turn the lamp on or off. They said she rode her horse through the prisoners' work area, slashing at them with her riding whip if they dared to look at her.

I guess one of the craziest stories they told about her was how she straddled a ditch that prisoners were digging, pulled up her skirts and dared any of the men to look - knowing they could be shot for doing that.

Oh, yes, and all those murders. They charged her with 35 murders or incitements to murder and dozens of incitements to

325

assault. If she were found guilty on half the charges, she wouldn't have much trouble qualifying as a true bitch.

The only trouble was, prosecutors were having a bit of trouble proving it all.

I got into the story a bit late. She had already been given the lurid title of "Bitch of Buchenwald." Some reporters, not wanting to look like copycats, made her the "Witch of Buchenwald." Still other writers tagged her the "Queen of Buchenwald." None of the different titles were as potent in stories as "Bitch."

The sober New York Times, scorning such lurid titles, simply called her Ilse Koch, widow of Karl Koch, a former SS officer who had served as commandant at the Buchenwald prison.

American newsmen discovered Frau Koch soon after the war ended. They started writing wild tales about her. They wrote of her fondness for lamp shades of tattooed skin, of flogging prisoners with her riding crop, of pulling gold teeth out of prisoners' mouths to finance high living for herself and Karl. Oh, it made good stuff for newspaper readers. I suppose, most of the reporters believed it. Even I believed it when I first heard about her. True, I was one of those reporters in Germany in that period. I knew how they sometimes cooked up stories.But a lot of real evil things had been uncovered in Germany after the war as the notorious Nazi regime crumble into dust. Why not a nutty bitch?

The American War Crimes Tribunal took the first crack at her in 1947. Even as the trial got under way, the first hints began to leak out that maybe it wasn't all true.

I didn't cover that trial so I could not know at first hand what kind of evidence the prosecution had been able to hurl against her. But if there had been any hesitation on the part of the judges they might have felt themselves under pressure of all that wild publicity and may have decided they couldn't afford to let her go. How could one explain the lamp shade business?

No matter the evidence, the judges at her first trial came up with a verdict of guilty and they gave her a life sentence. Now, perhaps, the people of the world could forget about their "Bitch of Buchenwald."

They couldn't forget her - or weren't allowed to. Somebody on the defense side of the picture pressured General Lucius D. Clay, commanding general of the American occupying forces in Germany, to order a review of her case. That was when things really went crazy. For, after a careful study by the review board of all the evidence, then a review by General Clay himself, the good general commuted her sentence to the four years she had already served. Including the months she had been locked up awaiting trial .

The press wolves began to howl. Obviously the ones who had been writing all those lurid lamp shade stories. How did General Clay dare let loose the notorious "bitch?"

Incidentally, that press was getting a bit of help from the woman herself. For, while in prison after her first trial, in the custody of the Americans, she somehow managed to get pregnant.

The press had a field day with that bit of news. Since the men and women at Dachau prison were supposed to be strictly separated, how had their "bitch" managed this one? One thing for sure, there would have to be a "thorough investigation," with those reporters covering every step and angle of it.

In the end, the investigators concluded that somebody had managed to loosen some of the bricks in the wall separating the men from the girls, made a hole large enough for a human body to squeeze through, and a lot of lusty fraternization had followed.

Nobody would say whether any of the other female prisoners had gotten in a family way but it did become abundantly clear that, in due time, Frau Koch was duly delivered of a baby boy. Under the circumstances it was promptly taken away from her and placed, under another name, in an orphanage. What boy, growing up in West Germany after the war, would want to be known as the son of a "bitch?"

In any case, using this new scandal, the press made it sound twice as urgent that something be done about this woman. As a result of all the hullabaloo, it was somehow decided that when the Americans released Frau Koch she would be arrested immediately by the Germans - and sent to trial in a German court.

If the American War Crimes Tribunal couldn't take care of her, perhaps the German courts could.

Some news analysts, waxing psychological, came up with the thought that the Germans might have an incentive to do a better job on Frau Koch than the Americans had.

The reasoning went something like this. First, there had been a huge war in which millions of persons had been killed. Entire cities shattered. The world was blaming Hitler and his gang of thugs for causing it all. After the war came the conquering armies. They discovered all that evidence of mass murders, the holocaust and the death camps. Buchenwald had been one of those camps. It was the sort of situation which could cause the people of the world to hate all Germans and all things German.

However, these same Germans, people who had not personally pulled any triggers or turned on any valves in the gas ovens, who liked to think of themselves as decent citizens, were trying to persuade anyone who would listen, "I had nothing to do with it."

Therefore, according to this theory, if the Germans could come up with a few sacrificial lambs, they could purge themselves of at least a part of the collective guilt the world was hanging around their necks. But could anyone suggest that Ilse Koch was a lamb?

It would also help if those sacrificial lambs happened to be tainted by prior sins. Yes, somebody like Ilse Koch. What made Ilse so suitable was the fact that the Germans, themselves, had labeled her husband a crook and stood him up against a wall and shot him.

There had been, apparently, another German SS officer named Konrad Morgan who had been assigned to the job of rooting crooks out of the SS ranks. Morgan had come up with damaging evidence against Colonel Koch.

The evidence indicated that Koch had used his position as prison camp commandant to extort money and jewelry from wealthy Jewish prisoners. That might have been all right if only he had turned the proceeds over to the German Reich, his government. The evidence on Koch indicated that he had used the money to line his own pockets. He had bank accounts all over the place.

It helped even further to know that Morgan had also suspected Ilse Koch of complicity in her husband's crimes. It was said that he detested her and did his best to find proof against her but had been unable to do so.

But all of that - her husband's proven guilt, the suspicions against her, the illegitimate child - all combined to make her fit so perfectly into the role of the despised sacrificial lamb.

However, if the Germans were going to put this woman on trial, it meant that I would become involved in the case.

You see, the Germans would be conducting the trial in German and since I was one of the few reporters on the United Press staff who spoke German, my boss assigned me to cover the new trial. It would convene in a German superior court in Augsburg on November 27, 1950. On that day I would set my eyes on the "bitch" for the first time.

It was when I arrived in Augsburg - a few days early to "get my feet on the ground" - that I heard more about that "guilt purge" theory which was becoming more popular as the trial neared. It was

328

coming mostly from the American reporters. Even the German reporters seemed willing to considerd it, though. Yes, maybe it was all true. The conclusion was, "They're really going to do a number on her."

In fact, I heard so much about this theory that I began to feel sorry for Ilse Koch. If that were possible. She didn't have a chance.

Not that I wanted to feel sorry for her. Who could feel sorry for a person who played with lamp shades made of human skin? On the other hand, I hadn't heard the evidence against her. I remembered the controversy over General Clay's commuting her sentence. I just didn't like the idea of hanging the woman before her trial.

Then came the big moment, my first glimpse of the notorious woman and the shock of disappointment.

I had seen pictures of her. Somehow I got the idea that she would have some semblance of glamour. Of feminine attraction about her. She would be a kind of sex symbol.

But here came two uniformed German policemen, leading between them this short, dumpy figure crowned by frazzly reddish hair over a blotched face. Not a single redeeming feminine feature could I find about her. One usually doesn't call a woman ugly but I was tempted to say it when I caught my first sight of this "star" of the coming trial.

True, she had been in jail now for more than four years. Such a life could not be conducive to beauty or glamour but now it was hard to look at her and imagine a time when she might have been attractive to anyone.

"Good Lord," I thought, "is this the woman everyone has been raving about?"

That other title that some newsmen used, "Queen of Buchenwald," came to mind. A queen? Ugh.

Then the trial began. It appeared to be heavy artillery that the German prosecution had marshalled against her. As a prosecutor they had chosen a lawyer who had a Jewish wife and, so they said, both had suffered at the hands of the Nazis.

With the assistance of American occupation officials, they scoured the new state of Israel as well as the United States for refugees who had once been prisoners at Buchenwald. Anyone who might know something about Ilse Koch during her reign as the "Queen of Buchenwald." They had a list of 240 witnesses scheduled to testify against her.

The implied promise, since some of these were new witnesses who had not testified at the first trial, was that the prosecution now had enough ammunition to convict her.

Then came a new shock to me. This time it was a creeping shock, coming slowly as the trial proceeded. As the long parade of witnesses began to testify I began to understand what had happened at the first trial. Most of the witnesses actually knew little about Ilse Koch except things they had heard others repeating. Some of them had not even seen Isle Koch before they were brought into the courtroom. In American courts, such hearsay evidence is given little credence.

At first, the lack of damaging witnesses did not bother me much. I supposed the prosecutor must be saving his big guns for the end. But the deeper and deeper they got into the trial, the more it became apparent there would be no big guns. I was beginning to understand why General Clay had been forced to commute Ilse Koch's first sentence.

True, prominently displayed on the table in the courtroom were several of the human skin lamp shades and a leg bone lamp stand with toe bone switch, along with several strips of tattooed human skin.

At least one or two witnesses were even able to testify they saw a human skin lamp in Ilse Koch's house. But when it came to proving that Ilse Koch had been connected in a direct way with slaying the prisoners from whom these skins were taken, the prosecutor fell flat on his face. He had no proof.

In an American court, a defendant would not even be called on to dispute evidence with which they were not connected. In Germany, the judges do the cross examinations and they have a bit more leeway. The judges asked Ilse about those lamp shades.

Then it came out. Ilse, and other witnesses, said the lampshades had been the brainchild of a young German doctor who was assigned to the prison camp imfirmary. The young doctor, apparently, was writing a thesis on the psychological types who allowed themselves to be tattooed.

"But he never had anybody killed to get their skin," Frau Koch said. "He only took skin from those who died of illness or other causes."

How about the lamp shades in her house? the judges asked her.

"He gave one to me. I didn't want it but he insisted."

Had she ever ordered any prisoner killed so she could have a lamp shade made from the skin?

"Absolutely not," the defendant swore. "I didn't even know they were making the lamps until the doctor showed me one."

The riding whip stories? A few of the witnesses said they had seen Ilse Koch, in her glory days, riding her horse around the areas where prisoners worked. However, there was disagreement as to whether she carried a riding whip or not. Some said she did. Others said they had never seen a whip.

Well, had she gone around slashing at prisoners with a whip, or not? Again the disagreement. Most said she did not. One or two said they had seen her strike prisoners when they got too close or reached a hand toward her. Were these prisoners making some kind of threat? Were they begging for food? Nobody seemed to know.

Were any of these prisoners injured? Nobody could say for sure.

One day the prosecution very nearly hit pay dirt. In fact, the court finally ruled that it was pay dirt. Two witnesses told the same story.

It seemed that many of the prisoners had been kept busy working in a stone quarry outside the barbed wire confines of the camp. Builders were still adding to the buildings inside the camp. So, the orders were that each evening, when the work day ended in the quarry and the prisoners were marched back under guard, each prisoner had to pick up a building stone, put in on his shoulder and carry it back to camp. It saved some horse cart and truck transport. Several hundred prisoners could carry a lot stones.

On that fateful day, it seemed, Ilse Koch, accompanied by a young SS lieutenant, had been standing beside the road. She watched as the tired prisoners trudged into camp, each lugging that heavy stone on his shoulder. It was a well known order that prisoners were forbidden to turn their heads to look at anyone standing beside the road as they marched. Certainly they were not to look at Ilse Koch, the wife of the commandant.

Now the testimony. "I was marching along with the stone on my shoulder when I saw Frau Koch and the lieutenant standing beside the road. The victim was some distance ahead of me in the line. He must have turned his head to look at her. She spoke to the lieutenant. He stepped out, knocked the prisoner down, picked up the stone the prisoner had been carrying and bashed the prisoner's head in with it."

Could the witness testify to what Ilse Koch had said to the lieutenant?

"No, I was too far away," came the reply.

If he was so far away, how had he managed to see what took place, especially since the prisoners were forbidden to turn their heads?

"I peeked out of the corner of my eyes."

The second witness told much the same story. Nobody was near enough to the lieutenant or Frau Koch to hear what was said.

Nobody knew the lieutenant's name. Nobody knew the victim's name or whether he was Jewish.

It was damning evidence. But, I had to ask myself, would such evidence be allowed to stand up in the American-British system of law? Frau Koch had not wielded the stone. It was not known what she said to the lieutenant. The victim, lost among the millions who died during the war, unable to testify either way.

Yes, Frau Koch was asked about the incident. Her reply was probably to be expected. "I don't remember the incident at all. I never gave orders for anyone to be killed."

Sure, most killers deny their crimes. But where was the proof to show she had ordered that prisoner killed?

Actually, Frau Koch did little to help herself during the trial. One day she began talking, a long string of rambling, incoherent sentences. The presiding judge ordered her repeatedly to shut up. She paid no heed.

At one point I could hear her saying, "What am I doing here? Why are all these people staring at me? I want to go home."

A police officer was finally able to quiet her. But on other days she repeated the performance. One day she said, "I am a sinner. I want to die." On one occasion she began to cry and became so hysterical they had to lead her from the courtroom. Under German law, the trial could proceed without her - and did.

Then one night there was that crazy incident . Locked in her cell in the downtown municipal jail, she smashed the glass window with her chamber pot and tried to pour the contents out the window. She began shouting all those obscenities through the smashed window.

"I want a man. Bring me a man. I want sex," she was quoted as shouting that night. They said she added a lurid description of what she could offer a man.

Finally, the jailors were called and she was given a sedative and led away to a more remote cell. One thing was certain, the solid Augsburg jailors wanted no more illegitimate babies on their hands.

I heard about the incident as soon as I arrived at the courthouse the next morning. Professor Englert knew about it. Was it an act or for real? he was asked.

The good professor was convinced it was an act although he was willing to concede that she may indeed have needed a man.

"I'm convinced she is putting on an act," he said. "What else can she do? She has no other weapon."

But such incidents certainly were not endearing her to the court or to her own defense attorneys who had been assigned by the German state.

The trial ground on, day after day, from November 27 to January 15, 1951. Even the matter of her husband's conviction and execution was brought up. She was questioned sharply about her involvement in any of his skulduggery. She was lucid enough on that day to emphatically deny that she had taken part.

In fact, I would learn, although this was not part of the testimony in the trial, there had been a bizarre development concerning this matter with Konrad Morgan who had investigated her husband.

It had been after the lamp shade stories began to circulate that American war crimes officials interrogated Morgan, still in custody of the Americans as a suspected SS war criminal. They attempted to persuade him to corroborate the lamp shade stories and to implicate Ilse Koch. He had refused to do so, saying he had no evidence to connect her to the lamp shade killings.

There were reports, published, that American interrogators beat Morgan, trying to make him sign an affidavit incriminating Frau Koch but Morgan simply would not sign. The Americans had met an honest SS officer. Morgan eventually was released and continued to practice law in Germany after the war.

So now, after Konrad Morgan's investigation had failed to do it, after the American War Crimes Tribunal had failed to do it, the Germans, in a third trial, were still unable to come up with the "smoking gun" everybody had been trying to put in the hands of this unglamorous woman.

The long parade of witnesses finally came to an end and it left the German judges with the same quandary that had faced the Americans, what kind of verdict they could produce. It would be inconceivable, after so much publicity about this "evil" woman, that they could publicly wash their hands of her and turn her loose. If they did that, how could the world ever be convinced that the Germans were decent people?

But even German judges in 1951, nearly six years after the end of the war, had to retain a semblance of integrity. Their act would part of history.

So, when it came time to read off the verdicts - more than a hundred of them - it came as no surprise to me that I would hear, "Count one, dismissed for lack of sufficient evidence. Count two, dismissed for lack of sufficient evidence. Count three, dismissed for lack of . . .

On and on. Until, finally, they came to that rock bashing incident. Here it was obvious that the judges had a struggle and went to great lengths to justify a guilty verdict.

Yes, the judges said, they had been troubled by this case, by the meagerness of evidence, with no one able to testify as to what Ilse Koch had said to the SS lieutenant.

But, they intoned after long deliberation, they had decided that the weight of the evidence was against her. "The verdict is guilty," said George Maginot, presiding judge.

And so the notorious woman was convicted on a single count of incitement to murder. Under German law, it carried the same weight as murder. She was once more sentenced to life in prison. The German people, if that was what they had wanted, now had the finger of guilt pointed at their sacrificial lamb, an unsavory member of their society. She would spend the remainder of her life in Aichach Prison, the court said.

Ilse herself was not present to hear the verdict. Dr. Englert had informed the court that she was in a state of hysteria and confined to a padded cell, her condition brought on by her repeated fits of simulated insanity. Or, had she really cracked up?

That should be the end of the Ilse Koch story except for a little sequel that cropped up during the trial.

Someone might get the impression from my story that I attempted to minimize the crimes committed by some Germans during the Nazi period, even the days of the holocaust. The truth is that a number of those witnesses at the Ilse Koch trial were able to tell stories of beatings, hunger, tortures, slayings, sadistic experiments which had indeed taken place at Buchenwald. Yes, many of them had actually witnessed such things. The problem being that they had been unable to link any of these crimes with Ilse Koch.

334

But that sequel. As the trial ground on, the name of a certain Sergeant Sommers began to register in my mind. I suppose that when I first heard the name, it did not register but as the days went on and the name was continually repeated, I began to take notice of it. Yes, the witness had seen this man Sommers take part in the beatings, the tortures, the slayings. It was clear that Sergeant Sommers had been, perhaps, the most bestial man at Buchenwald.

You could name the most sadistic crime against the hapless prisoners and there would be witnesses who saw this Sergeant Sommers doing it. His name popped up so many times that I began asking questions. Where was this horrible Sergeant Sommers? Why wasn't he in the prisoner's dock instead of Ilse Koch? Had he ever been brought to justice?

A member of the prosecution staff finally enlightened me.

"Yes," he said, "we would like to try Sergeant Sommers. We heard about him as soon as we began to investigate Buchenwald. And we tried to find him. We searched for him for months. We finally found him."

The prosecutor stopped here. I could sense that there would be a bit of drama in what he was about to tell me. He was almost savoring it.

"We found him in an American prisoner of war hospital. It seemed that as the war neared its end, and German manpower became short, they began taking some of the concentration camp guards and sending them off to war. Sergeant Sommers was assigned as a tank driver. One day his tank took a direct hit from an American anti-tank shell. He was severely wounded and was picked up on the battle field by the Americans.

"His condition was so critical he was expected to die. But with treatment by American doctors and nurses, he finally began to recover. But not completely. He is still paralyzed. Completely helpless - the man's mind is mostly gone. Not much more than a vegetable.

"We will never be able to bring Sergeant Sommers to trial."

Chapter Twenty seven - Bribe

A guy could always get a few "happies" out of being offered a bribe.

Especially if the offerer was a duchess. A real duchess.

And the boodle involved was something like four to six million dollars of crown jewels. At 1947 prices.

Even if the prospective bribee happened to be so young and full of moral righteousness he wouldn't dream of accepting a money bribe to kill a good news story. Not ethical.

Actually, if we tell the truth we will have to reveal that we were offered at least three bribes on that crown jewel story before it was over. Seems everybody wanted to bribe me. We had to accept the last one because it involved Army G-2 (Intelligence) and they pulled the old patriotic arm twist on us. "You wouldn't want to endanger the lives of Americans, would you?"

Plus the hint - here came another kind of bribe - that if we played ball with G-2 they might see fit to give us a break on another good story. And they did. Wow, what a story.

Perhaps the duchess, sitting there so prim, ladylike and proper in her old castle at Detmold, didn't really consider it a bribe. After all, she and her family owned those crown jewels, and maybe she just wanted to make sure those jewels didn't get lost.

Somehow, we've got to explain all this and the only way you get started is by remembering how World War II ended in Germany. They split Germany down the middle. The Russians grabbed the nearest half and left the rest to the West - to the Americans, the British and the French.

336

Word about the "divvy up" process got out before the war ended. A lot of the Germans, thousands and thousands of them, decided they didn't want to live any place where the Russians were.

That created a horde of refugees all heading west, choking the roads. Lots of them left with only what they could carry in a couple of suitcases. They were in a hurry. But then there were rich folks, too, like the duchess.

Which calls for more explaining. Everybody who studied German history in college knows that the country was once a whole series of little kingdoms, dukedoms and what have you. The country was chock full of royal families.

When modern politicians came along, folks like Otto Von Bismarck, and later Hitler, decided to unify the country. They took the political power away from all the little royal enclaves but left them their property - things like estates, castles and crown jewels.

Yup, believe it or not, a lot of these so-called royal families were still sitting around their castles during World War II. The men folks, naturally, were mostly off fighting the war. Not very happy about it but the Hitler decrees made for certain that all men, royal or otherwise, had to fight.

So there, at the end of the war was my duchess, the Grand Duchess Fedora of Sachsen-Weimar-Eisenach, sitting in the eastern part of Germany. At Heinrichan in Silesia - in the path of the invading Russian armies.

She packed up the jewelry and hustled off to another family estate at Zillbach, Thuringen, a bit further west but still in the Russian grab area. When the Russian armies kept on coming she decided to flee again. But now she was terribly worried about joining that horde of refugees while lugging all that jewelry around. So, she buried it.

There were a lot of folks doing the same thing, the wealthier ones, royal or otherwise. Too risky to be lugging the family jewelry, silver and heirlooms around on the roads, choked with refugees. So they buried the stuff. They would try to come back later and dig it up. They didn't realize, and neither did the West, that when the Russians once got their claws on a hunk of territory they didn't turn loose.

So, when all the smoke and thunder of the war faded into history, there sat all these millions of refugees in the American, British and French zones of occupation. The rich ones, of course,worried about all that stuff they had buried. My duchess had ended up on still another family estate at Detmold, in the British zone.

The Russians had clanged down their iron curtain across their half of Germany, for keeps. How were these folks with all their valuables buried in the Russian Zone going to get them out? By this time it was becoming more clear every day that the Russians were not nice folks to live with. Very, very few of these displaced Germans wanted to go home.

All of which gave rise to a new profession for a few selected Germans - smuggling. For a fee, usually a cut of the loot, slick operators would sneak back into the Russian Zone, past those border guards, bundle up the jewels and bring them into the American or British zones. Some of these smugglers were former residents of that Russian Zone and knew the country like a book.

Oh, it was risky, all right. On both ends. The owners of the valuable stuff always had to run the risk that their "smuggler" might just take off with the whole boodle. A few "elite" smugglers managed to convince their customers they were honorable and honest. They'd take their cut of two to seven per cent, and play it square. The other big danger was that either the Russians, their East German stooges, or the border guards would catch your smuggler. Then you lost it all.

The time came when Grand Duchess Feodora was spending sleepless nights worrying about all those Sachsen-Weimar-Eisenach crown jewels stashed away in Thuringen.

Besides, in those first years after the war, things were tough even for a duchess. The economy, what there was of it, was mostly black market. German money wouldn't buy anything. Gold and jewelry would.

Even a duchess had to eat.

It was also inevitable that, sooner or later, the duchess would hear about this new smuggling game. Could she find one of these smugglers she could trust? If so, could the guy sneak in, bag up the stuff and get out without getting caught?

We're getting to the bribe part.

Duchess Feodora found her smuggler and satisfied herself he would play it square. For two per cent in cash and five per cent of the jewels.

There was one more little conditon. Since the game was indeed so risky, the deal called for him to make several trips and bring it out in installments. That way, if he got caught they wouldn't lose the whole boodle.

It was going to be that installment thing that got me into the bribery part.

Our smuggler character - we'll call him Heinrich Mueller - had a pretty good racket on the Russian side. He had formerly lived in the eastern part of the nation. Now he was posing as a communist and had offered to be a kind of propaganda agent for the Russians and the new East German communists.

He offered to smuggle communist propaganda literature across the border into the American Zone and distribute it. That got him free passage around the countryside in the Russian Zone. Pretty smart trick.

One thing we've got to remember is that this was long before the Russians and the East German Communists built the Berlin Wall and set up all that elaborate surveillance equipment to keep Germans from sneaking across the border. But they did have troops patrolling that border, the Russians on the east side and the Yanks on the west side, plus newly established German border patrols that worked both sides. These German patrols were, of course, controlled by the Americans on our side and the Russians on their side.

I learned later that Mueller had done pretty well with his smuggling racket and had a clean record with his "clients." Unfortunately, his luck ran out on his first trip with the Sachsen-Weimar-Eisenach jewels. No, he didn't get caught in the Russian Zone but of all the bad luck, he had to get himself nabbed by the West German border patrol on the way out. They found the jewelry stashed under a pile of his communist progaganda stuff.

Since the U. S. Army, as the occupation authority in a defeated Germany, had set up the newly organized German border patrol and the Americans remained the boss, no sooner had they caught Mueller and discovered the "loot" than they went running to their supervising unit, an American C.I.D. (Counter Intelligence) outpost at Eschwege, manned by a German speaking American lieutenant and a couple of sergeants.

"Hey, look what we got," they said, or words to that effect.

It was when the young lieutenant, let's call him Lt.Schweitzer, started grilling Mueller that Mueller simply told him the truth. What else could he say?

He was caught. He had the loot, or the first installment of it, and he figured if he lied, some jewelry expert might identify the stuff as part of the Sachsen-Weimar-Eisenach loot and then he'd be accused of stealing it. He confessed that he was simply acting as an agent for the duchess to try to recover her crown jewels.

He even spilled the beans about the fact that he had only part of the stuff and there was more loot to come.

A little light bulb lit up in Lt. Schweitzer's head. He had concocted a brilliant idea - one that would get him in trouble and start the rockets going off at the United States military headquarters in Frankfurt.

His idea was to let Mueller go ahead and complete his job, bring the rest of the Sachsen-Weimar-Eisenach jewels out of the Russian Zone. To make sure that Mueller played it straight with him, Lt. Schweitzer - without consulting headquarters - decided he would send one of his German speaking "agents" with Mueller to keep an eye on him.

I always suspected that Schweitzer himself was that escort "eye."

This time Mueller and the "eye" got the jewels . They brought out all of them. Schweitzer immediately notified Frankfurt about the little coup he had pulled off.

The high command in Frankfurt sent an armored car escort to Eschwege to pick up the jewels. They were hauled back to Frankfurt where they were deposited in a vault for safe keeping while the chiefs made up their minds about what to do with them.

Mueller had not committed a crime. They turned him loose with orders to keep his mouth shut.

The duchess was upset when she discovered what was going on. With things being the way the were, she could see a fine set of wings sprouting on her jewelry box. Didn't conquering armies, throughout history, grab anything that fell in their hands from the enemy?

The duchess called on the authorities in Frankfurt and asked for her jewels.

"Sorry, we can't let you have them," came the answer.

At least, not for now. But somebody "with wings or a star on his shoulder" did give her a hint that things might blow over, quietly. The whole thing might be investigated discretely and then her precious jewels just might be returned to her.

She was told to go home, sit tight and keep her mouth shut.

That's when I became involved.

I couldn't claim credit for digging up the story about the duchess and her crown jewels. Pat Conger, my boss, and another boy at United Press, Dick Clark, stumbled onto it. Pat and Dick had good connections at Army headquarters in the I. G. Farben building. Somewhere along the way, somebody leaked word to Dick that some crown jewels were locked up in one of the headquarters safes. It was just a tip - not the whole story. It was just enough to get them excited.

Pat called me into his office and told me about the tip. He asked me to see what I could find out through my German sources.

This was the part I could do best because I spoke fluent German. With a pretty good German accent.

We knew just enough about the thing to know the jewels had been brought across the border near Eschwege where the Army had a counter itelligence post. We would try there.

I moved fast and was lucky enough to catch Lt. Schweitzer before the implications of the whole incident dawned on headquarters - and the lieutenant got a chewing out. I don't believe he had much experience in dealing with newsmen. He just didn't know how to handle a guy like me. I think he was dreaming of seeing his names in big bold headlines.

Yes, he said, he had helped bring the loot out of the Russian Zone. He even showed me photos he took of the stuff spread out all over a dining room table. He even told me where I could find Mueller and the duchess. The lieutenant was still floating around on a big soft cloud.

Next stop was Mueller's house. He tried to clam up. He remembered his orders to keep his mouth shut. But newsmen still went around in Army officers uniforms - orders from on high - and a lot of Germans had not caught onto our real status. We looked official, especially to people out in the country.

It was when I mentioned those crown jewels that his curiousity got the better of him. He had to find out how much I knew. He also was trying to figure out who I was. I didn't lie to him. I properly identified myself but he was still unsure. In the Germany he had known, Army press correspondents all had a sort of official status.

One of the first things I noticed about Mueller was that he lived in a brand new house. A pretty good sized house. Germans were not building new houses in those days unless they had access to something more than paper money. It was clear that Mueller, for a poor Russian Zone refugee, had been extremely successful at some kind of work.

"Nice house you have here," I said. I wanted him to know that I had noticed.

341

That put him on the defensive. We started sparring. On one hand, he wanted to toss me out and clam up but he was still trying to figure out who I represented and how much I knew. It was that curiosity that led him into my net.

"Yes, I have managed to build a house. But I'm honest. I'm not a crook," he said. He felt impelled to tell me that on the front end.

We got back to the jewels and he began to get nervous. He took a pack of American cigarettes out of his pocket and began smoking. Quick puffs. He offered me one. Normally it was the other way around. It was the American who had the cigarettes, prized on the black market.

"I can't tell you anything," he said. But then again that compelling need to assure me he had committed no crime.

"Who told you about the jewels?" he demanded.

"Oh, they told me about them in Frankfurt," I replied. I didn't elaborate on who "they" were.

In the end, in spite of his order not to talk, Mueller had to. He was exploding with curiosity mixed with fear of the unknown. He didn't know where he stood in all this.

"I did nothing wrong. I committed no crime," he insisted. Even the Amercian authorities in Frankfurt agreed on that. But these insistant questions from this red head. I'm sure he still had not figured out what my status was as an American press correspondent. The uniform worried him.

"But you did bring the jewels out of the Ruzzian Zone, no?" I said.

"They were not stolen. They are the property of the duchess. I was acting only as her agent. I have my reputation. I am not a thief."

Beyond that, I was able to get very little out of him. That may have been my fault for when he asked why I wanted to know, I told him the truth. For a news story.

Perhaps I should not have said that. Perhaps I should have pushed my advantage, using his curiosity without lowering myself to the simple status of a nosy reporter. In any case, once he was sure I didn't have some sort of official status, there was little more he would say.

Except for the bribe.

That came exploding out, as if he suddenly realized he had said too much already and now needed to cover his tracks.

"I could make it worth while to you not to print the story," he blurted.

Maybe I should have followed up on this sudden new advantage but there came all my young moral ethics bubbling to the surface.

"I'm sorry but I can't accept money to keep me from writing a story," I said.

That did it. From that moment on, not another word out of him.

Next stop, the anxious duchess at her old castle at Detmold, in the British Zone.

I went directly there. I am certain that Mueller had not been able to warn her. The telephones were not working well in Germany in those ripped up times. The military had dibs on most of the lines that still worked.

But the duchess was a bit more sophisticated and refused, at first, to even see me. Through a house lady - a servant - she informed me that she did not wish to speak to the press.

When I sent a message back that I wished to speak to her about the crown jewels, word came back quickly. "The duchess will see you in a few minutes."

She slipped quietly into the room. Tall. Prim. Regal. Ladylike, a true German lady in her fifties. I never found out what happened to her husband, if she ever had one. Maybe a victim of the war. She apologized for the big room being so cold in the winter. "Coal, it is so difficult to obtain," she said. And then, directly to the point.

"What is this about the crown jewels?" she said. "Where did you learn of them?"

I gave her the same answer that I had given Mueller. "They told me about them in Frankfurt," I said. Now she quickly demanded to know who I was and in what capacity I was asking such questions of her. No dummy, the duchess.

I told her the truth, as I had told Mueller, that I was a reporter trying to get a news story. Her reaction was quite different.

"Why is this news? The jewels belong to my family. I have only tried to recover our family property," she said.

I tried to explain that people liked to read about crown jewels being smuggled out of the Russian Zone.

The lady was honest. Yes, she had been in touch with the American authorities in Frankfurt. They had told her they held the family jewels. They could only hint that, after things calmed down a bit from the war, the relationship with Russia and all these things, then the jewels might possibly be returned to her. It was her great hope and she wished to cooperate with the Americans in the matter. They had told her not to talk about it. To anyone.

"Now, if you insist on printing this silly story, my family may never recover the jewels," she said. "I appeal to you, please, do not print it."

Now it was my turn to let her know that I was only an employe. I had been assigned to do the story. My superiors in Frankfurt would have to decide about printing it.

"Who is your boss? How may I speak to him?" she now asked.

That was when I had to slip the knife into the poor duchess.

"Actually, my boss in Frankfurt is only a part of the thing," I said. "He also has bosses - in London and New York."

She gave a gesture of dismay. This thing was becoming a bit too complicated for her to understand. She didn't say it but I could tell that she was fighting with the certainty that these Americans were a crazy people. So hard to deal with. Army officers - and nosy reporters.

So she said it.

"How much money do you want to forget this story?" she asked.

Once again, that righteous ethic coming up in my throat. I had to tell her, just as I had told Mueller, "Sorry, I can't take money for that."

"Maybe I could make it worth more to you than the story is worth to your agency," she said.

I didn't know how to handle this thing with diplomacy. In a sense, I felt sorry for the lady in spite of the fact that she was one of the defeated enemy now.

I was certain she had not stoked any of the fires at Dachau. Knowing what I did of the surviving German aristocracy, it was a pretty safe bet that the duchess and her family had not had much use for a character like Adolph Hitler. Few of them did.

But I had a job to do. I told her again that I could not accept money.

So she indicated that our interview was at an end. Hers was now a feeling of hopelessness. There was little to be gained by further conversation with the nosy reporter who seemed so stubborn.

I was equally helpless. Caught in my own kind of trap. I would simply have to report to my bosses what I had learned.

That was when all the rockets started exploding out the roof of the G-2 offices inFrankfurt.

By the time I returned to Frankfurt, G-2 knew all about my visit with Lt. Schweitzer at the border. What really upset them was that the lieutenant told me about sending an agent across the border with Mueller after the rest of the jewels. G-2 issued an urgent summons for my boss, Pat Conger, to appear in the office of the G-2 commander. Pat reconstructed for me the meeting he had with the colonel.

"Look, Mr. Conger," the colonel said, "we don't know how you got your tip on this crown jewel thing but it seems a young reporter with red hair has pretty well dug out the whole thing.

"The worst part is that our Lt. Schweitzer, very young and inexperienced as he is, was stupid enough to tell your reporter about his man going into the Russian Zone with Mueller. In the first place, he had no authorization to send one of his men in there. He should have checked with head-quarters first. We would have said flat no. It was a private matter, not involving the business of the military and he shouldn't have done that. But even worse, blabbing to your reporter all about it. He's been slapped good for it. We'll probably have to transfer him.

"Now we know you operate a private, independent news agency. The military is not supposed to interfere with the freedom of the press and all that. But I'm going to ask you, as an American citizen, not to dispatch that story out of Germany."

Well, Pat was no novice. He immediately asked why. The colonel squirmed a bit but finally came clean.

"You see," the colonel said, "while the war was going on, we were allies with the Russians. Since the war ended, things have gotten a bit sticky with the communists. As you know, they insisted on dividing up Germany. Then they clamped security on the border between their zone and ours. We had to agree - and put it down in writing - that we would not interfere in any way with what they were doing in their zone. It's a pretty high level thing. Interfering means things like sending undercover agents into their zone. Now, if word gets out that we sent an agent into their zone, they'll raise all sorts of hell and accuse us of violating the agreement."

It was Pat's turn to remind the colonel that the agent only went along and the mission was only to recover private property. He really wasn't on a spy mission.

"Do you think the Russians would believe that?" the colonel asked. "Even if they did, they'd still use it as an excuse to raise a lot of hell."

Then he blurted out the rest.

"It's top secret, of course, but I'm sure you realize both sides have been violating that agreement to keep hands off. They've got agents operating in our zone and we have agents in theirs. Officially, not a word has been said about it on either side. They are just waiting for an excuse to raise hell with us. If you insist on publishing that story, it might endanger the lives of our own men working in their zone. I might have to pull them all out in a hurry - and some might not make it. I'm asking you, as a duty to your country, to kill that story."

Pat probably hemmed and hawed a bit, trying to decide what kind of an answer to give the colonel when the G-2 man suddenly sweetened the pot.

"Mr. Conger, if you'll agree to hold up on this crown jewel story, I'll make it up to you some way. We'll see that you get a break on one of the next big stories that comes out of this headquarters. I'll promise you it will be a better story than this crown jewel thing."

I believe Pat would have agreed to stop the story, anyway. Gosh, he didn't want to do anything that would hurt his country's interest. Or endanger the lives of American agents.

"I told the colonel we'd sit on the crown jewels story," Pat told me when he got back. "For now, at least."

The pill was on the bitter side to swallow but Pat had done the right thing.

We had been offered a total of three bribes on this story.

What a pay day. A few weeks later, Conger got another summons to the colonel's office. The colonel greeted him and pointed to a big stack of papers on his desk.

"There is the big scoop that we promised you," he said. He went on to explain.

"While the war was going on, Adolph Hitler gave orders for two stenographers to be present at all staff meetings of the German High Command and take down every word they said. He wanted it all for posterity so that when historians wrote about World War II and the great victory of Germany, they would have the whole record. The stenographers took everything down for years.

"But in the closing days of the war, when it was apparent that Germany was going to lose and Hitler was planning suicide, he gave orders for all those stenographic notes to be destroyed. He turned them over to a group of trusted SS officers with orders to burn them.

"They had taken the papers down to Bavaria and were in the process of burning them when one of our advance Army units caught them and stopped the fire before all the papers were burned. Some were charred but still readable.

"Our intelligence officers have been going through all that stuff ever since the war and now the Army has decided to make it public. Up to now, no newsman has seen a single sheet of these papers. They are all in the German language and haven't been translated. I am going to give them to you 5 days before we give them to other news agencies. That will give you a chance to have someone read them and tanslate the important parts. Then you can write your stories and have them ready on the day we officially release them to everyone.

"You've got to promise me not to break the release date but you will have all your material translated and ready to go. Nobody will be able to catch up with you."

I guess the colonel got a lot of satisfaction out of reminding Pat about his promise. "I told you I'd give you a break. Now you've got it and we are even."

Wow. It was a much bigger scoop than the crown jewels story every could have been. I didn't know how he was going to explain to our competition how United Press got their story out so fast after the Hitler notes were released.

The next thing I knew, Pat walked into the office and plunked that whole stack of papers down in front of me.

"Here's your big scoop," he said, explaining the deal. For the next five days, I was locked in a room, reading and writing like hell. Extracting all the newsworthy items out of what Hitler and his generals had talked about during the war.

On the day of release, I was ready. All we had to do was feed our stories into the teletype. One big story each day. Our competition had to spend days, translating and writing, trying to catch up with us. They never did. I could sit back in the glow of all those beautiful messages coming in from London and New York about our great scoop. My byline was on headlines all over the world.

The whole world in 1947 was hungry to hear every word they could about what had gone on in Hitler's mind during the war. And his top commanders. Talk aboout a scoop - we had it.

A beautiful twist to the whole episode came about 6 months later. The same colonel at G-2 called us in one more time.

"You can release that crown jewel story now," he said. "If you'll just promise to leave out the part about our agent going into the Russian Zone. A lot of things have happened in the last 6 months. The Russians have been raising so much hell about so many things. They couldn't raise much more about a little thing like this. Besides, the German smugglers have just about got all the big stuff out of the Russian Zone. So, that part doesn't matter much any more."

What a twist. He had paid us off big to keep us sitting on the lid of the crown jewel story - and then let us use it after all. Like having your cake and eating it, too.

We had one more question.

"What happened to the crown jewels?"

"I'll answer that question if you promise not to use it yet," the colonel said after a moment.

We promised.

"The high command has been discussing those jewels. We've decided to give them back to the duchess and her family. But we want to do it quietly."

I was sort of glad the lady got her jewels back.

Even if I didn't pocket any bribe money.

Chapter Twenty eight - Jolt

The prophets sent no heralds on that bright June morning to foretell the fury with which the forces of evil would strike on that day.

Nor did they foretell that in the evening I would be alive, able to measure the margin of my victory by the sheerest strand of a spider's web.

Or that the instrument of evil would be something I had held in my hands so safely a hundred times. On this day its docile nature would errupt into jolting, stunning, smashing horror.

The setting for the struggle was so simple and tranquil. My privet hedges lined my woven wire fence with such precision that I swelled with pride at my neighbors' comments at how straight they were trimmed.

But the hedges were so near the fence that it was necessary to reach down from above with my electric hedge trimmer, between hedge and the wire fence, to keep the hedge neatly spaced from that fence.

I had done it dozens of times, so often that the job had bred a sort of boredom. I have never learned why the safe process I had known for so many hours suddenly exploded into a fury of threatening death.

I looked at my watch. It was nearly noon. The thought crossed my mind that in a few minutes my wife would be calling me for lunch. With a healthy appetite and her home cooking, the thought could only have been a pleasant one.

The next move was to shift my bench a foot or two for the next cut. My right hand was operating the electric clipper and my left hand gripped the wire fence for balance. The stance I had used for hours.

I never learned what happened inside that machine to transform it, in one explosive instant, from a tame and willing machine into an instrument of fury.

To a person who has never experienced electric shock, there is no way to recreate the wild savagery, nor the suddenness of such a jolt.

One moment I was standing on the bench, calmly contemplating the next swing of the buzzing clipper. The next - a jolting, pounding surge of electric current ripping through my body.

I confess that it was not the first time I had been shocked by electricity. As a do-it-yourself man, I have been bitten at least a dozen times by electricity. At times only a tingle. At other times, a bit intense, depending on the voltage and how well the current was grounded. I had, on a number of occasions, felt the shock from an auto's ignition, painful as a hot spear but not deadly.

What was hitting me now was something so utterly different. The full, surging force of everything a high amperage 120 volt line could deliver when fully grounded. My entire body had suddenly become a living lightning bolt, if that were possible. Jarring. Ripping.

Much of what I felt in the first moments is lost in a black nothingness. My brain slipped into a near unconsciousness. For at least a second or two, the thought processes must have stopped for, when my brain did begin to tell me what was happening, I was lying on my back on the ground.

I had been knocked off the bench. The upper edge of the woven wire fence was still gripped in my left hand. I had ripped that fence from its steel posts as I was flung to the ground.

My right hand was still gripping that once docile hedge clipper, suddenly gone berserk. But the jolting fury had not gone. It was still slamming through my body like a million red hot ice picks. Stabbing. Jarring. The nerves and the muscles of my arms in a seeming evil dance of death.

It has been said that the human mind is capable of recognizing the moment when death seems certain and only seconds away. I can remember a time when I was a child and dashed out into a street filled with cars. I heard the screech of tires and saw a car bearing down on me.

My brain told me that in a moment I would be dead. My mind braced for the impact. I believe I closed my eyes, prepared to be dead. Then I opened my eyes. The driver somehow had been able to avoid hitting me.

Now, once more on this June day, my mind had reached that moment of "exquisite certainty" that in a matter of seconds I would be dead.

Someone might be tempted to suggest that, since I was now conscious and able to think, why didn't I simply cast that evil thing out of my hand. Rid myself of any contact with the jolting force. Electricity doesn't work that way.

If you are gripping something when the current strikes, your nerves and muscles force you to grip the thing harder. The will is powerless to open the hand and free the person from the circuit of fire.

After one black moment when I was hurled from the bench, ripping out the fence, my brain returned to a kind of awareness. The muscles locked but my thought processes told me, with vivid clarity, what was going on.

Folks say that at moments like this, when a man faces death, the events of his life pass before him. In my case, there was no movie of my life. Popping into my mind was a name - Ed Reeves.

Reeves had been chief of police and I had known him well as a reporter covering his office. He later became sheriff - and soon after died from electric shock while working on a swimming pool pump in his back yard.

His name and face flashed into my consciousness, telling me, "Now I am dying as he died."

I was staring up into the cloudless sky which now seemed so utterly blue. So inviting to the living, not to the dying.

"This is a stupid way to die," I thought. Then, "God, if only someone would see me and come knock this thing off me."

Then came another thought. A realization? The one that might save. Somewhere in the midst of the jolting I was aware that my legs were not paralyzed as my arms were. In fact, they were kicking as if they were detached from my body.

The current was entering my right hand and arm, passing through my head, neck and chest and out through my left hand that clutched the wire fence. The upper half of my body was paralyzed, locked in rigidity. The current was not going through my legs.

I could see them kicking wildly and without any conscious effort. Was it the throes of the end?

Now came a thought that could mean salvation. I was still able, to some degree, to direct my thoughts. What if I could direct my kicking legs in the direction of that fence I gripped so tightly? Could I kick the fence loose from my hand?

For the moment, the legs were simply threshing wildly, involuntarily. Without aim or direction. If only I could somehow obtain enough control over them to send the kicks in the right direction.

I willed it. I decreed it with my brain. If I were capable in that frenzied moment, I might have prayed for it.

It didn't work. The legs continued threshing about without control. The plunging surge of electricity ripped through my chest and arms.

How long could a man stay alive, conscious, with this monstrous force jolting every nerve with merciless impact? At some point, death would come. It was inevitable now. Ed Reeves had died this way. Others had died this way. Would it take 10 seconds? Twenty seconds? Thirty? A minute? A man can die only once and the act of dying can never give birth to a measurement of time.

Somehow, even the act of trying to will the direction of my kicks was so desperate that it brought a moment of collapse. Some kind of exhaustion beyond which even the will could not function.

I lay back and stared at the beautiful blue sky. It was, for a moment, my surrender. I had kicked. I had tried so hard to force my legs to strike that fence. To jar it loose. I had failed at that. What more could I do?

In a moment would come peace. Quiet. The fading into darkness. But at least I would be free from the jolting horror that was ripping my body and brain. I would be free - gone forever.

"I don't want to die!" It was a scream of desperation. Not from my lungs and my lips but my brain - my soul.

"Try. Try. One more time. Try to kick the fence loose." It was a gritting order to my tortured body and nerves. I was trying to send the message to my legs.

"Kick. Kick. Kick. At the fence. At the fence. You must. You must."

It would be impossible to say how long I lay there in the grip of that monstrous force. Perhaps it all took place in seconds. Seconds which became hours in the imagery of the infinite mind. Perhaps it was indeed a minute or more.

I cannot even say that the conscious willing of a direction to my kicks played a part in it. All I do know is that - with the suddenness that it had begun - it ended. It was all over. The shocking surge of that deadly force was suddenly gone.

Peace. Peace. The glowing wonder of peace had returned to my tortured brain and body. I lay there for long moments, staring up into the beautiful sky. Breathing the peaceful breath of life. My line of vision included the gently waving branches of the big weeping willow tree behind me. It was beautiful, too. More beautiful than it had ever been.

I was alive. The horror was gone.

I must have lain there for several long minutes, simply laughing inside. At the joy of being alive and free from the blasting danger. Peace. Perhaps this was the way heaven was supposed to be. If not, it was all the heaven I wanted at the moment.

Then I began to move a little, looking around me. Now that the jolting was gone, my normal senses began speaking to me again. I could still feel pain but it was a normal pain now. From my hands. I looked down and saw the blood. Both hands were torn. Probably from the ripping force of the fall, tearing the fence down as my fingers gripped it rigidly.

On my right hand, the middle finger was numb. Dead. It had been the central gripping force on the clipper, the entry point for the electrical current. It would be months before normal feeling could return to it.

As I rolled over, I could see that clipper lying there, its plastic handle broken. Somehow it seemed like a rattlesnake, coiled and still deadly. Menacing. I was careful not to touch it.

Slowly I got to my feet. A bit wobbly but I could stand. And walk. The only pain now came from my bleeding fingers. Even that didn't seem important. I looked at the wire fence, torn off its posts. The wires twisted. The bench lying on the ground. So violent had been the physical force imposed on them.

I must have still been in my moment of rapture, happy at being alive, able to breath the clean air and see the blue sky - when I heard Ruth calling. She had chosen that moment to call me to lunch.

Perhaps she was also a bit mystified when I walked up to her, put my arms around her and kissed her. Laughingly, she pushed me away.

But then she saw the blood. The residue of horror in my eyes.

"What happened?" she demanded, a touch of panic in her voice.

"Honey, you almost lost your husband a few minutes ago," I said. Then I told her.

353

I took her out in the yard and showed her the ripped fence. The broken hedge clipper. But there was really no way to tell her what had happened. The jolting, murdering force. The gripping hands, unable to loosen their grip on something that was bringing me death. The kicking legs. The forcing of the will in an attempt to guide the direction of the kicks.

I tried to pick up a glass of iced tea from the table and found my hands trembling like the hands of an old man. I remembered how desperately I had wished Ruth would come and find me while the danger lived. To see me - to save me.

Now I suddenly remembered something I had forgotten in all those moments of rending shock. The old warning that a person found being shocked by electricity should not be touched. For, in the touch, the shock transfers to the second person and can indeed bring death to both.

Then I was glad Ruth had not come.

It must have been some time later that a portion of the drama forced itself into her mind. Filled with a sudden wave of womanly compassion it was she who came to me and put her arms around me. It was the only comfort she could offer for the terrible experience I had been through. But it was the comfort of heaven to feel her warm soft body against mine.

If I had gone, that warmth, too, would have been gone forever.

"Honey," I whispered in her ear, "I didn't want to die. I'm glad I'm still here. I love you."

Chapter Twenty nine - Dearest Darling

Dearest Darling could not have known about the flying typewriter.

The machine went flying out a second story window at Police Headquarters and narrowly missed hitting a pair of cops coming out of a door below onto the sidewalk.

She could not have known because her Joe Dear, who had thrown that typewriter, was a Two Guy man - a split personality.

Pouring drinks for the boys at his home during poker games or for Dearest Darling, when he went to visit her in Florida, he was a fine Kentucky Colonel. A true Gentleman of the Old South. The smoothest, the most gracious, the most generous host.

On the job, however Joe Dear donned his alternate ego as a police reporter for the local newspaper. He didn't walk the corridors of that headquarters in search of news - he prowled like a tiger. You could almost see the hair stand up on the back of his neck when he caught the scent of a story that was about to break.

He had been there so long, police said, that he probably was there when the massive stone headquarters was built. They simply built headquarters around him. He not only knew police officials and detectives - he had something on every one of them.

The anger, the wrath, the temper of Joe Dear were legend. A typewriter hurled out the window. Telephones ripped from their cords and smashed on the floor. The curdling threat. "I'll rip your goddam liver out and feed it to the pigs.

He didn't cow reporters on the other paper. He cowed the police. Damn them if he caught one of them giving a story to anybody but Joe Dear. Joe himself was the tradition, the fixture, the full embodiment of the spirit of that building and all its inhabitants.

DEAR GOD, I'M ONLY A BOY

I always cringed, just listening to his threats. For fear he would turn his wrath on me one day. Until I learned that he never mouthed those threats when the object of his wrath stood in his presence.

Oh, he had his ways of getting revenge on any policeman foolish enough to arouse his anger. He did it in print. It hurt more that way. He wasn't supposed to do it but he had his ways. Little tricks he had learned over the years. He would credit a big catch to Detective X when it was Detective Y who deserved the credit. Or he could simply skip the name of the guy who had made a big catch. Best of all, wait until somebody made a big blast against one of his erring cops and then print it. On the other hand, he could cover up the goriest sins of the men who played the game his way. It didn't take long for the cops to learn they'd better cooperate with Joe Dear - or else.

Then there was the telephone. Joe didn't mind venting his wrath over the telephone. Especially if his target was one of our girls who worked the telephone switchboard at the office. If they didn't get him his number fast enough. Those poor girls caught so much of his blood and guts they kept threatening to resign unless someone fired that "foul mouthed fiend." Only nobody was going to fire Joe Dear - he was just about the best damned police reporter ever invented.

He couldn't spell and his grammar was lousy. Nobody cared. That guy was always turning up with all the big stories at police headquarters. The rewrite men back at the office could clean up his writing.

Occasionally, but not often, the Police Commissioner might give a story to the other paper. The funny thing was, every time he did it he cleared it first with Joe.

"Joe," the Commissioner would say, "you know you've been getting too many breaks around here. I've got to give the opposition one. They've been ripping me apart. I'm going to have to let this one break on their time."

Joe would growl a bit but usually he went along with it. Especially if it was some kind of a departmental policy story. He didn't care much about that kind of story anyway. So long as the Commissioner saved the gutsy ones for him.

Under the rules of the game, the Commissioner released all the big stories. Department heads could release the routine stuff. As for detectives, the best way to get fired was to leak a story to the press.

That didn't keep them from doing it. They made sure they leaked to Joe Dear. His network of informers reached through the department like the arms of an octopus. You'd see one of the detectives sneak into the press room when the other reporters weren't around, whisper a few quick words to Joe and then disappear. If somebody caught them at it, they were just "talking about a fishing trip." Most of the time, detectives slipped up to Joe in the hallways. The best place to meet was in the john.

Sometimes one of the bureau chiefs might rip loose on a man suspected of tipping off Joe Dear. "God, boss, I swear I didn't tell him a thing about this case," the guy would say. Chances were that the detective really had said nothing directly to Joe about it. He passed it on to Joe through somebody else in the building who had nothing to do with the case. The bureau chiefs knew there was no way to keep a secret from Joe.

He smelled the news. He knew how to read the "Indian signs." He spotted the flurry of activity around one of the bureaus when they came in from a big hit. Guys would slip in and out of the Commissioner's office for conferences. The bureau chief would clamp his lips like a clam. They locked the office doors. Secretaries outside tried to act as if nothing was going on inside.

Joe would start hanging around like a love sick dog on the trail of a bitch in heat. He'd collar the Commissioner. The chiefs. The bureau chief. But it all had to wait until everything was properly nailed down. Then the door of the bureau chief's office would open a crack. The chief would peer out. If he spotted Joe - and he usually did - he would say, "Come in, Joe. We have a little story for you."

If a reporter from the other paper was hanging around outside, the Commissioner would simply slam the door shut again. Joe knew that sign, too. He'd head back to the press room and wait for a phone call. It always came in a matter of minutes. Then he'd go loping off to meet the chief somewhere else. They had their "safe rooms."

When one of those deals was in the cooking stage, Joe would be itching and stomping around as if he had fire ants in his pants.

Joe had one other big obsession. It was women.

He had a wife who was just about the sweetest little lady I ever met. A "real lady" type. Good looking. Neat. Clean. Good cook. She kept the house so clean that when you walked in, you'd almost swear the painters had just walked out the back door.

I never knew the details about Joe's relationship with her. He seldom talked about her and that was none of my business. I just knew she threw him out of the house, from time to time. He'd get a room at the University Club for a few months. One time he lived in that place more than a year.

Joe Dear did plenty of talking about his other women. That really wasn't any of my business, either, but Joe kept telling me all about them. Day after day. I had a running account of his conquests.

In the afternoons, after the paper had been put to bed, he'd spend his time on the telephone, talking to all those sweeties. Seems he was always in love with two or three at the same time. At least, that was what he was telling them on the phone.

He described them all as "lucious dolls." If you could believe him, that old horse was conquering the most beautiful women God knew how to construct. I guess I believed it, or at least part of it, until one day when I dropped in at his cabin at Hairpin Lake. It was Dorry, one of those girls I had heard him drooling about on the phone. One of his "really beautiful" ones. I had to close my eyes to look at her.

It was the beginning of my disillusionment and I soon found out that Joe Dear used the same imagination in his news stories about women. If a murder victim was a "lucious doll," I knew she might be decent looking. One of our rewrite men back at the office said, "If Joe says she's 'beautiful' she might be a passable middle aged horse. If he says she's an 'attractive blonde' she's probably as ugly as sin."

Every time the vice squad made a raid and brought in some women, Joe Dear would go galloping off to "interview" them. God knows why. The paper never used such stuff.

But Joe liked to tell about the old days when a reporter wore a pistol and a badge, just like the cops, and made runs to a big story in one of the squad cars. It was back in those days, he liked to say, that the chief of the vice squad was a good friend of his.

When they rounded up a bunch of girls for their fortnightly venereal check, the vice squad would pick out a good looking girl who was "clean." They'd phone Joe to come pick her up. They'd turn the girl loose with no problem if she'd promise to give Joe a free date. Joe repaid the favors by giving the vice squad a good ride in the news.

When vice made a "porn" raid and brought in a load of pornography - it was hot stuff then - Joe always got the chief to give him a bundle of it. He'd sit for hours, drooling over the girlies. Then he'd stuff it all into his personal filing cabinet. He had drawers full of the stuff. Every once in a while he'd haul out a load and drool again.

"Wow. Look at that bitch. Ain't she a pip?" He'd hand one of the pictures to me for an ogle.

He liked to do his brags about his physical ability, too. I guess I had to listen to a million of his women stories and even after he passed 60 his brag was, "I'm just as good as I ever was. Just give me time. I can still take 'em all on. One at a time."

It was only after Joe died, and I had to clean his stuff out of the press room, that I found out he had saved every love letter he ever received. Some of them dated all the way back to 1923.

Finally, there was Dearest Darling. Maybe they all were - but this one I knew more about. Joe met her on a vacation to Florida a few years before he died. He never took his wife on those Florida vacations.

She had been an airline stewardess. Another of those gorgeous blondes. I never saw her. All I knew was that Joe was drooling over her like a moon struck teen-ager. They talked on the phone at least twice a week. Every day he sat down and wrote her a letter. They always started the same way, "Dearest Darling." It didn't seem to matter that he was still dating Dory back home.

After Joe met his "Dearest Darling" he managed to get down to Florida at least once every month or so. He spent all is vacations down there, plus many weekends in between. Back home he'd fill me in on what a super gal his Dearest Darling was. It was a wonderful story but, somehow, I wasn't believing so much of his stuff any more.

It was his super temper that gave me one of the best of the Joe Dear stories.

As the years went by, I should have become used to the temper. I lost count of how many telephones he ripped from the wall and smashed on the floor. The phone company replaced them for a while free. Then they began sending bills for replacing the smashed phones. It was clear that Joe's story about how he "dropped them" wouldn't hold water any more. Then our company paid for the phones a while. It got to be too much even for them. So our city editor called and told Joe if he smashed any more phones the cost would be deducted from his paycheck. Joe kept on smashing them.

Then, one day, Joe was looking for the telephone Blue Book. It was a special telephone book used by reporters to check addresses against phone numbers. Joe couldn't find the book and he started going through the desk of the reporter for the other paper. It was an old fashioned wooden desk with no locks on it. To keep Joe from prowling, the other reporter had screwed a hasp onto it and hung a padlock on it.

The padlock sent Joe's temper into orbit.

"I'll bet that sonofabitch took my Blue Book. He's got it locked up in his desk. Where is that bastard? I want that book. Now," he screamed.

I had long ago learned that when Joe's boiler blew, it was best for me to shut up. To stay out of it. But the boiler just blew and blew.

"I know that sonofabitch has it in his desk. If I get my hands on him I'll beat the shit out of him."

A minute later he was cutting the other reporter's liver out and dividing it up among a school of sharks.

"If I get my hands on him I'll stomp him into the floor," he shouted.

By this time the noise level was high enough to travel beyond the doors and walls of the press room. Detectives started peeking in to see what was going on. It really wasn't necessary. They all knew. Joe's temper was part of the legend - and it was a good show. Joe Dear was having one of his famous blows.

I kept pounding on my typewriter. Or trying to. Joe stalked out a few times but he always came back and cranked up again.

"Where is that sonofabitch? I'll rip his balls off."

By this time, Joe's steam pressure was so high there had to be some kind of relief. He found it by grabbing a desk lamp with a heavy metal base and using it as a hammer to pound away at the padlock. Crash. Crash. After a couple of blows the lamp was shattered but the metal base stayed together and he kept pounding. He finally knocked the hasp loose.

Joe Dear now yanked every drawer out of the desk and pawed through them. Papers flew in all directions. No Blue Book.

"That sonofabitch hid it somewhere just to make a fool out of me. I'm going to kill him. I'll stomp him into the floor."

It was about this time that I finished my story and went to lunch. I didn't want to listen any more.

When I got back, everything was quiet as a church on Monday morning. I eased up to the door of the press room. Joe

Dear was inside. The other reporter was standing there, near his desk, hands on his hip and watching Joe. Joe Dear was down on his knees. He really was. A screw driver in his hands, silently screwing a new hardware hasp onto the desk.

They did not hear me. I backed away and left. What I had seen was justice but a bit much of it. I was happy that it was all taking place quietly.

The Joe Dear legend came to an end one day. The living part of it. I was home in the evening. It was my wife's birthday and we were planning a quiet evening of celebration. The phone rang. One of our rewrite men who played poker at Joe's house said, "He just dropped dead at home."

Joe had walked in from work, sat down in front of the television set and his wife came in with a beer. He was dead before she got across the room to him. The doctor said a major artery in Joe's head just blew up.

I never understood why it had happened when he was quietly at home. How come it did not happen in the middle of one of his famous temper tantrums at police headquarters?

That was when I became involved with the contents of Joe Dear' personal filing cabinet - and with Dearest Darling. The city editor told me to take care of the contents, do what Joe would have wanted me to do.

Joe had been explicit about his two cabinets. A dozen times or more he told me, "This one belongs to the office. I keep all my police files in that one. But the other one is my personal property. I paid for it with my own money. That stuff in there is all mine."

I had seen that cabinet opened often enough but, beyond the girlie pictures, I had no idea what was in it. I called Joe's wife and told her about Joe's private cabinet.

"What's in it?" she asked.

"Oh, just some old papers, letters and things," I said.

There was a pause. I believe she knew what she would find.

"Would you do me a favor?" she said. "Would you please take all that stuff out and burn it? I don't want to see it."

I promised. But before I kept the promise the phone rang. Dearest Darling was on the line from Florida. She was asking for Joe Dear. Nobody had told her.

Her daily letters kept coming but Joe Dear hadn't been sitting there every afternoon, writing his Dearest Darling letters.

How to tell her? "I guess you don't know what happened to Joe?"

"Oh, God, tell me what. Is he hurt? Is he sick or something?" Her voice dripped with anxiety.

I didn't know any other way to put it so I just blurted out.

"He's dead. Had a massive cerebral hemorrhage."

I could hear an explosion of sobs on the other end of the line. Some girls do love the craziest people. And she probably didn't know that there were several more like her, here at home, doing their share of sobbing, too.

The next day she called again. Her voice a bit more calm.

"I wrote Joe a lot of letters," she said. "I know he kept them. I'd like to have them back. Will you please pack them up and send them to me? I'll pay the postage."

So I packed them. It was a big shoe box full, crammed tight. A huge bundle of "Joe Dear." I never saw her - what I remember most is the sobs.

I took all of that stuff Joe left in the cabinet and hauled it out and burned it. Most of it. I saved a few of the porn magazines for a while. Later I dumped them, too.

I had to call Joe's wife one more time. About that steel filing cabinet. It was a good one with four big drawers and a lock.

"What shall I do with this steel filing cabinet?" I asked. "It is a good one, with a lock. It doesn't belong to the company. Joe said it was his personal property."

"You can have it," she said. "I don't want to see it."

Which explains why I have at home a nice big steel cabinet - minus its old contents.

That would be all of the Joe Dear story except for one thing. The funeral.

Cooper, one of his best friends, arranged the funeral. Together with Joe's wife. Cooper called me and asked me to be one of the pall bearers.

The police department sent an honor guard. They just never supplied honor guards to ordinary citizens. They might turn out for the mayor, or the commissioner, or men in blue killed on duty.

We were on our way, riding in one of those big black limousines when our old veteran city editor looked out the window at those crisply uniformed police officers on their sharply polished motorcycles, wearing white gloves. The escort.

"Joe would have liked this," the old editor said.

Joe Dear would have loved it.

Chapter Thirty - Kilo

I said goodbye to Kilo and then I shot him in the head.

"I'm sorry, Kilo, that I have to do this," I told him moments before.

"I had been approaching the decision for almost a year - reluctantly.

I could have ducked out - asked the vet to do the dirty work. Thea had taken Kilo to the vet one day and talked to him about it. He said the law required him to dispose of the body by cremation.

Thea, for reasons of her own, wanted Kilo buried in the back yard. That was against the law, the vet said. But who would know? I had already buried Bitsy back there when she died at the age of nearly 20.

Must a man justify shooting his own dog? Even if he liked him. Liked him a lot.

I started to say I loved Kilo but that might be a bit more than the truth. The only dog I really ever loved was Pedro, that lovable imp I grew up with. I had owned dogs since and liked all of them. Including Bitsy, the clown who knew so many tricks she should have been in the circus.

In fact, Kilo was not really my dog. He had been a Christmas gift to Bernie when the lad was eight years old. Bernie had grown up and gone off to school, leaving Thea and me to take care of Kilo - just at the point in time when Kilo began to have all his problems.

You could look out the window, 12 years ago, and see the boy and his pup rolling on the lawn. That tumble-charge-yap game that only a boy and his dog can play. Alone. Just the two of them.

that only a boy and his dog can play. Alone. Just the two of them. In their own little corner of the universe, oblivious to anything else going on around them.

Kilo, it sometimes seemed, was born under an evil cloud. Oh, he had fine breeding. His papers said one of his grandfathers had been a champion Alsatian back in Germany. He was born of proper parentage on Long Island and shipped by air to an eagerly waiting Bernie.

At the beginning, the biggest worry had been whether he would ever be able to hold his ears up properly, the way all German Shepherds must. Those ears just flopped around like dishrags until he was about a year old. In time they would snap to attention like a German feldwebel.

I guess one of the things I disliked about Kilo was that he was terribly big and strong.

When Bernie grew up and got involved in football and things, he didn't exercise Kilo enough. That left Thea and me with the job of taking him out for walks. If you could call them walks. Kilo took all the fun out of walking. Walks became endless battles with a beast so strong he was constantly yanking you off your feet. At the sight of a cat. At the sight of another dog. Or just a big bush. I tried wearing protective gloves. I tried winding the leash around my arm. I tried a choker leash. Nothing tamed that beast.

I felt that if I put him under the hood of my car and harnessed him to the wheels, he would take us tearing down the street like a hotrod. Especially when he spotted a cat.

His problems started about the time he was five. Heart worms almost killed him but the vet squeaked him through. Then he got that big tumor in one eye. The vet said it looked cancerous and he couldn't remove it. Thea doctored him with Vitamin E and the tumor went away - leaving one bad eye.

After that came the bugaboo of German Shepherds, osteo-malacia-displasia. Ouch. Hip disease. X-rays indicated there was a growth on his spine. One morning I went out to the kennel and found him crawling on his front feet. His hind legs were dragging, unable to support the rear end of his body.

Thea and the vet finally got Kilo back on his feet. But never properly. He swayed and lurched around like a sailor full of beer.

Sometimes his body would simply do a flop. Then he'd get up and try again. It was no fun watching that.

If all that hadn't been enough, his ears became infected. Thea and the vet cleared that up, too, but it kept coming back. Kilo would stand there, shaking that great head of his, as if trying to shake off a fly.

It was about the time that all of this stuff ganged up on the poor guy - hips, eye, ears - that we first began discussing whether it wouldn't be the thing just to let the guy go on. It was really only a matter of timing. When? How?

Oh, there would come times when we deluded ourselves into thinking that Kilo was doing much better. We'd postpone it. A few weeks of grace. Or was it truly grace when the poor guy was wobbling all over the place and constantly shaking that huge, classic head of his? He never could tell us exactly how severe the pain was. But you always wondered.

He still had that deep, authoritative bark which left the illusion that he was still boss of the back yard. But the fire had gone out of his lungs. He was no longer the magnificent animal we had been so proud of.

When Bernie came home that summer from school, and later at Christmas break, he took over the nursing routine. They'd still try going for walks. Not so far as in times gone by. Nor so fast. But Kilo wobbled his bravest. Still proud that he could go out with his young master who had grown so big. A guy playing defensive end on the team now.

Somehow it almost seemed as if Kilo actually improved a bit when Bernie was around. But mostly it was wishful thinking. Things never really got any better - only worse.

If a man in our day suggests taking a dog out in the country and puting him to sleep with a gun, chances are that he will hear a gasp of horror.

"You wouldn't. You couldn't."

Especially, the women. A lot of men, also.

Gee, does a guy have to justify it? Shooting your own dog?

I know it jarred Thea a bit, the first time I suggested it. I could see a tear in her eye. She knew it was inevitable that he go, sooner or later. Better soon.

"Could you really do it?" she asked, looking me squarely in the eye.

"Yes, if it is necessary," I said. I felt impelled to say that.

Such things were part of your growing up, out on the Oklahoma prairie. You survived by doing what had to be done.

If the horses or cows got cut on barbed wire fences, you doctored them yourself. You didn't get a vet. Nobody could afford a vet.

When lightning struck and killed three of our cows, we bit our tongues a bit at the enormity of the loss and then buried them. By hand. Big job.

When it came butchering time, to make sure we had meat in the cellar for winter, we killed and butchered our own animals. Even my mother, the most gentle and God fearing of women, would chop off the heads of her own chickens. She had learned her rules of living the frontier way.

Beyond that, in later years I was a hunter. Not a killer type but just someone who enjoyed the challenge of it and that communion with the woods in the early hours of a borning day. With sometimes the chance to bag a deer. Or a rabbit. Maybe a squirrel.

When I bagged an animal I dressed it myself - and ate it. Thea had turned into a superb venison cook.

So, if this thing had to be done, what was wrong with it?

The idea continued to worry Thea, the tender hearted Thea.

"Are you sure he wouldn't suffer? Would it be quick?" she asked.

I knew. If properly done, it would all be over in a fraction of a second. Faster than the vet's deadly needle. Just as painless.

The cost factor, too. We had spent hundreds of dollars on Kilo during his lifetime, trying to keep him healthy. The results had been less than glowing. If the decision was made to let him go, there wasn't any use spending more. We weren't that rich.

And by doing it my way we could bring him back to our own backyard as Thea wanted.

A trip out of town that Thea was planning, to be gone several weeks, sort of forced the decision on me. I knew that to do it while she was gone would be the best way. Fewer tears. Or pleas for a reprieve that could never truly be a reprieve.

Day after day I continued to postpone it.

Until that one morning when I looked out the window and saw it once more, that constant shaking of the big head. Still trying to shake that pain. Thea would be home in a couple of days. If I was going to do it, I would have to do it now. Today.

Kilo came when I got the leash and called.

When I lowered the gate of the station wagon he tried to jump in, as he had done so many times before on trips to the country for a romp. He couldn't make it. His hips collapsed and he tumbled to the ground in a heap. A yelp of pain. That was the way things were now.

So I picked him up. God, what a monster of heavy weight. And then, once more, as I put my arm under his rear end to lift, another yelp of pain.

"You won't have that pain much longer." I really didn't say it but it was my thought.

Again, out on that lonely country hillside I had chosen, I had to help him out, listen once more to the protest of hurt as I lifted his hind legs. Only a minute or two, now.

Suddenly it wasn't easy any more. My heart was doing things I didn't like. I found it hard to look at Kilo, into those trusting eyes, knowing that in a minute I would be aiming a gun barrel at him with deadly intent. Even Kilo seemed to sense that something was wrong and refused to look at me. He moved nervously back and forth, as if seeking some kind of shelter. There was, however, no sanctuary. For him or for me.

I tied him with a short tether to a tree. He lay down then but still refused to look at me. I had been so resolute when I told Thea I would do what was necessary. But now I wanted to load him back in the car and hurry home. But would that not only prolong the hurt?

I was trembling. Why? I hadn't trembled like that, at the prospect of aiming a gun, since that long ago day when I had shot my first deer. I had shot hogs and steers at butchering time. Now it was almost as if I were the one who was in mortal danger.

In the end, I managed to do it. Just as I had said I would, as I had long ago learned to do things because they had to be done. The loud "wump" of the heavy gauge gun as it went off. As I had promised, there wasn't a sound or whimper from Kilo. In that tiny fraction of a second it had all come to an end. He would have no more pain.

Now I was the one to suffer. Comforted only by the necessity of what I had done.

Later, as I was digging the grave and he lay there so quietly beside me, my thoughts were a tangle of memories. That deep, authoritative bark he had used so many times, to awaken us at night when something disturbed the peace and quiet of our back yard. A prowling coon, perhaps. Or always the thought that it might have been a prowler.

Those wild, powerful lunges at the sight of a cat. Or a squirrel. The look of automatic respect which came over the faces of strangers when they first saw him, awed by his size and that commanding bark. The wild plunges around the back yard when one of the neighbor dogs approached our fence. Perhaps most warming of all, the way his giant tail would whip when some member of the family appeared at the back door. The jump up against the fence on his back yard dog run, standing there waiting for the human hand, the scratch to his ears. The petting stroke.

Little Peppy, our only surviving dog now, had been locked up while I took care of my "chore." She would miss him, I knew, but the vet had said it would only be for a few days. "A dog forgets quickly," he said. I wasn't so sure.

The two of them had always been friends, since the day we brought the tiny beagle puppy home. Barely seven weeks old. When Bernie had taken Kilo out for his daily walk, the tiny puppy that was not much more than the size of two fists, would trot mightily along behind, trying hard to keep up with the long strides of the big dog. So big - so little. The whole neighborhood laughed at the sight.

She had always curled up against Kilo in the big doghouse at night. On colder nights it had been a friendly, warming thing. Now that big, warm body wouldn't be there any more.

When it was all finished and I freed Peppy, she whined and immediately began searching for her friend. Eventually she found the grave, sniffed at the spot where Kilo had been lying while I dug the grave so deep. Somehow it didn't seem to tell her what she wanted to know. She continued her search.

That night she tunneled her way out, under the fence, and prowled the neighborhood. Sniffing. Searching. When we found her gone in the morning, we knew where she had gone. At the sound of our voices she came. We didn't scold.

For days, Peppy searched for her friend. Whining. Sniffing. Sometimes at the grave but for once her sense of loss was not answered by what she found there.

In time she came to accept it. She, too, had said her goodbye, as best she knew how. The search. The whines.

As for me, I was the one who found it harder to forget and could never feel quite at ease with what I had done. Something vaguely disturbing. Not so much at Kilo's death but because I, his trusted friend, had been the one to fire the shot.

"Goodbye, Kilo. I'm sorry I had to do it."

368

Chapter Thirty one - Susie

I had been appointed Lord High Excutioner in the case of Squealing Susie.

None of us were very enthusiastic about imposing a death penalty on her, especially in view of her beautiful babies. They were twins.

Beyond that, it was impossible not to admire her for her uncanny intelligence and her impudent courage.

But Susie had more or less brought it on herself by squealing on us. Not once or twice but every chance she had. If she wasn't taken out of the picture, she was going to ruin everything we had been working on. All the time and money we had spent on our big project out there in Monticello woods.

I suppose I should explain that Susie was a deer. A female deer. A doe. A mama deer who showed up every spring with beautiful twin fawns frolicking at her heels.

Susie was more than just a deer. She was Superdeer.

Everybody knows that all deer have super senses - of smell, sight and hearing. But Susie seemed to have been born with a bit more than that. She had some kind of sixth sense - or was seventh or eighth - a way of detecting human beings that went far beyond anything I had ever seen in a deer. Even when the wind was against her and it shouldn't be.

Then, too, the fact that she used that extra super sense to squeal on us. God, what noise she would make. Gee, deer aren't even supposed to make noise.

I had started to say Susie was the most intelligent deer I ever saw. But if that had been, how come she didn't use that super sense

369

of hers to hike her pretty little butt out of sight every time we showed up? No. There she would be, so defiant and challenging, flaunting herself and those two beautiful little fawns almost as if daring us to do our worst.

It was almost as if she had still another super sense - a ninth maybe - which told her something about the nature of men and the rules they make up. For example, the rule that during the summer, deer were out of season and a man wouldn't shoot. Are deer supposed to know those things?

Beyond that, none of us really wanted to kill her. If only she had kept her mouth shut like other deer do.

In fact, most veteran hunters won't even shoot a doe, not even on those few occasions when it is legal. Shooting a doe, somehow, does not fit the macho image most deer hunters like to keep intact.

I had been hearing about Susie for about two years now. Other hunters scouting around the south end of Dr. Jim Collins' hunting preserve knew about her and had been telling me the story. But none of it prepared me for what really happened when I met her.

During the summer, on weekends we would sometimes sit in our deer stands to watch the deer. It was fun and gave a man a chance to learn something about the habits of deer.

I was sitting in Dr. Jim's high tree stand on the south end of his big field one day, watching a doe and a buck out in the milo field, snitching milo heads. The doe would arch her neck saucily, reach up and snag her milo heads. Not the buck. He mostly kept his head down and, by watching carefully, I could see he was knocking the milo stalks down with his feet and then reaching down to nibble. That way, he didn't have to show his head. Or that six point rack of his. Smart, those bucks. Keeping their guard up, even in summertime.

I guess I had been sitting there about a half hour when I suddenly heard that noise behind me. It was more of a snort than anything else. I turned around and there was Susie.

She was standing in the entrance of an old logging road that led into the woods to my left. Her head was high and she was looking right straight up at me. That was a surprise, for I had been quiet as a mouse and the wind wasn't even in her favor. But there she was, looking directly up at me and snorting. Every few seconds, to emphasize her snort, she would stomp one of those dainty front feet of hers, sharply on the ground.

370

Her message seemed clear. "I can see you - you dumb human. I don't like you. Get out of my territory."

Many veteran hunters, even some writers in hunting magazines, claim a deer never looks up and never sees anything above eye level. I had learned long ago that this was a bunch of horse radish.

If I had ever needed any convincing, I had it one day, years ago, when I had been sitting in another deer stand. It was overlooking the crossing of two logging roads in the forest. The hunting season was open. It was about three in the afternoon. I happened to be looking west when I heard the sound of deer feet just behind me. I turned and there was a buck. He stopped. I carefully and slowly swung my rifle around and released the safety.

It was the click of that safety release that did it. Just a tiny sound you could barely hear. But my buck heard it. In one swift movement he swung his head so he was looking right straight up at me. He wasn't more than 40 yards away and I was 25 feet above the ground.

Then, with one jump, and before I could get him into my scope, the buck was gone. After that day I never again believed that old idea that a deer never looks up. In any case, now it was Susie, standing down there, looking right up at me and very clearly letting me know she knew I was up there.

The sound. I called it a snort. Maybe it was more like a baa. Or a maa. Or a bleat.

Most western writers, and even the people writing the hunting books, say it is a sound a hunter seldom hears. Some hunters never hear it. The reason is because a deer seldom makes it. All true, except that those people had never met Susie.

Years ago, when I had first begun deer hunting, I had heard about that sound. In fact, some hunter supply catalogs listed a deer caller. You blew in it and it was supposed to reproduce that sound. The catalogs said it would attract deer. So I ordered one.

I read the instructions that came with it. The sheet said a deer seldom made that bleat. So, they warned, you blow only one little short bleat. Maybe two. Then you were to shut up and not blow again for at least half an hour.

I tried blowing the darn thing but I never could be sure whether it sounded like a deer or not. I had never heard a real deer sound off.

Then, when I took the thing to the hunting camp with me and blew it, I could see by the look on the faces of some of the veteran hunters that they were not impressed. In fact, they proceeded to inform me, if I went into the woods and blew that thing I'd scare away every deer in the country.

You see, they told me, that sound wasn't intended to attract deer at all. Just the opposite, it was a warning sound. When a deer made that bleat, it was to warn all other deer within hearing distance - and deer could hear it a mile - to hike their butts out of the area.

Several years after that, I did hear the sound. On several occasions. That first time - it was early morning and still dark - I was climbing up into my stand when I heard that sound coming from the woods behind me. It must have been a warning because I never saw a deer that day. Much less a buck.

Now here was Susie, violating all the rules in the book by snorting over and over again. It almost sounded as if she were trying to sing an aria. Not that it sounded like one. But Lord, what a defiant sound.

Somewhere behind her I could see two fawns flitting around in the bushes.

After Susie had stood there, snorting and stomping her foot for several minutes, she simply and defiantly walked out into the open field and began nibbling on some wheat shoots. The fawns joined her. But every few minutes she would look up at me, snort several times and stomp that pretty foot. She was making it very obvious that she didn't like my presence.

I was simply enchanted. Also puzzled. If Suzie knew I was there, and that I represented danger, why would she flaunt herself so openly? The idea was teasing. Was it really possible that Susie could know about men and their hunting seasons?

Susie must have displayed herself and her act for at least a quarter of an hour before she suddenly looked up at me, snorted once more and then hiked her tail and whirled towards the woods.

Even when she fled she made an act of defiance out of it. Instead of dashing straight into the woods, she whirled a few times, flipping her tail. And then, with the fawns at her heels, she was gone.

It had all been so fascinating I just sat there, almost unbelieving, for minutes after she had gone. I had to see more of this crazy deer. I made it a point to go back to that stand in the late afternoon, again and again. She never failed me. Always that same incredible performance.

At times she would approach from a different direction. I would hear her behind me in the woods, out of sight. But then, suddenly she would be there, defiant and cocky as ever. Always looking up at me. Snort. Stomp. No matter how quiet I had been.

Somehow, the whole thing troubled me a bit. Couldn't she know that if she continued this crazy behavior that it would, sooner or later, get her into trouble?

Then, one day as I sat watching her impudent act, the thought suddenly hit me that perhaps she was acting as a mother, training the prettty little fawns about the presence of humans. The odor. The danger.

What lent some credence to this thought was the way she used her tail. It is universal knowledge among hunters that when a white tail deer snaps its tail to attention, exposing that snow white underside, it is a danger signal to all other deer.

I had begun noticing that when Susie did her exit act, she never flashed her white danger signal immediately. She would go through her whirling snort stomp act a few times before she would flip that tail up and dash into the woods. The fawns always at her heels.

But then there remained that nagging question - if indeed all this act was a training session for the youngsters, to alert them to the danger of the sight and sound of a human, why would the mother flaunt herself so openly? If the presence of a human meant danger, didn't it also mean danger and possible death to her?

The only answer I could think of was that suggestion that Susie was a Superdeer. She knew more about humans than a deer was supposed to know. Otherwise, how come we never saw any other deer doing what Susie was doing?

When I first told my buddies, Dr. Jim and Kerry, about what I had seen out there - they just laughed. They knew all about Susie.

But as the summer wore on, the subject of Susie came up again and again. It was no longer a laughing matter. What if she kept hanging around during the hunting season with that snort act? It would, we knew, scare all the other deer away from the area.

It was Dr. Jim, who had lot of work and money tied up in our hunting project, who finally came up with it.

"Looks as if somebody is going to have to do her in."

But I don't believe we ever really thought about it seriously until, late that summer, the Arkansas Game and Fish Commission announced that there would be a special pre-season hunt for hunters using the old fashioned muzzle loading guns. The old Davy

Crockett guns. Above all, during that special season, the announcement said, doe would be legal targets.

I had never shot a muzzle loader. I didn't even own one. I wasn't even enthusiastic about them. Their effective range was limited - not more than about 50 to 70 yards. You were not allowed to use scopes on them. To me, it seemed a good way to cripple a lot of deer.

Suddenly it seemed the discussion about Susie was becoming serious. I remember that little "council of war" in the cabin one night. The Game Commission had handed us a legal solution to taking Susie out of the picture. We could legally protect our buck hunting.

Then, after everyone agreed we should give it a try there was the question of who was going to be delegated the job of shooting.

Suddenly I began to sense a lot of non-enthusiasm in the room. Yeah, who was going to do it? That was when Dr. Jim turned to me and asked, "Do you want to give it a try?"

And that was when I suddenly found my own enthusiasm level dropping. But I had agreed it had to be done. Dr. Jim was a good friend and I owed him a lot. With as much bravado as I could muster, I said, "Yes."

The next step was to take me through the elementary steps of how to shoot a muzzle loading rifle. The guys had been goading me to buy one but one of my excuses was my bifocals. Without a scope I couldn't see the sights on a rifle. Or so I said. The "muzz" didn't have a scope.

Even that excuse wasn't as valid as I had believed it to be. One day I had sneaked a peek at Kerry's muzzle loader. The sights didn't seem too bad. Apparently the people who made those things were selling them to other bifocal characters, too, and had put special wide sight aperatures on them. But I hadn't said anything about that and hadn't bought one.

Then that crazy thing had to happen the day I fired my first shot with the "muzz" gun. We went through the routine. You measured the powder and poured it through a special funnel into the barrel. Then, with a patch and a ram rod, you shoved home the bullet. Wow, what a hunk of lead that .56 caliber gun took. Last, you inserted the percussion cap. After that, Kerry showed me how to set the trigger. You pulled one trigger to cock the firing trigger. What he didn't tell me was that the final trigger was one of those "hair" jobs. It would go off at the slightest touch.

They had hung a white plastic antifreeze can on a bush about 50 yards away. Several of the guys had been practicing and managed to nick the corners of the big jug.

I sat down, rested the heavy barrel on my knees, took aim and put my finger on the trigger. It wasn't even ready to shoot when I touched that trigger. The gun jumped in my hands - a mighty boom and a blast of smoke out of the front. I was sure I had missed the target for I hadn't expected that trigger to pull that easily.

Next thing I heard, as the smoke cleared away, was somebody hollering, "He hit it dead center." I couldn't believe it. There was a hole right smack through the center. Funny how impish a guy can become at a time like that. I didn't dare confess it was a freak for it was too much fun basking in the glow of being a muzzle loader expert on the first shot.

But the worst part of it was that now I didn't have the slightest chance of backing out of the Susie deal.

All of which was why, on that first day of the muzzle loading season, there I sat in Dr. Jim's high tower stand waiting for Susie. And wondering what I was going to do when she did show up.

It was around 4 o'clock in the afternoon when I first detected signs that she might be around. A couple of flitting shadows in the woods behind me. The twin fawns. They had grown a lot during the summer and it was nearly time for them to go off on their own, without mama. Perhaps they had, for I saw no signs of Susie.

In a few moments, the fawns walked right under my stand, out into the wheat field and began nibbling on the tender green wheat shoots. They were so close I could see their little pink tongues wrapping around each bite of wheat. But no Susie.

It was odd, for when she did finally appear it was from a completely different direction, to my front and left, from the edge of the woods about 70 yards away.

At first I had doubts that it was Susie. For one thing, she hadn't come with the fawns. And she wasn't putting on her act. In fact, she was acting very strangely today. As she moved around, she seemed always to be keeping a bush or two between herself and the deer stand. This was more like a normal deer. I had already made up my mind that if it wasn't Susie I wasn't going to shoot.

But it had to be Susie because, after she appeared, the fawns went dancing over to her side. Beyond that, after the fawns arrived at her side, and after grazing a minute or two longer, there it came. The snort and stomp act.

At that moment, I became a very indecisive hunter. Almost as if it was my first deer. Was I actually trembling?

But I had to make a decision very quickly. Either shoot or admit I couldn't, for she was slowly moving away from me and getting very close to the limits of muzzle loader range. And keeping those bushes between us. Then, just for a step or two, she was out in the open. Some 65 yards away. I either had to shoot now or she would be gone.

I did. I took careful aim and pulled the trigger.

Now it was my turn to be surprised. The percussion cap popped but the big boom and the cloud of smoke didn't come until half a second later.

In that half second, I had taken my eyes off Susie and looked down at the gun. Questioningly. The thunderous boom answered my question. It had been a "hang fire." Muzzle loaders sometimes do that.

But Susie had heard the pop of the cap before the big boom. It had been loud enough to send her into a giant, flying leap and she must have completed that leap when the big boom came. It meant she had been out of the line of fire. In fact, I probably had moved the gun off center. Hardly a chance of hitting her.

Or had I? As she dashed those 25 yards to plunge into the edge of the woods it seemed that I could see a dark spot on what, otherwise, was the pure white of her underbelly. Below the gray.

Feeling just a bit frustrated, but also a bit relieved, I climbed down from the stand and walked over to the spot where she had been standing when I fired. The cardinal rule of the hunter required that I look for signs of blood, even if I was sure I had missed. I didn't expect to find any and I didn't.

But the unwritten rules also required that I trail her into the woods and, when I lost the trail, to begin circling. Looking for signs of blood or a wounded deer. First 25 yard circles. Then 50. Then 100.

I had actually been able to trail her by her tracks for almost 300 yards. After that, I circled until I had covered at least a half mile. No trace.

I wondered about that "hang fire." The only explanation I could think of was that the gun had been loaded the day before and had not been fired. The instruction book said that if you hunted with a muzzle loader and didn't shoot it during the day, to fire the charge off when you returned to camp. Then start with a fresh load in the morning.

I hadn't done that. It had been raining and perhaps just a trace of moisture may have crept into the primer hole.

The dark spot on her side? Probably a bit of dirt. I was certain now that I had missed.

Oh, I had missed a few other deer in my life. When it happened it always made me angry. At myself. But now, with Susie, I was somehow relieved. Almost happy.

I had given it a good try. I had my sights on her, good. It was fate. That "hang fire" had made me miss. I was pretty sure my story would stand up in camp for several of the other guys had experienced them, too. A muzzle loader just wasn't that reliable.

On the other hand, that little scenario kept running through my mind, over and over, like a little strip of memory film running over and over. The careful aim. The trigger pull. The pop. Then the big smoky boom. The sight of Susie galloping towards the sheltering woods. The fawns at her heels.

Disappointing? Yes, in the fact that I had another black mark on my hunting record. Disappointing in the fact that I had failed in my mission for Dr. Jim and Kerry, to get rid of the squealer.

I couldn't rid myself of the picture of that dark spot on her side. Was it possible my bullet had hit her low? So low it may not have been fatal? The bullet trajectory of a muzzle loader at 70 yards would make it drop at least that much. Those guns didn't shoot flat like my .303 or my 30.06.

And I couldn't forget the fact that Susie hadn't quite acted her normal self that day. She had not started her squealer act until the fawns came. She had always tried to keep a bush between herself and me. Was it possible, after all, that her act had been for the purpose of training the fawns? And now that the hunting season had come near, she had decided it was time to be a bit more cautious? I know, it sounds crazy to credit that much intelligence to a deer. Even Susie. Almost as if she could read the newspapers.

But how else could you explain it?

Back at camp, I had to tell my crazy story. I had to listen to those special chortles the guys reserved for occasions like this. But in the end, most of the guys had to believe my "hang fire" story. Kerry had one of his own, the day before, in a practice shot. In any case, they never pressed the matter and didn't try to cut my shirt tail off as they did, by ritual, when a guy missed during the normal hunting season. When we were shooting our "real" guns.

As the days went by, as Dr. Jim and Kerry and the others went back to the woods, I kept waiting for reports on Susie. Had anyone seen her? Was she still putting on her act?

In time, it became clear that nobody had seen Susie. Or, if they had, she had never given anyone signs of her identity. Dr. Jim thought he heard her snorting one evening but if it had been Susie she never showed herself.

I went back, too, looking for my crazy deer. But never saw her. All winter long. No signs of the deer that had been so impudent and sassy.

As the months went by I suppose we all forgot about Susie. Someone would mention her once in a while. For one thing, I bagged a nice buck during the regular season, in November, and that helped take my mind off Susie.

It was late the next spring, after Dr. Jim had been prowling around that Susie territory again that he came into camp one day with strange news.

"Susie is back," he said with a sheepish grin.

I couldn't believe it. Where had she been all winter?

"She has new babies," he said. "Twins again. Pretty little things."

"Are you sure?" I asked.

"Yup, it's her, all right. Same act. Same squealing. No deer ever did that except Susie," he said.

I thought about it for a moment. I really didn't want to say it but, like a dummy, I blurted it out anyway.

"What are we going to do with her now?"

"Nothing," he said. "I guess we'll just leave her alone. Seems she didn't bother us much during the hunting season after all."

Suddenly, I didn't mind being a dummy.

Chapter Thirty two – Temple of Prayer

It was when I heard the happy gurgle of water from the first flushing of the new indoor "john" that I began hatching my litte crime of arson.

To celebrate the completion of Mom's and Dad's new bathroom I was going to set fire to that ramshackled, smelly old john standing outside.

At night it would make a nice little celebration blaze. The neighbors would come running to see what was on fire. There wasn't a fire department within 15 miles. It would burn down.

I suppose it was a mistake to tell Dad about what I was planning. He immediately said no. An emphatic no.

It didn't bother me too much. I had defied Dad plenty of times before. Of course, that was all long ago in the distant past, in the days when I was a stubborn teenager.

I simply told Dad I was going to do it anyway. "You've got the new one inside. You don't need that old crapper any more," I said. "Besides, after using that smelly old thing all these years, we need some kind of celebration."

But Dad was insistent about his no. "Something might happen to the new one. We might need it again. No, don't do that."

That sounded a bit lame but I also detected a note of urgency in Dad's voice as he argued to keep that old outdoor toilet, a bit of anxiety. Something lay beyond the mere possibility of a breakdown of the new plumbing. I wondered.

Then, that night, it all came back to me. That smelly old crapper was Dad's temple of prayer.

He was out there now, praying. Long, very loud and with a voice that seemed to be trembling with emotion, almost with sobs of hysteria. And one of the main subjects of his long prayer out there that night was the state of my soul.

Oh, I knew that Dad considered me the Number One lost soul of the family. I had known that for 20 years or more. In fact, I had stayed away from home for a long time because of it. I felt pretty bitter about Dad in those days. I felt that I had my reasons. Plenty of them. Dad had broken so many promises to me.

But I loved Mom and, as time went by, I lost most of my bitterness towards Dad. I started going home again to visit. But every time I did, Dad would crank up on that soul business again. He didn't want to die, he said, without being assured that I would meet him in heaven.

At first I tried to ignore him but when he became so insistent I finally got tired of it and laid down my rules.

"Dad," I said, "I love Mom and I love you. I want to come home and visit once in a while but if you don't stop this preaching everytime I come home, I'll just have to stay away."

Dad didn't give me a direct reply. I could see I had hurt him almost as if I had slapped his face. I could even see traces of tears in his eyes. But I knew he got the message.

The next few times, when I came home Dad kept his side of the bargain. Oh, he would let it creep into his prayers at mealtimes. I let him get away with that much. But then, some months later, when we were saying goodbye, he hesitantly brought it up again. I stopped him.

"Dad, remember our deal. If you want me to come home to visit, you'll have to stop it."

After that, he mostly kept his part of the bargain. At least, the direct part. But I never could stop him from mixing it in with the mealtime blessings. "Dear Lord, remember our prayers for the souls of our children." At least, he kept it short.

It was in his main prayer session with God that he would lay it on, full blast. In his bedroom at night, or out there in his prayer temple, he would let it all hang out. So loud. As if not only God but everyone must hear.

At times it became so intense one could almost imagine him clawing with his hands at his own rib cage, as if to rip it apart and release such full power of his spiritual being as to force God to hear and act. But then, always in between, the remembering of his role as the "humble spirit," the beseecher, the pleader. Never with the

380

assurance - but only the hope - that God would hear and exert his awesome power.

For an understanding of all this, one almost had to be born into that hypnotic atmosphere of the "old-time religion" which had come to possess him, body and soul, with such utter finality.

In this sense, it could be said that Dad was born into his fate. Into a world through which God strode with eternal power, governing all things and all mankind. If God failed at times - in Dad's life it was mostly failure - failed to provide all those bountiful blessings he had promised, there was always a hidden reason. God's own reason.

If a poor guy like Dad, mucking around in the dirt and dust below, failed to perceive that reason, it was not God's fault. Never. It was always the poor pilgrim's fault. It mean he hadn't prayed hard enough. He hadn't whipped his kids hard enough, thus failing to shape them into the humility and image God wanted. If ever one wished to rebel against any of this, there was always the story of Job, the eternal sufferer, hurled from one plague or affliction to another until his spirit was completely crushed and he was willing to submit to the worst that God could impose.

Oh, this thing could become a bit hellish if you wanted to pursue it far enough. Sometimes it seemed that Dad was not far from being a Job figure himself. Forever the groveling, crawling, praying, beseeching pilgrim.

I can remember little real joy in their lives. Except, possibly, in those evening years of struggling together, and after all eight of the children were scattered to the far corners of the country, they entered into a sort of tender relationship with each other. It seemed to mellow Dad's soul. It had been a love affair and a marriage which had endured one hulluva lot. The tender closeness we saw between them in those last years may have been the biggest blessing and the most happiness the two of them every had.

But about Dad's gut-ripping pilgrimage, his constant search for the "real peace." I guess I could never have accused Dad of having conscious doubts about his faith. If he had them, they had to be buried deep inside his subconscious. And manifested only by the way he trekked from one church to another, dragging his family along. He had started with the Mennonites, for that was the church he was born into. Somewhere, somehow, this stern old fundamentalist church had failed my father.

He had gone to Oregon and for a time had embraced the doctrine of the Apostolic Faith Mission until it was the "apostles" who threw him out because he failed to live up to their expectations. He had sampled the teach-ings of the Pentecostal Holiness Church. Even the Baptists and the Methodists. He had ended up pledging his soul to the Church of God.

Formally, at least, this was the church he remained with until he died. But even that loyalty never put an end to his search - or his suffering.

Right now, Dad was out there in that weather beaten, leaky and smelly old outhouse, praying as if his heart and soul were breaking apart.

It was really supposed to be a joyous occasion in several ways. For one thing, it was the first time in 25 years that all the kids were home together. We had come to celebrate the Golden Wedding anniversary of Mom and Dad. We had been planning it for months. The neighbors and relatives were helping to make it quite a bang. They would bring gifts, food and cakes to heap on the tables at Community Hall. I had been asked to "make a speech."

But beyond all that, the offspring of that long marriage between Mom and Dad had done something a bit special. We had all decided we wanted to give our parents a meaningful gift, something that would be of service to them in their evening years. It was one of my sisters who suggested they needed an indoor bath. Nearly all their lives they had been forced to make those daily treks to the outdoor house of necessity.

It didn't take much to persuade me. Just the picture of dear Mom on a cold, rainy night, pulling a shawl around her shoulders and trudging out to expose her personal anatomy to that cold wooden seat at age 68, was enough to convince me. In fact, I wondered why it had taken us so long to do this.

I, as the son of the family most gifted with the use of tools, volunteered to take two weeks of my vacation and go out to do the plumbing. We all shared the costs. New bathtub. New wash basin with hot and cold running water. New hot water tank.

A whole crew of volunteers sweated to dig a hole for the septic tank with the drainage leading out into Mom's vegetable garden. It would be a greening blessing to the parched plants under the hot Oklahoma sun.

Finally, that supreme blessing of all, the seat of comfort which gurgled so merrily when you pulled the flush lever.

The whole project should have brought joy and happiness to Mom and Dad. I know they appreciated it. A lot. Dad even joined in, helping with the digging and hauling of dirt despite his 70 years.

On Mom's gentle face, a look of contentment, despite the way her neatly kept house was being ripped apart to make way for plumbing it had never had. Especially as the project neared completion and all her kids started drifting in. So a part of her contentment and joy was having her brood around her once more. Even my brother, Ernie, who had his share of arguments with Dad, too, had refused to come home for 25 years. He was coming.

It was Saturday night. The whole project done and competed. The big celebration would be tomorrow. Sunday. So why was Dad out there in that outhouse, praying as if his heart would break?

It really couldn't be a secret. All you had to do was listen. For the Bible clearly stated that it was duty of every man of God to make certain that his children followed his footsteps. Dad, over the years, while the complete and fulfilling peace eluded him, had come to believe that the reason God had "punished" him so much, withholding the fullness of his blessings, was because at least three of his children had failed to accept his view of the Almighty.

I had been the first and the oldest to bring it out into the open. It had been a time when the full fire and fury of Dad's wrath descended on me. I would have been thrown out of the house except that my labor and earnings were sorely needed.

But that didn't stop Dad from making a full scale battle out of it. Nor did it leave me without scars. Yes, I had indeed defied Dad before.

The years had at least partly healed the wounds and I no longer hated Dad. In fact, I was willing to concede that I even loved him now. I had learned to understand that he had been the victim of his environment - so stern and unrelenting the environment that made him the man he was.

But now, on this night, on the eve of the great Golden Wedding celebration, Dad's spirit and mine were once more locked in battle. In a symbolic sense, at least. There was not the slightest thought on my part of capitulating, of granting him his prayer. Never again would I put my soul at the mercy of that meat grinder which had once made my life a living hell.

After all, he was praying to his God, not mine. I just happened to be the subject of his prayers. In fact, I even suspect that he turned his volume up loud because he wanted the subjects of his prayers to hear him. As if some subconscious doubt had suggested to him that his prayers might rise no higher than the roof of that smelly outhouse. No, that isn't fair.

But on the other hand, perhaps the thought on his part that if the subjects of his prayer were indeed listening, this tearful supplication might soften their hearts without waiting for the message to travel all the way to the heavens and wait for God, in his time, to take action.

Somehow, I can still hear it. Strident, yet pleading. "Dear God. Merciful God, look down with mercy upon your humble servant. You know how hard we have worked and prayed to bring our children into your fold. Show your servant, oh, Lord, in what way we have failed. Forgive us if we have sinned in any way against these children. Open their hearts, oh, God, that thy love and mercy might be received."

Oh, there was a lot more to it than that. There had to be for something that went on for more than an hour. Or was it two hours? Sometimes, in looking back on it now, it seems that the only way Dad could sustain one of those sessions for so long was to work himself into an emotional frenzy that gave him super strength. Even so, I wondered how he could do it.

I do know that when Dad emerged from one of those sessions, he seemed almost drained of his blood. Pale. Weak. Trembling. Waiting for a sign that God had heard and would act. Even as I had waited, as a child, for the answers to my prayers.

The next afternoon, in public, I gave my answer to Dad's prayer.

The people of this little pioneer town, Bessie, that had been home for Mom and Dad for some 25 years now, had made quite a thing of this celebration. Other people had come for miles. Relatives and family had come from as far as California, Pennsylvania, Tennessee, Texas, Illinois and Kansas. Some of the people were customers of Dad's Watkins sales route, who wanted to show their respect for his honest dealing with his fellow men over the years.

They had come bringing their offerings, food and gifts, to load the tables of the little community hall.

My brother and my sisters asked me to make a "speech." So I did.

First, I reviewed briefly the history of the Mennonites as they trekked from country to country, seeking freedom to worship God in their own way, free from the burden of bearing arms.

The story of the young man who had awakened on that long ago October morning with a song in his heart. The young man who had hung bells on the harness of his little mare, Dolly, as he hitched

384

her to the buggy. To trot off to church to claim his bright eyed bride of 19.

I reviewed the marriage which had endured so much. The nine children brought into the world, eight of them still alive and present. I spoke of Mother, whom I remembered as the uncrowned queen of mothers. The woman who had toiled in the fields beside her husband with pitchfork and hoe. I gave my respects for my father, "the man who has always plowed a straight furrow" in his dealings with his fellow man. The man who had remained faithful to his God.

In the end, I paraphrased something from his own Holy Book. Standing there before these hundreds of his relatives, friends and children, I spoke on behalf of my sisters and brother, "These are our beloved parents in whom we are well pleased."

It had been for me a labor of love. I had done my best. I had given Dad the only kind of answer I was capable of giving to his prayer. I could give him my love but not my soul.

The editor of the Washita County Enterprise, the little weekly newspaper that had served this Washita Valley community for so many generations, thought well enough of my tribute to print it - in its entirety. I was amazed at the results. As long as 20 or 30 years later, when I would return to that valley to visit, people would still pull out faded clippings of my "tribute" to Mom and Dad.

That "eternal" marriage lasted another 12 years. Until death did them part. For the most part, during those last 12 years, Dad kept his part of that bargain with me. The few lapses I chose to overlook.

And then, on that day in 1966, my phone rang in Memphis. It was Mom, in Bessie. "Dad is in the hospital," she said. "He had a heart attack. The doctor said that if any of the children want to see him, they had better come now." I went.

I'm not exactly sure why I felt impelled to go. None of the other "children" came until he was gone.

Did I, because of that mighty conflict over the years, feel that I owed it to Dad? Some kind of subconscious need on my part? I could never truly answer that question. I knew there could never be any question but that I would not present to Dad on his deathbed the surrender from me that he had prayed for so long. I would keep possession of my soul.

But I would go. I would offer him what comfort and love I could. I would give my support to Mom.

After traveling all night, I arrived in Cordell, some 12 miles from Bessie. There was no hospital in Bessie. It was another instance of my father's stubborn will.

"It actually happened four days before he called a doctor. If he had come immediately after it happened, we might have been able to save him. As it is, the damage to his heart is so great. He doesn't have much chance," the man of medicine said.

When I saw Mother, she told me the rest. "I knew something was wrong," she said. "But he refused to go to the doctor. He stayed on his feet for four days and then he simply collapsed. We had to call an ambulance."

As for Dad, he was now conscious and alert, if not strong. He was happy to see his eldest son at his bedside. He talked and talked.

The doctor and the nurses tried to hush him.

"Try not to talk, Mr. Duerksen," the doctor said. "You haven't much strength and you are going to need all of it if you are going to make it. You want to make it, don't you?" He was talking to a man of 83.

The stubborn reply. "I'm going to talk all I want to. This is my son and I'm going to talk to him. I know I am dying. But I am ready to go. God is waiting for me. My soul is ready."

The doctor walked out. I believe I detected even a bit of trembling of the lip on his part.

As for Dad, he lasted four more days. I brought Mom, at least once every day. They had their little communions of love, their faithfulness unto death. My emotions were not immune to the beauty of it. Their enduring love. Their faith.

During those four days, Dad finally broke his promise to me about the status of my soul. Perhaps, as he felt no compulsion to obey the orders of the doctor, he felt no compulsion any longer to obey my orders either. And now I could not forbid it. I couldn't walk out on a dying man. My father.

So I stayed. I listened but I made no promises. It would serve no purpose.

In the end I could only bear witness to his own abiding faith in a God who had failed me. A God who, in my opinion, had also failed Dad in so many ways. But I had to see it, Dad's faith remained intact to the end.

On the fourth night I was alone with Dad. I had taken Mom home. She knew what was coming but, for reasons of her own, she wanted to do her waiting at home. She had her own tears to shed.

Sometime during the evening, with his strength slowly slipping away, his breathing becoming labored, I could see Dad's lips moving. I could barely hear him and I moved closer.

He was singing one of his old beloved gospel hymns.

"Rock of ages, cleft for me. Let me hide myself in thee."

And then he was gone.

It was beautiful. It was courageous. It was the ultimate act of abiding faith.

Somebody might suggest that it was the classic death scene for a Christian. I would have to agree.

Oh, I almost forgot.

On that night, 12 years before, on the eve of his Golden Wedding Anniversary, when he had prayed so passionately for my soul, I had not been able to provide him with the answer to his prayer. But I made another decision that night, as I listened.

I decided to grant him his wish to allow his temple of prayer to stand.

It was still standing on the night he died.

Chapter Thirty three - Unto the Bitter End

Dante failed to add the final hell to his inferno. The hell reserved for those humans required to witness the death of someone they love. A hell made doubly cruel by the fact that it is love which compels a man to offer his soul to such a demanding trial. And love which permits the dying to accept the gift.

You see, I wanted my Ruth to die.

In my heart I prayed and pleaded for her death. Not because I hated her but because I did love her and knew that she was beyond any desire to help her. She had more courage than I. She had what I would have called the spirit which refused to cry.

There is something about a woman, I suppose, which demands a certain pride, even in a time of terminal illness. She wanted no sympathizing friends hovering over her in those last weeks. When they came, even the closest of friends, she asked me to send them away. Perhaps it had something to do with an undying vanity about being seen in such a condition. All feminine charm and beauty sacrificed to the ravages of cancer. Perhaps it is even something else, a rejection which we cannot understand.

She did accept my presence. She let me know that she desired my presence even when she told me no. Perhaps, because we had shared so many other intimate things in our 24 years together, she knew it was only I who could now share her last days and hours.

So it was I who spent those last two weeks together with her in the hospital room, nursing her unto the hour of her going. Accepting, because of love, the cruel blades which ripped at my heart.

388

It was I who sat transfixed with horror during her last half hour of battle with death. And yet, refusing to call a nurse or doctor who might come running with means of prolonging the battle for a few more hours or days. I wanted her to go, and go quickly, because there was no other way. She needed that end to the hopeless battle which had been going on for a year.

The real story started, I suppose, five months earlier, the day of Ruth's surgery. That was the day when the hell began. For more than five hours, I sat alone in her hospital room, waiting for the verdict. And somehow knowing - because dread has a message of its own - what the verdict would be. I guess I died a bit myself during those five hours.

And then, when Dr. Fleming came, I suppose I could read it in his face.

"There is a liver involvement," he said, "and there is really nothing we can do. We might keep her going a few months but..." He shrugged his shoulders. And that was it.

I don't believe I wept then. Or when, some time later, they wheeled her into the room. A tube in her nostril and other tubes down below, glucose dripping into her veins. This was not the time for tears.

But I wept that day when I left to go home and saw her car standing there on the parking lot. It was the first new car I had ever bought for her and it had made her so happy. She was so proud of that little white hard-top she had chosen herself. And now it was the car which made me cry because I suddenly realized that Ruth would not be driving it any more. It was a symbol of happiness that could never be reclaimed.

Later, during those five months, there were times when I indulged in a bit of hope - despite what Dr. Fleming told me. Perhaps it was because of the indestructible courage of this woman herself. There were times when she could almost convince you she was not really ill. And when she insisted on getting up in the morning to fix my breakfast. When friends came to visit and she would bounce into the room with a spring to her step that was utterly deceiving. Is it any wonder that some of them refused to believe she was a dying woman. Or, at times, that I found myself believing that perhaps a miracle was taking place.

They were giving her cobalt treatments. Injections of a new drug. Maybe these things would work. At this time I desperately wanted Ruth to live. The prospect of living without her was a frightening one.

But the other side of the coin was showing, too. Anybody could see it, especially being with her day after day. Her time on her feet was growing shorter each day. There were the times when I caught her in the kitchen in the morning, sitting down to fry my egg because she did not have the strength to stand. Spending more time in bed. Her daily battle with the emptying of her colon through the new opening in her body became a more desperate struggle, depriving her of her strength. The time came when she could barely hobble to the bathroom and I had to get her a bed pan.

And then there was our last day together at home - on our wedding anniversary. May I weep now in remembering it? It was 24 years now since our romance started. An experience which had its moments of cruelty and pain but, in the whole, had been a thing of beauty and love.

I had brought her those seven red roses and found when I gave them to her that somehow - incredibly - she had managed her gift for me, too. She had baked a cake.

It had been a tradition for her to bake a cake on our anniversaries. And now, without the strength to go to the kitchen, she had demanded a white sheet to spread over the bed and all the ingredients of my favorite Buttercremetorte to be brought to her bed. It is not an easy cake to make but somehow she managed it. Assembling the four layers with the filling between. and the impeccable icing. A thing of art and beauty as she had always done it.

Smiling an impish smile, she presented it to me. A smile which was meant to say, "You didn't think I could do it, did you?"

No, I had not.

It was this act of giving, of offering herself in these last days of her illness, which put her in high spirits that night. In bed together that night, we held hands and we talked. I knew she was thinking about death then but she did it in a manner that became an act of defiance.

"We had a lot of good times together," she said. We kissed and I put my arms around her fragile bone-thin body. She could barely bear the weight of my hands and arms because of the pressure of that cruel tumor growing within her.

This was our last night in bed together, the end of 24 years of sharing. We had always said goodnight this way: a last kiss, a last embrace and holding hands. A strange irony that it should end on the night of a wedding anniverrsary, a journey of 24 year which started on a hectic day in Frankfurt, Germany.

The next morning it happened. I was in the bathroom shaving, preparing to go to work, when I heard her call. "Dirk, come here. Something is happening," she called.

I went to the bedroom to find huge globs of blood tumbling from her stoma - that new surgical opening in the side of her abdomen. And from her rectum. In desperation, as if clutching life itself, she was trying to stop the bleeding with her fingers. I ran for a towel to press against the stoma. And for the bed pan I had just bought the day before. She had even laughed about the odd gifts for her wedding anniversary.

"Hold the towel tight," I said and telephoned for an ambulance. As always, when you want something to hurry it seemed it would never come. I hoped they would have pads to wrap around her body.

When the ambulance attendants did come, Ruth had to submit her now unbeautiful but nude body to the stare of strange men as they wrapped bandages all the way around to hold the pads and stop the flow of blood. Then that ride through seven miles of city streets. All the way, she looked into my eyes with a quiet, desperate fear. But not a whimper. I sat and held her hand. There was nothing else I could do. I was no doctor, and even a doctor could not help her now. Nor was I God, with the power to somehow say, "Rise up and walk."

There was only the tumbling flow of fearful thoughts. How shall it end? When?

If I had known. The ordeal in the emergency room itself lasted five hours. At first they did nothing, except provide a bed pan for the bleeding. Dr. Fleming came. "It is the face of the raw tumor bleeding. There is nothing we can do to stop it. Surgery would not help now," he told me.

He ordered intravenous glucose containing a blood coagulant. And a blood transfusion. And then he left. He had surgery scheduled with some other stricken person, a rendezvous with destiny. He knew, and I knew, that for Ruth it was only a matter of time. Perhaps he could save that other patient waiting upstairs.

Perhaps it is a sin to suggest that my part of this was an ordeal. Ruth was the one who was facing death. But my heart was in pain, too. At times, tears welled up, but how could I cry when Ruth refused to. She only smiled, wanly.

A nurse came and tried to insert a needle into one of Ruth's veins but the arms were so thin, the veins so shrivelled, the nurse couldn't make it. After three or four tries, she gave up. They called Dr. Fleming. He could not come from surgery. They called a staff doctor. And we waited. The ordeal had started at 5 o'clock in the morning. It was now the middle of the morning. Nine. Ten. Eleven o'clock. They allowed me to stay with her. To wait. To curse silently beneath my breath at the utter inefficiency of this place which they saw fit to call an "emergency room."

Ruth was frightened, too. You could see that. The look of a frightened animal - wondering at the long wait. I could see the terrified questions in her eyes. "Why don't they do something for me?" But she didn't say it. She never cried. Sometimes she talked quietly. Perhaps to ask for the bed pan when the blood began to flow again. She still had strength enough in her legs to lift herself.

But how could she lose so much blood and still live? Still remain conscious and aware of what was happening. Still have that strength.

Waiting. Waiting for that staff doctor to arrive.

Sometime during that wait, we had an accident. Because she needed the bed pan frequently, we had left it standing beside her on the emergency room cot. It was too painful to remain on it constantly. There was blood in it. In struggling to move, Ruth kicked it off onto the floor with a terrible clang. Blood splattered 10 feet across the floor, with dark red globs against the curtains surrounding the cubicle.

For a short moment I experienced a feeling of annoyance. Why did she have to do this? To embarrass me like this? What cruel thoughts invade a man's mind at moments like this. How could you be angry with a dying woman? A woman you loved? A subconscious reflex?

At the sound of the clang, everyone turned for a moment to look. Then they turned their backs again and ignored it. I went to look for someone to clean it up. When I found one and explained what had happened, it was their turn to give me a look of annoyance. Now they were blaming me for the mishap. I was already angry and impatient at the long wait for help from the doctor.

When the cleaning woman came with the mop it was Ruth herself who did the apologizing. "I'm sorry I made such a mess," she said. This apology was ignored.

About half an hour after the cleaning woman had gone, a porter came with a clean curtain. He took the soiled one down and then, after a long period of fumbling, decided it was the wrong one and left. Now we did not even have a curtain to separate us from the traffic of the main emergency room.

Somewhere in the midst of all this, the staff doctor finally arrived. Doctors are supposed to know everything, to take over when a nurse gives up. This one apparently didn't. First, he sat down to read the directions with the intravenous needle. Then he made a mess of it, too. Instead of getting glucose and blood flowing into Ruth, there was more bleeding because of the bungled insertion. In fact, it was not until later, after Ruth was finally taken up to her room, that staff nurses on the floor finally got the needles inserted properly, with blood and glucose feeding into Ruth's starved veins.

After two blood transfusions Ruth rallied a bit. The glucose dripped on constantly for three days. It was her only nourishment. For weeks, now, she had been eating less and less. She had blamed it on the food. Eating caused gas pressure and distress, she said. For weeks I had been chasing from one store to another, trying to find something she could eat.

But it had not been the food at all. It was the pressure of that growing malignant tumor, constantly growing and creating pressure in her abdomen. By the time she got to the hospital, the amount of food she ate in one day could almost be placed on one spoon. They brought food to her in the hospital. She simply shook her head.

On the fourth day, the vein in which Ruth was receiving the fluids hardened and refused to accept it any longer. Slower and slower dripped the glucose until it finally just stopped. It meant changing to another vein on the other arm. Both her arms were scarred and blue from all the fumbling with the needles.

A nurse came with the equipment and was struggling to find a spot where a vein would accept a needle. She was having trouble, too. The veins were even thinner now. It was at that moment that Dr. Fleming walked in. He stood watching the nurse for a moment. He was making a decision. "You may let it go," he said. "I believe we'll leave the glucose off a while." Everyone in the room knew what that meant. No food. No glucose. Nothing to sustain life. I felt tears welling up in my eyes for, in a sense, it was like a hand on the gallows trigger.

No, this is not fair! At some point the decision had to be made. We all knew - even Ruth knew it now - that the glucose was merely prolonging an agony. In the end, the results would be the same. She accepted it quietly without a word. There was no sign that she realized the finality of Dr. Fleming's words. Or the meaning when the nurse packed up her equipment and walked out.

Ruth lived 10 days more days after that. How, I'll never know. Dr. Fleming, speaking quietly to me out in the hall on his daily visits, said he also could not understand from where her strength came. But she stayed, with her constant and labored breathing to remind me that the struggle was going on and on.

These were 10 days of hell.

I stayed with her almost constantly. Leaving only for a brief time to dash home to take care of urgent chores. To see Omi weeping and demanding constantly to know what was going on at the hospital. Dashing back to the hospital, back into the hell, hating it but compelled by an inner force to do it. Because of love. Or duty. Because this woman had given me her love and her life for 24 years.

During those 10 days I took over almost all the nursing duties, except the injections of pain killers. The nurses allowed me to do it. Ruth made it clear she wanted no private duty nurse. She allowed me to do it.

They say nursing is for giving life. Mine was a ministration unto the dying. She only demanded water. And help. To move. To assist her on the bed pan which she needed a hundred times a day. There were still dribbles of blood.

At first she still had enough strength in her legs to help lift herself onto the bed pan. But she became weaker, day by day, until she could not even bend her knees. I had to learn how to get leverage with my elbows beneath her to lift.

There came a time when the skin on her bony back was worn through. I rubbed talcum and cream on it.

During those days of hell, I brushed her teeth, propped her up in bed with a chinpan held tightly to catch the drippings as she attempted to rinse her mouth. I brushed her parched and cracking lips with a glycerine swab as they burst and peeled. Later, even her tongue became dry and blistered. I swabbed the inside of her mouth.

Her voice constantly grew weaker until I had to lean near her lips to understand what she wanted. I learned from the nurses how to brace myself at the head of the bed, place my arms under hers to shift her up in the bed. It was a procedure that had to be repeated a hundred times a day because of her restless shifting.

Sometimes it hurt her in spite of my efforts to be as gentle as possible. She cried out in pain.

She finally became so weak she could not roll over without help, not even when she pulled on the railing.

Only that constant, labored breath, telling me that the fight was going on and on.

There came a time when she could scarcely swallow water. I would place little chips of ice on a spoon, drop them into her mouth and let them melt. Sometimes she choked and coughed, even on that. What was keeping her alive?

"She's using all her strength just to breath," the doctor said.

During one of those last days when Dr. Fleming paid his daily visit, Ruth looked up at him and made a desperate, whispered appeal.

"Can't you give me something to end all this?" she pleaded. She was not crying. She just felt the futility of it all and knew now that there could only be one end.

Dr. Fleming shook his head quietly. There was a forced smile on his face as he said, "No, we doctors have a bad enough reputation without doing things like that."

She never asked again.

Somehow, I told myself during those last days, when the end came it would come quietly. The breathing would simply stop. I had seen men die in battle but I had never seen a person die in bed from cancer.

There were many times during those last days when I thought I saw it coming. These were times when the labored breathing slowed or paused momentarily. My heart would beat rapidly for a moment, in apprehension. Then the breathing would start again, on and on with that labored, desperate sound.

I could see the blood pulsing through those veins in her starved neck. I counted the pulse rate sometimes and wondered when it would slow or stop.

There were even times during those days when a desperate thought entered my mind. It was a terrible thought and not one I summoned consciously. But you cannot always control these intruding thoughts. From somewhere they come.

Why - these thoughts argued - couldn't I just take a towel or a pillow while she slept, heavily drugged, and press it tightly over her mouth and hold it a few moments? That would end this terrible ordeal.

What if a nurse walked in while I was doing that and saw it? The doors on these hospital rooms have no locks. What if Ruth woke up in the midst of it and saw what her husband, who professed love, was doing to her? Would there be horror in her eyes? Or acceptance? Perhaps even thanks? She had asked the doctor to do it and he had refused.

But each time these thought intruded, I knew I could not do it. No. I would simply have to wait. Death would have to choose its own moment to come.

Yes, at times there was even boredom, a desperate kind of boredom, with this tragic vigil. In those 14 days of waiting, there were times when she was asleep from the heavy sedation and I tried to read books or magazines. There were times, lost in utter weariness, I felt drained of all emotion.

But then the impact always came back - the visitation of tragedy unfolding before my eyes. Then I would be overwhelmed with the pain of what was happening to her and to me. I suppose a hundred times during those days, in moments when she was asleep, I wept. I tried not to let her see me cry.

There were other times during those days of hell when I paced the corridor outside when she slept. Going down to the snack bar for a cup of coffee. Then worrying and hurrying back.

Or, stopping to chat with other people also waiting for death. There was a policeman on the floor, also on a death vigil with his wife, but his had been going on for two months. How can the human soul take this?

Just across the hall, another woman was undergoing almost the identical agony as Ruth. She died the same day Ruth died, within two hours of the same time.

Occasionally, friends came by, wanting to see Ruth. I never let them in. Ruth told me she did not want to see them.

One day, Omi came. She had gotten a friend to bring her. She did not believe what I was telling her. She wanted to see for herself. Until the very last she insisted she still had hopes that Ruth would somehow get stronger, get well. I had long ago lost that hope.

Of course, I had to let Omi in. You cannot bar a mother from the death bed of her daughter. But Omi stayed only a few minutes. Now she saw the ghastly mask of death already showing on this woman still alive. The skin stretched taut over the bones of the face. No flesh. Omi never came back. From then on, the vigil belonged to me alone - and Ruth.

Even the nurses on the floor seemed to realize what was going on. Had they seen something like this before? Perhaps many times. They surrendered to me, voluntarily, most of their duties to Ruth.

I learned how to roll a patient to insert a bed pan. I learned that bed pan routine so well. The elbows propped against the mattress for lifting power. Then, emptying and flushing the foul, odorous discharge. Spraying the pan with deodorant. Then drying the edge, sprinkling it with talcum powder to keep it from sticking to the chafed and sore infested skin.

In the end, I even wiped her dry. An intimate task no woman would surrender to a man unless she was completely helpless.

There came a day when she groaned with pain on the pan and I discovered a huge red swelling. I called the nurse. She looked and had a medical name for it. A plague that comes to people who live in bed. With so little flesh for padding.

We didn't talk much now. It was a strain for her. She could barely form words with her mouth. It was only a whisper. "It is affecting her voice muscles," said Dr. Fleming. It was something I was going to be thankful for at a certain time.

Each day I told her, perhaps a dozen times, that I loved her. She would whisper back, "I love you, too." She would kiss the tips of her fingers and toss the kiss to me. It was a little gesture I had treasured in former years, something she did when we were across a room from each other.

"I'll never stop loving you," I told her now. I meant it.

In those last days, with the weakness, came restlessness. The pressure from the tumor was still growing. This was the one place on her body which constantly became thicker while her face, her arms and legs became only outlines of bones.

She would ask me to roll her onto the side to rest her sore back. First right, then left. Then she would ask me to raise the bed. I'd raise it and a moment later, back down again. Towards the last, she no longer asked to be rolled onto her left side. Perhaps it was the pressure on her heart. She was too weak to explain.

At times, just for the comfort of a move, she wanted her knees raised. In the beginning she could do it herself. Then the utter helplessness of those final days when she whispered, "Can you raise my knees?"

When I did, if I released them, they flopped down again. God, what bitter helplessness. But still alive. Her chest heaving in labored gasps.

Each day, the doctor told me it could not go on. But it did. She was barely able to swallow a few drops of water. When she could no longer raise her head, I got the nurse to bring me a little syringe. I dribbled water into her mouth as she lay. But that did not work, either, for it choked her. I gave it up and went back to the little chips of ice.

Yes, death finally came that Tuesday. I suppose I sort of sensed it in the morning. There was a wild, erratic pounding of the pulse where you could see it in her neck artery. The beat of it was mad, racing, faster than I had ever seen it, with a frenzied irregularity.

She was still conscious. Perhaps she also sensed what was coming. One time, during the morning, she beckoned to me with feeble arms and made a motion with her lips. She was asking me to kiss her for the last time.

I did, with tears flowing from my eyes. This time I made no attempt to conceal them. I bent and kissed those hot, parched and cracking lips that had once been so soft, so desirable.

I saw, rather than heard, her lips forming the words for the last time, "I love you." She was trying to embrace me with her arms but it was only a feeble attempt. I was weeping openly.

Sometime that morning, Dr. Fleming came in. He felt her pulse and watched her quietly for a few moments. I was trying to read his face. So many times during those past two weeks I had thought the end was coming and it had not come. Was this another false alarms?

It could not be. An end had to come, sometime. How could a person grow any weaker and live? Without nourishment? Barely able to swallow a few drops of water.

And she was so restless, too, constantly requesting to be moved. Up. Down. Over. Again and again. She demanded to sit up, although that was obviously impossible.

I followed Dr. Fleming into the hall and reminded him of what I had seen. Of course, he had seen it, too. The terrible restlessness.

"Yes, I know. There is no reason for her to be in such distress. I'll order something to make her more comfortable."

It was a doubling of the strength and frequency of her sedation shots.

I remembered once before, when Ruth had been restless and I had asked a nurse for a shot before the scheduled time. She had refused, saying it would be dangerous.

How ironic, that. How could anything be dangerous to a life that had already reached its terminal?

Did Dr. Fleming realize this and, in making such a drastic change, had he finally decided to grant this woman her wish after all? I could not know. I could only guess.

Some time during that morning, a group of student nurses were brought up to the tenth floor by a nurse instructor. I learned it was part of their training. They would visit various wards for a time, helping out the regular nurses. Asking patients if they could be of any help.

Several of them wandered into Ruth's room that morning. Two of them, one quite pretty, came back several times. It was almost as if, in spite of their fledgling training, they sensed something was happening in this room. A human life in crisis.

The pretty one stayed the longest. As she stood at Ruth's bedside I could not help but notice the contrast. This fresh, young, pretty bit of feminine humanity. Compared to that wasted, ravaged body on the bed.

I could not order her to leave but I wanted her to. I wanted to be alone with Ruth now. I had been thinking about it all these days. "When the end comes, I want to be alone with her."

I don't really know why. There could be no joy to such an occasion. Yet I felt that compulsive desire to be with her, to share with her, as we had shared our joys, this bitter end. It was something I owed her and myself. It was at noon when the instructor nurse called her charges together and took them to lunch.

It was during that lunch hour, sometime between noon an 1 o'clock, when death came. And I sat watching in desperate fascination, almost as if hypnotized.

It really started while I was out of the room. I had stepped out for a moment and when I returned Ruth was tossing frantically in bed and screaming.

I said screaming? But actually she was only trying to scream. Her mouth was working frantically, and a faint cry was coming. As loud as she could make it.

"Help me. Help me sit up. I want to get up. I want to get up," she was saying in that strained, shouting whisper. Her body was jerking as she tried to pull herself up, but without the strength to do it.

Perhaps the normal reaction for me should have been to run for help, or ring. But this I refused to do. I now sensed fully what was coming and I felt that it must come without interference.

399

I had hoped, even believed, that when the end came it would come quietly. Just an end of breath, in a quiet sleep. I had never anticipated this wild terror in the eyes of the woman I loved.

The forced screaming was constant now. The stark stare of tragedy. To answer her pleas, I rolled the bed up as high as it would go. But then came the increased pressure on her abdomen. "Down. Down."

We went down but then she wanted up again. Perhaps she did not realize what she was saying or doing. "Help me up."

"Honey, you know you cannot get up. It is impossible," I told her. "You can't get up." Perhaps there was a note of hysteria in my voice now.

My heart was pounding. And there were the tears. Tears of sorrow and pain at being so helpless and yet knowing it must, it must come. I wanted it to happen - and then end. To end this ghastly nightmare which had me trapped in its hypnotic clutch.

The silent screaming, the struggle must have lasted nearly half an hour. Yes, I could have called the nurses. A doctor. But they had already given her that enormous dose of sedation. What more could they do?

Perhaps there are other last desperate measures doctors take in times like this, but it would not change the end. I clenched my teeth and resolved to let her go. I even prayed that a nurse would not come at that moment. And it was now I who was thankful that the screams could not be heard because of the crippled voice muscles.

Then the gasping silent screams began to fade. Her efforts to sit up became weaker. Once during that struggle, as she pleaded to get up, I weakened and took her in my arms, attempting to lift her. But it was impossible. She was a wasted bit of fading humanity in my arms. Trembling desperately but without strength.

Finally, she lay back on the pillow. Her lips in feeble gesture of supplication, making hardly a sound. That pulse in her neck leaped wildly. Sometimes it stopped. Her breath coming in shorter, wilder gasps.

But weaker by the moment. The eyes staring almost sightlessly now. But the breath going on.

Then suddenly it stopped. For a long moment. No breath. No movement.

"I guess she's gone," I told myself. But in that moment it began again. For a couple of minutes and then, again, silence.

At least four times this act of "dying" took place. Each time the breath came back again. Each time for a shorter period and each time weaker.

Then she was truly gone. Utter quiet, her eyes and mouth open in silent supplication.

Only once, after that, for a brief moment, a faint shadow of breath passed through her lips. Once, twice. Just barely visible. Then silence forever.

I stood up and tried to close her eyes. Her mouth. The face was a twisted, ghastly mask, bearing no resemblance to the woman she had once been, glowing with life and love. Desirable.

This face lying here before me could have been the face of a very old woman, even 90.

For long moments, I sat there quietly, in a silent last communion of husband and wife. I was weeping but there was no one to see. It did not matter.

One more time I spoke to unhearing ears. "I love you, darling. I'm glad it's over."

This was a moment that would live forever in my soul.

Finally, drying my tears with a handkerchief, I slowly and calmly walked to the nurse's station. Three floor nurses were chatting, their backs turned. I did not shout or demand their attention. I had no emergency. I waited until one of them turned and noticed me.

"I believe Mrs. Duerksen is gone," I said quietly.

These words, as I knew they would, set off a flurry of frenzied activity. The three of them each grabbed something and ran. One with a stethescope and another with a blood pressure gauge.

Let them run, I said to myself, she is beyond their reach now.

I followed them to the room but now I, the husband, who had been allowed to nurse her those past two weeks, was barred from the room.

"Will you please leave?" the nurses said gently, but firmly. They had certain chores to do now and even the husband should not be a witness to this.

So I left.

I had already had my communion of death with this woman I had loved. We had been together in her death for long moments of silence before I had even told the nurses she was gone. Let them do now what they had to do.

One of the nurses took me by the arm and led me into a little private office. She brought me a glass of ice water. Perhaps she wished it could be a highball.

I telephoned Omi and told her that her daughter was gone. I could hear the frantic sobbing on the phone.

About 20 minutes later, the nurse came back with a little envelope containing Ruth's wedding ring, her watch and the little silver cross she had worn around her neck for many years. It had been a gift of another wedding anniversary and she had said, "I'll never take it off. " She hadn't.

They told me I could go back to her room now, to gather up the remainder of Ruth's things. I went and the bed was empty now.

I picked up the comb and brush she had no longer had the strength to use. The toothbrush I had used for her. Skin cream. Flimsy little items of underwear she had not worn. A new housecoat from Christmas she had hardly had a chance to wear.

I simply dumped all these things into a sack and walked out. I was turning my back forever on this empty room which had been a living hell for 14 days.

Now only a paining sorrow was with me. And tears. But the terrible pressure my soul had borne these days was gone now. And emptiness had taken its place.

Now I was going home without her.

Forever.

Chapter Thirty four - The Miracle

Thea believes in miracles. The kind, she says, that God arranges.

I, having a somewhat lesser faith, must take my miracles as they come. By chance. By quirks of fate. By the odds. Such as when some lucky character wins five million in a state lottery. It does happen, occasionally, but I doubt that God would want to take any credit for it.

Thea and I do have one area of agreement, however, and that is that one particular happening was, and is, some kind of a miracle. For her part, God arranged it. For my part, well, it happened and I am willing to accept it as a grand and a glorious gift. And that "happening" is simply the fact that we found each other on that incredible day in 1970.

Since almost everyone agrees that miracles don't happen every day, at least not the to same person - in this case, to two of us - it became a bit of a story.

When it all began, I was willing to lay claim to being the most lonely person in the world. A loneliness so vast, so crushing, I almost feared to face the future. It was something I had not anticipated in those last days before Ruth died.

I had never considered as a most remote possibility that there would ever be another woman in my life. There couldn't be. But then, when her irrevocable absence came crushing down upon me, it became that enormous loneliness. I needed her. But she was gone. Forever.

There were a few times, in those first lonely nights, when I would turn on the tape player to recapture her voice as I had recorded it on a Christmas Eve. The cheery, healthy voice of a happy woman supervising the opening of gifts. It helped a bit but not much. After a few hearings, I couldn't even listen to it any more.

Somewhere, in the midst of my loneliness, it may have been several months after Ruth left me, I ripped out a hunk of the misery from my soul in the form of a bit of tortured poetry.

BEREFT

Splinter of being;
unmoored.
Given unto the furied storm.
Flung. Frenzied,
unwilled.
Borne of a tempest,
untamed.

Anchor of soul;
unchained.
Unmercied, the guideless heart.
Torn, harried,
driven.
Cry for a peace;
Forbidden.

Menno Duerksen, summer, 1970

It didn't help much. But it had exploded out of me and, for the moment, at least, it relieved a bit of the pressure.

And then life went on. It had to. I had my job. Ruth's mother, Omi, was still in the house. Although she was well into her 80's, she was still relatively healthy and even helped keep things going in the house.

And then there was Peter, Ruth's retarded son whom I had accepted as my own, and had helped rear as best I could. I'll have to agree that Ruth and her mother had done most of that.

But then this is supposed to be the story of a miracle.

It was, perhaps, some 8 months after Ruth had died when I made that totally unexpected trip to New York. I had been, more or less, offered a job with a New York publication and had been asked to come up for a job interview. I was almost certain that I would not take the job. I had too many years of job tenure on the paper in Memphis. But, since they were paying for the plane ticket, I decided on an impulse to go.

And this "happening" begins to take on the proportions of a miracle when we consider that I had not been to New York for nearly 17 years, even though I had once lived there for nearly a year while on another kind of job training during World War II.

My plane whooshed in over the water for a landing at La Guardia. Downtown on Manhattan, a friendly interview and a confirmed job offer. Maybe it was an ego boost I needed, just to know I was still wanted. But I didn't take the job. Just as I had known that I wouldn't.

But then, at La Guardia again, checking in for my return flight to Memphis - that crazy miracle.

Somewhere nearby I heard the chatter of a couple of feminine voices. And one of these voices was grabbing my attention. That German accent.

How could I miss it? I spoke German. I had spent 7 years in Europe, mostly in Germany. I had married Ruth over there. She, the daughter of a gentleman from Hanover, where they spoke the purest of German.

The "voice" was speaking English. Normally, I'm the shy type who never makes the bold approach to a stranger. Much less a woman. But now it was almost as if I were compelled to do it. I blurted out, in German, "Apparently, the lady also speaks German?"

The "lady" in question turned to me, a sparkle of mischevious laughter in her dark eyes, and replied in German, "Of course, I speak German. I'm from Augsburg."

Something had clicked. That crazy miracle was coming to life.

I mentioned that I had covered the Ilse Koch (Bitch of Buchenwald) trial in Augsburg. It was something to keep the conversation going.

So - we had a few moments of chit chat. I learned very quickly that she was an employe of the airline, had been in the United States some 17 years, that she was a widow, the mother of four, three of them born in Germany.

Then, when it came time to board my plane, I did that other crazy, impulsive thing, so out of character for me. I handed her my business car and made it a challenge. "Why don't you write me a letter?"

"I won't promise," she replied. "My friends say I'm the world's worst letter writer."

And then I was gone, my plane winging it back to Memphis, so far away. Perhaps never to see New York again for another 17 years. Or ever. Except that now a miracle was at work.

I had been back home and back at work perhaps a week and I was in the process of forgetting about that little chat at La Guardia. I couldn't have contacted her for I didn't even have her address. But then that little envelope with a Long Island return address landed on my desk at the office.

Who can explain things like that? Was my heart thumping a bit as I opened the envelope? Had I detected the slight odor of perfume? Was it possible?

For the "worst letter writer in the world," the little note inside was deceptively bright and cheery. And somewhere in it the question, "Where in the world is Memphis?"

And then we became acquainted by letter. I learned all about Thea Folkerts.

She, her husband and their three small children had come to the United States after the war, to "seek their fortune." Their fourth, Bernie, had been born in New York.

Her husband had been a test pilot for Messerschmidt during the war but in America it had been tough going at the beginning. Then he had landed a job with TWA, the airlines, finally ending up with the responsible job of trouble shooter. The man who was sent out to bring planes home when they developed mechanical or electrical problems.

Then tragedy struck. Four years before, she wrote, her husband had drowned in a sail boat accident on Long Island Sound.

Bernie, now eight, had been only four years old when it happened and he had been with his father when it took place. The child had been found floating in the water, unconscious and more dead than alive. The fact that he had somehow survived and was now a healthy, growing youngster had been duly noted by his mother as another of those "miracles" she owed to God. Thea sent me a newspaper clipping about the accident.

Beyond that, the airline where her husband had worked, offered her a job so she could take care of her family. Bernie was staying with his grandmother while Mom worked, driving 50 miles to La Guardia each day.

Of course, I also told her, in my letters, about losing my wife, about my job and a bit more about my experiences in

406

Germany. I had always been a reporter so the writing came easy for me but the surprises were in her letters. Coming from someone claiming to be such a lousy letter writer, they were little gems of cheer. So revealing of a character one would like to know more about.

In one of my letters I became bold enough to ask if she had a "boy friend." Her reply, yes, she had a few admirers, a few dates but "I don't have time for a boy friend. I'm too busy working and taking care of my family."

At the beginning, we never in our letters made any overt suggestion that we would be seeing each other again. But as the letters continued, the whole thing had to be leading in that direction.

When I began to think seriously about that possibility, I became frightened. It wasn't even fair to her. There was still an aged mother-in-law who must be cared for. The retarded Peter. The long distance to New York. I had a few middle age problems that frightened me. Then, too, it was apparent that Thea had her roots pretty well planted in Long Island. Her mother and her sisters, who had also come to the United States, were all living in that area. Her older children who had grown up there were beginning to sink their roots.

It hurt a bit because I had come to enjoy the correspondence. But, I decided, the only fair thing to do would be to stop the crazy little letter writing affair. So I wrote her what I considered to be a goodbye letter. I explained why I was dong it, all about the problems I faced, and suggested we end it. I didn't expect to hear from her again. But I did.

For here, in a few days, was another letter with that familiar Long Island postmark. Once again I was aware of a pounding heart as I opened it. It was immediately apparent that my "sign off" letter had pained her a bit, too. Later, she confessed that when she read it she had sat down on the porch and cried. Even then I could almost feel the hurt and the tears in her reply.

No, she wasn't rejecting my idea of a sign off. If it must be that way, so be it. But then there was so much warmth and understanding in her letter my heart began to pound with excitement. I must see this woman again. To hell with the problems.

This time, I couldn't wait for a letter. I simply grabbed the phone and called her. "May I come to visit you?" I asked. The answer was yes.

So, after only a few months, here I was grabbing a plane for New York again. And there, at the La Guardia landing gate, she stood waiting. Against the chill of a November day she was wearing a long capelike coat. But when she took it off to get into the car I saw that she was wearing one of those colorful German dirndles, complete with apron. It was simply an eloquent expression of her German heritage.

To begin with, we had just smiled and she offered me her hand. The Germans are always dutiful in the hand shaking business. But then we were in her little BMW heading for Northport, 50 miles away. It was strange how little we had to say in those first moments, especially in view of the torrent we had poured out in all those letters. As she drove, we kept looking at each other, trying to size each other up. And saying so little. I remember I liked what I saw except, maybe, the hairdo. A half beehive. There were the dark, sparkling eyes, somehow asking questions. The pretty, open face. After all, hairdos are not forever.

There would be times, in the years to come, when Thea would ask me, in that bantering voice of hers, "When did you really fall in love with me?" It was a little game for we both knew the answer. So well I knew it.

It had been in her home on the afternoon of my first visit. She had been busy in the kitchen. I was in the living room, sitting on the floor, leafing through some of her family photo albums.

Her daughter, Meta, about to be married, was there. Friends and family drifted in and out. Then someone, I believe it was Meta, sneaked in and put a record on the record player. The sound came floating out into the room, old German folks songs I had heard so many times during my years in Germany and which I had come to love. It was the nostalgia of it all. Somehow, it brought emotions creeping up into my throat. I couldn't help it. I could feel a tear creeping into my eye and threatening to roll down my cheek.

It had to be exactly at that moment when Thea came in from the kitchen and stood for a moment, looking at me. Perhaps it is safe to say that she saw the tear, threatening to drop onto my cheek. She came towards me, bent down and planted a light kiss on my forehead. That was all.

She quickly retreated to her kitchen. No matter. The magic moment of a miracle happening had come. In that moment I knew that I loved her. And that my life would never again be the same.

Later in that day, her mother showed up with Bernie. He eyed me and I him. We were strangers. But not for long. I liked what I saw. Handsome, straw blonde hair, a bustling bundle of boy energy. His heroes, pro football players. "I'm going to be a pro

DEAR GOD, I'M ONLY A BOY

when I grow up," he announced. His slender build would prevent him from ever being a pro but it would come to pass that in his senior year at Harding Academy, in Memphis, he would be voted the most valuable player of a victorious Lions football team.

But, back to that first day in New York. Before the afternoon was over we were down on the floor, battling it out in a hotly contested game of marbles. Bernie kept winning.

I would have to wait until later in Memphis to get revenge - at carroms. Even if I had to pay for it with hours of hurling football passes for Bernie to catch, until my throwing arm ached with pain.

Was this the son I had wanted all these years? It was.

In any case, going back once more to that first visit in New York, it was later that night when, as if by previous arrangement, everyone except Thea suddenly disappeared. We were alone in the house. It was to give us a chance to become better acquainted. Suddenly the dam broke. Through all the letters we were better acquainted than we realized. We even found the right moment for our first real kiss. And it wasn't on the forehead this time.

But the next day I had to head back to Memphis. This was a heady weekend. There had been no spoken commitment from either of us but it was somehow understood that we would be seeing each other again. In the meantime, more letters. I tried to visualize the future. It wasn't easy. Despite the new, hopeful lift to my soul, there were still so many unanswered questions. Worries. One day I put my feelings into another little poem and sent it to her.

THE QUESTING HEART

Unto the day of my need,
she came.
Impetuous heart.
Wounded spirits, encountered...
Bereft.
Shorn of armor.

Endure, endure, joyed gift,
guardian
against the ebbing tide.
Relive,
each yearning day,
the pulsing hope.
Oh, cry of soul.

DEAR GOD, I'M ONLY A BOY

Beyond? Beyond this hour, this day
the veiled psyche.
Bursting,
a sunkissed dawn,
or unpierced mist?
My heart questing.

Menno Duerksen, winter, 1970-71

Her answer? Suddenly she was there, in Memphis. Our first real togetherness. And it was on that first night in Memphis when I found the courage to ask, "Do you love me?" Without hesitation came the reply, "Yes." As simple as that.

The next question had to follow. "Will you marry me?' Again, without hesitation came the quick reply, "Yes." We were committed.

Oh, we waited a few more months. We both wanted to be sure. She had her worries about quitting her job, moving to Memphis, leaving her mother and sisters, her grown children, all behind.

But by this time we knew we would not listen to our worries. There was something about the bubbling spirit of this woman that was bringing me to life again. The miracle of love. I found myself writing a different kind of poem now. Just a little snippet of a poem.

THE LAUGHING HEART

Deep in her eyes I saw,
the mirror of her soul.
T'was dancing stars I saw,
vivant, her spirit whole.

The laughtered joy of life, I saw,
enchantment, bursting through.
Enraptured by the glow, I found,
my heart was laughing, too.

Menno Duerksen, spring 1971

410

Yes, my soul was laughing again. No, I hadn't forgotten Ruth. In fact, I could now afford to remember that it had been Ruth who had told me, in those last tragic months of her life, when she knew she would soon be gone, that I must find a new love.

I tried to hush her when she said things like that. It was something I didn't want to think about. In that moment I knew there could never be another Ruth. Impossible.

But now there was. If not a Ruth, a woman named Thea.

At her christening, they had called her Theresia. But her friends had long ago shortened that to the German abbreviation, Thea. I had no quarrel with that.

So, in a little white chapel in Northport, with her children and family looking on, giving us their blessing, we were married.

Our honeymoon was something we would laugh about a lot. Later. A trip to Memphis by U-Haul truck, loaded with things she wanted to bring along. We wanted to hitch Thea's little BMW to the rear of the truck so we could, as properly and newly married folks, ride together. But the truck people told us the bumper on her little car was not strong enough. She would have to drive it, following along behind.

Impishly I told her, "If you follow me all the way to Memphis, I will know it is for real." And it was. In fact, there were times when she followed me so closely I couldn't even see her in my rear view mirror. The first time it happened, my heart skipped a beat, but she was there.

Tough, being separated that way on a honeymoon trip but at least we could have our nights together in the motels.

It was somewhere along the way, perhaps on the third day, when she said, "Now I am beginning to realize just how far it really is."

At night we talked about our future. We agreed to sell my house and get another one so we could make a new start in a new atmosphere.

And so it was that my Thea arrived in Memphis, hung her inscription on the diningroom wall of our new house and set about making it into a home.

Oh, yes, that inscription? I had seen it on the wall of her home in New York, a friendly little message in German. I hadn't really given it a thought. But now, when she brought it all the way to Memphis and hung it up again, it took on a new meaning.

DEAR GOD, I'M ONLY A BOY

In German it read -

> Begruesse froh den Morgen,
> den Muh' und Arbeit gibt.
> Es ist so schoen zu sorgen,
> fuer Menschen die man liebt.

Freely translated into English it would read something like this -

> Greet joyfully each morning,
> which chores and work will bring.
> It fills the heart with gladness,
> to care for those we love.

Brought to Memphis and hung on a new wall, it now became something of a statement of philosophy, a committment. For that I could only love her more.

So that makes me a male chauvinist? At least a latent one? I had married the woman so I'd have someone to take care of my house and baby me? I must deny it. Yes, perhaps every man has in his heart a bit of a desire to be babied. But my heart was also quite certain that I loved this woman and I was going to be certain she knew it.

I put my feelings into another bit of poetry -

TO THEA

> Tender grow the fibers of my soul
> when deep within me flows that stream of love,
> from you to me.
>
> Of grace, this gift, of self, of being.
> So rare, but rarer still the will of spirit
> which commands the giving
>
> May one command creation of such souls,
> keepers of that priceless gift?
> But nay, my friends, such gift is born of self.

412

DEAR GOD, I'M ONLY A BOY

No, I won't tell the story of our lives after that, except to say that the passing of time, the years, only served to confirm the miracle. It had indeed been for real.

Oh, we didn't live without our storms, our quarrels, even the ones we called "fights" and the weapons were bitter words. But somehow we always managed to end them with someone saying, "I'm sorry." Our arms around each other.

Thea even had one of her little German proverbs for these occasions. "Gewitter reinigt die Luft," she would say. "A storm clears the air." The resolution renewed, to look into each other's eyes each day and say, "I love you."

One day, after one of those storms had passed, I even managed to write a bit of poetry about it -

THE WINDS OF FATE

The winds of fate conspired and blew,
the two of us together.
The winds of fate, they also knew,
this love was meant forever.
But winds and fate have also know,
that storms are part of weather.

Our love may live and grow each day,
when peace and joy abound.
But love must also stand and hold each day,
each threatened bit of ground,
Against the blasts which bar the way,
to heavens we have found.

Perhaps if one consulted the esthetes, it might be suggested that I really wasn't a poet. It doesn't matter. On those occasions when I made the tries, what I had to say was the real me.

Of course, I also did it for the more joyful occasions. An anniversary, a birthday or, maybe, when I wanted to say, "I love you." Which is why I called one of them simply , Love.

LOVE

Ask not what spirits rule my soul;
which power guides the journeys of my soul.
No science known to man can toll,
the myriad travelings, where they start.

Nor where they end, these whisping dreams,
which wing so swiftly down the trails;
of mind and soul, alighting gleams,
where jungled dark so oftenly prevails.

So who can say where love is born,
what mystery sires the fiery glow,
which joins two souls beyond the scorn,
of scoffers who can never know.

So ask not, love, the whence nor why,
what magic flute the gods did play,
to pluck two soul stars from the sky,
weld heart to heart, forever and a day.

Oh, Thea is sentimental, too. Sometimes she insists that she loves me more than I love her. Which isn't possible.

Part of Thea's sentimentality is preserving memories. Photo albums, pictures, notes, newspaper clippings. About all the memorable happenings in her life.

It was several years after we were married when I discovered she had kept all those letters I had written her when we were discovering each other. She had them all tied up in a little bundle, with a ribbon around them. Together with the dried remnants of the first flowers I had bought her in New York, on an impulse when we happened to pass a subway flower stand. Somewhere she had also found the ones she had written to me and which I had stuck in a drawer somewhere. One night she got them out and started reading them to me, aloud.

We laughed at some of the crazy things we had written. But it had been our real courtship. Yes, it was fun to remember. I had my memories, too, so one day I told her about it in another poem -

MEMORIES

Those bits of life lived in our yesterday,
have now become the memories, alive in our today.
If they were warmed by love, those bits,
they now become a treasured hoard,
to which we cling as life itself,
because our morrows now have endings.

Those memories have their living glow,
a stroke of hand, a touch of lip,
a tender word, caressing smile,
a spark of love inside our eye,
the only treasure I have stored,
until the end of all my morrows.

Menno Duerksen, May 12, 1979

There would be a time, as the years went by, it would be my physical body, with new ailments, telling me I was not immortal. There would even be that day when I had my coronary occlusion and it would be Thea who rushed me to the hospital. I must, the medics told me, have heart surgery if I wished to live.

Perhaps it was, in times like this, when I realized that one day I would really be gone, and that I wanted to tell Thea, that selfless woman of the generous spirit, who had given so much to me, how much I treasured her love. I said that, too, in another poem.

TO THEA

There is a passing,
of time, unyielding.
There is an ending,
for each to wait.
There is an age,
when every man has known,
that evening, fading,
cannot wait for long.

But I may wait,
while moments linger,
in joy and not in fear,
because the heaven earthbound men have sought,
was not withheld beyond my eventide,
but granted as a golden gift,
in life, because you loved me.

Yes, Thea, it was a miracle!